To Julie
Speak Freely.
Best David

KILLED

Great Journalism Too Hot to Print

Edited and Introduced
by
David Wallis

Nation Books · New York

Killed: Great Journalism Too Hot to Print

Compilation Copyright © 2004 by David Wallis

Published by
Nation Books
An Imprint of Avalon Publishing Group
245 West 17th St., 11th Floor
New York, NY 10011

Nation Books is a co-publishing venture of the Nation Institute
and Avalon Publishing Group Incorporated.

Library of Congress Cataloging-in-Publication Data

Killed: great journalism too hot to print/edited and
introduced by David Wallis.
     p. cm.
  ISBN 1-56025-581-1
  1. Journalism--United States. I. Wallis, David.

PN4726.K55 2004
071'.3--dc22

                2004042639

9 8 7 6 5 4 3 2 1

Book design by Paul Paddock
Printed in the United States of America
Distributed by Publishers Group West

CONTENTS

Introduction

Superb journalism is often the progeny of a dedicated writer and a supportive editor. Now meet the bastard children of such liaisons gone wrong.

Like committed parents, dedicated writers invest time, energy, money, hope, ego and love into their articles. They talk of finding a "good home" for a piece, and they mourn when their cherished creation meets a bad end. Consider *Killed* a kind of literary orphanage, albeit one with high standards, that rescues remarkable stories that editors commissioned, then abandoned.

Most editors perform a valuable service as journalism's gatekeepers; they may kill assigned articles for any number of legitimate reasons: A competitor gets the scoop first. Vital photos are unavailable. News events outpace the story. A dropped ad shrinks the available editorial space. The publication unexpectedly dies, or the subject of the article does. (In 1997, *Playboy* pulled Glenn O'Brien's piece, "How to Pick Up Princess Di," which was filed days before her fatal accident). And finally, honest disagreements occur: with some of the pieces that follow, the editors were simply less enthusiastic than I am.

But most of the stories collected here were killed because they somehow disturbed the commissioning editor or the magazine's lawyer or the publisher or perhaps the publisher's pals. This book strips a layer of gloss from the pages of magazines and cracks open the door of the newspaper editor's inner sanctum, granting readers a glimpse at the sometimes sordid process that determines what you read and what you can't. The media elite didn't want you to know about the seamy side of the circus. They kept you in the dark about a missile-sized hole in airline security. They suppressed a satire of Hollywood's publicity-industrial complex so as not to offend powerful flacks. They banned book reviews that were tough on cronies. And they folded rather than fight a hypocritical CEO who misled consumers.

To better understand the many murky permutations of press self-censorship, though, requires an examination of more than the twenty-four stories in this book. Consider a few cases from the annals of editorial cowardice:

> • On February 3, 1972, a few days after what became known as "Bloody Sunday," Murray Sayle and Derek Humphry of London's *Sunday Times* filed a bullet-by-bullet account of the shooting attacks that took the lives of fourteen unarmed civil rights protesters by British paratroopers in Londonderry, Northern Ireland. The devastating article concluded that the attack was premeditated, and that it "presented the IRA with the most resounding victory they have had since 1916." The British government reportedly threatened the *Sunday Times* with action if they ran dispatch from Londonderry. The paper fell in line and shelved the story, a decision akin to as if *The Washington Post* had not published the Pentagon Papers.

In a scene that could have been written by Graham Greene, the Sayle and Humphry article subsequently vanished from *The Sunday Times*'s newsroom, only surfacing twenty-six years later when a researcher discovered the document in an archive at the University of Hull. By withering under government pressure, *The Sunday Times* deprived Britons of a critical opportunity to question their country's Northern Ireland policy.

• In July 2000, former *Portland Press Herald* reporter Ted Cohen uncovered evidence that George W. Bush had been arrested for drunk driving in 1976 near his family's Kennebunkport compound. As Cohen later recounted in an *American Journalism Review* essay entitled "The Greatest Scoop I Never Had," his editor refused to pursue the story, judging it irrelevant given Bush's subsequent rebirth as a teetotaler. A Maine Democratic political operative later leaked word of the arrest to another reporter, and the bombshell broke just five days before the election. Coming so close to the end of an ugly presidential campaign, however, the news seemed more like a dirty trick by a political opponent than an honest attempt by an objective journalist to appraise a potential president's character.

• Not long ago, a reporter on assignment for a women's magazine exposed a few abortion providers as charlatans who injure patients. The piece called on certain states to strengthen regulations that govern those who perform the procedure. But the assigning editor aborted the article, admitting to the writer the worry that publishing the report would harm the pro-choice movement. That decision kept readers ignorant about a potential health hazard. Ultimately, the reporter backed out of publishing the exposé in this book because he was afraid that the potential cost of contributing—being blacklisted by women's magazines—was too high to pay. "If I give you this piece," the reporter lamented, "I could lose fifteen percent of my income."

• The Library of Congress—"a symbol of the vital connection between knowledge and democracy," according to its Web site—pressed editors at its now-defunct magazine *Civilization* to quash a 1999 profile of an Al Jolson impersonator by writer Joe Hagan. "The story," remembers an editor who worked at the magazine, "included a historic look at minstrelsy and blackface performance and how African-Americans and whites appropriated and exchanged musical and dance traditions. We loved it, and had found great art and photos. We submitted it to our liaisons at the Library and they said 'no way, we're not touching this.' It was well-known that the Library had been involved in a long legal battle with some of its African-American employees. I would not be surprised if that played a part, but no one connected the dots for us. That said, they avoided anything controversial, and race remains the third-rail in this country." A Library of Congress spokesperson, Helen W. Dalrymple, said she had "no recollection" about the article in question, but made a point of mentioning that ". . . the Library had a contractual right to advise *Civilization* of any objections it had to material that it deemed specifically inimical or harmful to the best interests of the Library in any material way."

Undoubtedly, intra-office politics stifles many worthy stories, particularly when publishers push editors to ditch articles that could offend advertisers. Indeed, the so-called Chinese Wall, which once sealed off editors from untoward business pressures, has now been reduced to a Chinese fence—a rickety one at best. In 2000, the Pew Research Center and the *Columbia Journalism Review* reported that approximately one-third of journalists they surveyed said they avoided articles that might rattle advertisers. (Imagine the blockbusters that never even get the chance to be killed.) An earlier study cited by the *Journal of Advertising* found that forty percent of business publication editors had "been told by the ad director or the publisher to do something that seriously compromised editorial" integrity. Less than half of those respondents said they would rebuff such a request.

The journalist and social critic Vance Packard, who exposed sleazy advertising practices in his 1957 bestseller *The Hidden Persuaders*, fretted about the Faustian bargain some magazines make with marketers. In 1954, *Reader's Digest* solicited a piece from Packard about motivational research but then dropped it—just at the time the magazine started accepting advertising. According to Packard's biographer Daniel Horowitz, even after *The Hidden Persuaders* proved a hit, its author confided to a friend: "I still feel my head is very much out on the chopping block as a writer for magazines which depend on advertising." But Packard soon savored vindication that few writers ever enjoy. Following his book's success, *Harper's Bazaar* ran his killed story, leading *Reader's Digest* to excerpt—and pay twice for—the very story they had earlier spiked.

Forty years later, Edward Kosner, then top editor of *Esquire*, apparently caved in to pressure from his magazine's advertising executives, pulling a short story with a gay theme by acclaimed writer David Leavitt that was already in page proofs. "As we got closer to publication, I changed my mind," Kosner told The *Boston Globe*. "No advertiser was consulted."

Merely editorial prerogative? The *Wall Street Journal* reported that Kosner's change of heart occurred only after *Esquire*'s publisher warned him that running the racy story would probably cost the magazine four pages of ads sold to Chrysler. The automaker, as Russ Baker pointed out in the *Columbia Journalism Review,* had previously delivered a chilling message to many magazines, including *Esquire,* through its ad agency, demanding notification "in advance of any and all editorial content that encompasses sexual, political, social issues or any editorial that might be construed as provocative or offensive."

Kosner's lack of *cojones* prompted *Esquire*'s Literary Editor, Will Blythe, to quit in protest. "Events of the last few weeks signal that . . . we're taking marching orders (albeit, indirectly) from advertisers," wrote Blythe in his resignation letter.

Here's another smoking gun. In 1985, the *New Republic,* which accepted ads for brands like Merit and True, flicked away a piece about big tobacco as if it were a spent cigarette butt. Ironically, David Owen's article spanked the media for velvety coverage of the tobacco industry.

In a version of his story that later ran in *Washington Monthly,* Owen wrote that Martin Peretz, The *New Republic*'s owner, "told me that he thought smoking was not as dangerous as doctors made it out to be and that, therefore 'this is a costly crusade that I am willing to forgo.'"

In the *Washington Post,* Peretz denied that the *New Republic* had even accepted Owen's article. "It was not a piece that was commissioned by us . . . I thought it was frankly a hysterical piece. I think this is a weighty scientific subject, and it requires a much more balanced treatment than this is."

As A. J. Liebling famously quipped, "Freedom of the press is guaranteed only to those who own one." Or, I would add, *have friends* who own one. Unflattering profiles of media heavies like

Miramax's co-founder Harvey Weinstein, tabloid publisher David Pecker, magazine impresario Steve Brill, owner of London's *Observer* Tiny Roland, and the late newspaper baron Robert Maxwell have all been scrapped in recent years.

When a media boss orders a rub-out, scant evidence remains unless the crime is particularly brutal. In 2001, the Freedom Forum, which bills itself as an "international foundation dedicated to free press, free speech and free spirit for all people," hired Michael Gartner to write a "warts and all" biography to honor its founder, Allen H. Neuharth, the man also responsible for *USA Today*. Gartner, the former editor of the *Des Moines Register* and a one-time president of NBC News, discovered a whopper of a wart. He planned to write about a woman who claimed to be Neuharth's shunned, out-of-wedlock daughter. The Freedom Forum abruptly canceled the book project and instructed Gartner to turn over his notes.

Unlike many media magnates, Otis Chandler, the powerful patriarch of the family that long controlled the *Los Angeles Times*, bragged about his seemingly successful bid to kill a story that hit too close to home. In 1996, *Los Angeles Magazine*, then owned by Disney, commissioned the award-winning investigative reporter Mark Dowie to write a feature on the Chandlers. The historical piece contained some embarrassing revelations, including details about the ugly divorce of Otis Chandler's son.

"I spoke to [Disney Chairman] Mike Eisner," Chandler later told David Margolick of *Vanity Fair*, "and said, 'Do you realize that you're going to do another—another—piece on the Chandlers?' . . . "He [Eisner] said, 'Don't see why,' and that was the end of it."

Days later, Michael Caruso, the editor of *Los Angeles Magazine*, killed Dowie's story, though he denied receiving an order from Eisner to do so.

Magnates who can't get Disney's chairman on the line can always wage a legal war against pesky publications. U.S. libel laws favor journalists but courts rarely throw out frivolous law suits and almost never force a losing party to pay the winning defendant's legal fees. "It's difficult to get cases thrown out in preliminary stages and its almost impossible to get legal fees and other litigation costs paid for by the losing party," noted Paul R. Levenson, a Manhattan attorney with vast experience in libel cases. Given the odds, some magazines and newspapers decide to spike a controversial story than shell out big bucks to defend themselves against nuisance law suits.

The late Robert Friedman, a renowned investigative reporter, accused *GQ* of cutting its losses when in 1999 it killed his hard-hitting profile of casino mogul Steve Wynn. "From the moment I got back from my ten-day investigative trip to Las Vegas, *GQ* was bombarded by letters from Wynn's attorneys," Friedman complained to the *New York Post*. It was not the first time Wynn and his lawyers mixed it up with the media; he had sued Barricade Books for putting out *Running Scared: The Life and Treacherous Times of Las Vegas Casino King Steve Wynn*. Given his reputation as a free-spending plaintiff, it's a safe bet to assume that few editors will order substantive probes of Wynn's business dealings in the future.

The breakneck pace of media consolidation will only produce more risk-averse editors. An increasing number of publishing companies are now publicly-traded corporations that compensate top management with stock. A 2001 survey by the consultant Youngs, Walker & Company found that nearly one-third of editors of large newspapers receive stock as part of their pay package. Are these shareholder-editors more or less likely to jeopardize their personal wealth by spiking a contentious story that could cause their company's stock to crater?

Other top editors see themselves not as Wall Street CEOs but as celebrities in their own right as they are chauffeured from premiere to premiere. Perhaps that explains why in the last decade some editors have come to regard working writers as extras on the set—essentially interchangeable faces. Can a wealthy editor who is fawned over by publicists and chased by paparazzi relate to freelance writers who earn, according to a 2002 study by the National Writers Union, less than half what they did in the 1960s? Too many editors indiscriminately kill worthy stories on a whim. While researching this book, I heard an anecdote that I can't confirm. But take it as a fable: The top editor of a men's magazine conducted a secret experiment: he assigned the same story to three different writers, planning to pick his favorite version and kill off the other two.

All of the above does not absolve writers of some blame for their devaluation. Again and again they sheepishly accept labor practices that would produce pickets in the rest of the business world. Many independent journalists, scared of being branded a "troublemaker" by cliquish editors, do not discuss scandalously low pay rates and sign, often without reading, take-it-or-leave-it contracts that give magazines and newspapers the power to arbitrarily deem an article "unpublishable"—regardless of quality—and pay a minimal "kill fee." Plumbers would not put up with such practices—why should writers?

Perhaps writers can learn something from one of their creative brethren. The legendary photographer Man Ray developed an innovative strategy to deal with skittish clients: "If [editors] expressed hesitation to the advisability of using one of my far-fetched works, asking for a reduction in fee, I replied to soothe my hurt vanity that in that case the fee would be double."

• • •

The other day, a colleague who helped me track down an article for the collection requested that I remove his name from the acknowledgments. He worried that his former boss, who receives a mild rebuke in this book, might notice the name of an ex-employee and occasional contributor, add two and two together, and put the kibosh on future assignments. Paranoia? Perhaps. Then my lawyer made a similar request. She reasoned that even the slightest chance of being dragged into a nuisance law suit outweighed any potential business generated by free advertising.

When I conceived of *Killed*, I initially thought the book would entertain more than it would unnerve, but that opinion changed as I began interviewing writers and editors. On several occasions, I detected palpable trepidation on the other end of the phone, expressed in awkward pauses, stammers, near-hang-ups. Are we back in the McCarthy era when whispers crushed careers? Not quite. But an unmistakable undercurrent of fear exists among many of the people traditionally charged with challenging powerful interests.

I trust *Killed* will provide a good read, but I hope that it will also provoke debate and outrage, as well as a realization that what is left unsaid, and unwritten, often has profound consequences, because when editors kill, readers often end up as unwitting victims.

David Wallis
New York

Editor's Note

The stories that follow, except for the book review by George Orwell and "A Ramble Through Lebanon" by P. J. O'Rourke, which are reprinted from the books *The Complete Works of George Orwell* and *Holidays in Hell* respectively, were edited to some degree. Stories by Todd Gitlin, Gerald Hannon, Erik Hedegaard, Ted Rall, and Carlo Wolff ran in various publications subsequent to being spiked and required only minor editing, as did Robert Fisk and Terry Southern. Mark Schone restored some cuts made to "Unfortunate Con" by *Oxford American*, which had picked up his piece after *Rolling Stone* rejected it. The remaining articles, all previously unpublished, received the care that they would have gotten had they not been killed. Each contributor was asked to write a precis, an admittedly subjective account of the killing of their article. Unpublished nonfiction articles underwent fact-checking to verify that they were accurate at the time they were written.

To submit a letter to the editor, visit www.killedstories.com.

Review of O. D. Gallagher's "Retreat in the East"

By George Orwell

Killed: *The Observer,* 1942

George Orwell's career as a writer was marked by almost continual struggles for the right to be published in the first place. He suffered from the cowardice of editors, from the rejection of manuscripts by publishers on overtly political grounds, and from the interference of government bureaucrats. Though these experiences occasionally embittered and annoyed him—he did not make anything that could be called a steady income until he was almost on his deathbed—they were of undoubted use in honing his criticism of the "intellectuals" of his day.

Many writers find their work being kept out of print with no explanation, and have to speculate about the reasons. (This quite often leads to authorial self-pity and paranoia.) In the case of Orwell, however, those who turned down his stuff were only too happy to tell him why. In 1937, as the Spanish Civil War raged, the New Statesman *informed him quite candidly that his reports from Barcelona were unwelcome because their implications were "unhelpful" to the Republican cause. T. S. Eliot and Victor Gollancz, who were among the giants of the publishing world, told him to his face that* Animal Farm *would not see print if they could help it, because of its latent "Trotskyism" and because its appearance might offend Britain's wartime Soviet* ally. Other publishers were encouraged to turn the book down, by an underhanded campaign on the part of a senior official at the Ministry of Information (who was later revealed to have been an agent of Soviet intelligence). The Observer, as you are about to read, rejected a commissioned review of a book that criticized the lavish lifestyle of expat businessmen in Singapore and Burma on the grounds that it might give encouragement to influential Americans—the sort who had made Britain's imperialism an excuse for staying out of the Second World War.

None of Orwell's would-be censors ever alleged that what he was saying was not true. They asserted, rather, that the time was not right, or the prevailing climate not appropriate, for such things to be said. In a letter from The Observer's editor Ivor Brown, the words "play into the hands of" occur twice, as if to say that "objectively" Orwell was doing more damage than he knew. Brown's note is a demonstration case of the fatuity of the censorial mind. It is hinted that, if opinions like those of Orwell were published, neither the USSR nor the United States would continue to fight against the Axis. A moment's thought might have prompted the saner reflection that Stalin and Roosevelt were at war for good reasons of their own, having to do with their respective calculations of national interest, and it seems improbable that they would have capitulated to Hitler and Hirohito because of any polemic written by a then-obscure English socialist. (The United States had entered the war against imperial Japan about nine months before Orwell wrote his review of Gallagher's Retreat in the East.) Then again, if the publication of undesirable thoughts about the British Empire were likely to hinder the prosecution of the war effort, it might be the original printing of Gallagher's book itself, and not of a short review of it, that would do the damage. But such thoughts, as we know, do not penetrate the mentality of censorship and "damage control."

Upon receiving a rejection letter from Ivor Brown, Orwell vowed to The Observer's literary editor Cyril Connolly that he would not write for the paper again after this episode, but he eventually did. There may be a lesson here for other struggling writers: don't make any proud and principled boasts on which you are not prepared to be consistent. (Within a few years, indeed, the owner of The Observer would be paying the expenses of Orwell's funeral.) The larger lesson was one that Orwell took to heart with some effect. The attempt to establish an official truth, and to deny or degrade the idea of the individual search for objectivity, is not just a property of the totalitarian regime. It exists in the mind of the apologist and the careerist, and it often comes dressed up with insidiously persuasive euphemisms. And it needs to be resisted, everywhere and all the time. —Christopher Hitchens

Though telling us too much about Mr. Gallagher and his fellow correspondents and too little about the various oriental peoples among whom they made their hurried journeys, this book contains interesting material. As war correspondent of the *Daily Express* Mr. Gallagher was on board the *Repulse* when she was sunk, and saw the Malaya and Burma campaigns at close quarters. It is a depressing story that he has to tell, though not a surprising one, and of course the villains of it are the *Burra Sahibs* and *Tuans Besar*,[1] the big businessmen and high officials under whose sloth and greed the Far Eastern provinces of the Empire had gradually rotted. Here is a picture of some of them in the Singapore club:

There lay the Tuans Besar, in two long rows of chairs. Attached to the arms of each chair were two leg-rests, which were swung out so that the sitter could lie flat out with his legs held up at a comfortable angle for him. The Tuans Besar were nearly all dressed in light-weight, light-coloured suits (not white, mark you, as only Eurasians wore white in Singapore; certainly not the exclusive, well-dressed Tuans Besar). Dark-red mouths opened and closed as they blew out great gusts of curry-laden breath. The bloated bellies heaved. . . .

While the Singapore businessmen, whose income tax had a ceiling of 8 percent, carried on with their normal round of golf, gin, and dancing, the fever-stricken troops in the jungle lived on bread and jam and chlorinated water. In Burma it was much the same story—an ill-armed, hopelessly outnumbered army with a frivolous incompetent civilian community behind it: the only redeeming features were the courage of the troops, the brilliant feats of the R.A.F. and the American Volunteer Group, and here and there the devotion and initiative of some minor official, who might be either an Englishman, an Indian, or a Eurasian.

A number of people, which Mr. Gallagher estimates at 300,000—even the Governor put it at 200,000—fled from Rangoon as a result of two air-raids which would have been petty ones by our standards. After that the defence of Burma became even more hopeless than before, because of the lack of labour. It was impossible to get ships unloaded, and thousands of tons of American armaments, originally destined for China, had to be destroyed before the Japanese arrived. Mr. Gallagher makes two charges which the ordinary reader has no way of verifying, but which ought to be investigated. One is that fresh troops were landed at Singapore long after its position had become obviously hopeless,[2] in spite of the protests of General Wavell, who wanted them diverted to Burma. The other is that Chiang Kai-shek's offer to send troops into Burma was only accepted grudgingly, and too late. It is also clear from his account that there was a good deal of favouritism in the matter of evacuation. Europeans, at any rate women, could generally get transport, but Indians had to fend for themselves. An interesting passage in the book describes a column of 4,000 Indian refugees on the 1,200-mile march back to India, with not a weapon between them and with Burmese bandits robbing them every night and murdering the stragglers.

Mr. Gallagher also spent some days with the Chinese army in Burma, and went as a passenger on a bombing raid on Bangkok. It is unfortunate that he says little about the political attitude of the ordinary Burmese population, an important question of which conflicting accounts have been given. Otherwise his book is a valuable piece of reporting, likely to ruffle some dovecots, which have needed ruffling these twenty years past.

[1] According to *The Complete Works of George Orwell*, edited by Peter Davison, "*Burra Sahibs* and *Tuans Besar* were terms of respect for important Europeans in Burma and Malaya respectively."

[2] This proved to be correct, noted Peter Davison, editor of *The Complete Works of George Orwell*, who adds: "Troops were landed and within a few hours were Japanese prisoners, many, of course, to die, and all to suffer, in the hands of their captors."

Are Women Wasting Their Time in College?

By Betty Friedan

Killed: *McCall's*, 1958

"You can use everything. You can use defeat as well as victory. You can use failure as well as success," Betty Friedan tells me over tiramisu at a trattoria near her home in Washington, D.C. The eighty-two-year-old feminist icon speaks from experience— initially a bad one.

In 1957, Friedan returned to her alma mater, Smith College for the fifteenth reunion of the Class of '42. Friedan had been asked to design and administer a questionnaire to profile her classmates and she presented her findings at the alumnae gathering. Since the project required a tremendous amount of work, Friedan planned to reuse her research in an article for McCall's, which had published her work in the past.

At Smith's campus in Northampton, Massachusetts, Friedan met several undergrads who had apparently bought into the notion—advanced by some magazines of the day—that too much education could deter women from finding husbands and a happy life. As she explained in her autobiography, Life So Far, Friedan positioned her subsequent article as an argument: "maybe it wasn't higher education making American women frustrated in their role as women, but the current definition of the role of women."

The top editor of McCall's—*a magazine that Friedan later spanked for assuming "women are brainless, fluffy kittens"—spiked the article and* Ladies' Home Journal *picked up the piece. But when editors there completely rewrote the article and radically changed its meaning (a practice still common in women's magazines), Friedan refused to allow them to publish it. "* McCall's *wouldn't print it.* Ladies Home Journal *wouldn't print it.* Redbook *wouldn't print it," recalls Friedan with a laugh, more Ha! than giggle. "That's when I knew I had to write a book."*

That book, published in 1963 and still in print, turned out to be The Feminine Mystique. —David Wallis

had come back in June to my college, to Smith, pioneer of higher education for women, pride of a century of daughters for its uncompromising intellectual standards. A suburban housewife with three children of my own, I walked again on the green campus in Northampton, Massachusetts, and felt the excitement that I felt as a young girl from a Midwest small town, when the life of the mind, and the wide horizons of the world, were opened to me.

I had come back for my fifteenth reunion with a soul-searching questionnaire on what we had become—members of the first generation of college women to follow the postwar pattern of woman's life, eschewing careers, marrying young, raising large families in the suburbs. We had all come back, as people do at a reunion, to see in each other the changes in ourselves—and to relive a little of our youth.

But as the weekend wore on, a strange Alice in Wonderland

feeling grew in us. We could not see our former selves in these pretty girls of '58, '59, '60. Watching the confident, clear-eyed seniors walk as we had walked through the ivy chain, carrying red roses against their white dresses, we said: "They're prettier than we were. It's their short hair." But it was more than that.

On the broad campus lane where we used to linger after classes, arguing what the professor had said in Science and the Imagination, the History of Western Civilization, Sociology, Chaucer, Economic Theory, Political Philosophy, I asked a blond senior in cap and gown what courses *she* was excited in. Nuclear physics? Modern Art? The Civilizations of Asia? She stared as if I were a prehistoric dinosaur.

"Girls don't get excited about things like that anymore," she smiled at me. "We don't want careers.

"Our parents expect us to go to college. Everybody goes, you're a social outcast at home if you don't. But a girl who got serious about studies, or going into research, would be peculiar, unfeminine. I guess everybody wants to graduate with a diamond ring on her finger, that's the important thing."

In front of the lab where I remember the sunset stillness, after finishing a difficult experiment, a sophomore in Bermuda shorts told me she'd changed her mind about majoring in science. "I intend to get married and have four children and live in a good suburb. My husband will probably be drawing a good salary from a large company. What good will it do me to study physics? Boys would think I was odd. Besides, it's too time-consuming. Science is something you can't do on the train. I couldn't leave early for football weekends."

In the coffee dive where we used to sit for hours, in passionate bull sessions about what-is-truth, art-for-art's-sake, religion, sex, war, and peace, Freud and Marx and what's-wrong-with-the-world, a senior said: "We never waste time like that. I guess we don't have bull sessions about abstract things.

Mostly, we talk about our dates. Anyhow, I spend three days a week off campus. There's a boy I'm interested in. I want to be with him."

Under the elms by the great library I knew so well, a dark-eyed junior said: "Privately, I like to wander around the stacks and pick up books that interest me. But you learn as a freshman to turn up your nose at the library. Sometimes, it hits you, that you won't be at college after next year. For a minute you wish you'd read more, talked more, taken hard courses you skipped. So you'd know what you were interested in. But I guess those things don't matter when you're married. You're interested in your home, and teaching your children how to swim and skate, and at night you talk to your husband. I think we'll be happier than college women used to be."

I discovered that the girls had an unwritten rule, barring "shop talk" about courses, intellectual talk, in the dormitory living room and dining room. I discovered professors resorting to desperate means to arouse their students' interest. Picking up the college paper which I once edited, I read the current student editor's rueful description of a Government class in which fifteen of the twenty girls were knitting "with the stony-faced concentration of Madame LaFarge. The instructor more in challenge than in seriousness announced that Western civilization is coming to an end. The students turn to their notebooks and write 'Western civ—coming to an end,' all without dropping a stitch."

My old psychology professor complained: "They're bright enough. They have to be, to get here at all now. But they just won't let themselves get interested. They seem to feel it will get in their way when they marry that young executive and raise all those children in the suburbs. I couldn't schedule the final seminar for my senior honor students. Too many kitchen showers interfered. None of them considered the seminar sufficiently important to postpone their kitchen showers."

And this attitude, I discovered, is shared by girls on all campuses today, with effects even more drastic than those I saw at Smith. Recent statistics show that 60 percent of the women who start college in the United States now drop out before they finish, one out of three after freshman year. Fewer and fewer women are preparing themselves for any professional work. They go to college, says Indiana educator Kate Mueller, because "the campus is frankly the world's best marriage mart." If they don't leave, at nineteen, to marry, they leave, says Harvard social scientist David Riesman, because they fear too much education is a "marriage bar."

I don't blame these girls. I blame those who have given them the picture that the fate worse than death of the unmarried career woman—or neurotic husband-and-child-destroying career woman—awaits a girl who takes college seriously. I blame those who have made these girls half-believe themselves that college is a waste of time, or worse, for women who want to marry and have children.

Ladies' Home Journal recently ran an article called "Is College Education Wasted on Women?" draped with editors' comments: "Let's face it, most females between eighteen and twenty-five are out to get a chap . . . Planning a career, unless they refuse motherhood, just means frustration."

"Do college-bred women feel unhappy when they become 'mere' wives and mothers?" asked *Newsweek* recently under the headline "College—the Seeds of Discontent?" In a special issue on women, *Life* magazine pictured the high divorce rate, alcoholism, mental illness, male impotence, juvenile delinquency, and all the restlessness, frustration, and last-third-of-life disillusion and defeat of women themselves as due to their education, stating: "A woman educated for some kind of intellectual work who finds herself in the lamentable position of being 'just being a housewife' can work as much damage on the lives of her husband and children, and her own life, as if she were a career woman."

Small wonder that girls are afraid to get interested in college—with all the warnings echoing Marynia Farnham and Ferdinand Lundberg's book, *Modern Woman: The Lost Sex*, that such interests lead to "the masculinization of women with enormously dangerous consequences to the home, the children dependent on it, and to the ability of the woman, as well as her husband, to obtain sexual gratification."

I think it's high time someone questioned the truth of this picture that is making the girls waste time in college. It seems fantastic, with 1,170,000 women in college in America today, to suggest that they may lose the right to higher education if they don't stop wasting it. But with Sputnik imparting national urgency in education, colleges may not continue so tolerantly to fill one out of three college seats with women who regard it merely as "a place to find a man."

The facts are that in the last ten years, while U.S. colleges generally have had their unprecedented growth, thirty women's colleges have closed their doors. The Danforth Foundation, largest donor of teaching fellowships, is no longer giving any to women—so many have wasted them. More and more voices are asking—in the words of *Newsweek*'s Special Education Report on the American Coed—"why the girls bother to go to college at all? . . .With earlier marriages becoming an American pattern, wouldn't it be simpler all around . . . if they just trained themselves for such domestic tasks as cooking and sewing and child-rearing?"

And the educators led by former Mills College president Lynn White who have been urging that women's education be limited to the "household arts" to prevent their "frustration" as housewives, are now being joined by those who point out that the space they are "wasting" can be used to train boys as scientists.

The girls have been warned of this danger, by educators, sociologists, psychologists. But against the threat of missing sexual happiness, fulfillment as women, they won't listen to professors' arguments. "It is simply that we are rediscovering our role as women, which has been so long neglected in America," a Smith senior wrote in answer to her professors.

"This attitude *will* perhaps lead to less stimulating class discussion and more cutting of classes," she went on. "However, looking at the differing role of women and men in life, perhaps this is only natural and a more healthy attitude for women students to have than the enthusiastic 'fighting for rights and out to conquer the world' type woman who, though undoubtedly a joy to her college professor, is often less than a joy to her husband, which perhaps has contributed to the high divorce rate."

Perhaps the women now at Smith might listen to two hundred women who are leading the very lives they want to lead—the women of my own Smith generation whom I questioned last spring, fifteen years after graduation. We could tell the pretty girls of Smith '58, '59, and '60—and all the other girls on all the other campuses who are wasting their time in college today—that they have it all wrong.

We are what you want to be—executives' wives chauffeuring stationwagonfuls of children through suburbia. We spend most of our time at home (eight rooms, Colonial to contemporary) with our husbands and our two, three, four, five, six children. We've lived through all the possible frustrations education can cause housewives. And the problems we have had, working out

our role as women, make us regret only one thing today—that
we did not work harder in college.

If one generation can ever tell another, we can tell you. By virtue of Pearl Harbor our senior year, we were the first graduating class to applaud a proudly pregnant classmate, receiving her diploma *cum laude* in a hand already encircled by a wedding ring. Before then, Smith girls were expelled for marrying in college.

We bridged the conflict as acutely as it could be bridged. In our prewar college years, the prettiest most popular girls—not just the brains—were serious about their work. Whether or not we had career ambitions—and 40 percent of us did—we became excited about ideas, issues, the world beyond our personal lives, the life of the mind. Not everybody, of course. But girls who took their full quota of weekends at Yale also browsed alone, without shame, in the library stacks. We got the most rigorous liberal arts education women could get in this country, unhampered by the fear that it was "unfeminine" to be interested in sociology, world politics, physics, musical theory, art history, Einstein, Plato, Bach. The only crime was not to think for yourself.

And then came Pearl Harbor. The lonely years when our husbands—or husbands-to-be—were away at war made us ready indeed to receive the doctrine of "Modern Woman: the Lost Sex" and "look for sole fulfillment in the home." We worked, using our minds, 90 percent of us, during the war—and feared, with reason, that we might miss fulfillment as women. And when the men came back, we gave up our careers (only 11 percent are working full-time now) glorying in the domesticity we might have missed, the babies we could have at last, one after the other—and almost wondering ourselves why we'd "wasted so much time," training our minds in college.

The answer we arrived at, not without pain, after fifteen

years of working out our role as women, is not the simple one you've been given. It can, I think, be believed. Sociologists say they would not have dared to ask us some of the soul-searching questions we asked ourselves on that questionnaire last spring. But we who drew it up (Anne Mather Montero and Marion Ingersoll Howell who helped me are sociology-trained housewives) and the two hundred who spent almost a whole day answering it, were motivated not by prying curiosity, or even cold sociological inquiry, but by the need to know ourselves, what we had become, where we were going. As postscript, one woman wrote: "It gave me a much needed chance to evaluate the meaning of my life."

Our education did not keep us from sexual fulfillment.

We are married (97 percent)—most of us within three years after college—to college men of our own generation, who are now $14,843-a-year executives. We compare our marriages to our dreams of marriage and find (80 percent) that our dreams were wanting. We enjoy being with our husbands more than anyone else (90 percent), making all major decisions "together" (93 percent). Heading toward forty, we (98 percent) neither feel over and done with sexually, nor are we just beginning to feel the satisfaction of being a woman. Sex to us has been satisfactory all along—and, for 85 percent, gets "better and better with the years." Only 3 percent of us have been divorced. Only 50 percent have even been interested in another man since marriage, and most "did nothing about it."

Our education did not bar us from enjoying motherhood.

We planned our children's births (86 percent), enjoyed our pregnancies (66 percent), neither feared nor were depressed in childbirth (75 percent). We breast-fed (70 percent) our babies, from one to nine months. Our homes, we say proudly, differ from the homes we grew up in because we "have more children" (five and six are more common with us than one; our average is 2.94) and we "do more together as a family." We take our vacations, spend our days and weekends, have made our friends, together. We admit (99 percent of us) to times when we "shout [at] or slap" our kids—and 99 percent of us "have fun with our kids." Only 10 percent of us ever feel "martyred" as mothers.

We might have been "frustrated" housewives—without the resources our education gave us.

We had problems working out our role as women (89 percent of us). Our education did not cause those problems. And they were not solved by telling ourselves "be happy, be fulfilled as a wife and mother" while we waxed the kitchen floor. Our main problem was to find the meaning of our lives—to find the strength for all our roles—to be a self, as well as wife and mother.

We found we could not live through our husbands and children.

Sex, we discovered (99 percent of us) is only "one factor among many" in marriage, in woman's life. We can say that sex "gets better with the years" and still find it "less important than it used to be." We share life with our husbands "as fully as one can with another human being" but find (75 percent of us) that we cannot share it all. (Only 25 percent can talk fully with our husbands about our deepest feelings. To a few of us this "wall between my husband and myself" is the chief frustration in life.)

Those of us who sought all satisfaction through our husbands and children were frustrated by "the inability of my children to live up to my expectations," and "the time and energy my husband must put into his job, leaving not too much for the family." A few of us, at first, had more problems than fun with our children because "I tried too hard to be a good mother, and took out my own frustrations on the kids."

Most of us (60 percent) cannot honestly say that we find our "main occupation as homemaker really fulfilling."

With every possible appliance from dishwasher to trash disposal and a cleaning woman once a week (only 12 percent have full-time help) we spend four hours a day on housework. We do it in Bermuda shorts, and we do not put the milk bottle on the table, and our husbands do not complain about our housekeeping, (they've had a hand at most of it themselves). But except for cooking and the decoration of our homes, we do not particularly "enjoy" it. We frankly "detest" scrubbing the kitchen floor, cleaning the Venetian blinds, picking up the clutter. Whether we would enjoy the drudgery of housework any more without our education, we do not know. But most of us can say that we frankly do not find homemaking "totally fulfilling" and still say we are "not frustrated" as suburban housewives. For we point (74 percent of us) to satisfying interests beyond our homes, or within ourselves—the serious interests our education gave us.

Our education did indeed unfit us for a woman's role confined to housekeeping. It gave many more dimensions to our role as women. It fitted us to meet the challenge of the new suburbs—where, with the men gone all day, women must do the pioneering to get a good education for their children, a spiritually good life for their families.

We started cooperative nursery schools in suburbs where none existed, when our kids were three . . . Cub Scout packs when they were eight . . . teenage canteens . . . libraries in schools where Johnny seldom read—"ordered and catalogued the books myself and got volunteers to staff it," said a mother of four. A great many of us teach Sunday School. We "teach the children French and music myself since they don't get it at school." PTA to us is no comedown from Plato—we fought to get better schools, in suburbs where the problems taxed all our intellectual powers. One of us, a mother of five, stood alone as a member of the School Board in a major town controversy over a new school. One of us was personally instrumental in getting 13,000 signatures for a popular referendum to get politics out of the school system. One of us publicly spoke out for desegregation of schools in the South . . . and one got white children to attend a de facto segregated school in the North. One of us pushed an appropriation for mental health clinics through a western state legislature. One set up museum art programs for school children in each of three cities she's lived in since marriage. We lead a suburban choral group . . . a suburban opera troupe . . . a $100,000 theater-in-the-round . . . a Great Books study group . . . a foreign policy group. In many suburbs, we have campaigned, canvassed, poll-checked to oust corrupt officials; 30 percent of us are active in local party politics. And over 90 percent of us read the newspaper thoroughly every day and vote regularly, in local and national elections.

We do not need to live life through our husbands and children, or find its meaning in the material possessions of our homes. For we draw increasing strength from the solitary life of mind and spirit our education gave us. We know who we are, ourselves.

Our complaint as suburban wives and mothers is not of boring, empty lives but of lives too *fragmented*. Where will we get the strength for "the multiplicity of roles—wife, mother, homemaker—often in competition with the endless demands for affection from all sides, including the dog?" Our greatest need, we sometimes feel, is more time alone (we have so little, an hour a day)—"time to myself when I could get my mind off the petty details of housekeeping, child-rearing, and answering 'mummy, mummy' "—time to read, to write, to study, to work on my art and music, to think about the meaning of life, to figure out where I'm going. One of us renews her strength in sculpture, another—mother of four— in studying geology. One of us sets aside time every day to study the great theologians. One paints three mornings a week. One writes—in odd moments between giving family haircuts, altering clothes, baking bread, cutting grass. As suburban wives and mothers, we find increasing meaning in philosophy, history, sociology, religion, in re-reading Dostoyevsky and Shakespeare (of the 15-to-300 books apiece we've read this past year, half were not bestsellers).

This other part of life which we enjoy alone—the life of the mind our education gave us—somehow renews our knowledge of who we are. In an era of suburban conformity, we do not (80 percent of us) do things, little or big, simply because everybody else does them or they are the "thing to do" in our community. We live according to our own individual values. We can look back over the changes the years have made in us and say, "I have a growing sense of self-realization, inner serenity and strength." "I have become more my real self."

And if we pay a certain price in frustration, now, for this rich full life, this self-realization our education gave us—in return, we do not fear growing old.

The chief frustration for most of us today is simply *time*—"not enough time after the children and housework to do all I want to do that is creative, challenging, fun." It is not an unbearable frustration (ask us the best time of our life and 70 percent of us say "now"—no regrets for lost youth, romance). And it has its own time limit, and reward. We are on the verge now of the "last thirty years," when our children will no longer fill our days, when we can no longer do everything as a family together. The prospect does not terrify us. We do not have the growing sense of disillusion and defeat supposedly so common to women our age. Facing forty, we frankly acknowledge that our hair is graying, our skin looks faded and tired—and we (70 percent of us) do not hate growing older. "How do you visualize your life after your children are grown?" we ask ourselves ("this is the $64,0000 question," someone said). Sixty percent of us have concrete plans for work or study, pursuing further the strong interests we acquired in college, the life of the mind that has nourished us through these hectic golden years of young motherhood.

We have only one profound regret today about our education. We regret (80 percent of us) that we did not study more seriously in college, study more intensively philosophy, poetry, physics, sociology, astronomy, when we had time.

If we could do it over again few (10 percent of us) would have spent college time on homemaking courses, though we admit "our education did not prepare us for the routine of housekeeping." We could complain that our education "lacked a feeling for the pattern of a woman's life"—that it gave us "no perspective for thinking in a household full of noisy kids and constant interruptions." That each of us had to work out for herself.

What we regret, more seriously (30 percent of us) is that we did not direct our education to a more serious end—that we did not prepare, quite frankly, for some serious work we could return to when our children were grown. For many of us who had no career ambitions in college—have them now. And it's hard, nearing forty, to start.

One of us recently tried to go back to the kind of job she held the year between college and her marriage; the agency refused to let her register, and she was told by the nearest university that she was too long out to go back for a master's degree.

Many of us are planning now to teach. One of us, a mother of five, who was too "self-conscious to get as much out of college as I should"—is taking education courses in summer school. A mother of four is preparing herself for professional social work by the time her youngest is in school all day, by taking one course a year over six years.

And for many of us there are no regrets. The serious interests acquired in college, that sent us pioneering in suburbia and gave us strength in the hours alone these years when our children were young, are our sufficient passports to the last half of life.

Many of us plan to pursue professionally after forty, work we undertook as volunteers in the community when our children were small. The board member of a mental hygiene clinic is studying to be a group therapist. The Republican precinct committeewoman intends to study law; the mother of four who fought for better schools will teach remedial reading; the League of Woman Voters leader plans to run for the legislature.

And the mother of five who paints three times a week will

become a serious artist. One of us plans to study astronomy at forty, the choir singer to get an advanced degree in sacred music, the museum volunteer to become an art historian.

Maybe one generation cannot tell another. But when we asked ourselves if we wanted for our daughters the kind of liberal arts education we had—the kind they say makes "frustrated" housewives—we said, 94 percent of us, "yes."

And so we warn you—as we shall our daughters—don't waste your time in college. Commit yourselves with passion to physics, philosophy, poetry. Find out who you are. Commit yourselves with such passionate hard work to the life of the mind that it is *yours,* for your whole life as woman. It may be too late to start, in the fragmented years ahead of you as wife and mother, when you have only an hour a day alone to read or think, alone in your house with no prescribed paths to follow as men have, with the children calling "mummy, mummy" and the pressures to conform.

You will need it, not for a career, but for your role as woman (though your role as woman may also include a career in ways you do not now anticipate, as we did not anticipate at twenty-one that we would want to teach at forty. Who knows how long science will make *you* live?) Sure, you'll have problems as woman; in the fast-changing years ahead of Sputnik and space they may be even more unexpected than the challenges of suburbia were to us. And you'll need a trained mind to solve them, even more surely than we did.

For America's new frontier is intellectual. And it will be woman's role to pioneer on that frontier beside her husband, as it was in America's past. Will you be able to share true companionship with your husband and children, in the world that is conquering space, if you aren't excited about the life of the mind? Will you be able to raise children to meet the intellectual challenge of our time without strong intellectual interests of your own? For educators say students get their values mainly from their mothers.

Will you find the happiness we have found as wives and mothers, if you do not know who you are? If you do not take your education even more seriously than we did, and frankly plan it toward some end serious enough to nourish you all your life?

Mathematics will not frustrate you waxing your family room floor, if you share the excitement of the new world of space in your mind as you wax, and the satisfaction of contributing to that world, in some hour when your waxing is done. But if you have a mind capable of conquering space, won't it frustrate you if your whole world is waxing that floor?

Maybe one generation does not need to tell another. For on my own old campus, in Northampton this past year, the freshmen instigated a year-long soul-searching about the unspoken rule against serious intellectual talk. The upperclassmen tried at first to laugh it off. But the freshmen organized a new literary magazine (the old one had died for lack of contributors) as well as an intellectual discussion group. "What we ask is a college life where we can, and are encouraged to develop, the values and insights which will be the real core of our later lives," they wrote in a letter, published on the college paper's front page. "The superficial tricks of the game we can pick up any time—we have only a few years in which to shape our investigations into the true nature of things."

To those members of the class of 1961—and to the fresh-faced junior who is reading books that are over her head instead of playing bridge—two hundred slightly graying suburban wives, struggling with the crisis in education and the challenge of the last half of woman's life, say with assurance: You are not wasting your time.

Check-up with Doctor Strangelove

By Terry Southern

Killed: *Esquire*, 1963

In the summer of '62, my father received a fateful assignment from Esquire *to interview Stanley Kubrick whose film* Lolita *was about to be released. Terry admired* Paths of Glory, The Killing, *and* Spartacus *and, despite the list of canned (mostly trivial) questions from* Esquire, *engaged Kubrick in a provocative discussion about film, literature, and politics. After submitting the piece through his agent, it was clear* Esquire *wanted something more "gossipy" on Kubrick. Hoping to throw the editors off their celebrity blood hunt, Terry responded:*

> *. . . trying to establish [Kubrick] as a 'wise-guy,' 'difficult,' or having the reputation as such, was so far off-mark that to have pursued it would have been altogether misleading. . . . He does not know what [actress Sue Lyon] is going 'to do next' . . . Similarly, he had no opinion on Elizabeth Taylor's behavior in Rome . . .*

As the interview languished at Esquire, *Terry began working with Kubrick on* Dr. Strangelove, *and in 1963 asked* Esquire *if he could do a piece on the movie. Incorporating bits of the squelched interview, he found the time to write the article during filming. In the piece that follows, Terry introduces the reader (and the masses)* to Kubrick, this revolutionary film, and the all-important (and ever looming) topic of the day: nuclear annihilation.

Much to his astonishment, the editors dismissed the article as a "puff piece" and prodded him to go more gonzo. Esquire's assistant managing editor suggested Terry "jettison most of the article" and instead describe life in London "with his friends, books, parties, and especially his own self."

Terry protested, quite presciently, that this was one of those "rare instances where something genuinely great was at hand." He wrote back:

> I have obviously failed to persuade you as to the phenomenal nature of the film itself—i.e., that it is categorically *different from any film yet made, and that it will probably have a stronger impact in America than any single film, play, or book in our memory. To say that the piece is a* puff *is, to my mind, like saying that a piece about thalidomide babies is* downbeat.

Kubrick's insights into America's military are eerily prophetic of the Bush administration, particularly the ideologues Wolfowitz, Cheney, Rumsfeld, Pearle, and their Project for a New American Century. "What has struck me," Kubrick told Terry, "is their cautious sterility of ideas, the reverence of obsolete national goals, the breeziness of crackpot realism, the paradox of nuclear threatsmanship, the desperately utopian wish fantasies about [an enemy nation's] intentions, and the terrifying logic of paranoiac fears and suspicions."

The idea of launching a "first strike," had been anathema to all government and military policy strategists since World War II. Amazing how now, pre-emption and even pre-emption with "low-yield" nuclear devices is part of the dry rhetoric of the United States. It is, as Terry warns in his article, "a curious self-deception which tends towards making the unthinkable thinkable." —Nile Southern

Ranged round the gigantic table in the swank and spacious War Room of the Pentagon are the President of the United States and his cabinet, flanked by the Joint Chiefs of Staff and the twenty-odd senior officers and advisors who comprise the National Security Council. It is a 3:00 AM meeting of the utmost and unexpected urgency; USAF's four-star General Buck Turgidson, chairman of the joint chiefs, is explaining how three dozen of his B-52 bombers (each carrying two nuclear devices of twenty megatons) have mistakenly received the so-called "Go-Code," and are now in fact screaming toward their Russian targets. It seems that the commandant of Strategic Air Command's 843rd Bomb Wing, Brig. Gen. Jack D. Ripper, has resorted to the seldom practiced (and never discussed) *Plan-R*—an emergency War plan which gives unit commanders authority to issue strike orders in case higher echelon has been wiped out.

General Turgidson is addressing the assembly, and has just referred to the last telephone conversation with General Ripper, before the latter shut down the 843rd's communications center.

> **GENERAL BUCK TURGIDSON** (GEORGE C. SCOTT)
> . . . And then, Mister President, the SAC Duty Officer asked General Ripper to confirm the fact that he had issued the Go-Code, and he said—
> *(Clears throat and reads from the communications monitor-sheet)*
> "Yes, gentlemen, they are on their way in—and no one can bring them back. For the sake of our country and our way of life I suggest you get the rest of SAC in after them . . . otherwise we will be totally destroyed by Red retaliation. My boys will

give you the best kind of start—1,400 megatons worth. You sure as hell won't stop them now, so let's get going—there's no other choice. God willing, we shall prevail—in peace, and in freedom from fear, and in true health through the purity and essence of our natural fluids. God bless you all!" Then he hung up.

PRESIDENT MUFFLEY (PETER SELLERS)
(Frowning terribly)
Did he say something about *"fluids"*?

GENERAL BUCK TURGIDSON
Yes sir, uh, let's see *(scrutinizes paper)* . . . yes, here we are—"We shall prevail—in peace and in freedom from fear, and in true health through the purity and essence of our natural fluids." *(grimly)* We are still trying to determine the meaning of that last phrase, sir.

PRESIDENT MUFFLEY
There's nothing to determine, General Turgidson. The man's obviously a psychotic!

GENERAL BUCK TURGIDSON
Well, Mister President, I'd like to hold off judgment on a thing like that until all the facts are in.

PRESIDENT MUFFLEY
(coldly)
General Turgidson, when you instituted the Human Reliability Tests, you assured me there was no possibility of such a thing ever occurring.

GENERAL BUCK TURGIDSON
(With a smile of gentle condescension)
Mister President, I'm sure you'll agree that it's hardly fair or reasonable to condemn an entire program for a single slip-up.

Stanley Kubrick, however, has taken the plunge and *has*, in fact, condemned the entire program for a single slip-up—or rather for the obvious and myriad possibilities of such a slip-up and its nightmarish consequences. This is something which everyone who thinks has thought about, but about which no one has been able to do much more than write an irate letter to the *Times* or *The Realist*. Then along comes a young man with two million dollars to spend making a movie, and he blows the subject apart at the seams.

In Kubrick's office, I counted sixty-three volumes concerned with nuclear warfare; they ran the gamut of possible approaches—from Unilateral Disarmament to The Preemptive Strike. But one has only to listen to know his concern with the subject.

"During the past six years," he said, "I've read almost every available book on the nuclear situation, including regular issues of *Air Force Magazine, Missiles and Rockets, Bulletin of the Atomic Scientists,* and so on. What has struck me is their cautious sterility of ideas, the reverence of obsolete national goals, the breeziness of crackpot realism, the paradox of nuclear threatsmanship, the desperately utopian wish fantasies about Soviet intentions, and the terrifying logic of paranoiac fears and suspicions. The present world seems very much like a neurotic paralyzed by incompatible goals."

It was in October 1961, at London's Institute for Strategic Studies, that Kubrick's hazy and incredible dream of "doing something about it" began to take on the bittersweet edge of reality. Alastair Buchan, director of the Institute, told him about a certain novel he had just read which he considered remarkable in its verisimilitude of how a nuclear war might start. The novel, published in 1958, was written by a former RAF officer, Peter George, and was entitled *Red Alert*. Kubrick read it and was intrigued by its suspense, and by its technical authenticity—which had also been strongly endorsed by Professor Thomas Schelling of Harvard's Center For International Affairs; he immediately bought the film rights.

The novel itself, though highly suspenseful, offered little more than a straightforward melodramatic attitude toward the subject—not unlike that presented by its 1962 successor, *Fail-Safe*. (The basic similarities, incidentally, between *Red Alert* and *Fail-Safe* are embarrassingly sharp—so much so that the authors and publisher of the latter are now embroiled in a plagiarism action brought against them by the English author Peter George.) In any case, the sort of standard or prosaic approach afforded by melodrama, to the most astounding phenomenon in the history of man, was not what Kubrick had in mind. "The present nuclear situation," he has said, "is so totally new and unique that it is beyond the realm of current semantics; in its actual implications, and its infinite horror, it cannot be clearly or satisfactorily expressed by any ordinary scheme of aesthetics. What we do know is that its one salient and undeniable characteristic is that of the *absurd*." And so what Stanley Kubrick has done is to create the blackest nightmare comedy yet filmed. *Dr. Strangelove: Or How I Learned to Stop Worrying and Love the Bomb.*

The "War Room" at Shepperton Studios outside London is one of the largest indoor sets ever built. It is 130 feet long and 100 feet wide, with a 35-foot high ceiling. The walls are made of huge electronic world-target maps which cast back in weird reflection from the high-gloss black floor. The mammoth circular table, seating the Prez and his council, is covered with green baize, like a monstrous gaming-table, and is 380 square feet in surface area. An equally important sequence of the film takes place in a B-52 bomber—representative of those on their way towards Russian targets. "I've seen a lot of airplane pictures," Kubrick said, "but I've never seen one where I got the feeling of really being inside a plane." To this end he spent $150,000 authenticating the interior of a B-52, and in sending a twelve-man camera crew to the far north in a specially equipped B-17 photographic plane, where they shot 40,000 feet of moon-like Arctic ice-pack and wasteland footage and it has resulted in some of the most convincing flying sequences ever filmed.

This accentuation of realistic detail is part of the overall concept which he has tried to impose on the film—including character interpretation. A note at the front of the shooting-script reads: "The story will be played for *realistic* comedy—which means the essentially truthful moods and attitudes will be portrayed accurately, with an occasional bizarre or super-realistic crescendo. The acting will never be so-called 'comedy' acting." This clearly derives from Stanislavsky's own theory for obtaining the highest comic effect from a given scene—namely, that if the situation is *inherently* funny, it should be played as though it were not—played, in fact, as gravely straight-faced as possible. It is the difference between seeing a custard pie hit the face of a clown or the face of Herbert Hoover—one is predictably funny, the other outrageously funny. "I think that *surprise*," Kubrick said, "whether it occurs in love, war, business, or what have you, produces the greatest effect of any single element. It gives the added momentum to the sort of see-saw of emotion from one position to another, and you get this extra push of thrill and discovery. I've always believed that in presenting realistic drama—as opposed to verse or impressionism—the only thing that justifies the time and effort of *making* it realistic is the power, the tremendous power, including the comic, which you can generate emotionally if you astonish the audience and allow them to discover for themselves what your meaning is. People don't like to be told anything—I mean I don't think they even like to be told their pants are open. They love to discover things themselves, and I believe the only way to do it is to lead them up to a certain place, and then let them go the last distance alone—taking the chance, of course, that they may miss your point."

There is little danger that the points of *Dr. Strangelove* will be missed—although for Mr. and Mrs. Front Porch Swing the suspense alone should suffice. For despite General Ripper's ultimate suicide, the recall-code is uncovered, and all but one of the planes are brought back; with this one, however, it is touch-and-go all the way. Its entire communications-system shot out, the "Leper Colony"—with veteran Texas pilot Major "King" Kong (Slim Pickens) at the stick—doggedly presses on. ("Well, boys" he drawls in the classic John Wayne manner, "I reckon this is it—nuklar *com*-bat! Toe to toe with the Rooskies! *San An-tone!*") Meanwhile, back at the War Room, President Muffley speaks on the "Hot Line" (another case of fiction preceding fact) with the Russian premier, in an all-out cooperation to help him intercept the plane and stave off mutual disaster.

By way of hitting at least one of his points right on the nose, Kubrick cast Sterling Hayden in the role of General Ripper. Sterling Hayden . . . is a bronzed, six-foot-four former marine captain with blond curly hair and a humorless Colgate smile. A more clean-cut and uncomplicated looking fellow-American simply does not exist outside the illustrations of the *Saturday Evening Post,* and one can well imagine the senior class at Des

Moines High voting him "Person Least Likely to Blow His Bonnet." This sets it up nicely for the following exchange between himself and his executive officer—to whom he is explaining his reasons for giving the Wing the Go.

> **GENERAL RIPPER**
> *(grimly)*
> Captain Mandrake, have you ever seen a Russian drink *water?*

> **CAPTAIN MANDRAKE**
> No sir, I can't say that I have.

> **GENERAL RIPPER**
> Vodka, that's what they drink. On no account will your Russian drink water—and not without good reason.

After some preliminary exposition, General Ripper gets to the heart of it.

> **GENERAL RIPPER**
> *Fluoridation of water*, Captain—the most monstrously conceived and dangerous communist plot we have ever had to face. . . . The fluorides pollute our bodily fluids, Captain! They clot them. Our precious bodily fluids become thick and rancid!

The Captain asks General Ripper when he first became aware of this . . . this so-called bodily fluids theory.

> **GENERAL RIPPER**
> I first became aware of it . . . during the physical act

of love, Captain. A profound sense of fatigue, a feeling, if you like, of emptiness followed. Luckily I was able to interpret these feelings correctly—*loss of essence*. I can assure you it has not recurred. Women sense my power, and they seek the life essence. I do not avoid women, Captain—but I deny them my essence.

CAPTAIN MANDRAKE

I see.

Kubrick's status among American film directors is most exceptional. At thirty-four he has directed seven features and two documentaries—including such divergent fare as the prize-winning *Paths of Glory* and the ten-million-dollar *Spartacus*. His real affinity however is with the European school who think of themselves not as directors but as filmmakers. The distinction is the area of responsibility assumed toward the film as a whole. Aside from directing, the filmmaker prepares his own script, supervises set design, imposes the lighting values, and finally spends eight hours a day in the cutting room editing the footage. Kubrick's interest ranges beyond that, into designing his own ads and translating foreign titles. When the French, Italian, Spanish, and German titles for *Dr. Strangelove: Or How I Learned to Stop Worrying and Love the Bomb* were designated by the studio and reached his office, he revised each of them in consultation with Oxford language professors, who, of course, readily agreed they were faulty.

Not since Chaplin or Welles has anyone achieved the kind of autonomy which Kubrick has vis-à-vis whatever major studio happens to be financing his film, and it is certainly unique for one his age. "It's the first time I've worked on an A picture," said George C. Scott, "where there wasn't somebody from the front office snooping around. I guess they're afraid of what they might see—I mean maybe they don't understand Kubrick or what he's trying to do, but they do know how good he is."

Kubrick himself is of a somewhat different opinion: "When the major studios started unloading their back catalogue of films onto the television networks, movie attendance—which was already in a steady decline—took a nosedive that was really alarming. Now these studios are beginning to realize that to get people back into cinemas they have got to produce films of a different order from those being shown on TV. A new group of farsighted men, like Mike Frankovitch of Columbia, are leading the way in this—and it is extremely encouraging, not only for the creative people in the industry, but for movie-goers, and for the culture generally."

Kubrick has a frightening amount of controlled energy; he sleeps little, and while his assistants are reduced to an almost straight diet of dexies in order to keep abreast, he coolly munches a sedative and plays blitz-chess, at a pound (sterling) a piece, during the lunch break. He also possesses a curious Eastern-like facility for dropping into states of complete repose, seemingly at will. During one of these I ask him what was the best way to become a movie director—and his answer should be an inspiration to every young cineaste.

"The important thing," he said, suppressing a yawn, "is to start at the top."

Oddly enough, this is in keeping with his own self-made career, which he began at twenty-one, by doing a sixteen-minute documentary called *Day of the Fight*—a day in the life of a boxer, from the time he wakes up in the morning until he steps in the ring that night.

"How much does it cost to make such a film?"

"Well," he said, "I knew this fighter, Walter Cartier, a very good middleweight boxer, and so I put up the money and shot it, and we were supposed to share the profits. As for actual costs, the camera—a 35-millimeter Eyemo—was ten dollars a day, and the cost of the film, developed and printed, is about ten cents a foot. The only expensive thing on this film was doing an original music score. The whole film cost 3,800 dollars, and 2,800 of it was for the sound."

"And what did you do with this film?"

"Well, I didn't know what to do with it—but I called up RKO, because they were using a lot of shorts at the time, and asked them to have a look at it. They did, and they bought it—for 4,000 dollars, so I had picked up a quick 200 on it. I mean it only took about four months to put it all together . . . but the important thing was they advanced me 1,500 to make another one."

"And then what happened?"

"Well, these small things led from one to another until I met James Harris, a very courageous and perceptive young man, and he was able to raise some money so we formed our own company. Up until then I hadn't been able to consider the *content* of a story or anything like that—I had to use whatever material came to hand, simply to keep functioning in the medium. But now we were able to start thinking in terms of buying good stories and taking the time to develop them. We bought a novel called *Clean Break*, by Lionel White, and make it into *The Killing*. That's the first film I made with decent actors, a professional crew, and under the proper circumstances."

"And then you made *Paths of Glory*?"

"Yes. That was a book I had read when I was about fourteen, and one day I suddenly remembered it."

"Wasn't there some controversy over the ending of that film—where the French soldiers are executed for desertion?"

"Well, it wasn't a controversy—I mean there are always a lot of people around a film studio who like to give artistic advice, and they said 'You've got to save the men at the end!' but, of course, it was out of the question. It would have been like making a film about capital punishment in which the innocent man is saved—it would have been pointless."

"Now what about your involvement with Marlon Brando on *One-Eyed Jacks*?"

"Yes, that was a curious involvement. We became friendly, and he told me about this 'western' he wanted to do—and I was to direct it. So we spent six months working on the script—Marlon, Calder Willingham, and myself, along with Guy Trosper, George Glass, Carlo Fiori, Walter Setzer, Frank Rosenberg . . . and maybe some others. But it's really a much too complex and Kafkaesque story to go into now."

"I have here a quote from Brando about you—'Stanley is unusually perceptive and delicately attuned to people. He has an adroit intellect and is a creative thinker, not a repeater, not a fact-gatherer. He digests what he learns and brings to a new project an original point of view and a reserved passion.' What do you say to that?"

"Well, Marlon is very generous, of course—but surely it's possible for two 'adroit, perceptive and delicately attuned people' not to agree in any way, shape, or form."

"I understand that the only picture you've done where you weren't your own boss was *Spartacus*—how did that occur?"

"When the thing with Marlon didn't work out, I had nothing to do, and they asked me to direct *Spartacus*. So I did that. Yes, it's the only picture where I was *employed*—and I found that's the wrong end of the lever to be on. In a situation like that the director has no real rights, only the rights of persuasion. And very often you fail to persuade—and even if you do, you've wasted so much time you may find you've overlooked some even better ideas than those you had to push for."

Kubrick and Harris first read *Lolita* in the original Olympia

Press edition, and they bought the film rights to it for $150,000 before it became an American best seller. Shortly afterwards they declined an offer of $500,000 for the book. Kubrick himself now admits to a keen interest in affairs of high finance, and he is by all accounts an astonishingly adroit businessman.

"I love to gamble," he said, "and games of logic and intuition have always fascinated me. The financial aspect of filmmaking is like a three-dimensional poker game, composed of logic, psychology, and instinct. It's a game the filmmaker has to play, and to win—or he simply will not be in a strong enough position to make the kind of films he wants."

"Did *Lolita* present any problems which were different from those of your other films?"

"Yes, I think the process of trying to gradually penetrate the surface of comedy which overlies the story, and reach the ultimate tragic romance of it, put it in a category apart from the others. In terms of format, all of my other films, including *Dr. Strangelove*, have been strongly plotted, whereas *Lolita* was more purely a mood piece—like music, a series of attitudes and emotions that sort of sweep you through the story."

"Do you feel that the totality of your work has any specific goal or direction?"

"Perhaps, in a very personal sense. In making a film I generally start with an emotion. The theme and the technique come as a result of the material passing as it were, through myself and coming out of the projector lens. It seems to me that a genuinely personal approach, whatever it may be, is the goal. Chaplin, Bergman, and Fellini, for example, although as different in their outlooks as possible, have achieved this, and I'm sure it's what gives their films an emotional involvement lacking in most work."

During my visits to the *Strangelove* set I heard a number of interesting anecdotes about Kubrick's gifts as a director—that is to say, as a manipulator of the human personality in creating a film. One of the most striking of these was told by his English associate producer, Victor Lyndon, who worked with him in Germany on *Paths of Glory*. This is a film about the French Army in World War I; several hundred German police were used in the movie to portray the French infantry regiment on which the story is focused.

"They were the most disciplined extras in the world," Lyndon said. "They would do exactly as they were told, and between takes they would sit for hours without saying a word—rather frightening actually. Well, in this particular scene they were supposed to advance across about a hundred yards of broken terrain under heavy shell fire. The first time they did it so fast, so efficiently fast, that it was hardly more than a blur in the lens. Kubrick told the interpreter to tell them to do it one-quarter as fast. The second time, it was still much too fast and likewise with the third, fourth and so on, despite these renewed instructions each time. There seemed to be no way to get these chaps to slow down. Well, Kubrick sat there staring at them for a while, and then he went over to the interpreter and said, 'Listen, tell them to remember that they're not German soldiers now, they're *French* soldiers.' The interpreter said this, and a great bloody roar of laughter went up—the only sound they had made all day—and when they crossed that field again, by God it was perfect."

From beginning to end, *Dr. Strangelove* is, among other things, an unrelenting indictment of the specious logic and the conveniently flexible semantics which have served militarists and politicians in such good stead from time immemorial. When President Muffley is first confronted with the horrible fait accompli of a squadron of nuclear bombers having been given the Go, his reaction is exactly what one might expect.

PRESIDENT MUFFLEY
(greatly irritated)
But General Turgidson, this is impossible—*I* am the only person authorized to order the use of nuclear weapons.

GENERAL TURGIDSON
(reassuringly)
That's right, sir, you are the only person authorized to do so—and though I hate to judge before all the facts are in, it's beginning to look (*tone becomes grim and accusing*) as though General Ripper . . . has exceeded his authority.

Sophisticated nuclear strategists also speak a language all their own. They are gradually evolving a terminology which is free of moral, or even human, connotation. They do not, for example, use any form of the word *attack*, but use instead the term *preempt*—which, of course, sounds like something in a bridge game rather than what it is. One of the most outlandish of their new words is *megadeath*—thus allowing the estimates of loss of human life (in case Russia should preempt) to be expressed in an easily digestible form: "New York Area, 12.7 megadeaths" (whereas should *we* pre-empt and so only have to absorb the limited counterstrike, the same area is rated at "4.3 megadeaths"). Preempt is supposed to mean "delivering the initial strike in the knowledge that an enemy strike is in preparation"—naturally the words *in preparation* are variously interpreted. Behind the use of such euphemisms as "preemptive strike" and "4.3 megadeaths"—instead of spelling it out as "attack" and "four million, three hundred thousand dead"—is a curious self-deception which tends towards making the unthinkable thinkable.

Probably the most sophisticated concept now on the boards is that of the "ultimate deterrent"—the so-called *Doomsday Machine*. This world-suicide apparatus is formed by a complex of gigantic nuclear devices (as the bombs are called) encased in a cobalt compound and buried in the earth. Dr. Strangelove, director of Weapons Evaluation and Research, explains:

DR. STRANGELOVE

It is extremely simple, Mister President. The nuclear devices are sealed and linked to computer and tape-memory banks. A specific set of requirements for detonation is programmed into the tape-memory banks, which are connected to a complex of data input-sensors. These sensors monitor heat, ground shock, sound, atmospheric pressure, and radioactivity. The device is triggered when its requirements are met.

The theoretical value of the Doomsday Machine is that it dramatically negates the usefulness of a nuclear attack on the nation possessing it, because the cobalt-casing means that the bomb, if exploded, will produce a lethal cloud which within six months will enshroud the surface of the earth, destroying all life, plant and animal, for a duration of ninety to one hundred years. The final sophistication of the machine is that it is so designed that it *cannot be untriggered*, even by the nation possessing it—thus its effectiveness is not to be impaired by threats or bluffs. Should a nation convert its defense strategy to the use of a Doomsday machine, it would need no other nuclear armaments. Some strategists foresee this eventual like-lihood for both Russia and China, whose economies could be more advantageously geared to projects other than armament production.

When President Muffley gets the Soviet premier on the phone and "explains" that a wing of nuclear bombers is mistakenly on its way to Russian targets, and asks for his assurance that this will not be regarded as a hostile act, he is dismayed to learn that Russia does, in fact, now have a Doomsday Machine—it was to be announced at the People's Congress the next day—which lends a bit of spice to the already mounting suspense, for it is set to trigger if an explosion of the twenty-megaton range occurs anywhere in the Soviet Union. Finally, when all efforts to recall the one remaining plane have failed, it appears that the end of the world is well at hand, and a pallor of despair engulfs the War Room. ("Mister President," says a presidential aide gravely, "how are we going to break it to the people—it's going to do one hell of a thing to your image.") But it is Dr. Strangelove again who, with characteristic presence of mind, saves the day.

DR. STRANGELOVE
Mister President, I would not rule out the possibility
of preserving a nucleus of human specimens. At the
bottom of our deepest mine shafts.

PRESIDENT MUFFLEY
(numbly)
At the bottom of . . . mine shafts?

DR. STRANGELOVE
Yes, radioactivity would not penetrate mine shafts of
sufficient depth. In a matter of weeks suitable

improvements for dwelling space could be provided. It is quite possible that as many as 200,000 persons could be accommodated, utilizing mine shafts throughout the nation.

Selection should be made, Dr. Strangelove continues, on the basis of youth, health, sexual fertility, and a cross-section of necessary skills. "It would of course, be vital," he adds, "that our top government and military men be included, to foster and impart the necessary principals of leadership and tradition." The arrow does not miss its mark, and throughout the War Room there is a noticeable amount of sober nodding and murmurs of agreement. "With the proper breeding techniques," Dr. Strangelove explains, "and starting with a ratio of, say, ten women to each man, I should estimate that the progeny of the original group of 200,000 would emerge a century later as well over 100 million. Naturally the group would have to continually engage in enlarging the original living space."

General Turgidson, USAF, has a question: "Doctor, you mention the ratio of ten women to every man. Wouldn't that necessitate abandoning the so-called monogamous form of sexual relationship?"

"Regrettably, yes," is Dr. Strangelove's reply, "but the sacrifice is required for the future of the human race. And I just add that since each man will be required to perform prodigious service in that regard, the women must be selected on the basis of sexual characteristics of the most stimulating order."

Having faced up to this prospect, General Turgidson again feels the heavy cloak of responsibility of his station—and this gives rise to one of the most delightfully incisive moments of the film, and one with a finality all its own.

GENERAL TURGIDSON
(gravely)

Mister President, I think we would be extremely naive to imagine that these . . . these *new developments* will basically affect the Soviet expansionist policy. We must be increasingly on the alert for their moves to take over other mine-shaft space in order to breed more prodigiously than we, and so knock us out through superior numbers when we emerge . . .

(Close-up of General Turgidson;
he speaks with tremendous authority)

Mister President! WE MUST NOT ALLOW A MINE-SHAFT GAP!

A Ramble Through Lebanon

By P. J. O'Rourke

Killed: *Vanity Fair*, 1984

The following article was spiked by Vanity Fair *in 1984 for political reasons. Or so a humorist would say, believing that no reasonable political view can be held without a sense of humor.*

I had spent the first ten years of my working life making modest fun of politics at the old National Lampoon. *By the early 1980s I wanted to make more ambitious fun. I told an editor friend of mine at* Vanity Fair *that I could "combine the traditional foreign correspondent's role with the skills of a humor writer" (or some such line). Thus I wrangled an assignment to cover the Lebanese civil war. But I had never been in a war zone. Indeed, I had never been overseas except as a tourist. I was frightened. Also, I was laughing. The Lebanese were very funny. All over Lebanon militias of fanatical Sunnis, Shiites, Christians, Druze, and what-have-yous had set up roadblocks where people were pulled from their cars and robbed, beaten, and killed for not being fanatical Sunnis, Shiites, Christians, Druze, or what-have-yous. The response of ordinary Lebanese was to make checkpoint jokes.*

A Syrian soldier stops a Volkswagen Beetle and demands that the driver open the trunk. The driver begins to open the luggage compartment at the front of the car.

"No!" says the Syrian, "I said the trunk."

"This is the trunk," says the driver.

"I am not a donkey," says the Syrian, pointing to the back of the car. "Open the trunk!" So the driver does as he's told, exposing the VW's engine. "Aha!" says the Syrian, "You have stolen a motor. Furthermore, you have just done it because it's still running."

I completed the assignment, traveling to unnerving Christian East Beirut, to scary Muslim West Beirut, to the Bekka Valley where the terrifying Hezbollah held sway, and to Sidon and Tyre occupied by the equally terrifying Israeli army. Then, when I had boarded my return flight, takeoff was delayed due to mortar fire. I sat in a big, obvious target of a kerosene-filled jet plane listening to ka-booms get nearer. And I thought, "If I get out of here, I'm never going to worry again." Even at the moment I realized this was an overstatement. I have a fretful nature. "Well," I thought, "I'm never going to worry about things that won't kill me. I'm never going to worry about the rent. I'm never going to worry about articles being rejected. And I'm certainly never going to worry about earning a living as a humorist, because, if I can make fun of this, I can make fun of anything."

I turned in "A Ramble Through Lebanon." My friend at Vanity Fair told me that editor-in-chief Tina Brown had a one-sentence response to my piece: "You can't make fun of people dying."

EDITOR'S NOTE: This article, which was killed in 1984, subsequently appeared in a collection of O'Rourke's travel essays, *Holidays In Hell*, and includes a few parenthetical addenda.

Bassboat." "Bizport." "Passboot." "Pisspot." It's the one English word every Lebanese understands and no Lebanese can say. The first, deepest and most enduring impression from a visit to Lebanon is an endless series of faces, with gun barrels, poking through the car window and mispronouncing your travel documents.

Some of these faces belong to the Lebanese Army, some to the Christian Phalange, some to angry Shiites or blustering Druze or grumpy Syrian draftees or Scarsdale-looking Israeli reservists. And who knows what the rest of them belong to. Everybody with a gun has a checkpoint in Lebanon. And in Lebanon you'd be crazy not to have a gun. Though, I assure you, all the crazy people have guns, too.

You fumble for passes and credentials thinking "Is this Progressive Socialist or Syrian Socialist National party territory? Will the Amal militia kill me if I give them a Lebanese Army press card: And what's Arabic, anyway, for 'Me? American? Don't make me laugh'?"

The gun barrels all have the bluing worn off the ends as though from being rubbed against people's noses. The interesting thing about staring down a gun barrel is how small the hole is where the bullet comes out, yet what a big difference it would make in your social schedule. Not that people shoot you very often, but the way they flip those weapons around and bang them on the pavement and poke them in the dirt and scratch their ears with the muzzle sights. . . . Gun safety merit badges must go begging in the Lebanese Boy Scouts.

On the other hand, Lebanon is notably free of tour groups and Nikon-toting Japanese. The beaches, though shell-pocked and occasionally mined, are not crowded. Ruins of historical interest abound, in fact, block most streets. Hotel rooms are plentiful. No reservation is necessary at even the most popular restaurant (though it is advisable to ask around and find out if the place is likely to be bombed later). And what could be more unvarnished and authentic than a native culture armed to the teeth and bent on murder, pillage, and rape?

One minor difficulty with travel to Lebanon is—you can't. There's no such thing as a tourist visa. Unless you're a journalist, diplomat, or arms salesman, they won't let you in. And if you believe that, you'll never understand the Orient. Type a letter saying you're an American studying stabilization of the Lebanese pound or something. (Sound currency is one thing all factions agree on. The Central Bank is the best guarded and least shelled building in Beirut.) I had a letter saying I was studying the tourism industry in Lebanon.

"The *tourism* industry?" said the pretty young woman at the Lebanese Consulate.

"Yes," I said.

"Tourism?"

I nodded.

She shrugged. "Well, be sure to go see my village of Beit Mery. It's very beautiful. If you make it."

Middle East Airlines is the principal carrier to Beirut. They fly from London, Paris, Frankfurt, and Rome—sometimes. When the airport's being shelled, you can take a boat from Larnaca, Cyprus.

There are a number of Beirut hotels still operating. The best is the Commodore in West Beirut's El Hamra district. This is the headquarters for the international press corps. There are plenty of rooms available during lulls in the fighting. If combat is intense, telex Beirut 20595 for reservations. The Commodore's basement is an excellent bomb shelter. The staff is cheerful, efficient, and will try to get you back if you're kidnapped.

There's a parrot in the bar at the Commodore that does an imitation of an incoming howitzer shell and also whistles the

Marseillaise. Only once in ten years of civil war has this bar been shot up by any of the pro-temperance Shiite militias. Even then the management was forewarned so only some Pepsi bottles and maybe a stray BBC stringer were damaged. Get a room away from the pool. It's harder to hit that side of the building with artillery. Rates are about fifty dollars per night. They'll convert your bar bill to laundry charges if you're on an expense account.

Beirut, at a glance, lacks charm. The garbage has not been picked up since 1975. The ocean is thick with raw sewage, and trash dots the surf. Do not drink the water. Leeches have been known to pop out the tap. Electricity is intermittent.

It is a noisy town. Most shops have portable gasoline generators set out on the sidewalk. The racket from these combines with incessant horn-honking, scattered gunfire, loud Arab music from pushcart cassette vendors, much yelling among the natives, and occasional car bombs. Israeli jets also come in from the sea most afternoons, breaking the sound barrier on their way to targets in the Bekka Valley. A dense brown haze from dump fires and car exhaust covers the city. Air pollution probably approaches a million parts per million. This, however, dulls the sense of smell.

There are taxis always available outside the Commodore. I asked one of the drivers, Najib, to show me the sights. I wanted to see the National Museum, the Great Mosque, the Place des Martyrs, the Bois de Pins, the Corniche, and Hotel Row. Perhaps Najib misunderstood or maybe he had his own ideas about sightseeing. He took me to the Green Line. The Green Line's four crossings were occupied by the Lebanese Army— the Muslim Sixth Brigade on one side, the Christian Fifth Brigade on the other. Though under unified command, their guns were pointed at each other. This probably augurs ill for political stability in the region.

The wise traveler will pack shirts or blouses with ample breast pockets. Reaching inside a jacket for your passport looks too much like going for the draw and puts armed men out of continence.

At the Port Crossing, on the street where all the best whorehouses were, the destruction is perfectly theatrical. Just enough remains of the old buildings to give an impression of erstwhile grandeur. Mortars, howitzers and rocket-propelled grenades have not left a superfluous brush stroke on the scrim. Turn the corner into the old marketplace, the *Souk*, however, and the set is a Hollywood back lot. Small arms and sniper fire have left perfectly detailed havoc. Every square inch is painstakingly bullet-nibbled. Rubble spills artfully out of doorways. Roofs and cornices have been deftly crenulated by explosion. Everything is ready for Ernest Borgnine, John Cassavetes and Lee Marvin in a remake of *The Dirty Dozen*, except the Lebanese can't figure out how to remove the land mines.

We went back and forth across the Green Line six times, then drove into Beirut's south suburbs. This area was once filled with apartment buildings housing the Muslim middle class. The buildings were destroyed by Israeli air strikes during the invasion of 1982. Modern construction techniques and modern war planes create a different kind of ruin. Balconies, windows, and curtain walls disintegrate completely. Reinforced concrete floors fold like Venetian-blind slats and hang by their steel rebars from the buildings' utility cores. Or they land in a giant card-house tumble. Shiite squatter families are living in the triangles and trapezoids formed by the fallen slabs. There's a terrible lack of unreality to this part of the city.

Outside the areas controlled by the Lebanese Army the checkpoints are more numerous, less organized and manned by teenagers in jeans, T-shirts, and Adidas running shoes. They carry Russian instead of U.S. weapons. Some belong to the

Shiite Amal militia, others to the even more radical Hezbellah. All have strong feelings about America. Fortunately, they can't read. One even held my Arabic press credentials upside down, picture and all, and tipped his head like a parakeet to see if I matched my inverted photo. At the most dangerous-looking checkpoints, Najib said something that made the guards laugh and wave us through.

"Najib," I said, "what are you telling them?"

He said, "I tell them you travel for pleasure."

Finally, we got to a place where we could go no further. Down the street the Sunni Muslim Mourabitoun militia was having it out with the Shiite Amal militia—part of the long-standing Sunni/Shiite dispute about whether Muhammad's uncle Abbas or Muhammad's son-in-law Ali should have succeeded the Prophet and, also, about who gets the take from the south-side gambling joints.

West Beirut can also be toured on foot. You'll find the city is full of surprises—a sacking of the Saudi embassy because of long lines for visas to Mecca, for instance, or shelling of the lower town by an unidentified gunboat or car bombs several times a day. Renaults are the favored vehicles. Avoid double-parked Le Cars. Do not, however, expect the population to be moping around glassy-eyed. There's lots of jewelry and makeup and the silliest Italian designer jeans on earth. The streets are jammed. Everyone's very busy, though not exactly working. They're rushing from one place to another in order to sit around drinking hundreds of tiny cups of Turkish coffee and chat at the top of their lungs. The entire economy is fueled, as far as I could see, by everyone selling cartons of smuggled Marlboros to each other.

It turns out I didn't miss much on Najib's style of guided tour. The *Bois de Pins*, planted in the 1600s by Emir Fakhr ed Din to protect Beirut from encroaching sand dunes, had all its foliage blown off by Israeli jets and looks like a phone-pole farm. The *Place des Martyrs,* so-called because eleven nationalists were hanged there by the Turks in 1915, is right on the Green line and now all that much more aptly named. Most of the buildings on the Corniche have literally been face-lifted. The old American Embassy is here, in the same state as U.S. Middle East policy. The British Embassy down the street is completely draped in antibomb nets imported from Belfast. Hotel Row was ravaged at the beginning of the civil war in 1975. The high-rise Holiday Inn is a delight to the eye. Who, when traveling around the earth faced with endless Holiday Inns, has not fantasized blowing one to flinders? The National Museum is bricked up and sur-rounded with tanks—no nagging sense of cultural obliga-tion to tour this historical treasure trove. I couldn't find the Great Mosque at all.

A surprising lot of Beirut stands, however. A building with a missing story here, a lot with a missing building there, shat-tered this next to untouched that—all the usual ironies of war except with great restaurants.

The Summerland Hotel, on the beach in the ruined south suburbs, has good hamburgers. The wealthy Muslims, including Shiites, go here. All Shiites are not stern zealots. Some have string bikinis. And, like an American ethnic group with origins nearby, they wear their jewelry in the pool. (It was at the Summerland where the Amal militia feted its American captives during the 1985 TWA hostage crisis.)

Downtown on the Corniche you can lunch at the St. Georges Hotel, once Beirut's best. The hotel building is now a burned shell, but the pool club is still open. You can go water-skiing here, even during the worst fighting.

I asked the bartender at the pool club, "Don't the water-skiers worry about sniper fire?"

"Oh, no, no, no," he said, "the snipers are mostly armed with automatic weapons—these are not very accurate."

Down the quay, pristine among the ruins, Chez Temporal serves excellent food. A short but careful walk through a heavily armed Druze neighborhood brings you to Le Grenier, once a jet-set mob scene, now a quiet hideaway with splendid native dishes. Next door there's first-rate Italian fare at Quo Vadis. Be sure to tip the man who insists, at gunpoint, on guarding your car.

Spaghetteria is a favorite with the foreign press. The Italian specials are good, and there's a spectacular view of military patrols and nighttime skirmishing along the beachfront. Sit near the window if you feel lucky.

Addresses are unnecessary. Taxi drivers know the way and when it's safe to go there. Service at all these establishments is good, more than good. You may find ten or a dozen waiters hovering at your side. If trouble breaks out, the management will have one or two employees escort you home. When ordering, avoid most native wines, particularly the whites. Mousar '75, however, is an excellent red. Do not let the waiters serve you Cypriot brandy after the meal. It's vile.

The Commodore also has restaurants. These are recommended during fighting. The Commodore always manages to get food delivered no matter what the situation outdoors.

Nightlife begins late in Beirut. Cocktail hour at the Commodore is 8:00 PM, when U.S. editors and network executives are safely at lunch (there's a seven-hour time difference). The Commodore is strictly neutral territory with only one rule. No guns at the bar. All sorts of raffish characters hang about, expatriates from Palestine, Libya, and Iran, officers in mufti from both sides of the Lebanese Army, and combatants of other stripes. I overheard one black Vietnam veteran loudly describe to two British girls how he teaches orthodox Muslim women to fight with knives. And there are diplomats, spooks and dealers in gold, arms, and other things. At least that's what they seem to be. No one exactly announces his occupation—except the journalists, of course.

I met one young lady from Atlanta who worked on a CNN camera crew. She was twenty-six, cute, slightly plump, and looked like she should have been head of the Georgia State pep squad. I sat next to her at the Commodore bar and watched her drink twenty-five gin and tonics in a row. She never got drunk, never slurred a word, but along about G&T number twenty-two came the stories about dismembered babies and dead bodies flying all over the place and the Red Cross picking up hands and feet and heads from bomb blasts and putting them all in a trash dumpster. "So I asked the Red Cross people," she said, in the same sweet Dixie accent, "like, what's this? Save 'em, collect 'em, trade 'em with your friends?"

Everyone in Beirut can hold his or her liquor. If you get queasy, Muhammad, the Commodore bartender, has a remedy rivaling Jeeves's in P. G. Wodehouse's novels. It will steady your stomach so you can drink more. You'll want to. No one in this part of the world is without a horror story, and, at the Commodore bar, you'll hear most of them.

Dinner, if anyone remembers to have it, is at ten or so. People go out in groups. It's not a good idea to be alone and blonde after dark. Kidnapping is the one great innovation of the Lebanese civil war. And a Reuters correspondent, Jonathan Wright, had disappeared thus on his way to the Bekka Valley a few days before I arrived.

If nabbed, make as much noise as possible. Do not get in anyone's car. If forced in, attack the driver. At least this is what I'm told.

Be circumspect when driving at night. Other cars should be given a wide berth. Flick headlights off and on to indicate friendly approach. Turn on the dome light when arriving at checkpoints. Militiamen will fire a couple of bursts in your direction if they want you to slow down.

Clubs, such as the Backstreet near the Australian Embassy, keep going as late as you can stand it. There's some dancing, much drinking and, if you yell at the management, they'll keep the Arab music off the tape deck. Cocaine is available at about fifty dollars a gram and is no worse than what you get in New York.

Beirut nightlife is not elaborate, but it is amusing. When danger waits the tables and death is the busboy, it adds zest to the simple pleasures of life. There's poignant satisfaction in every puff of a cigarette or sip of a martini. The jokes are funnier, the drinks are stronger, the bonds of affection more powerfully felt than they'll ever be at Club Med.

East Beirut is said to also have good restaurants and nightclubs. But the visitor staying on the west side probably won't see them. No one likes to cross the Green Line at night. And, frankly, the East isn't popular with the westside crowd. All the window glass is taped, and the storefronts are sandbagged over there. It gives the place a gloomy look. No one would think of doing this in the West. It would be an insult to the tradition of Oriental fatalism, and nobody would be able to see all the cartons of smuggled Marlboros stacked in the window. Anyway, the eastside Christians are too smug, too pseudo-French, and haven't been shelled enough to turn them into party reptiles.

To travel to the rest of Lebanon you just hail a taxi. The country is only one hundred and twenty miles long and forty miles wide, and no Lebanese cab driver has to call home to ask his wife if he can take off for a couple days. Settle the price first. This won't be easy. It's not the way of the Levant to come to the point. I asked Akbar, one of the Commodore's taximen, how much he'd charge to take me through the Israeli lines and into South Lebanon.

"I have been in this business twenty-seven years," he said.

"Yes," I said, "but how much is it going to cost me?"

"I will tell you later."

"Give me a rough idea."

"Would you like a coffee?"

"What's your hourly rate?"

"Across the street—fine rugs at the best price. I will get you a discount."

"What do you charge by the mile?"

"I have a cousin in Detroit."

"Akbar," I shouted, "what's it going to cost?!"

"If you do not like my price, I tell you what," Akbar gestured grandly, "you do not hire me anymore again."

Make sure your driver knows English well enough to translate. Lebanese English is often a triumph of memorization over understanding. "I come from the village of Baabdat," the driver will say in quite an acceptable accent, "it is very beautiful there in the mountains."

"Right," you'll say, "but you'd better pull over, that guy behind the sandbags is leveling an antitank gun at us."

"You do?" the driver will say, "Is that in Texas? I have a nephew in Houston."

Wherever you go, it's important to leave early in the morning. Those who think the war is dangerous have not seen the traffic in Beirut. It's a city of a million people with three stoplights and these aren't working. There are some traffic cops, but they are on no account to be minded as they tend to wave you into the path of dump trucks going sixty miles an hour. All driving is at top speed, much of it on the sidewalks since most parking is done in the middle of the streets. The only firm rule is: Armored personnel carriers have the right of way.

Once outside Beirut there are, of course, other difficulties. The only land route into the Israeli-occupied South goes through the Chouf mountains to a crossing point in the town of Bater, which is separated from Beirut by forty miles of armed Druze. You can also take a boat to Sidon from the Phalange-controlled docks in East Beirut if you're a Christian. I am, but there seemed to be some difficulty anyway. First they said they would have to ask Israeli permission because I was a journalist. Next they told me they didn't speak English. Then they quit speaking French.

On the way to Bater my driver took me past "Green Beach," the former U.S. Marine emplacement and very interesting to students of military history. It's as defensible a position as the bottom of the air shaft in the Plaza Hotel. There's hardly a spot in Lebanon from which you can't fire a gun and hit it. Don't get out of the car. The beach is now an Amal military base under heavy guard because it's next to the orthodox Shiite women's bathing area. They wear ankle-length chadors in the water, which may explain the lack of a world-class Shiite women's swim team.

In the Chouf mountains, the land is green and exquisite, cut through with precipitous gorges. Even the steepest slopes have been terraced and planted with fruit trees, vineyards, olive groves, and gun emplacements. The road is narrow with no railings or shoulders, and traffic is slow because the Druze are usually moving artillery around preparing to blast the Phalangists on the coast. Be sure to keep a mental note of such things. It's considered good manners to convey information about military movements to the next faction down the road. This takes the place of celebrity gossip in Lebanese small talk.

The Druze militiamen were good-natured. "Do you speak Arabic?" asked one. I shook my head, and he said something to another soldier who poked face and gun into the car and shouted, "He just said he wants to fuck your mother!" At least, I assume this was good-natured.

The Druze villages are built in the Ottoman style, graceful, foursquare sandstone buildings with balconies, arched windows, and fifteen-foot ceilings. The low-pitched hip roofs are covered in red tile. Tidy gardens surround each house. Peasants in white skull caps and baggy-crotched jodhpurs ride donkeys along the road. Herds of goats meander in the streets. It's all quite timeless except for the videocassette rental stores, unisex hair salons, and Mercedes-Benz sedans all over the place.

The Bater crossing was another matter. A couple hundred Lebanese, mostly old people, women and children, were jammed into line behind barbed wire, waiting for the crossing to open. Several hundred more squatted in the dirt or milled about disconsolate. These, apparently, did not have their papers in order. Some had been there for days. A few tents had been provided but no toilets. There was no running water and no food other than what people had brought with them. Soldiers from the Israeli-hired South Lebanon Army were yelling, pointing guns, and threatening everyone. The sun was hot. A few of the women and all of the babies were crying. The smell was horrendous.

There seemed to be no way to tell when the crossing would open. My driver, Akbar, didn't have any ideas. I was not about to get in line behind the barbed wire. It looked too much like Bergen-Belsen. No one in sight, as far as I could tell, was in charge of anything but pistol waving.

On top of an embankment about a hundred yards on the other side of the crossing was a machine-gun nest with the star of David flying over it. I took my passport out and, holding it shoulder high, walked through the barbed wire and tank traps. I fixed the South Lebanon Army guards with a stare I hoped would remind them of Grenada. *"American,"* I said. They backed away, and I headed as coolly as I could for the muzzle of the Israeli .50-caliber machine gun now being pointed at my chest.

Israelis are not well liked in West Beirut. During 1982 the Israelis besieged the Moslem part of town. There was no electricity and little food or water. The shelling and air strikes sometimes went on for twelve hours at a stretch. Beirut's journalists call the Israelis "Schlomos" and consider them war criminals and also real squares.

Personally, I was glad to confront the only armed maniacs in the Middle East who aren't allowed to shoot U.S. citizens. I hoped they remembered.

"That's *my* helmet you're wearing," I was thinking. "Those are *my* boots, and *I* paid for that gun so you can just go point it at someone else." Not that I said this aloud. The hole a .50-caliber bullet comes out of is *not* small. It looks as if you could put your whole foot in there.

The Israelis motioned for me to come up, and I climbed the embankment. They held the machine gun on me until it became clear I was not a peroxided Iranian. "You must speak to the captain," they said.

He proved to be a boy of twenty-five. "Do you speak English?" I said.

"Gee, sure," said the captain. The Lebanese kept a respectful distance until they saw him talking to me. Then they descended in a horde waving unlikely looking slips of paper and shouting the interminable explanations of the east. The captain's escort chased them away with shoves and curses. The women, children, and old folks pressed back with no apparent fear. Finally, they pushed the officer and me under a guard tower. "Welcome to Lebanon" is the phrase everyone uses whenever anything untoward or chaotic breaks loose.

"Welcome to Lebanon," said the Israeli captain. He read my credentials and smiled. *"Tourism?"*

"Yes," I said, "I'm the only tourist in Lebanon."

The captain laughed. "Oh no, you're not. I'm a reservist, you know, and this is my vacation, too."

The Israelis wouldn't, however, allow my car through. I told Akbar to meet me there in two days and then hiked across no-man's-land to a line of taxis on the other side.

There were three stages in crossing the Israeli lines. Once through the checkpoint at Bater, I had to go by taxi to an interrogation center a few miles up the road. From the interrogation center I took a bus eight or ten miles to another checkpoint in Jezzine.

At the interrogation stop I was searched and questioned by Shin Bet, the Israeli FBI. An enlisted man apologized for the inconvenience. Less auspicious-looking travelers were being led off to be grilled in windowless huts.

In Jezzine I was questioned again by the South Lebanon Army, an interesting process since we had no language in common.

I hired another taxi to take me the fifteen miles from Jezzine to Sidon. It took five hours to get through the Bater-Jezzine crossing and a total of eight hours to make it from Beirut to Sidon. Before the war it was an hour drive on the coast road.

Sidon and Tyre, the two coastal cities of southern Lebanon, were once the principal towns of ancient Phoenicia and spawned a mercantile empire from Turkey to Spain. Important archaeological work has been done in both places, exposing six millennia of human misbehavior. Lebanon has been overrun in turn by Canaanites, Egyptians, Assyrians, Babylonians, Persians, Greeks, Romans, Arabs, Crusaders, Arabs again, Turks, French, more Arabs, Israelis, and occasional U.S. Marines. Perhaps by means of the past one can begin to comprehend the present. Or learn which way to run from the future.

I hired a Palestinian Christian driver named Simon and had him take me twenty-five miles down the lush coast littoral to Tyre. We passed through ten or a dozen Israeli guard posts. These are heaps of sandbags with anxious eyes and many gun barrels sticking over the top. They look down upon a series of "Khomeini gates," cement barriers that jut into the road like meshing-gear teeth and force vehicles to zigzag slowly between them in single file. If you stall in the middle of these, you die.

The roadsides all over Lebanon are piled with trash, the coast road especially so. Beaches and parks are even worse. There's something about a civil war that brings out the litterbug in people.

Tyre is an awful mess of dirty modern architecture, offal, and the detritus of battle. The Elissa Beach Club Hotel, on the south shore of the Tyre peninsula, may be one of the few oceanside hotels anyplace where none of the rooms faces the sea. But it's clean, the hot water is not actually cold, and the food's passable. Also, there's nowhere else to stay.

Simon went home for the night, and I was left on the hotel's roof terrace about a thousand miles from the nearest example of the Four Freedoms. "I have a cousin in Cincinnati" was the only English anyone could speak. I watched the sun go down behind the ruins of some previous attempt to bring the rule of law to these climes.

I'd hoped at least for a good night's sleep. There'd been quite few bombs going off in Beirut. I'd heard five the night before, starting with one at midnight in a bar a few blocks from the Commodore and winding up with a spectacular attempt on the life of the minister of education at 6:00 AM. This took windows out for three blocks around and shook the furniture in my room. The minister survived but my repose did not. But this night, it turned out, was the beginning of the Hajj, the Muslim holiday marking the return of the Mecca pilgrims, and the urchins next door celebrated with a six-hour firecracker fight in the street. Then at 2:00 AM there was a truly horrendous explosion.

No use looking around the next day to see what's been blasted. Everything has been already.

Later I read in the Beirut newspapers that while I was in the south there were four sniping attacks on Israeli patrols, the South Lebanon Army had stormed a section of Sidon, there was a riot at a Palestinian refugee camp near Jezzine, and the coast road was heavily shelled. I noticed none of this. On the other hand, no explosion in Tyre was reported. This illustrates the difficulty, in Lebanon of knowing what's happening, even to yourself.

In the morning I visited the principal archaeological digs. These are all decorated with small blue-and-white signs saying the ruins are national treasures protected by the convention of the Hague of May 12, 1954, and in case of armed conflict notify UNESCO. I suppose I should have phoned.

The oldest and most extensive excavation, near the ancient port, has revealed Phoenician house foundations, a Hellenistic theater, a long, colonnaded walk from Roman times, and parts of a Crusader wall. Some pretense is made of keeping these in order. They are guarded by one desultory fellow in a fez. After I'd wandered beyond the palings for an hour, he whistled at me to get out. Nearby a newer dig has uncovered a Roman temple now being used as a garbage dump.

Half a mile or so inland is a much larger site, which I couldn't find mentioned in any guidebooks. Not that there are many Lebanon guidebooks. I couldn't find any in U.S. bookstores. And the Hachette guide I purchased in Beirut was twenty years old. Other than this I was relying on a 1876 Baedeker I found in a New England thrift shop. It was not without useful advice:

The transaction of business in the East always involves an immense waste of time, and as Orientals attach no value whatsoever to their time, the European will often find his patience sorely tried.

Many travelers rejoice in displaying a stock of revolvers and other arms, which add greatly to their importance in the eyes of the natives, but are not often brought into actual use.

The larger excavation contains what looks to be an aqueduct, another theater, and a vast Roman necropolis. Simon had come back to get me at the hotel, and I had him drive me into the middle of these ruins. Garbage was being dumped here, too, and burned automobile seats, Pepsi cans, and lots of spent ordnance was mingled on the ground with ancient pot shards and mosaic tile chips. Simon picked up an amphora handle. "How old you think?" I told him about two thousand years. He nodded, "Two-thousand-year-old garbage."

Antiquity hunters have been at work in Tyre. All the Roman tombs are broken open, and many of the fracture marks in the marble are fresh. I peeked inside one grave, and there was a muddle of antique bones. It was, by sheer chance, the only dead body I saw in Lebanon.

I'd been given the name of a Lebanese-American, Billy Hadad, who has a farm on the coast near Sidon. We drove around looking for him. It's hard to know what your driver is doing when he talks to the natives. He'll pull up somewhere and make a preliminary oration, which draws five or six people to the car window Then each of them speaks in turn. There will be a period of gesturing, some laughter, much arm clasping and handshaking and a long speech by the eldest or most prominent bystander. Then your driver will deliver an impassioned soliloquy. This will be answered at length by each member of the audience and anybody else who happens by. Another flurry of arm grabbing, shoulder slapping, and handshakes follows, then a series of protracted and emotional good-byes.

"What did you ask them?" you'll say to your driver.

"Do they know of your friend?"

"What did they tell you?"

"No."

Eventually, we were directed to an old fortresslike farmhouse near the shore. There on the terrace was a big American preppie kid in chino pants and a button-down shirt. He looked at me and said, "Awesome. Man, I haven't heard English in months!"

The farm near Sidon has been owned by the Hadads since the time of the Ottoman Turks. Its 230 acres are irrigated by springs and planted in avocados, bananas and other fruit. The house dates from 600 A.D., with Arab and Turkish additions. It stands on a rock outcrop above a pool in use since Phoenician days. Centuries-old ficus trees grow over the walls, and flowers bloom all around it.

Billy's father was Druze, his mother from Oregon. They met at college in California. In the middle of the civil war Mr. Hadad was killed in, of all things, a skiing accident on Mt. Lebanon. Mrs. Hadad took the younger children back to America, and Billy, just graduated from a Connecticut boarding school, came out to Lebanon to manage the property. He has five families, some thirty-five people, working for him.

We had lunch with one of his tenants and sat around a low table under a loggia indulging in Arab table manners. These are the best in the world or, anyway, the most fun. For the midday meal there are a dozen large bowls of things—salad; hot peppers; yogurt; a chickpea paste called hummus; kubbeh, which is a kind of meatball; and things I have no idea the names for. You get a flat loaf of pita bread and make flaps to grab the food. The bread is your napkin, also your plate. We had too much Arak, the regional version of absinthe, and drank endless tiny cups of drug-strength coffee. You can smoke in the middle of the meal, and no one considers it impolite.

The tenant brought out his guns. It's like an Englishwoman showing you her roses. There was a Soviet AK-47, a Spanish Astra 9mm automatic pistol, a Smith and Wesson .38 revolver, an old British military rifle, and a very nice Beretta over-and-under shotgun. This is a modest collection. More militant people have mortars and the like. Serious gunmen favor the rocket-propelled grenade, or RPG, which is something like a bazooka. It's inaccurate and tremendously noisy, a perfect Lebanese weapon.

After lunch we went for a swim. This far south of Beirut the ocean is clean. From out in the water distant rumblings could be heard. I thought it was artillery in the Chouf. "Dynamite fishing," said Billy. (Dynamite is one bait fish always rise to.)

There was a wedding party in a nearby village that night. Lebanese wedding parties are held on the eve of the marriage. Thus the groom is given an excuse for looking green at the altar. A hundred or more chairs had been placed in a circle behind the bride's house. A few lightbulbs were strung in the grapevines and a huge table had been laid with food, Scotch and Arak. Parties in Lebanon start slow. Everyone sits primly in the chairs, neither eating nor drinking, and talking only in low voices. Or they would usually. In this case the men and boys must all discuss politics with the American. Every one of them has cousins in Texas.

"Just tell them what you think," said Billy. I couldn't very well do that. After a week in Lebanon what I thought would hardly make fit conversation at a wedding feast.

This was a Christian village. "If the Muslims take over," said a young man (Billy translating), "they'll close the bars during Ramadan. But we won't make them drink at Christmas if they really don't want to." A lather of self-justification followed. Justifying the self is the principal form of exercise in Lebanon. The principal form of exercise for a visitor in Lebanon is justifying American foreign policy. The Marine incursion was the question of the hour. Muslims wanted to know why the Marines were sent here. Christians wanted to know why they left. And Druze wanted to know why, during the Marines' brief stay, they felt compelled to shell the crap out of the Chouf.

My answer to everyone was that President Reagan wasn't sure why he sent the Marines to Lebanon. However, he was determined to keep them here until he figured it out, but then he forgot.

Nobody held it against me personally. The Lebanese never hold anything against anyone personally. And it's not considered rude to root for the home team. There were a number of Muslim guests at the party. The villagers had nothing but affection for the Druze Billy Hadad, who towered over most of them. One teenager, summoning all the English at his command, told me, "*Billy, il est. . . le homme vert, tu connais, 'Credible Hulk!'* " Billy said the only real trouble he's had with his neighbors and tenants was when he tried to convince them that professional wrestling is fake. It's the most popular program on Lebanese TV.

About ten o'clock there was a change in the festivities. Acting on some signal I couldn't perceive everyone suddenly began to drink and shout. A little later the bridegroom was carried in on the shoulders of his friends accompanied by drums, flutes, and the eerie ululation Arab women use to mark every emotional occasion. Awful tapes were put on a large Rasta box. There was bad Arab music, worse French rock and roll, and

Israeli disco music, which is the most abominable-sounding thing I've ever heard in my life. A sister of the bride got in the middle of the circled chairs and did quite a shocking traditional dance.

There was something of the freshman mixer to the party. The young men and women held to opposite sides of the crowd, eyeing each other furtively, and being shoved out to dance only after prolonged giggling and conspiracy among their fellows.

"I haven't been laid since I was in Beirut last June," said Billy. "Out in the country it's marriage or death."

Good-fellowship in the Middle East can be a bit unnerving. You'd best get used to being gripped, hugged, and even nuzzled. I was taken aback the first time I saw two fully armed militiamen walking down the street holding hands. Large amounts of Arak aid in acclimatization. The sense of affection and solidarity is comforting, actually, when you realize how many of the men throwing their arms around you have pistols in the waistbands of their pants. A Mercedesful of gunmen kept watch on the road.

Eventually I was thrust onto the dance floor and matched with a hefty girl who had me do Arab dances. This was, justly, thought hilarious. But my discotheque dancing made an impression. I gather the locals are not familiar with the Watusi, the Jerk, and the Mashed Potato.

The whole celebration was being videotaped, and every now and then one of the revelers would use the Sony's quartz-halogen light to dry the skin on a snareless Arab drum.

Sometime in the early morning Billy and I returned to his farm. There was protracted questioning from his housekeeper on the floor above. She wanted to make sure we were us before she threw down the door keys. We locked ourselves in with five dead bolts.

I never did get to see the historical points of interest in Sidon.

The overland crossing going north was a horror. The Israelis run Betar and the midpoint interrogation center, and conditions there are ugly but organized. However, the clumsy and violent South Lebanon Army has control of the Jezzine checkpoint.

There were about a thousand angry and panicked people in the small town square when I arrived. Most of them were poor Shiites, and all of them seemed to have screaming children and every earthly possession with them. One group of two or three hundred were fighting with fists to get on a bus. Soldiers ran through the crowd screaming and firing Uzis in the air. It was only ten in the morning but already ninety degrees. I looked for Israeli officers. There were none. I sent Simon into the crowd. He returned in a few minutes.

"No ways but bus across," he said.

"How do I get on it?"

"You cannot."

I paid him off and sent him home. I was sick with the dysentery every foreigner in Lebanon suffers. My head ached from the wedding party Arak. There was, it appeared, a man with a gun selling bus tickets. But every time he tried to sell one a crowd of three hundred would rush him like a rugby scrum. The man fired his pistol directly over the people's heads. Bullets smacked into nearby masonry. The crowd quailed and ran backward, trampling each other. Then they gathered themselves and rushed the ticket seller again. He grew purple with shouting, reloaded, fired again. The crowd moved away and back like surf. Then with one great surge they chased him on top of a truck.

Most of these people had been camping at Jezzine, if that's the word for sleeping in the streets for days with your children and no food. They were desperate and fully insane. The crowd began running against itself, into walls, up the sides of buildings.

I was at a loss. I might be at Jezzine still if my arm hadn't been grabbed by someone who said, "I ken you're new here." It was a magnificent Scotswoman, tall, thin, and ramrod straight. With her was a gentle-looking Lebanese girl. The woman was Leslie Phillips, head of the nursing school at a medical center near Sidon. She was on her way to get textbooks in Beirut. The girl was named Amal, the same as the militia. It means "hope." She was headed to America for college.

Miss Phillips placed us in a protected corner and said, "I'm going to speak to the man with the gun. I always go straight for the man with the gun. It's the only way you get anywhere in this country." She vanished into the melee. The crowd went into a frenzy again and made right for Amal and me. I suppose I would have been filled with pity if I'd been in a second-story window. As it was I was filled with desire to kick people and I gave in to it.

Miss Phillips was gone for two hours. She emerged from the donnybrook perfectly composed and holding three bus tickets. I asked her what all the shooting was about. "Oh," she said, "that's just Lebanese for 'please queue up.' " An ancient horrible Mexican-looking bus pulled into the crowd smacking people and punting them aside. Amal was carrying a coed's full complement of baggage in two immense suitcases. I handed my kit bag to Miss Phillips, grabbed these, and made for the bus. Or tried to. Three steps put me at the bottom of a clawing, screeching pile-up, a pyramid of human frenzy. I heard Miss Phillips's voice behind me. "Don't be shy," she said, "it's not rude to give a wee shove to the Lebanese." I took a breath, tightened my grip on the suitcases, and began lashing with Samsonite bludgeons at the crowd of women, old men, and children. If you ask me, it *was* pretty rude, but it was that or winter in South Lebanon. I fought my way to the side of the bus. There was a man on top loading luggage and kicking would-be roof rack stowaways in the head, knocking them back on top of the crowd. I hoisted one of Amal's fifty-pound suitcases onto my head, waved a fistful of Lebanese money at the loader, kept hold of Amal with my other hand, and fended off the mob with both feet. This doesn't sound physiologically possible, but it was an extreme situation.

I got both suitcases on top at last. Then we had to scrimmage our way to the bus door in a flying wedge, Miss Phillips leading the way. Just as we were getting aboard, a worse brawl yet broke loose in the throng. One of the South Lebanon Army guards leapt into the middle of it and began beating people in the face with the butt of his pistol. The crowd exploded. Miss Phillips was heaved inside. I was squashed against the bus door and lost hold of Amal, who was sucked into the maw of the Lebanese. Miss Phillips reached out the bus window and tapped the pistol-whipping soldier on the arm. "Pardon me, lad," she said, "but those two are with me."

The soldier left off his beating for a moment, pushed me into the bus, and fished Amal out of the crowd. I pulled her inside, and the soldier went back to hitting people. Everyone in the crowd was yelling. I asked Amal what they said. "They're all claiming to be someone's cousin," she sighed.

About two hundred people were packed inside the bus, which was built to carry fifty. More kept wiggling in through the windows. It was well over one hundred degrees in there. Every now and then a soldier would get in and climb across the top of people to beat one of the illegal passengers. There was more shooting outside. I found myself in a full body press with a Shiite girl. She was rather nicely built but over the top from claustrophobia and shrieking like a ruptured cow. "What's Arabic for 'calm down'?" I yelled.

"As far as I can tell," said Miss Phillips, "there's no such word."

We did eventually get under way, the bus backing over people then swaying horribly in blinding dust on the half-lane-wide mountain road. We were only stopped, unloaded, searched, interrogated, and held at gunpoint several times.

Fortunately, the Lebanese are a clean people, even the very poor ones. It wasn't like being packed into a bus on a sweltering day with a bunch of French or anything.

Akbar was waiting at Bater. I found out later he'd also come up from the city the day before and waited all afternoon in case I got thrown out or evacuated or tried to get back to Beirut on foot.

Travel to the North is less arduous. George Moll, the video editor at ABC-TV's Beirut bureau, and I went on a trip to the Bsherri Cedars. Traffic on the coast road north of the city is stalled by checkpoints. Amazing what a few guys standing around with guns can do to create gridlock. "I ♥ Lebanon" bumper stickers are popular with the motorists. "Kill them all—Let God sort them out" T-shirts are popular with the militias.

It's important to remember, when dealing with these militias, that the gunmen are mostly just kids and they're getting a big kick out of the whole thing. I suppose this is only natural when young people lack proper recreational facilities and well-supervised activities to keep them out of mischief. They need sympathy and understanding. Or a sixteen-inch shell from the battleship *New Jersey*.

I wanted to visit the gorge of the Nahr el Kelb, the River of the Dog, a strategic point on the Lebanese coast just north of Beirut where for more than three thousand years invading armies have carved stelae commemorating their passage. A tunnel for the coast highway now cuts through the gorge wall, and the carvings are reached via a ramp above the traffic. The cuneiform characters of Nebuchadnezzar II, the stela of the

Pharaoh Ramses, the Assyrian bas-reliefs, a Latin inscription from the Emperor Marcus Aurelius, Greek carvings from the Seleucid empire—they've all been completely effaced by air pollution.

Don't go to the famous Jeita Grottoes at the source of the Dog River, either. These have been turned into a military training base. Although what kind of military training goes on among a bunch of stalactites lit by colored spotlamps, I can't tell you.

A few miles north of Nahr el Kleb is the Casino de Liban on Juniye Bay. This was prewar Lebanon's attempt at Monte Carlo and used to have elaborate floor shows featuring plump blondes who were out of work in Europe. You can still gamble there, though just being in this part of the world is a gamble enough for most people. The blondes are gone.

On up the coast road, twenty-four miles from Beirut, is Byblos. Since the Christians were run out of the Beirut airport, the Phalange has taken to landing planes on the highway here. Expect another traffic jam. Byblos was considered by the ancients to be the oldest city in the world. In fact, it has been an established metropolis for at least six thousand years. Main Street, however, looks most like the oldest part of Fort Lauderdale.

By the seaport, however, is an Arab fortification atop a Frankish castle constructed with chunks of Roman temples which had been built over a Phoenician town that was established on the foundations of a Neolithic village—quite a pile of historic vandalism.

The war has not touched Byblos except to keep anyone from coming here. We found one consumptive tour guide playing solitaire in a shack by the entrance to the ruins. He took us through the deserted remains spieling, with pauses only to cough, a litany of emperors, catastrophes, and dimensions.

The Lebanese are chock-full of knowledge about their past. Those who *do* learn history apparently get to repeat it of their own free will. The whole business filled me with inchoate emotions and a desire for lunch.

The Byblos Fishing Club at the base of the Crusader sea-wall has wonderful food and no other customers. They don't speak English anymore so I went back to the kitchen and picked out what I wanted. Seafood got with dynamite fishing is very tender, it seems. On the wall of the Fishing Club are dusty photos of better days—Ray Milland, Ann-Margret, David Niven, Jean-Paul Belmondo. "Now this," said George, "is archaeology."

There's a very good hotel in Byblos, the Byblos-Sur-Mer, whose owner hadn't seen anyone in so long he bought us drinks when we stopped to use the pay phone.

You can proceed to Tripoli on the coast road, but shouldn't. The Arab Democratic Party, which supports Islamic unification, is having a big fight there with the Islamic Unification Party, which is in favor of Arab democracy. And the Syrians are shooting at both of them.

We turned east toward the mountains at the Syrian lines near Batrun. There's a medieval Arab castle here that's worth seeing. It sits in the middle of a cement plant.

Once into Syrian-controlled territory the checkpoint scrutiny becomes severe. Ahmed, our driver, began making long explanations to the glowering soldiers. He wouldn't quite confess what he was saying, but I have an idea it went something like: "I have the brother of an important American strongman here and the president of England's cousin. They are traveling in secret as journalists so they may see the justice and resolve of the great Syrian army in its struggle against Zionist oppressors everywhere. Soon they will return to their homeland and tell rich men there to drop a bomb on Tel Aviv."

The Syrian army has dozens of silly hats, mostly berets in yellow, orange, and shocking pink, but also tiny pillbox chapeaux, peaked officer's caps with half a foot of gold braid up the front, and lumpy Russian helmets three sizes too large. The paratroopers wear shiny gold jumpsuits, and crack commando units have skintight fatigues in a camouflage pattern of violet, peach, flesh tone, and vermilion on a background of vivid purple. This must give excellent protective coloration in, say, a room full of Palm Beach divorcees in Lilly Pulitzer dresses.

The rest of the scenery is also spectacular—Californian, but as though the Sierras had been moved down to Santa Barbara. The mountains of Lebanon rise ten thousand feet only twenty miles from the sea. You can ski in the morning and swim in the afternoon. Actually, of course, it's raining on the beach that time of year, and the skiing is mediocre at best. But it's the kind of thing that made for great Lebanese travel-brochure writing in the old days.

We drove to Bsherri on the lip of the dramatic Qadisha Valley, 650 feet deep and only a half-mile wide. This is the heartland of the Maronites, seventh century A.D. Christian schismatics who sought refuge among these dangerous hairpin turns lacking guard rails and speed limits.

Bsherri was the home of Kahlil Gibran and also where Danny Thomas's family comes from. Thus, the two great cultural figures of modern Lebanon, though in many ways opposites (Danny Thomas does not write poetry; Kahlil Gibran never did spit-takes), are linked. Or so I was told. I wouldn't spoil that piece of information with research.

We visited Gibran's house above the town. It's probably the world's only example of the California bungalow style carved out of living rock. Interesting but damp. The place is decorated with a hundred or so of Gibran's artworks. He was a dreadful painter—the gentle insouciance of Rodin and the technical abilities of Blake, all done in muddy earth tones. Gibran's coffin is bricked into the wall of his bedroom if that says anything about the man.

While we were asking directions in Bsherri, a young man named Antoine attached himself to us. He got us into the Gibran house, which was supposedly closed for repairs, then took us home for a Lebanese sit-around with his mother, aunts, sisters, cousins, etc. Hospitality is a must in the Middle East whether anyone wants to have it or not. Pomegranate juice is served, lots of cigarettes are smoked, and tiny cups of coffee are drunk while everyone smiles and stares because you can't speak Arabic and they can't speak English, and Lebanese are the only people in the world who pronounce French worse than Americans.

Antoine's house was extraordinary. Like Gibran's it was carved into the side of a hill. The main room was windowless, floored with layers of Persian carpets and hung wall and ceiling with ornate cloths. There were stuffed falcons, brass things, photographs, and religious statuettes all over the place and a dozen Mafia-Mediterranean-style dining-room chairs. Antoine let us know he thought Kahlil Gibran's house was underdecorated. Antoine's mother told us that she'd lost five sons in the war so far, though that may have been the usual polite exaggeration of the Levantine.

Ahmed, though Muslim, was a great hit with Antoine's family. He brought them up-to-date on Beirut politics and then told Syrian checkpoint stories. Syrian checkpoint stories are the Polish jokes of Lebanon.

A Syrian soldier stops a Volkswagen Beetle and demands that the driver open the trunk. The driver begins to open the luggage compartment at the front of the car. "No!" says the Syrian, "I said the *trunk*."

"This *is* the trunk," says the driver.

"I am not a donkey," says the Syrian, pointing to the back of the car.

"Open the trunk!" So the driver does as he's told, exposing the VW's engine. "Aha!" says the Syrian, "You have stolen a motor. Furthermore, you have just done it because it's still running."

Another of Ahmed's stories—and he swears this one is true—is about a checkpoint on a hill where the Syrian soldier wanted to inspect a car trunk. "I can't get out," said the driver, "I have no emergency brake, and I must keep my foot on the brake pedal or the car will roll away."

"Don't worry," said the Syrian, "I will sit in the car and hold the brake pedal." So they changed places. "Now open the trunk," said the Syrian. The driver opened it. "All right," yelled the Syrian from inside the car, "is there any contraband in there?"

What the Syrians are looking for in your trunk, by the way, are *Playboy* magazines. Be sure to carry some.

We sat and smoked more cigarettes. Lebanon is not the place to go if you're trying to give that up. Everyone over the age of six chain-smokes. Long-term health effects are not, these days, a major concern, and it's the worst sort of rudeness not to offer cigarettes at every turn. George fell in love with Carmen, Antoine's sister, a beauty of about fifteen. George could talk of nothing else for the rest of the trip but getting married and becoming Maronite. Maybe the feeling was mutual. Antoine took me aside later and asked me if George was a Christian. I assured him most blond, blue-eyed Americans over six feet tall are not Druze. He then nicked me, instead of George, for the two hundred Lebanese pounds it allegedly cost to get in the Gibran house.

We went on up into the mountains to the Cedars, one of only three small groves of these trees left. Once the country was forested with them, a hundred feet high at full growth and forty feet in circumference. It was from these the tall masts of the Phoenician galleys were made and the roof beams of Solomon's temple and so forth. The trees in the Bsherri grove look like they need flea collars, and the grounds are a mess.

We found a good hotel, the La Mairie, about ten miles west of Bsherri in Ehdene. Ehdene is notable for the country's best-looking martyr pictures. There are martyr pictures everywhere in Lebanon. The Phalangists put up photographs of the ox-faced Bashir Gemayel, who got elected president in '82 and blown to bits within the month. The Shiites plaster walls with the face of some dumpy Ayatollah who went MIA in Libya. The Druze have Kamal Jumblatt, who looked dead even before the hitmen ventilated his limo. Ehdene, however, is the headquarters of the Giants militia, led by the very photogenic Franjieh family. In 1978 the Phalangists attacked the Franjieh home and killed a handsome son, his pretty wife, and their little daughter, too. If you have to look at pictures of dead people all day, they might as well be cute.

From Ehden, with light traffic and no mood swings at the checkpoints, it's only two hours back to Beirut.

The remaining great thing to see in Lebanon is Baalbek, site of three immense Roman temples, among the largest in the ancient world. Baalbek, however, is in the Bekáa Valley, where Israeli and Syrian forces are faced off and where Israel has been making periodic airstrikes on Syrian missile emplacements. Take sturdy and practical clothing.

Baalbek itself is controlled by an extremely radical pro-Khomeini Shiite group called Islamic Amal. The leader of Islamic Amal is Hussein Mussawi. He has close ties to Iran, and many people believe he personally ordered the suicide attacks on the American Embassy and the U.S. Marine base at Green Beach.

The Islamic Amal people are so far out there that they think *Syria* is a puppet of international Zionism. When I first arrived in Beirut, the Syrian army had Baalbek surrounded with tanks and was shelling downtown.

I went to Baalbek with ABC's chief Beirut correspondent, Charles Glass, and two drivers, one Syrian and one Lebanese Shiite. (Glass was later kidnapped by radical Shiites, possibly this same Islamic Amal; after two months in captivity, he made a harrowing escape.) The ride over the crest of the Lebanese range is breathtaking. The arid reaches of the Anti-Lebanese mountains rise in the distance. Below is the flat, green trough of the Bekka, where Syrian and Israeli lines are lost in verdant splendor. The thin neck of the fertile crescent is spread out before you, cradle of the civilization that has made air strikes possible. It's overwhelming.

At the foot of the descent is the large Christian town of Zahle, a Phalange outpost surrounded by Muslims. The Syrians shell this sometimes, too. Zahle has a good hotel, the Kadri, and an arcade of outdoor restaurants built along a stream in the Wadi Arayesh, or "Valley of Vines."

The road north to Baalbek runs up the middle of the Bekka. Marijuana fields stretch for miles on either side. This is the source of Lebanon's renowned hashish. Don't try to export any yourself, however. The airport customs officials won't search you when you arrive, but they're very thorough when you leave. Taking hashish out of the country without payoffs is one of the few crimes they still prosecute in Lebanon.

Bedouins from the Syrian desert camp beside the hemp fields. They're not very romantic up close. Their tents are made from old grain sacks, and everything around them stinks of goat.

The ruins of the Roman temples at the Baalbek are, words fail me, big. The amount of mashed thumbs and noses full of stone dust that went into chiseling these is too awesome to contemplate. The largest, The Temple of Jupiter, is 310 feet long, 175 feet wide, and was originally enclosed by fifty-four Corinthian pillars, each sixty-six feet high and seven and a half feet thick. Only six are left standing now. The temple complex was three centuries in building and never finished. The Christian Emperor Theodosius ordered the work stopped in hope of suppressing paganism and bringing a halt to a very lively sounding cult of temple prostitution.

Once again we found a lonely tour guide who took us around, spouting names and numbers, and pointing out things that are extra odd or large.

The ruins are policed by the Syrians, who are doing a better job than the Israelis at Tyre. The captain in charge came up and introduced himself. His English consisted of "Hello." "Hello," he said and shook hands. "Hello," he said and waved good-bye.

Outside the ruins, Baalbek is a tense and spooky place. All the Christians, Sunnis, and Druze have fled. Giant posters of Khomeini are hanging everywhere. There are few women on the streets, and they are carefully scarved and dressed down to the feet. The men gave us hard looks and fingered their weapons. The streets were dirty and grim. Syrian soldiers stayed bunched together. The tanks are still dug in around the city. You cannot get a drink or listen to Western music or dance or gamble, and you'd better not whistle "The Star-Spangled-Banner."

The tour guide led us directly from the temples to a souvenir store. There was something about risking my life to visit a pesthole full of armed lunatics and then going shopping that appealed to me. The store looked like it hadn't been visited since the Crusades, except all the ancient artifacts were new, made this month, and buried in the yard for a week.

The nonsense you hear about bargaining in the Orient is,

like most nonsense about the Orient, perfectly true. I had not been in the shop three seconds before the owner was quoting prices that would do justice to a Pentagon parts supplier and flopping greasy, ill-made rugs in every direction—like somebody house-training a puppy with the Sunday *New York Times*. There's a charming banter that goes with all this. I mean, I suppose there is. Some of the verbal flourishes of the Levant are lost in a minimal English vocabulary. "Good, huh? Real good, huh? Good rug! Very good!"

"He has a cousin in St. Louis," added the tour guide, helpfully.

It seemed I had to hold up both ends in this legendary duel of wit in the Bazaar. "Tell him," I said to the guide, "his goods are of the greatest magnificence and pleasure flows into my eyes at their splendor. Yes, and I am astonished at the justice of his prices. And yet I must abase myself into the dust at the humbleness of my means. I, a poor traveler, come many miles over great distances . . ." And so forth. Out came bogus Egyptian dog-head statues, phony Roman coins, counterfeit Phoenician do-dads, and more and worse and bigger rugs. After an hour and a half I felt I had to pay for my fun. I settled on a small bronze "Babylonian" cow with some decidedly un-Babylonian rasp marks on the casting. I bargained the shopkeeper down from $200 to $30. Good work if the cow hadn't been worth $0.

Charles Glass has spent years in the Middle East and was completely bored by this, however. He said we should go meet Hussein Mussawi.

Our Shiite driver was sent to negotiate. After the customary amount of temporizing and dawdle, Hussein consented to see us. We were taken to a shabby and partly destroyed section of town, where we were surrounded by nervous young gunmen. Though whether they were nervous about us or nervous that they might get a sudden invite to make like a human Fourth of July,

I don't know. We were marched into a tiny and dirty office and told to sit down. We waited. Then we were marched to a larger office furnished Arab-style with couches around the sides of the room. Khomeini pictures abounded. We were served tea, and Charles and I, though not our Muslim drivers, were very thoroughly searched. Charles's tape recorder was taken apart with special care. Our guards were pleasant, but small talk did not seem the order of the day. We waited some more. Finally, another group of armed young men came and took us through a warren of narrow filthy alleys to a modest and well-protected house. We were put into a small study lined with Arabic books and decorated with more pictures of Khomeini. There were two young men who spoke English waiting for us. They asked in an affable way what was going on with U.S. foreign policy. "After all," said one, "this part of the world has a Muslim majority. Is your government crazy or what?"

Half an hour later Hussein came in and shook hands with everyone. He's a thin man of middle size, about forty-five. He was dressed in a sort of semimilitary leisure suit and was very calm and dignified in his bearing but had, I swear it, a twinkle in his eye.

Hussein ordered a gunman to bring us coffee and cigarettes. The young man who spoke English less well acted as translator. "Were you responsible for the bombing of the marine base?" asked Charles. I nearly lit my nose instead of the Marlboro. Hussein answered with equanimity, pointing out that any number of people, including the American Democratic Party, stood to benefit from the attack on the marines.

"How long will this peace last in Lebanon?" asked Charles.

"This is not peace."

"When will there be peace?"

"When there is Islamic justice everywhere," came the answer.

"Everywhere?" asked Charles. "Will there be a place for Christians and Jews under Islamic justice?"

"Islam allows a place for everyone," said Hussein. The translator paused and added on his own, "Except, you know, Zionists and imperialists and other types."

"The Zionists will have to be driven out?"

"Yes."

"That may take a long time," said Charles.

Hussein fixed him with a smile. "Long for you. Short for us."

Hussein expounded upon the destiny of Islam and a believing man's place therein. The translator got himself tangled up with "Allah's great wishes . . . I mean, large would-be's . . . That is . . ."

"The will of God," I suggested.

Hussein turned to me and spoke in English. "Do you understand Arabic?"

"No," I said, "I just recognized the concept."

He said something to the translator, who said to me, "He wants to know if you believe in God."

I didn't think I should quibble. "Of course," I said. Hussein nodded. There was intensity in his look and no little human concern. He continued on subjects theological.

"To get back down to earth for a moment . . ." said Charles.

Hussein laughed. "Oh," said the translator, "all this is *very much* down to earth."

Charles continued to ask questions. I continued to ponder Hussein. He was practically the first Lebanese I'd met who didn't tell me he had a cousin in Oklahoma City. Although, as it turns out, his brother is a petroleum engineer who used to work in Dallas.

Charles asked Hussein about Jonathan Wright, the missing Reuters correspondent. "I hadn't heard about this," was the reply. "Also, he wasn't headed this way."

Hussein told Charles he should study the Koran.

At length we took our leave. As we were being escorted back to our car I noticed a woman on a nearby roof wearing a chador and hanging out lacy black lingerie on the clothesline.

Less than a week after our visit, the U.S. embassy annex in East Beirut got blown up. I hope it wasn't anything we said.

The hotel at Baalbek is the Palmyra, built in the 1870s. It's a massive Ottoman structure furnished with antique carpets and heavy mahogany Victorian furniture. The leather-bound guest register bears the signatures of Louis Napoleon, the duc D'Orleans, the empress of Abyssinia, and Kaiser Wilhelm II. There's an air of twilight and deliquescence to the place. Only the owner and a couple old servants are left. No room had been occupied for months, and only an occasional Syrian military officer comes to dinner.

Charles and I sat alone that night in the vast dining room. Pilgrims were still returning from Mecca, and celebratory gunshots sounded outside. "Happy fire" it's called. The electricity guttered in the bulbs and cast the long tables and tall ceiling into gloom. The forces of darkness and barbarism seemed to gather around. It was as though we were the last two white men in Asia. We sat up past midnight drinking the bottle of Arak a grizzled waiter had smuggled to us, talking politics and literature and citing apt quotations:

> Turning and turning in the widening gyre
> The falcon cannot hear the falconer;
> Things fall apart; the center cannot hold;
> Mere anarchy is loosed upon the world,
> The blood-dimmed tide is loosed, and . . .

. . . and you just can't find travel like this anymore.

Travels with Bassem

By Mike Sager

Killed: *The Washington Post Magazine,* 1988

When I was new to journalism, a wise old editor explained to me that the best magazine stories were a team effort—a consummate blend of writer, editor, subject, and publication.

"Travels with Bassem" bore him out perfectly—only in reverse.

I started my career as a copy boy at the Washington Post *in the fall of 1978. In those days, the paper was not yet computerized. I was assigned to the wire room, the paper's link to the outside world.*

On my first night, at 1:50 AM, the Reuters machine starting dinging. Pope John Paul I was dead. I stripped the wire, hustled out to the foreign desk.

In short order, the night news editor was barking: "Stop the presses!"

I was hooked.

For the next six years, I learned newspapering the old-fashioned way, writing everything from three-inch police shorts to long features. It was an intense experience; I lost most of my hair. What I learned I still use every day.

Grateful, but ready to move on, I left the Post in 1984. My objective: to work for New York glossies.

Two years later, the Post brought in a well-known, if somewhat offbeat, New York editor named Jay Lovinger. His objective: to make the Post's Sunday magazine more like a New York glossy.

At our first meeting, on a cold November morning in 1986, Lovinger was wearing one of his trademark goofy ties. "Why don't you go to Tahiti and find Marlon Brando?" he suggested.

The result ran fourteen thousand words. I never did talk to Marlon.

Come Monday morning, New York was calling. It was the breakthrough I'd been waiting for.

However, Ben Bradlee—the Post's legendary executive editor—was not so pleased. Recalls Lovinger: "Of anything I ever did at the Post Magazine, Bradlee hated [the Brando story] the most. I think he saw it as a thinly disguised criticism of journalism—which it was, of course."

And so it was that I met with Lovinger again a few months later.

We came up with the idea of me living with average Palestinians in Israel. The first Intifada had only recently begun. On the nightly news, there was lots of footage of kids throwing stones, of soldiers shooting gas canisters and rubber bullets. To most Americans at the time, the word Palestinian was synonymous with the word terrorist. In my mind, the concept of the story was simple: Palestinians must be people, too.

Lovinger loved it.

Before I left for Israel, the Post's Foreign editor summoned me to his office, a glass-walled affair in the middle of the newsroom—just about the same spot where, some ten years earlier, I had delivered the urgent wire to the night editor.

Be careful about what you say and do and write, the Foreign editor warned me, "There are larger considerations here." He also told me, "You're on your own."

Shortly thereafter, word filtered down that even though I would be traveling on a Post expense account in a war zone, I would not be granted a Post press card.

For the record, I forged one. Also for the record, I entered Israel carrying a formal "letter of assignment" written by a sympathetic Lovinger on Post stationery. With that I managed to secure press credentials from the Israeli government.

After spending six weeks in Israel, I submitted my story in the early fall of '88. One week later it was announced that Lovinger was "stepping down." Several tense weeks after that, I was informed that my story had been killed.

Honestly, I can't remember who delivered the news, but I remember receiving it in a phone booth just outside Ratners kosher restaurant on Manhattan's Lower East Side. And I remember sobbing uncontrollably as I rode uptown in a cab, heading to an appointment at Rolling Stone, where I had become a contributing editor.

Some people might say "Travels with Bassem" was suppressed by the Post—in vainglorious moments I could say that, too, I suppose.

But it is probably closer to the truth to say that nobody at the paper ever even read it. My rabbi at the paper, my patron with the goofy tie, had been shit-canned. To the powers that be, my Marlon story was emblematic of his whole madcap reign. "Travels with Bassem" never stood a chance.

Bassem is calling, collect from Jerusalem. He's been missing for two weeks. I've been worried.

The line hiccups and clicks, spits static. Then I hear his voice.

"They arrested me," he says, the accent thick, a tone of outrage. "Right after you left, they take me from my house. They put me in jail. The whole time I just sit there like an animal. They didn't even ask me one single question. Then they let me go. Just like that. They are really after something, Mike. I don't know what it is."

The words skip across the ocean like hard, flat stones. I was afraid something like this would happen. Bassem and I went through a lot. I keep his picture on my desk, a five-by-seven glossy in a simple Lucite frame. I look at it while he speaks.

He is sitting, right knee crossed over left, on a pile of Bedouin rugs beside a tray of trinket earrings, in his family's shop in the Old City. He's wearing designer jeans, a silk shirt, a gold chain, white socks, tan loafers. Though he is looking straight at the camera, his eyes, one of which is set deeper than the other, seem to be saying two different things. The right one is focused and wary; it is in his world right now, a place where anything can happen at any moment. The left one appears unfocused and wistful, dreamy. It seems to be in another place, a place that may never be.

In these weeks since my return from Israel, I have looked often at Bassem's picture, for there is much to remember, even more to try and comprehend. Bassem showed me Israel, his Israel, a place he calls Palestine. He translated Arabic and Hebrew into English for me, got me a discount on a rental car, invited me home, fed me his mother's stuffed grape leaves, guided me to illegal places, floated with me at midnight in the Dead Sea, beneath a million ancient stars. We drove all over the country; he took me to meet his friends. There was Ziad, the Bedouin accountant. His family's lone remaining camel was tied to a stake in the middle of their compound—under Israeli law, the Bedouins were no longer allowed to roam the desert. Naser was a civil engineer. He made water pipes out of irrigation tubing stolen from Israeli settlements. Mohammed was a graduate of the Bethlehem University School of Hotel Management. Poona lived in Dahisha, the oldest of the refugee camps. Her neighbors called her Mother of the Camp; she served us endless rounds of orange soda, mint tea, Turkish coffee. Samir, in Gaza, had a seventeen-year-old Peugeot with a trunk full of cruddy tires. He'd stop here and there and chat a while, leave a tire behind. Later, the tire would be burned, a crude roadblock, a feeble but symbolic attempt to keep out Israeli soldiers. Taher rented a room in the Jerusalem that was seven hundred years old. Every morning before work, he rode his exercycle, listened to reggae music through his headphones.

Bassem did a lot of things to help me; he saved my ass and I saved his. And though I paid him a good wage to be my translator, he wasn't in my service. (From time to time, in fact, I had the distinct impression that I was in his.) From that day in the West Bank, when the soldier cocked his M-16 and commanded us to come or die, Bassem and I were friends. "This is the life," Bassem would say, when we were stopped at a checkpoint, when we visited wounded boys in the hospital, when the soldiers threatened to beat us, when the refugees ran us out of their camp, when the Israeli waiter pretended we didn't exist, when we had to stay inside for days at a time because a town was under curfew. Bassem shared the life with me. He let me in.

Now he is on the phone, collect from Jerusalem. He's in trouble. There is nothing I can do.

"Mike," he says, "you can't even believe this. Ziad is

arrested. And Samir, he is arrested, too. Mohammed is in the hospital. He is unconscious. The doctors cut off his right arm.

"I think they were following us, Mike. In Gaza. In Hebron. In Akko. In Bethlehem. But it is not only this. Even in the American Colony Hotel. Remember the photographer? The men in the garden? I have to go see my lawyer. I have to talk to some people. They are really up to something. I have to find out what it is."

The plane rolled to a stop in the middle of the runway at Ben Gurion airport, far from any buildings, and everyone clapped and chanted prayers. Late June 1988. A flight to Tel Aviv, full of Jews. Blond Jews and bearded Jews, Jews with videocams, Jews in fur-covered hats, Jews speaking Spanish, English, French, Russian—all of them making *aliya,* the blessed return to the Promised Land, a right and a privilege bestowed by both the Torah and the State of Israel.

Myself, I was a Jew making *aliya* on assignment. It was my first trip to Israel. I'd been warned. Be careful of danger, they said. Be careful what you write: there are larger considerations at stake. I gathered my knapsack and my trepidations and walked up the aisle, stepped through the hatch. The sun was already strong. The wind blew grit. I put on my sunglasses, waited my turn behind grandmothers and kids.

Down the gangway, two steps on tarmac.

A beefy guy started hollering. He pointed at me and ran in my direction. Four others followed.

I was surrounded: Three men, two women, all of them wearing identical sport shirts and chinos. The first guy jab- bered at me in Arabic. Another reached slowly for the bulge beneath his shirt. There was panic in his mirrored sunglasses, my reflection. . . .

Things were not well in Israel. For the past seven months,

the Intifada, the struggle, had been raging in the territories seized during the Six Days' War of 1967.

Beginning in December of 1987, the two million Arabs indigenous to the territories, the Palestinians, had erupted spontaneously in mass protest. Local committees were formed. Children and mothers were demonstrating. An ordered, primitive, effective, grassroots uprising was taking place on the front pages of newspapers around the world. The Palestinians protested and struck and built road blocks, threw stones at the formidable Israeli troops. The soldiers, great grand-children of the Holocaust, countered with tear gas and automatic weapons, the bullets sometimes rubber, sometimes real.

Since the Intifada began, two hundred Palestinians had died, two Israelis had died. Thousands of Palestinians, the majority of them teenagers, had been shot or beaten. More than fifteen thousand Palestinians had been arrested; at least fifteen hundred were being held without charge on "administrative detention" by edict of military commanders. More than thirty Palestinian houses had been destroyed. Long the victims, the Jews were beginning to look like the oppressors. The Palestinian terrorist on the six o'clock news was beginning to look a lot younger. And he was beginning to look like the good guy.

Clearly, Israel was troubled. Born in 1948 into a state of war, faced always with the possibility of extinction, the Jewish homeland had grown, but she had not matured. The institutions set up forty years earlier in a state of military alert were still in place, but they no longer accommodated the needs of the burgeoning, modern nation that Israel had become. Over the years, ad hoc had become status quo. The Israelis hadn't even gotten around yet to writing a constitution.

In the coming six weeks, while I was in-country, Israeli doctors would call a full-fledged strike and all ambulance service would be suspended. The nation's district court judges would threaten to resign "en bloc" in a dispute over a Knesset plan to reorganize the court system. Jewish factory workers would storm the Ministry of Finance, wielding clubs in protest of government plans to lay off almost three hundred. The Education Minister would warn the cabinet that because of budget cuts, "The Israelis are gradually becoming a nation of mediocrities." The Central Bureau of Statistics would report a $1.3 billion decline in share value on the Tel Aviv stock exchange for the first six months of 1988.

The country, its systems, its institutions, even the buildings in its hastily assembled model city, Tel Aviv, were crumbling around the edges from neglect. A raucous national election was in progress. The nation was traumatized and split by the dirty war of attrition in the territories. Neighboring Arab countries were announcing arms deals with China and France. The war between Iran and Iraq was heading toward a truce; the lull in headlines was sure to focus even more attention on the plight of the Palestinians. King Hussein of Jordan was about to absolve himself of responsibility for the Palestinians in the occupied territories, leaving the United States and Israel faced with the almost certain possibility that the Palestine Liberation Organization would have to be recognized if negotiations were ever to convene. The world—even the United States, even some American Jews—was beginning to lose patience with the stark, ugly news footage of soldiers shooting at children. "Our relations with many countries have been reduced to the level of constant justification," a Foreign Ministry official would be quoted as saying.

And so it was that my plane landed at Ben Gurion and I was surrounded by plainclothes government agents, one reaching for his gun. Everything on the airfield had screeched to a halt. Everyone was staring—the passengers on the gangway, the stewardesses, the baggage handlers, the engineers, old and young, Spanish and French and American and Israeli—all of them Jews, all of them scared to death, sure that their worst fears were coming true and that any moment I was going to run amok or take hostages or blow something up.

I removed my shades, raised my hands in surrender. I'm short, dark, and bearded, wear an earring in my left ear. Like many Jewish men, I am half-bald on the top. Unlike many, I complete nature's work with a razor. At home, my friends often joke that I look like a terrorist.

At the moment, it didn't seem so funny anymore.

"It's okay, I'm Jewish!" I said, forcing a smile. "No problem! I'm Jewish!"

Two other agents went for their guns.

Bassem is calling, collect from Jerusalem.

"Mike, everything is shit," he says.

"The other day I was threatened by the Israeli security. They saw me in Salahadin Street. They say, 'You're out of prison, but don't think you are as free as you really think. We know what you are doing. We're just waiting for the right time and the right charge. This is your end, that's it.'

"I cannot stay here. I need to go someplace for a few months so my name will be forgotten here, or not even to be forgotten, but for things to start quieting down. They are putting this chain around my neck. They are making it tighter."

At sundown on Sabbath the Old City glowed; the muezzin at the mosque sang a strange nasal *sura*. Three boys in shorts and kneesocks and long black coats hurried through the Arab Quarter, arm in arm in arm, sidecurls flying beneath wide-brimmed hats. Leaves of cardamom and pieces of trash skittered across the narrow cobbled streets, which echoed the ancient, solitary clip-clop of a donkey. Soldiers clustered in archways on folding chairs, guns in laps. On the Via Dolorosa, where Christ carried his cross, a man in a long, dresslike *jalabia* carried a refrigerator on his back.

The Jews call this city *Yerushalayim*, the City of Peace. The Arabs call it *al-Quds*, the Holy. Set along a ridge of strong stone hills the color of sand, Old Jerusalem is a fortress behind a thick, saw-toothed wall. To the east is the desert, the land of milk. To the west is the fertile plain, the land of honey. For four thousand years, men have fought over the ownership of Jerusalem. It is the city where David ruled, where Christ died, where Mohammed ascended. The streets here are mentioned in the Bible; you can stand in places where miracles occurred. Jerusalem stands as a monument to the religious beliefs of half the people on Earth. Since its beginnings as a Canaanite city-state in the Bronze Age, Jerusalem has been ruled, alternately, by Jews, Macedonians, Egyptians, Seleucids, Greeks, Jewish Hasmoneans, Romans, Byzantines, Persians, Umayyads, Abbasids, Fatimids, Ayyubids, Crusaders, Mameluks, Ottoman Turks, British, Jordanians, and now again the Jews.

I was headed out of the Old City, through the Arab Quarter, toward the Damascus Gate. I'd been to the Wailing Wall for the Friday evening service.

I'd climbed up high near a barbed wire fence to watch. At the Wall, black hats and yarmulkes bobbed in prayer. Behind them, tourists circled guides. The name of God was spoken in many languages. Young soldiers cruised the massive courtyard, scanning for trouble, scoping the foreign girls. The Wall itself is one hundred feet high. It is made of great blocks of Herodian stone. Actually, it's a retaining wall: it holds back the western face of Mount Moria, the Temple Mount. Over a period of one thousand years, in a repeating pattern of defeat, exile and return, the Jews laid claim to this hallowed plateau, a reign by the God of Israel which ended in A.D. 70, when the

Roman emperor Titus destroyed the Second Temple and slaughtered and enslaved the Jews.

High above the soldiers, worshippers, and tourists, above the Wall itself, on that very same hallowed plateau, the gold Dome of the Rock hunkers beneath an Arab crescent. The Al Aqsa mosque was built in A.D. 691. It is the third most sacred site in all of Islam. One of the duties of a good Muslim is to make three pilgrimages in his lifetime—to Mecca and Medina in Saudi Arabia, and to Jerusalem, to this mosque. At the heart of the complex is a huge, tan-colored rock formation, the exact place where Muhammad mounted his winged steed and flew to heaven to meet Allah. To this day, in bas-relief in the rock, you can see Muhammad's footprint. Hanging above it is a glass canister. Inside are three hairs from the prophet's beard.

I'd just arrived in Jerusalem from Tel Aviv. I'd been in Israel four days. Being here, among my people, was not like being in other foreign countries. Everything was so familiar. I didn't know the language, but I was fluent in the customs. Everything about the place was Jewish. The restaurants had all the stuff we used to eat only on holidays. The faces of the Jewish people reminded me of every Jewish face I'd ever known. The words in people's sentences were the same words I used in the prayers I'd repeated as a kid, only they were using them to talk about the weather. I had this strange feeling, like someone had taken all my furniture and arranged it exactly the same way in a different room.

But it was more than that. The way the lady in the hotel bookstore admonished the eleven-year-old who was paging through *Hustler*: "What do you know from such trash?" she said, shooing him with both hands out the door. The way the older man in the sundries shop, after I told him I didn't need a bag for my postcards, urged, "Take it, it's better in a bag." The way the hotel operator had admonished: "There's nothing wrong with the phone. It must be you."

In *Fodor's Guide to Israel*, the 1988 edition, it is explained that Jews are "generally warm, friendly, generous people. They can also be prying, rude, and exasperating." I guess I would have to agree. It's how the world thinks of us; it's how I think of us, too. My best friends from college were Jews from Long Island. It could be said, with apologies to them, that they were prime examples of the archetypal ugly American Jew: gold chains, loudmouths, a certain air of entitlement. Becoming close friends with these guys helped me learn a very important lesson: Someone can act like a jerk but still be a great guy. It's an extension, I suppose, of something my parents taught: You can love someone even if you don't like what they do.

You need to know these things in Israel, if only to acclimate yourself to the attitude. It is part of the heritage, the upbringing—the way Jewish kids are taught that they are loved, that they are special. Jews like themselves. They have great amounts of self-esteem. They believe they can accomplish things. It has something to do with the religion, I believe. Jews aren't born encumbered with an original sin; we don't start life with a theological strike against us. We do, however, start life with a cultural strike against us.

My parents always had a keen sense of their Jewishness, and I suppose I have it, too. Both grew up in small towns in Virginia. Things were not easy. Some of their neighbors actually believed they had horns.

"It was mostly verbal stuff," my Dad has said. "Damn kike. Something that would come up. But it was more than that. It was the idea that was hard. They never forgot you were a Jew, and they never let you forget, either. You couldn't be a Jew and be part of the rest of the world too. That's how they made me feel."

After they were married, when I was young, my parents moved to Pikesville, Baltimore, a neighborhood the Jews themselves called a "golden ghetto." There were six temples along a two-mile stretch of Park Heights Avenue; growing up, no one ever made me feel like there was something inherently wrong with my existence on the planet. But no matter where you grow up Jewish, you're made to remember—from the slaves in Egypt to the death camps in Nazi Germany—how it has always been for your people, what it means to be Jewish.

Now I was in the Jewish homeland, a member of the majority. Walking back to my hotel from Sabbath services at the holiest of Jewish places, the Wailing Wall, I headed along a narrow street in the Arab Quarter of the Old City, filled with the odd sensation that, for once in my life, I was in a place where being Jewish was actually an advantage.

Up ahead, however, there were nothing but Arabs. The street was dark, close, menacing. Men smoked and played cards. Little boys played soccer and rode bikes. My leather sandals, bought that day in the market, clicked too loudly on the cobbles. As I came closer, everything stopped.

Then someone yelled at me: "Hey, Kojak!"

The little ones surrounded me, and they laughed and pointed, and then one of them got the courage to touch my shaved head with his fingertips, and then all of them, maybe twenty young boys in all, began to reach and touch and laugh, squealing "Kojak! Kojak! Kojak!" referring, of course, to the popular TV detective with the shaved head. Reruns of the series were broadcast in Israel. A boy named Nasser spoke a little English. He asked me to give him five, and I did, slapping his palm at waist level. Then I taught him a new way, and everyone took turns slapping palms high in the air.

Nasser locked his fingers in mine, walked me over to some

older guys who were sitting around drinking tea outside a store called Holy City Souvenirs. He introduced me to everyone, and most rose in turn to shake my hand. One, however, refused to rise. Like the rest, he was wearing designer jeans and a dress shirt, open almost to his navel. He nodded in my direction, barely cordial.

I took a seat with the men and little Nasser brought me sweet mint tea. The boys gathered around. We drank and smoked cigarettes, talked of this and that in broken English. Then Nasser made his close: "You want to buy something in shop?"

"I am not here to buy," I explained. "I'm a journalist. You understand journalist?"

They understood. There was much to tell.

One boy spoke about his two brothers in prison. Another showed me his broken arm, made chop-chop motions like a billy club—the other tool of the soldiers—across the plaster cast with his good hand. A third pulled a picture from his wallet, his dead cousin. A fourth pulled a picture from his pocket, his dead brother.

Their litany was long and horrifying, even in broken English. Houses demolished, land stolen, children shot, babies dead from tear gas. "The Jewish do this," each repeated in turn. "The Jewish."

I was gut-shot. I had no idea. This was 1988, seven months into the Intifada. No one had any idea, not really. No one outside of Palestine, anyway.

The stories continued until well after dark. I didn't have my tape recorder with me. "Maybe I should come back tomorrow," I said. "Maybe we can talk some more?"

Everyone looked to the skeptical guy. He was in his late twenties, roughly the same age as me. He was sitting on a pile of Bedouin rugs. He hadn't said a word all evening. He stroked his mustache, looked me up and down. Finally, he spoke:

"Mr. Mike," he said, with much formality. "Are you, by chance, a Jewish?"

Palestinians have this way of making you wait. They say they'll call on Saturday afternoon, so you wait in your room until Saturday night. On Sunday, you wait in the garden courtyard of the hotel, running back and forth to the front desk to remind them to transfer the call. You wait three hours and drink six cups of thick Turkish coffee, and then you go the bathroom.

That's when they call.

And they leave an admonishing message.

So it was on my third day in Jerusalem. I was waiting for a call back from a Palestinian urologist.

An organization in Washington, D.C., the American Arab Anti-Discrimination Committee, had set me up with the doctor. The idea was that I—the son of a Jewish gynecologist—would live with him and his family for a week or two, experience upper-middle-class life in the occupied territories. I'd had this notion that the world didn't really see Palestinians as people. They were an issue. They were numbers, quotes, and footage.

I'd met some Palestinians in Washington before I left. When I thought about it, they seemed a lot like Jews. They valued family and education. Many were well off. People hated them. They had their own Diaspora—college-educated Palestinians were settled all over the Arab world; they held the kind of important, background positions that Jews have always held. Palestinian kids are taught that they are loved, that they are special. Palestinians like themselves. They have lots of self-esteem. They believe they can accomplish things. I wondered if maybe this was a clue to what was happening in Israel. As time went on, I would form this picture in my mind: someone boxing his own mirror image.

And so it was that I, the son of a Jewish gynecologist, had arranged to stay with a Palestinian urologist and his family in the West Bank. Now, if I only could divine at what hour on which day he would choose to return my call, I could begin my research in earnest.

I was staying in Arab East Jerusalem, in the stately oasis of neutrality called the American Colony Hotel. Built in 1840 for a Turkish pasha and his four wives, it was a ten-minute walk from the Damascus Gate. In 1917, the Arab mayor of Jerusalem used one of the American Colony's white sheets to surrender to the British army. In 1948, during the war for Israeli independence, the owner of the hotel turned the lobby into a hospital. In 1967, the hotel was caught in the crossfire of the Six Days' War, taking more than twenty direct hits during the battle for East Jerusalem. More recently, U.S. Secretary of State George Shultz had scheduled a meeting here with Palestinian leaders, a first tiny step toward recognition of the "outlaw" regime as a legitimate voice of the people.

Those Palestinians kept him waiting, too. Indefinitely.

Now, sitting in the garden courtyard of the American Colony Hotel, I was reading the introduction to a book called *Arab and Jew,* written by Pulitzer Prize–winner David K. Shipler in 1986.

> This is the land most burdened and enriched by history, most scarred and coveted by the Jews and Arabs who now face each other in combat, in distaste, in regard, in accommodation, in strange affinity. . . . Both peoples are victims. Each has suffered at the hands of the outsiders, and each has been wounded by the other.

The Jews, he said, "have been subordinated, despised, vilified, imprisoned, and slaughtered. Throughout their history, they have been haunted by a corrosive sense of illegitimacy. . . . And they have stood and fallen alone. Nobody has rescued them except incidentally, as the Allies liberated many from the concentration camps after defeating Hitler's Germany."

The Palestinians, he continued—in a passage written some two years before the Intifada began—have "suffered powerlessness and deprivation of liberty but never genocide. Their sense of distinctiveness as a Palestinian people has come not from an ancient source but largely in reaction to the creation and growth of Israel on part of the land where they lived. In contemporary, personal terms, then, many Palestinian Arabs have been the victims of expulsion, displacement and war. They have found themselves scattered and rejected in the Arab world at large. . . ."

"Is this how you report your story, Mr. Mike? You sit in the garden of the hotel and read a book?"

I twisted around. It was the skeptical guy from the Arab Quarter.

Over the last few days, in between bouts of waiting for Dr. Jibril, the urologist, to call, I'd gone back to Holy City Souvenirs. I can't say I was welcomed, exactly. The older guys I'd first met didn't want to talk anymore. The skeptical guy made a point of not even noticing me. I don't think he'd believed me when I told him I was Greek—just like Kojak. Mostly, I'd spent my time with little Nasser. He took me around the old city, showing me the sights, stopping here and there for a high-five. I certainly hadn't told anyone where I was staying.

"Well, see," I stuttered, trying to explain, "there's this Palestinian doctor—"

"Let me tell you something, Mr. Mike—" he motioned to the chair, raised his eyebrows. "May I sit down?"

He said his name was Bassem. I reached over and shook his hand. He crossed his legs, looked around the garden restaurant.

It was nearly empty. "A few months ago," he said, "if you came to this hotel, hundreds of journalists were here. Upstairs, downstairs, in the garden, in the restaurant. They were all of them from press. They thought the Intifada was going to last for three months, or even two, or even four months. And then, after four months, they start asking, 'What are we doing here?' They are fed up with it.

"To them, it was only a matter of very important news. They want to be famous. They want to show their people back in their country, 'Look, I got this story. I'm a good reporter or even I can be a famous reporter.' For them, it's a chance to get a big story, to get lots of attention for himself, especially if he is a young reporter, like you."

I raised my hand in protest, but he continued. "Mr. Mike, I have been watching you. I have seen you in the Old City. I have seen you here and there. But I have never once seen you with a camera. I have never once seen you writing things down. I have never once heard you ask any questions."

Bassem looked at me for a long moment. He shook his head slowly. *Tsk, tsk.* I didn't know what to say.

"I have decided," he said at last, flourishing his hand in the air like a sheik ordering the dancing girls. "I will get you your story, Mike. I will get you a *very* good story. You can count on me."

Bassem is calling, collect from Zurich.

"How did you get out?" I ask.

"I used a travel document."

"They gave you a travel document?"

"I pay money to get it. There is an Arab man who work for security. I go through him. Then, when I went to the airport, they stopped me. They say I can't leave the country. They say I have to bring this paper from the court.

"I need this file from 1982, so the next morning, I go to the court. I go from office to office, from place to place. Nobody's willing to help, nobody's willing to listen. Everybody was using his phone, everybody was having a meeting, no one would say anythings to me. It took me three fucking days to get the paper.

"And you know, the second time I come to the airport, they never even mention this paper! But they did search me. Ten times they search me. Three times they make me take off my clothes. I told them listen, I'm very offended to this."

"What are you going to do now?"

I have no plan yet," he says. "I need to go to Germany, and then I will have a plan. I need to see the country. I don't think I can live in such places like this. It is something to do with the view you see around here, the kind of country it is. Everything not right here. This is not what I am used to. It is imitation to me. It is not like Jerusalem. Nothing's real."

At three in the afternoon on a stifling day in early July, three months earlier, Bassem and I were speeding down the highway, through Ramullah in the West Bank, driving back to Jerusalem. Dry, dusty wind whistled though the windows of my rented Renault. Scenery eddied over the asphalt; silence baked between us. Past watermelon stands, donkey carts. Everywhere seemed deserted.

"Look at this!" Bassem exclaimed. "Park over there."

The sun bleached the hills, scorched the backs of our necks. We scrambled down a rocky embankment, stood behind a waist-high wall. Five hundred yards away, down in the valley, a rock-strewn road through a little village, a truck full of Israeli soldiers.

Three of the soldiers had set a perimeter—points north, east, and west from the truck. A fourth directed a work party of civilians. A young boy and a woman wearing a veil worked together to roll a medium-sized boulder to the side of the road. Six teenagers attempted to pull a burned-out car from a gully. Others swept and picked up stones.

"This is how they clean the streets," Bassem whispered. "They go to the houses and take the people out. They make them take down the rocks and the barricades. When the soldiers leave, the people put them back up."

"What's the point?"

"This is what means *occupation*. The soldiers have to drive through the village one time or maybe two times every day. Then they can say they are occupying, or even that they are in control. When the soldiers come, the demonstration comes."

"So if the soldiers didn't come in, the people wouldn't riot?"

"Yesssss, Miiiike." It was tone I had come to know well, reserved for such occasions as this, dripping irony, a song of the obvious.

"Let's get closer," I said. I swung a leg over the wall.

"*Tal!*" shouted a soldier, the one on the northern perimeter. We'd been spotted.

"What is he saying?" I asked.

"He says to come."

"*Tal!*" the soldier repeated. Then he cocked his rifle. You could hear it five hundred yards away, the familiar metallic *click-shick* of lock and load. He raised the weapon, fit it to his shoulder. It was American-made, an M-16. He laid his cheek to the stock and aimed . . .

I approached holding my press cards high overhead, dancing them on the chain. The soldier kept his rifle shouldered. He yelled something in Arabic.

"I speak English," I said indignantly to the barrel of his loaded weapon. "If you want to speak to me, speak in English! I'm American!"

We'd spent the morning visiting the wounded of the Intifada, a hospital in the old Arab city of Nablus. I met a fourteen-year-old with a bullet-hole in his back, a seven-year-old with a cluster of three bullet wounds in his calf—Olympic-caliber marksmanship. I met kids with broken arms and legs and missing eyes. I learned that a so-called "rubber bullet" was really a solid cylinder of lead with a rubber coating around it. A twelve-year-old had taken two rubber bullets to the face at close range. The damage was indescribable.

One ten-year-old had taken a bullet in the thigh. The artery had been shredded: the leg was gangrenous. I stood at the end of the bed with my tape recorder. "Are you scared?"

The boy's lip quivered. "No," he squeaked.

I had to leave the room.

The hospital, called Al Itihad, was a charity hospital, one of the few in the territories that was operated, staffed, and funded totally by Palestinians. It had space for sixty beds. Already, they'd squeezed in ninety-two.

That very morning the Israeli government had announced new rules for medical care for Palestinians. Starting today, any Palestinian who went to the Israelis for treatment would have to pay in advance for three days' care. If you participated in a demonstration, for instance, and were shot by a soldier, it would cost you about one thousand dollars—up front—to receive emergency treatment.

The new medical rules were part of larger plan. Besides the obvious measures invoked under the Israeli's new "iron fist" policies—the midnight searches of houses, the billy clubs and rubber bullets, the administrative detentions, the torture, the deportations—the Israelis were laying siege to the Palestinian economy. Subtly, surgically, they were cutting the flow of resources to the territories.

Sometimes the government would turn off the telephones,

sometimes they'd cut the water or the electricity, or stop the shipments of fuel. Already they'd shut down several Palestinian produce markets, cut international communications, and imposed restrictions on travel, on building houses, and on the amount of foreign currency an Arab could bring into the territories. Hundreds of thousands of Jordanian dinars and American dollars had been seized at Ben Gurion Airport and at the Allenby Bridge, the crossing from Jordan.

Towns, villages, cities, and refugee camps were intermittently put under curfew. When I was there, Jalazun, a refugee camp, had been under curfew for more than a month. On any given day in June or July, eight or ten or fourteen different locations were under military siege, declared "Closed Military Areas" by the regional command. Journalists were turned away at checkpoints many kilometers down the road; sitting in the garden at the American Colony, reporters joked about playing a game called "Hunting the Intifada." You drove around, played hide and seek with the soldiers, trying to see for yourself what was going on.

Under curfew, all entrances to Palestinian towns or refugee camps were sealed. Nothing was allowed in, including food, and no one inside moved. People shuttered the windows and sat still, stayed in one room. Men and women relieved themselves in jars and pots, afraid even to cross open courtyards to their outhouses for fear of Israeli sentries posted on the roofs nearby.

The government was also cracking down on tax scofflaws. The Palestinians were withholding tax payments on the basis that their money was being used to finance the war against them. But the Israelis controlled the roads; all drivers in the occupied territories had to pass through military check points. Soldiers were checking tax rolls. Cars were being seized on the spot as payment. In some areas, like Gaza, there were hardly any autos left on the road.

Perhaps the most powerful weapon yielded by the Israelis was the "Identicard." By law, every Palestinian had to be registered. The cards—made of paper and holstered in a shirt-pocket-sized plastic sleeve—contained a picture, a name, an address, and a registration number, which corresponded to a central file in Tel Aviv. Failure to have an Identicard in possession could mean immediate arrest. Often, soldiers would drive through a village, round up a work party, confiscate Identicards, leave for an hour or so. The soldiers knew that the Palestinians, Intifada notwithstanding, wouldn't move an inch without their Identicards. It was another little tweak, another indignity—same as pissing off the roof in plain sight of a Muslim woman, or throwing rocks at kids from the machine gun nest. In July, one youth in the West Bank would die when a large rock fell off a roof where a soldier was sitting. The death was ruled accidental. It was that kind of confrontation—deep and mean.

All of which, I suppose, had made me angry and ashamed. All of which made me speak to the Israeli soldier the way I did, despite the fact that he was holding a weapon.

I wanted to make something perfectly clear to him. I wanted him to know that I am American. That he couldn't fuck with me because I have a country to protect me.

One of the jobs of a country, if you believe in Rousseau's social contract, is to stand up and claim each citizen as her own. He is mine, the country says to all the other countries in the world. If you have a problem with him, you have to deal with me.

The Palestinians have no country. They have no stamps, no currency, no law, no police, no passport, no Olympic team. They have a flag, but it is outlawed. They have a government, but it is in exile. They have leaders of the Intifada, but they are hiding. There is nothing Palestinian, except people. There is no country to bestow and defend their rights. In the grand historical game of musical chairs, the band has stopped, and there is a nation of people who can't sit down.

And so it was that I stood on my American rights, and the soldier took the gun out of my face. A lieutenant called us over to the truck nearby. The soldier walked behind.

Upon closer inspection, the truck was actually some kind of lightly armored personnel carrier, It had huge, tractorlike wheels and an open cab, behind which was a flatbed holding two long benches of soldiers, all of them slouched in the shade of an olive-drab canvas awning. The lieutenant was up front, in the passenger seat, high off the ground. He dangled a black boot over the side.

I told him I was a journalist, and that Bassem was my translator. I told him we were just touring the area.

The lieutenant said we had to leave. "You will make a riot. It is because of press that the Arabs riot."

I had no camera, no shoulder bag. My tape recorder was in my pocket, and it was running, but no one could see. I did not look like a journalist. "Why would people riot?" I asked.

"You will make a riot. You have to leave," he shot back.

Then he snapped his fingers at Bassem, turned his palm up. Bassem handed up his Identicard.

The lieutenant studied it a moment. "You live in Jerusalem?" he asked. "What are you doing here?"

Bassem smiled, a shit-eating grin. "Ramullah is a beautiful town. There is nice breeze here, Lieutenant."

"Tell this story to your grandmother," the lieutenant said disdainfully.

"This is the story I have," Bassem shrugged.

The lieutenant spit. "This is a Closed Military Area," he declared.

"No, it's not," piped a soldier from the back of the truck.

The lieutenant twisted around on his high seat and muttered something. Then he turned back to us. He pitched Bassem's Identicard into the desert. It flew like a Frisbee.

He leveled us with a menacing stare. "The other day," he growled, "we beat up three journalists, and we beat up two translators. We put them in the hospital. If I see you here again, you two will not be so lucky. You will not make it to the hospital alive."

"Why should I clean up the streets?" Bassem was saying, "I don't even clean up my own room."

We were on the porch of his family's concrete house in the Mount of Olives, sitting in metal chairs beneath an arbor of green grapes, talking with Bassem's little brother sixteen-year-old Omar. His mother wanted Omar to be a doctor. He and Bassem shared a room. They were very close.

Thirty years old, Bassem still lived at home, as do most unmarried Palestinian men. Though he sometimes rankled at the arrangement, considering himself a modern sort who would someday occupy his own bachelor pad, he had put his own plans on hold for the time being, in favor of keeping an eye on his little brother. Omar went to private school, was fluent in French and English, liked Hemingway, Camus, Madonna, and George Michael. He wore Pub aftershave, though didn't yet shave, and used Brylcreem in his auburn hair, which he combed in a rakish dip over this right eyebrow. Omar dressed like a kid from the American suburbs: Lee stonewashed denims, unlaced high-tops, oversize T-shirts with the sleeves rolled up over his biceps. A year or so ago, Bassem came home to find Omar had decorated their room with posters of Rambo, Ralph Maccio, Knight Rider, Samantha Fox. He'd scribbled graffiti on the walls with a magic marker: DIRTY DANCING near the light switch, SOS FOR LOVE near the bookshelf in which he kept his collection of teddy bears. A girl in Toronto keeps sending the bears, along with letters about flunking algebra and her screwed-up parents.

Before this year, Omar had been an outstanding student. His slide could be attributed partly to the government closures of his school in the Christian Quarter of Jerusalem. But part of it was something else. One night, Omar told Bassem he was "spinning around inside, all confused." He said he was tired of his friends, tired of talking about girls, music, videos. Lately, Omar had been hanging with college-age kids, talking politics, staying out to all hours. It used to be that Omar would sleep in Bassem's bed so that Bassem would have to wake him up when he came home from a night out. Now, Bassem was usually the one awake and waiting. He was worried that Omar would get himself arrested.

Where Omar was a private-school suburban, Bassem was a city streetwise. He'd been born in the kitchen of a house in the Old City, near the Damascus Gate, that his family had owned for two centuries. When he was still a little boy, he sold wooden camels, beaded rosaries, and brass menorahs to tourists from behind the counter in his family's shop. By the time he was twelve, he'd learned English, Hebrew, German, and some French, and he was hiring himself out as a personal tour guide. He'd wait around the Damascus Gate until he could pick up a family of tourists, preferably one with a pretty young daughter. He'd show them the Holy Sepulchre, the Arab souk, the Western Wall, the Dome of the Rock, chattering away about the mysteries and miracles of the Old City that he'd memorized from books. He never asked for money; he always came away with a generous tip. More recently, just before the Intifada, he had gone back into sales, specializing in fine Bedouin antiques.

Bassem had the gift of gab in many languages, especially

Arabic, and when he walked through the streets of the Old City people waved and slapped his back. Once, a guy reached into my knapsack in the crowded market. Bassem called him by name, told him to lay off. I hadn't even noticed the hand in my bag. It was a tiny little village within the walled city. Bassem was a native son.

Bassem was the third of four brothers in a family of ten children. They had moved from the Old City to the Mount of Olives during the Six Days' War. One brother was studying psychology in London. A sister was married to an engineer and lived in Saudi Arabia. She visited rarely; permits were hard to obtain. All the rest of the grown children lived at home, in the way of most Arab families, which operate in communal fashion, each member of giving what he can, each taking what he needs. One family under one roof. A tiny nation.

The roof, the home, is most important to Palestinians. In Islam, the land is the mother, and the mother is revered. It is she who carries on the generations, she who nurtures the present and the future. So, too, the house. When Palestinians build with concrete, they leave the top unfinished, steel rods exposed and waiting for the addition of the next floor. A Palestinian man's highest goal on earth is to house all of his family together. Out in the countryside, they build ranch-style, adding rooms, spreading out. In the city, they build apartment style, adding floors, moving up.

After his father died, Bassem's eldest brother became the head of the family. Assad favored $500 Hugo Boss sport coats, wore a Rolex. While I was visiting, he would twice travel to Germany on business. Each time he returned with a different German girl on his arm. The first one, the ex-wife of a West German bank robber, took a liking to Bassem. One night he borrowed my rental car and took her out on the town. After that, Bassem and Assad spoke even less frequently. Since their father died and

Assad took charge, well . . . Bassem was a man of strong convictions. He didn't like being told what to do. He wanted to do what *he* wanted to do—that was his problem with Assad. It was also his problem with the State of Israel. To date, he'd been arrested seventeen times.

Between the ages of fourteen and thirty, Bassem said, he had spent a total of three years in prison, the longest stint being three months. He had been arrested for several barroom brawls with soldiers, all of them in Jewish West Jerusalem, all of them over girls Bassem was having drinks with. He'd also been arrested for throwing rocks, for throwing Molotov cocktails, for other reasons not specified in his records.

Though he remembers the Arab soldiers during the Jordanian occupation, and the fighting during the Six Days' War, Bassem's first personal memory of the Israeli occupation dates from age eleven. He'd been in his father's shop when word spread that a Jew had set off a bomb in the El Aqsa mosque.

"We heard of the bomb," Bassem remembers, "and everyone just ran through the market to the mosque. There is a big fire inside, and I see people carrying water to throw on the fire. And here I was carrying water, too, not too much, just a small bucket, because I was small. I carried it and the big people would throw it. I mean, it was the mosque. I always prayed at this mosque when I was a kid. Of course, I wanted to help to save it from the fire. Afterwards, you could see everybody in the Old City wearing black, everybody sad. You don't see anyone smiling around the city for a long time."

Bassem was thirteen the first time he witnessed the death of a friend. Muhammad was a champion bodybuilder in the West Bank. Tell a Palestinian father he has a handsome boy, and he won't be particularly pleased. Among Palestinians, the highest compliment you can give is "strong." Mohammed was the strongest of the strong. When Bassem would go lift weights at the gym in the Old City, "Mohammed would give me advises about what to do with my body."

Mohammed was in the act of throwing a stone when a soldier shot him in the head. "I was in shock," Bassem said. "It took me forty-eight hours even to talk. He was shot, and then we had to steal his body from the hospital. We stole it and walked it all around the city, and everyone came with us. His blood was on my shirt. Afterward, we take his body to the mosque. I didn't want to go home, I wanted to be next to his body."

Within a year after Mohammed's death, Bassem was arrested for the first time. He was fourteen.

"One time there was a call over the loudspeakers at the mosque. There were Jewish people inside the mosque, trying to pray there. They claim this is their Second Temple and this is where they belonged.

"I answer the call, I come to the mosque. And I see one of them praying, one of these Jewish. And I jumped into him and I started to fight with him, and I catched him from the neck. I was strangling him. He was a bigger body than me, or even taller, and maybe over thirty years old. And then I started kicking him, and then there is the police catching me. I was really mad. I pushed the policeman and I tried to run away, but I wasn't lucky. I was caught.

"I stayed twenty-two days in jail before my trial. My mother, for twenty-two days, she never ate anything. She never smoked. All she did was drink coffee twenty-four hours a day and sit on the balcony waiting for me to come back. She was really upset. She refused to cook anything. She refused to let anyone turn on the television or even the radio.

"Among the Arabs, prison is something very bad. It means you have been stealing or killing or using drugs or all different bad things, bad things that dishonor your family. But the people in prison were OK. They talked about politics, about the Palestinian state. They told me listen, I should not be ashamed in prison. Being a political prisoner is something completely different. Being there gave me a clear picture of what it is meaning to live under occupation.

"They push you into a corner, the Israelis. This is the reason for the demonstrations. It is like a chain. It gets long and long and long, and this chain, it keeps going around your neck. And every time it's getting more tight and more tight. You know this is your homeland. You know you have the right to be here. You can't stand up and see people being shot in the street without doing anything, without feeling anything. If Gandhi himself was here, he would be turned into violence. Gandhi himself, honest to God. I mean, Palestinians have a hell of a life.

"How do you want me to feel? I want to live. Sometimes I really want to live. I want to go out there. I want to go to the beach. I want to be able to go out with a girl and have a good time. Maybe sometimes even you have a good time, but then you walk in the street and there is something else coming up to you to eat your heart, or even to eat your feelings, or even to fill you with lots of sorrows. You cannot enjoy a life like this. Always you know. Always you remember. To them we are a people who should not be here."

Allahu akbar! Allahu akbar! Allahu akbar!

We were in the middle of a riot.

Six hundred angry Palestinians, children and teens, mothers and fathers and grandparents, residents of a refugee camp in Gaza. They were throwing fists in the air and stamping their feet. They were yelling, "God is most great! God is most great!" The chords in their necks were straining, their eyes were fixed with hate.

Hatred for me.

Fingers were pointing, and then one finger was jabbing me in the chest, and then a hand pushed my left shoulder, and then another one pushed harder from the back and I almost lost my balance. A pebble hit the top of my head, a little pebble, arched from close range. And then a rock hit the hood of our car, and then another, and it sounded like the first drops before a heavy rain—tentative, pregnant, imminent . . .

Bassem and I were being kicked out of a refugee camp. It was the second time in two days.

Over the last month or so, members of the Shin Bet—Israel's internal security service, the same people who'd greeted me at the airport—had been playing a little game in the territories. They'd been going into Palestinian cities, villages, and refugee camps in unmarked cars. They carried press cards and video cameras, posing as journalists. They'd interview people, the whole charade. They'd ask about throwing rocks, demonstrations, politics, friends. When the interviews were done, they'd make arrests.

News of these tactics had passed through military censors and was published in both Hebrew and Arabic newspapers. The government did not deny the story. Israel knew that as long as the Intifada stayed on the front page, world support for the state would continue to deteriorate. Their hope was to turn the Palestinians against the press.

It appeared to be working.

Yesterday, in a village in the West Bank called Edna, Bassem and I had made friends with some *shebob*, the teenage soldiers of the Intifada. We'd spent all day with them, going from house to house, hearing the litany of indignities and horrors heard in every camp and every city, the same stories out of different mouths, the same stories all the time.

The people of Edna were particularly strong in their faith in the Intifada. They were farmers and herders who lived in an ancient town built in the rolling hills near Hebron. Not long before I came, they'd managed to keep the soldiers out of their village of seventeen thousand for twenty-five days, repulsing the daily patrols of jeeps and trucks with rocks and Molotov cocktails. On the twenty-sixth day, according to the villagers, the army attacked with helicopters and paratroopers. The battle lasted six hours.

Edna, like most of its sisters in the West Bank, was a fortress camouflaged as a sleepy village. There was one main road in and out, littered with an obstacle course of boulders and mufflers and bed springs. Just before the first house, a large truck sat halfway across the road. As we came toward it, a small boy in the cab of the truck blew the horn. Three older boys then stepped out from behind. They questioned us. Bassem passed muster. One of them got in our car.

We drove slowly up the hill, toward the village proper. The *shebob* we'd picked up had his head out the window. He signaled his comrades on the rooftops, telling them to hold fire. Meanwhile, Bassem and I waved like two Shriners on a parade float. *"Alafi shebob!"* we called, over and over again, Hello guys!

Through the village, past the battlements, toward the town square. As we went, I thought about one of the *shebob* I'd met in the hospital in Nablus. His name was Faisal. He was studying to be a nurse. He'd wrestled a gun from a soldier, then slammed it onto the pavement, breaking the stock. Then he threw it down and ran. He'd been shot in the back.

I asked him why he didn't use the rifle to shoot the soldiers while he had the chance.

He shook his head, *tsk tsk*. "*They* shoot guns. *We* throw rocks. This is the point of Intifada," he had said.

It was this kind of simple, perverse, effective logic that had been the best ally of the Intifada since its beginnings. *En masse,* the Palestinians boycotted Israeli products, withheld taxes, stayed away from jobs in Israel. Palestinians who worked for Israel as tax collectors, civil servants, and police resigned their posts. Those who failed to resign, or who collaborated with the Israelis, were attacked or killed. Under the unofficial guidance of the United National Leadership of the Uprising in the Occupied Territories, known as the UNLU, the Palestinians were doing everything they could to pester, annoy, wear down, and piss off the Israelis. They couldn't overrun them, perhaps, but they could drive them to distraction, make them crazy like a man being swarmed by mosquitoes.

Over the months of the Intifada, in a series of numbered communiqués, UNLU had ordered flag days, days of fire, days of stones, days of sit-ins, days of demonstrations, days of commemorations, days of general strike. They'd asked merchants and professionals to lower their prices, organized food deliveries to curfewed villages, kept communications open between the territories. Though competition between factions in UNLU was becoming increasingly divisive, the people themselves were solid. Every Palestinian was linked in his or her desire for a homeland, and everyone seemed to know the score: The illiterate goat herder spoke passionately against American imperialism. The taxi driver derided the military industrial complex. The mother in the refugee camp complained of the influence of New York Jews on American government policy. They were a nation of people exceedingly attuned to current events. A nation of people with one goal: a homeland.

In Edna, Bassem and I had gotten as far as being assigned a room for the night. Then, as the daylight faded, a throng of *shebob* gathered outside the house. One of them told my host that I looked like an Israeli settler he'd seen once, a guy with a shaved head and a beard.

And that was that. We were escorted out of town.

The next day, we saddled up for Gaza.

Thus far, over the past five weeks, my travels with Bassem had taken us all over the country, from the ancient Arab coastal city of Akko to the Dead Sea, the lowest point on earth; from the West Bank to Gaza, from Bethlehem to Beersheba, from the Golan Heights near Syria to the Egyptian border. I'd met Mohammed, the graduate of Bethlehem University School of Hotel Management, and Nasser, the civil engineer. I'd made rounds at a hospital in Ramullah with Dr. Jibril, the urologist, toured Nablus with his brother, a lawyer. We'd been in many places, met many people. But always, as night fell, the hospitality would dry up, and we'd be ushered out of town.

Always, as we left, we'd see soldiers marching in.

Everywhere we went, the Palestinians told of the horrors of the night. But no one would let me stay to witness. They were afraid what would happen if the soldiers found us in their house. They were afraid we knew the soldiers. They would talk to us for a little while, but they wouldn't let us into their lives, and I guess I didn't blame them. They didn't know who I was. I had two press cards, but one of them was written in Hebrew. I was suspect. Everyone kept saying I looked like a Jew. I wondered what Bassem thought.

Bassem had a Bedouin friend named Ziad who lived in Khan Yunis, near Gaza. Ziad had a friend who had some friends in the Beach Camp, known locally as the Shati camp, a teeming complex along the wide, sandy coast of the Mediterranean. Built originally in 1948 to house some 23,000 Palestinians— refugees who were displaced from their homes by the creation of the Jewish state and the ensuing war. Forty years later, the camp held upwards of 100,000 people—including several generations of Palestinians who had known no other home.

Ziad's friend Samir was the one who had contacts in the Beach Camp. His seventeen-year-old Peugeot plowed through the deep sand like a 4x4. Just outside the camp, about a half mile shy of the checkpoint, he turned a quick left onto a donkey path.

The sand in the camp was particularly deep, and it was black, the color of burnt tires. Sewage flowed at speed towards the sea in open, foot-wide trenches. Garbage in the streets festered in 115-degree heat. Electric wires hung overhead—the wires themselves were hung with illegal Palestinian flags, American-made tear gas canisters, pairs of old shoes. The houses, built of crumbling concrete and mud—some large and approaching grand, some merely shacks—had high walls and open courtyards, were huddled together haphazardly on narrow lanes that spilled, eventually, into a large central field of sand.

I was slumped down in the back of the Peugeot. Samir turned into one of the lanes, pulled in front of a small house, and stopped. We were hurried to a back room. The walls and roof were made of tin. It felt like an oven.

We sat on carpets on the floor, drank coffee, smoked cigarettes. Samir and his friend talked and argued a while, and then the friend left. He returned with a plastic bag. The substance inside was black and gummy. It was passed around in a gesture of friendship. Everyone took a little on the tip of a matchstick. You sucked a while, and then chewed. It was gritty and sour. Then you washed it down with coffee.

The talk continued. More coffee was served. As usual, not knowing the language, I felt a bit left out. I looked around the room, tried to make eye contact, tried to follow what was being said. By now, after more than a month in the occupied territories, I could pretty well catch the drift of the conversation—the tones and the gestures, the body language, the occasional proper noun, the look in people's eyes.

Usually in these negotiations—there had been many over the weeks—I would sit this way and listen for while until I got the feeling that it was time for me to speak for myself. (Though

I sometimes wondered who was truly in charge of this little journalistic enterprise, I couldn't let Bassem do *everything*. After all, *I* was the reporter.) For shorthand we called it The Big Close.

Giving The Big Close, I would speak and gesture forcefully, the way the Arabs did. Bassem would translate. I'd tell them that I was not an Israeli, that I was not a Shin Bet, that I was not, gulp, a Jewish. I'd tell them that I was looking only to see the truth with my own eyes, that I didn't want to hurt anyone, that I wouldn't take any names. I'd tell them about the one million American readers who would get my story on their front porch on some future Sunday morning—important people, senators and congressmen, even the president. And I'd tell them how public opinion was turning. I'd tell them that American Jews were not as powerful and popular with the leading American WASPs as they might think. It was a helluva speech; it came from my heart. It had gotten us *this* close . . .

Now, sitting in the hot tin shed, a bit woozy from the opium, I felt it was time to get to The Big Close. We'd come a long way. I'd been here five weeks. My expense account was totally gone. I reached over, knocked Bassem on the knee. I whispered in his ear, "Ready for The Big Close?"

No response.

I shook his shoulder. "Bassem?"

Both of his eyes were fixed and unfocused. His pupils were pinholes. His complexion was an alarming shade of olive green. "I think I need some water," he said in English, and then he said something in Arabic. Our host led him out of the room.

The talk continued around me. I had no idea what was going on. Then, from just outside the shed, I heard a thud. It was a sickening sound, like a side of beef falling onto a concrete floor. A moment later, our host dragged Bassem through the door, feet first. He was out cold.

At first I didn't move. I was a stranger, a white American

stranger. One thing I've learned over the years is that in a situation like this, in a place like this, you can't act like a know-it-all. Through the history of colonialism, white people have always acted that way. We can see now where this has gotten us. I was alone in a refugee camp without any translator. The best thing to do was to show deference, to be cool. They were men. This was their home. They knew what they were doing. They'd take care of Bassem, I was sure.

Our host set Bassem in a heap against the wall, placed an electric fan next to him. Then he took his old seat in the circle, resumed partying.

The fan oscillated back and forth. In the dim light of the shed, it appeared that Bassem's lips were beginning to turn blue . . .

In a little while I had him on his feet and walking, and now he was sitting next to me, semialert. Everyone was smiling at me, like I was Florence Nightingale, and I was feeling pretty good. Surely this would convince them I wasn't Shin Bet. Surely this was proof of my good intentions.

"Bassem," I whispered.

"Yesssss, Miiiike."

"Could you try the Big Close now?"

Just then two men entered. A discussion ensued. Bassem was not really operational. I gathered from the gestures that they wanted me to meet some people in the camp, some elders, perhaps. That was fine with me. I had nothing to hide. I followed them out of the room, alongside a house, toward the dusty street.

A crowd had gathered. One of them spoke to me in English. "May I see your press card, please?"

His name was Sharif. He worked as a stringer for a news organization, he said. He'd of course heard of the *Washington Post*. He showed me his own press card. I mentioned some names of Palestinian journalists I'd met in Jerusalem. I mentioned Dr. Jibril. I mentioned the lawyer. He knew them all.

"Come," Sharif said. "They want you to walk around the camp. The people want to see you, then maybe you can stay."

We walked down the lane toward the large central field. Samir and Ziad followed in the Peugeot. As we walked, more and more people joined the procession. Behind the car, Bassem walked with the help of a pair of *shebob*, each holding an arm.

As we reached the central field, the crowed gathered and grew. Hundreds of faces surrounded me, pushing closer, laughing and shouting and pointing. Then one of the kids yelled out "Shamir," the name of the Israeli prime minister, and everyone stamped on the ground and pointed their thumbs down. Someone else yelled "Reagan." Someone else yelled "Shultz." They stamped their feet. They pointed down.

I got the picture: I did the same.

I stamped and thumbed down. I made a terrible face.

Everyone cheered.

Then someone put a Palestinian flag in my hand. It was home-sewn, a triangle of red, green, and white—the outlawed flag of the PLO, in my hand. I could be shot just for holding it. I wondered if the soldiers at the checkpoint had heard the ruckus and were on their way. Everyone around me was silent. What would the journalist do now?

I did what I had to do. I raised the flag, this illegal PLO flag. I raised it high in the air, raised it repeatedly, punched it up there as convincingly as I could, like some demented cheerleader. I screamed at the top of my lungs: "PALESTINE! ALLLLL-RIGHT! PALESTINE! YEAHHHHH! PALEEEEEEESTIIIIIIINE!!!!!!"

They screamed. They squealed. They loved it!

They began chanting my name: "Mike! Mike! Mike! Mike!"

It was beautiful. I was in. Finally, we'd made it.

And then in the distance, another chant.

Allahu akbar! Allahu akbar! Allahu akbar!

I had won over *this* group, yes. But word of a Jewish interloper had already spread through the camp. They hadn't seen my flag bit. They hadn't heard the chant: "Mike! Mike! Mike!"

I looked up across the sandy field. People were pouring out from every lane, from every direction, coming at me fast across the open plaza, hundreds of them, with stones in their hands, a full-blown riot, *Allahu akbar! Allahu akbar! Allahu akbar!*

A pebble hit my head. A rock hit the car.

"I'm very sorry" Sharif said. He pushed me from behind, hurrying me toward the vehicle. "Perhaps you can come back again."

I jumped in, slammed the door. The starter ground.

Finally, it caught. Samir began to pull away.

"Wait!" I said. "Where's Bassem?"

Samir kept rolling, very slowly through the crowd. They were banging on the car. I banged Samir on the shoulder. "We have to get Bassem!"

I jumped out. Samir stopped the car. I raised my palms in submission to the mob. "It's okay. It's okay. We're going," I said, pointing toward the exit. "I just want to get my friend."

They let Bassem pass. He had a loopy grin on his face. I piled him into the back seat and Samir floored it, fishtailing though the sand in hail of stones.

Outside the camp, a collective nervous laugh spread through the car. Samir switched on his lights, made a slow U-turn to avoid the military checkpoint.

Suddenly, a bright spotlight.

Israeli soldiers.

We'd been spotted.

Bassem is calling, collect from Stuttgart.

"I called my lawyer back in Jerusalem," he says. "She say to me, 'Bassem stay where you are.' "

"What does that mean?"

"Well, Mike, they have arrested eighty people from Jerusalem, and already eighteen of them are people I really know."

"It says in the newspaper that the Israelis have been rounding up organizers of the Intifada. Are they saying you're an organizer?"

"Yes, they believe I am."

"Why?"

"I don't know. This is what I need to find out. I have to wait for the court cases of the ones already arrested. Especially two certain people."

"Wait a minute. Do you think they really have something on you?"

"I don't know."

"Is there something to have?"

"Well . . ."

"Bassem."

"Yes, there is, Mike."

"For organizing things?"

"Well, I used to know a few leaders. I used to sit with them. You know—"

"Go on."

"Well . . . we used to do these things. Writing the papers, the leaflets, saying when there is a strike, saying what is good for the people to do, you know, discussing what times the shops would open, or even not to have them open at all."

"You were one of the organizers?"

"Yessssss, Miiiike."

While we were in Gaza, trying to get into the camp, Bassem's little brother, Omar, had been studying for finals. All across the city, kids were cramming in groups, trying to make up for time lost to the Intifada began. Since December, the government had closed schools for a total of four months.

On Tuesday, the day we'd left, one of Omar's classmates, a boy named Nidal, had bicycled from his house in the Old City to a well-to-do Arab suburb just outside Jerusalem, to study with some friends.

According to press reports, Nidal was returning home when some kids threw rocks at a bus. On the bus were six armed men—three soldiers, three civilians. According to eyewitnesses, after the bus was pelted, the driver pulled over. The armed men jumped out of the bus and laid down fire. Both the Jerusalem police and the army denied any involvement. Nidal was killed.

Omar was heartbroken. He'd known Nidal all his life. After a sleepless night, Omar went to knock around with another friend from school, Faisal. Palestinian boys and men are very close. From a young age, in Islamic culture, males and females are separated. In an family's house, the boys have a room, the girls have a room. Men eat with men, hang out with men, sleep in a room with men. Younger men serve older men. Older boys take care of younger boys. Neighbors and cousins are always around. Palestinian men hold hands, lock arms, rest a hand on each other's knees or thighs. It's not sexual. It's affection. They grow up together. Their feelings are very strong.

To reaffirm their feelings, to soften their grief, Omar and Faisal went to a photo store in the Old City to have a photo taken together. The man gave them the choice of several different backdrops. They almost chose the tropical beach with palm trees. In the end, they settled upon the alpine forest; they sat on a bench and held hands.

Then, as luck would have it, on the way out of the shop,

they ran into the middle of the demonstration that had been called to protest Nidal's death.

Now, Omar had been in jail for two days. Bassem was beside himself. His mother was hysterical. She cried and cried. She washed all the floors twice, slamming a rag mop across the tile. We had no idea where exactly Omar was, or whether he was injured, or whether he'd been beaten. We had no idea about anything concerning Omar. All we knew were the possibilities.

"When I was there," said Bassem, "they didn't torture me every day. Just every few days. They'd put this sack on your head, a really rotten sack with shit in it. Or they'd put those handcuffs on your hands behind your back, or even you are hanging from the wall, half standing, half sitting, with your hands tied behind your back and then tied to the wall. And sometimes they put you in a cold shower when it's really cold, and then they put you in front of an air conditioner.

"You're in your cell, and they put you into psychology things. You never know when they're going to come. Maybe late at night, or maybe in the morning, or maybe not at all this day. First they will sweet-talk you, these sweet sugar words, making you to feel safe. Then another guy wants to beat you up, jump on you, or he says, 'we will screw your mother, we will screw your sister,' we will do this, do that."

Outside the jail, in the Russian Compound in Jerusalem, we waited for word of Omar. Bassem was sitting on the steps, his brother Assad was standing behind him, wearing a six-button blazer in the stultifying heat. Their mother was holding a place in a long line outside a metal door.

At eye level in the door was a window with a sliding cover. The man at the head of the line kept inching open the cover, trying to steal a look inside. He'd open it slowly, stealthily, a millimeter at a time. Then someone inside would slam it shut. Then he'd start again. Like everyone else in line, he clutched in his free hand a little slip of blue paper, a permit to bring clothes and food to a loved one being held without charges in jail.

Occasionally, the guard, a very large man in uniform, would open the door. He'd inspect a bag, ask a name, take the bag inside, close the door again. Sometimes he'd decide that two apples had to be taken out of a bag. Or that grapes were OK, but bananas were not. Or that all the food in *this* paper bag had to be placed in *that* plastic bag.

It was late in the afternoon. We had spent the morning going from one office to the next. From the Old City to the Russian Compound. From the jail to the lawyer. From the press office to the office of the chief of police. A maze of offices, a shroud of run-around. We weren't asking for much. We just wanted to know where Omar was. We wanted to know what he was charged with. We wanted to visit him.

They would tell us nothing.

It would go like this:

"I need a permit to visit my brother."

"We don't know anything about your brother. We don't handle the young ones."

Two officers walk by, escorting a teenager in handcuffs.

"Listen," said Bassem, "if you want to play this game with me, go and come. Just say it to me."

"OK," the man said. "I will. Maybe I can help."

"Yes?"

"On one condition. All I need is for your brother to sign a paper—"

"Forget it!"

We ran around and around and around. No one would help. I became outraged and got into it, too. I took my American citizenship and my press card and went from office to office to office. I wanted to know the policy on press visiting prisoners. A simple question. "What is the policy?"

Rivka in the government press office sent me to the chief of police's office. Both of his spokesmen were unavailable. They sent me to another office. They sent me somewhere else. I ended up in the tourist complaint center. "Please wait," they said.

So now we were waiting in line with a permit for food, something anyone could get. Perhaps that way we could at least confirm that Omar was here. Every twenty minutes or so the guard would take in a package. Every so often, the metal door would open and a couple of agents would escort a couple of boys in handcuffs out of the door, across the compound, to the police station to be booked.

At four in the afternoon, the guard opened the door again. "*Ma salami,*" he announced, smiling sadistically. "Good-bye, all." Then he closed the door. The lock clicked.

Nobody budged. Bassem's mother tapped her high-heeled foot. Assad chewed his moustache. Bassem lit a cigarette.

"You know, Mike," he said, exhaling, "this Intifada is going to last for a long time. Here we are. Fighting against weapons, fighting against everybody. Nobody's helping, but it's okay, it's really okay. We have a saying in Arabic: nothing can scratch your skin except your own nail. You know, no one is going to scratch your skin for you. . . . I mean, the Palestinians are not waiting for Jordan to make a war against Israel because they know it will never happen. They know Saudi Arabia will never stop the oil and say to the Americans, 'Listen, if you want the oil, give the Palestinians a state.' We know these things will never happen.

"It doesn't matter. I'm one of the people who believe that if I want to grow an olive tree in the garden, I have to wait at least five years to get an olive. You know, after taking care of this tree, looking after it, taking really good care, this tree would start giving me olives. But then for the next years in my life it would keep giving me olives. And even for my grand-grand-children. When every you go around any Palestinian village, you will see a lot of olives. Olive is a very patient tree. It is the tree of the Palestinian people. . . ."

Fifteen minutes passed. Twenty-five. A half hour. We waited. For what I didn't know.

Then, behind us, the metal door opened. Everyone turned their heads.

Two agents exited, followed by two boys in handcuffs, followed by two more agents. They moved past us, toward the parking lot.

Omar!

We stood—Bassem, Assad, Mom, and me—glued to our different positions. The back of Omar's shirt was torn. His pants were dirty. His hair was uncombed.

Bassem dropped his bag of fruit and dashed across the parking lot toward Omar. Assad took off after him.

The distance between them closed. Thirty yards, twenty, ten. As he ran, Bassem reached inside his shirt and pulled out . . . a Cadbury chocolate bar. He tore off the wrapper.

Dodging an agent, Bassem leapt for Omar, shoved the candy into his little brother's mouth. Another agent caught him with fist behind the ear. Down he went.

Assad was right behind with a banana. One of the agents knocked it from his hand, punched him in the stomach. He crumpled.

I ran to them and knelt helplessly—Assad fetal, Bassem on his back. I looked up in time to see Omar's back recede, his arms pinioned by two agents. Omar's head was held high. He was strutting.

I was in my room, packing my bags. It was two in the morning.

I had to be at the airport at four, leaving enough time for the inevitable search and questioning. Bassem slouched in the armchair beside the bed. As a present, he had brought me a *jalabia*, a long, silk shirt-dress. Every Palestinian man had at least one.

"I have something to tell you, Bassem."

"What?"

"Have you figured it out yet? About me?"

"What?"

"I'm Jewish.

He regarded me a moment. Then he said, somewhat triumphantly, "I knew you were a Jewish."

"You knew?"

"Come on, Mike, you have a Jewish name."

"I do?"

"Assad said this. Ziad said this. It is no surprise."

"It doesn't matter?"

"No. I don't give a damn shit."

"You're sure? I mean, I feel . . ."

"Listen, Mike," he said, looking deeply into my eyes, "If you first iron that *jalabia* before you wear it, it will look very nice. I know that all the womens at home will be falling all over you."

Bassem is calling, collect from Stuttgart.

"The people here are very boring here, very cold," he says. "Everything is like a computer. There is no excitement in the life."

"That's because there are no Israeli soldiers."

"At least at home, I used to have an argument every day with a soldier! They ask me for my Identicard. They stop me at checkpoints. They bother me. I get mad. I get used to this!"

"Maybe you'll get used to Germany. Maybe things will get better."

"Maybe. There are one hundred maybes in this world, Mike.

There's one hundred maybes. Maybe maybe maybe. It's far away from reality."

"Bassem, you have to try."

"Here I am so isolated. You hear nothings about Jerusalem, nothings about the West Bank or Gaza. I went all over Stuttgart and I finally found a newspaper in Arabic. It was three days old. Six people were shot, one person was killed in the Beach Camp, seventy-five people released, another hundred people was arrested. The usual game they always play.

"I want to go back. Soon as I can. Soon as I see everything's clear out in front of me. Now if it's four years in prison, I'll go back. I'll spend those four years. At least you know you are in your home. At least you know you are there. That's it. To me, four years, five years, I can do it.

"You'd rather go back home and go to prison?"

"Yesssssss, Miiiiike."

Missile Crisis

By Daniel Asa Rose

Killed: *Condé Nast Traveler,* 1990

A humorous essay is always a bit of a stretch for a glossy travel magazine, especially one as photography-driven as *Traveler.* It was precisely to get it in under the radar, as it were, to make it as palatable as possible, that I sugarcoated my piece—which raises serious questions about airline security—as a letter-to-camp, a faux-naif feuilleton. Nevertheless, as an historic document it speaks to a fascinating phenomenon. Here it is: As far back as a decade before 9/11, a number of writers—journalists and poets alike—sniffed something in the air: trace puffs of wrongdoing, vagrant inklings of evil. What I sniffed was nothing so venal as the image of a passenger plane hitting a building full force: all I came up with was the almost quaint picture of a child's airborne plaything revealing itself as a weapon. But the incongruity was there—the proximity of planes and mayhem, the obscenity of seemingly innocent things being put to deadly use. Not that any of our inklings would have prevented a single act of terrorism, of course, but still it seems a pity that those inklings were never given a chance to see the light of day.

Dear Marshall,

I trust you are enjoying camp. I have some news to share with you, so I hope you are sitting down.

Remember the 90-mm anti-aircraft missile grenade your big brother Alex assured you was completely safe when he sent it to you from France earlier this summer before you left for camp? The one you were juggling around the kitchen and I wanted to check out to make sure it wasn't loaded? And you said, "Dad, don't be such a wimp?" Remember?

Well, I thought I'd check it out anyway. So I threw it in the car and drove it to the local police station and brought it in and four or five cops immediately turned blue. "Put it down right there and don't make a move," they shouted. Feeling rather bashful in my summer shorts and T-shirt, I started to explain. "You see, my fifteen-year-old son Alex was traveling with his mother in France this summer looking for the perfect present for his eleven-year-old brother Marshall and he found this completely safe 90-mm anti-aircraft missile grenade in a flea market in Grasse. Pretty cool for ten francs, eh?"

"How'd he get it here?" they demanded.

"Regular airmail," I told them. "He just put it in a fruit box and covered the box with brown paper and dropped it in a post office slot. *Et voilà.*"

"*Voilà?*" the police said. "*Voilà* over the ocean? *Voilà* in a jet?"

"Yup," I said proudly. "Pretty enterprising, eh?"

"Take it out of here now," the policemen ordered.

So I tossed it in the back seat and drove it to the local National Guard post and darned if I didn't get the same reaction there.

"No, you don't understand," I said with a lot of patience. "The flea-market vender assured my son that it's been dead for years but I thought I'd just make sure so I'm letting you check it out. But just to show you how safe it is I'll bang it on this table . . ."

At which point a squad of National Guardsmen persuaded me not to bang it on the table.

"See this pin in here?" They pointed with a yardstick, not daring to touch. "Never been fired."

"Oh," I said.

"It could've blown up your house and everybody within fifty yards," they explained.

"I see."

"Not to mention the plane it flew in from France, and all the passengers."

"Yes, quite," I said.

"But don't worry, we'll get the Air Force to detonate it for you," they said.

"That would be kind of you," I said. And drove quickly to the nearest phone booth with a number of questions in mind. To wit:

How is a fruit box wrapped in brown paper screened for international mail?

According to Ken McFadden, General Manager of International and Military Mail Operations Division of the U.S. Post Office in Washington, it's generally not. "Some countries have export controls, but most don't. It varies from country to country, depending on the threat assessment."

Who transports such packages?

"Not having aircraft of their own, the post office usually contracts with commercial airliners of the country-of-origin."

A passenger airline?

"Yes."

What happens when it gets to America?

"It goes to one of several International Exchange Offices as the first point of entry, where it may or may not be subject to an on-site customs inspection before being turned over to the U.S. Postal Service for delivery."

So, a fruit box wrapped in brown paper is not necessarily inspected in either the country-of-origin or the United States?

"Not necessarily. It's like anything else in life, you can't screen 100 percent."

And so, Marshall, my question to you is: At any given moment, how are big brothers, wimpy fathers, and innocent airline passengers to know they are not sitting atop a live 90-mm anti-aircraft missile grenade?

Answer: They aren't.

Yours,
Dad

P.S. How's your juggling?

Moonstruck: The Reverend and His Newspaper

By Ann Louise Bardach
Killed: *Vanity Fair,* 1992

I became interested in the Reverend Sun Myung Moon and the Washington Times *while reporting on the Clarence Thomas Senate hearings for* Vanity Fair *in 1991. The* Washington Times *aggressively covered the Thomas hearings both on the front page and in its editorial pages—with multiple stories about the identity of the suspected leaker of Anita Hill's explosive testimony. During this period, I learned that* Times's *reporter Dawn Weyrich Ceol, daughter of conservative icon Paul Weyrich, had resigned from the paper claiming that her coverage of the hearings had been rewritten and politicized by her by editors.*

I was further interested when I learned that the paper's deputy editor at the time, Josette Shriner, hailed from the same town that I had. I remembered her father, James Sheeran, a former World War II paratrooper and FBI agent and the Republican mayor of West Orange, New Jersey. Few could forget his public anguish during his battle with the Unification Church to win back his three daughters who had become converts. Indeed, it was Mayor Sheeran's tenacity that triggered investigations into Moon—with Senate hearings in 1977 and subsequent tax evasion and perjury charges that eventually sent the reverend to prison. The fact that the fiercely proud Irish Catholic patriarch had won his battle against Moon—but lost his daughters—was the stuff of Greek tragedy (though Josette reportedly left the Church a few years ago and presently serves as the Bush Administration's Deputy Secretary Trade Representative).

My editor Tina Brown seemed keen on the story—and dispatched me back to Washington. I spent nearly a month there—at some expense—interviewing dozens of staffers as well as boosters and critics of the newspaper. The conventional wisdom that reporters, famously thin-skinned, resist the spotlight when turned on themselves, proved not to be the case with this story. It seemed that everybody in Washington wanted to talk about the Washington Times. The most generous and garrulous sources turned out to be among the most influential players in the conservative establishment.

I spent another two months doing research into Moon and his Church. It was within his Church that I encountered the veil of silence—with the exception of former Moonies. But some of the stories from the Reverend's ex-disciples were as bizarre as science fiction. Consequently, I made the decision to tape all interviews relating to the story.

Because of the tapes, I thought I was home free. But alas, as I would learn in ten years at Vanity Fair, there is no guarantee of publication until the magazine hits the stands. Stories were sometimes killed even after they went to "blues"—an advanced and expensive stage of print production.

I was never given a specific reason why this story was killed. However, reservations were expressed about litigious Moonies. I think it is fair to say that taking on a billionaire mogul, especially one who happens to believe he's the Messiah, with powerful pals in the White House, and more money (and lawyers) than God, was the primary factor.

I n May, the *Washington Times* will celebrate its tenth anniversary as "the conservative alternative to the *Washington Post*," with a month long party. While launching a second newspaper in a major city is an extraordinary achievement in ordinary times, sustaining it through a recession that has silenced dozens of newspapers nationwide, is nothing less than astonishing. Not only has the paper survived, it has carved a niche for itself inside the Beltway, championed by no less than a current and past president. "Quite simply, life would be hell in Washington without it," says William F. Buckley, founder of the *National Review* and the guardian of American conservatism. However, the existence of the *Times* owes virtually nothing to its circulation numbers or advertising revenues, the traditional criteria of a newspaper's health, but rather to the munificence of its owner, the controversial Reverend Sun Myung Moon.

Though the *Times* is technically a part of News World Communications, a media conglomerate owned by Moon's Unification Church, few doubt who the power is behind the checkbook. Nearly a decade of public relations' work assuring the public that the *Times* had no ties to the reverend flew out the window last July when the seventy-two-year-old Moon made a surprise appearance at a party at the newspaper's downtown headquarters.

The reverend, who has described himself as the Messiah, addressed some 200 staffers, wearing a beige suit and a snug-fitting silk shirt. According to one guest, Moon spoke to the gathering in "rapid-fire, high-pitched peals of oratorical Korean alternating with incomprehensible English," with both languages requiring the translation services of Moon's close ally, *Times* executive, Bo Hi Pak. Bristling with emotion while thumping the podium, he told a stunned audience that he had already poured a staggering $830 million into the *Times*. Moreover, he said that he personally raises the $7 million dollars each month needed to keep the paper afloat.

If Moon's figures are correct, they are a record-shattering sum for the newspaper business, surpassing previous estimates of $35 million to $50 million annual losses for the paper. Time-Life pulled the plug on the *Washington Star* when its losses hit $30 million while the *Dallas Herald* owners closed their doors after less than $20 million had seeped into the red. Nevertheless, Moon told his audience that it was his privilege to fund a newspaper which was part of the fight for a new, moral, and Christian America—one free of drugs, crime, and homosexuality.

According to John Podhoretz, an editor at the paper at the time, the evening's most embarrassing moment came when Reverend Moon demanded of his audience of paid employees, "Do you like me? . . . Some people don't like me. . . . You don't like me, do you? . . . Do you want to see more of me here?" After a protracted silence, a scattering of applause broke out, primarily from the two dozen Church members present. His remarks concluded, Moon vanished into his Rolls Royce limousine.

For the editors and staffers who have doggedly pursued respectability and acceptance in the nation's capitol, it was a demoralizing evening. Once again, they would have to face charges of being a Church-controlled organ and hear their newspaper, which even *Times*'s critic Michael Kinsley describes as "perhaps graphically the most beautiful paper in America," contemptuously dismissed as "the Moonie-paper." Their fears were soon confirmed. Six months later, a *Frontline* segment on Moon hurled a volley of charges—the most serious being that the paper is in violation of America's Foreign Registration Act, as a political entity financed by Korean and Japanese money. Nor was it the first time the charge has been made.

Worse, credible rumors persisted that Reverend Moon, despite his boasts to the contrary, had recently taken some mighty punches with record losses in several segments of his empire. How long can the Reverend throw away $84 million annually on a newspaper that has yet to turn a profit?

The paper's birth in 1982 could not have been more auspiciously timed, only months after the *Washington Star*, the sole challenger to the *Post*'s supremacy, had died. Conservatives, at the apex of their power with Reagan's presidency, lamented the *Star*'s demise and hungered for an alternative newspaper that spoke to them. Although many had misgivings over Moon's ownership of the paper, the hiring of veteran editor James Whelan from the eminently conservative *Sacramento Union*, owned by right-wing crusader Richard Mellon Scaife, did much to soothe jitters. Whelan says he signed an iron-clad contract which stipulated "there could be no direct contact between any of the editorial staff and the Moon organization," and was able to assure staffers that "Church officials understand the only way the *Washington Times* can become anything is for them to keep their hands off of it."

To further bolster credibility, Smith Hempstone, whose venerable Republican family had once owned the *Star*, was brought on board as executive editor. When asked at the time whether he had misgivings working for a Moon-owned enterprise, Hempstone quipped, "I've worked for lots of publishers who thought they were God."

Soon, an extraordinary romance bloomed between right wing ideologues and Church members—a courtship fueled not by common interests but by a common enemy: the dragon of communism. In 1982, communism was still, if not a national obsession, a Republican one. Ronald Reagan was lambasting the former Soviet Union as "the evil empire," while Reverend Moon was telling followers that communism was the earthly manifestation of Satan.

As no one else was about to fork over the bucks to start a major newspaper, there was a great urgency to make the marriage work. According to Arnaud de Borchgrave, who later became the *Times's* editor-in-chief, "I went around cap in hand all over the country to raise funds after the *Star* folded and I talked to the one hundred wealthiest people in America. All everyone wanted to know was when they were going to get their money back."

At the *Times's* lavish debut gala, held at the Corcoran Gallery of Art, some two thousand guests showed up for lobster and crab claws. While protestors outside picketed the event with placards reading, "You've Been Duped by the Moonies," and *"The Washington Times* Is a Moonie Paper," inside staffers and Church officials were rubbing shoulders with conservative heavyweights of the day like Moral Majority cofounder Richard Viguerie and S. I. Hayakawa, the late Republican senator from California.

From the outset, no expense was spared on the paper. More than twenty million dollars was spent converting a shabby warehouse on the outskirts of D.C. into a sparkling ode-to-God office building, replete with marble floors and walls, bronze fittings, oversized doors, cathedral windows, and a state-of-the-art, computerized newsroom. "The office joke is," noted one staffer, "that if the newspaper fails, they can always turn the building into a church." With unlimited funds on tap, Whelan and his staff were able to put out an impressive, lively, well-illustrated newspaper. In its early months, the paper didn't even solicit advertisers. Free introductory subscription offers drenched the nation's capital and bright orange boxes selling the daily sprouted up at every street corner—right next to the *Post's* boxes. A host of toys and ploys were offered to new subscribers including a raffle for free Caribbean vacations. Some residents complained that even after repeated calls to halt delivery, the paper still arrived at their doorstep.

But circulation grew—slowly but steadily to roughly 100,000, where it remains today. Although never a threat to the *Post*, with a circulation of 830,000, the *Times* established itself as a voice and presence to be reckoned with.

The paper's most powerful booster, President Reagan, let it be known that he "reads the *Times* first thing every morning at breakfast." It quickly became apparent that the Reagan administration was doing more than just reading the paper; the *Times* received numerous leaks and exclusives, including coveted interviews with Reagan. The paper was the first to report the president's intention to seek reelection, the resignation of James Watt, and the defection of KGB honcho Vitaly Yurchenko, among other scoops.

Although its critics charged that the paper was little more than a house organ for Administration policy, the *Times* was the first to break the story that former Reagan aide Michael Deaver was lobbying former contacts with unprecedented greed—charges that led to Deaver's conviction on perjury—and even investigated charges about an alleged callboy ring servicing high-level Republicans (the charges proved unfounded).

Ace journalists at the paper include foreign correspondent Paul Bedard, national reporter Rowan Scarborough, who revealed the navy's scandalous handling of the explosion on the battleship *Iowa*, which killed forty-seven sailors, and eagle-eyed Paul Rodriguez who dug out stories on the House check-cashing scandal months before it became news elsewhere.

Notable among the paper's first staffers were the children of conservative luminaries, a group dubbed the "mini-neocons." They included John Podhoretz, whose parents Norman

Podhoretz and Midge Dexter are a veritable conservative institution, Liz Kristol, Irving's daughter, Danny Wattenberg, son of *Times* columnist Ben, and Dawn Weyrich Ceol, daughter of conservative icon, Paul Weyrich.

The thirty-year-old Podhoretz, who left the *Times* last October after five years as a columnist and an editor, describes his tenure at the paper as a "wonderful and extraordinary opportunity." Known for his encyclopedic memory (he was a five-time *Jeopardy!* winner), Podhoretz says he had little patience with colleagues who complained about the Church owners, who, he says, stayed clear of the editorial side "99 percent of the time. There was exceptional freedom at the paper, but the price of working there was that sometimes you had to carry water for a madman."

Podhoretz spent time with the "madman" on four separate occasions, including the July party where Moon spoke for nearly forty-five minutes. "He was ranting and pacing behind the podium," remembered Podhoretz. "He wanted credit for the paper and wanted to be thanked and no one felt very grateful. He was saying things like, 'Maybe I should shut this place down?' in this rhetorical style and then he'd say, 'But I'm not going to!' He started telling us this parable with nautical imagery about how he was the fuel of our boat but then he tripped over the parable so it made no sense. He was more histrionic than just whining. There was a pall of embarrassment over the room. Basically, he was there to remind us how grateful we should be."

Podhoretz describes his decision to leave the *Times* as a "personal one which I will not discuss." However, some of his colleagues say that he was deeply troubled upon his return from an Alaskan fishing trip he took with Moon last August. Moon used the occasion, say sources, to expound on his "Zionist conspiracy theories" and what Podhoretz perceived to be undiluted anti-Semitism. Indeed, some of Moon's teachings contend that the Jews have "suffered four thousand years of punishment for killing Christ."

"Everyone knows there's a price for working at the *Times*," said former reporter Mary Belcher. A current staffer notes that the newspaper "knows they have to offer more to get people to work here. I don't know anyone who wouldn't leave for a job at the *Post*, "despite generally higher salaries at the *Times*. Jack Shafer, editor of D.C.'s alternative weekly, *City Paper*, and a longtime *Times*'s critic, derided the broadsheet's payroll as "Moon welfare."

Charlotte Hayes, who wrote a hilarious and snarky memoir in *The New Republic* entitled "I was a Moonie Gossip Columnist," still laments the loss of the generous expense account she had at the paper. "This is on the Rev.," Hayes, a thoroughbred conservative, would tell sources as she lunged for meal checks. "The *Times*," she added drolly, "is a place for free-market conservatives to escape the free market."

Despite the financial perks, many reporters have been unable to make the leap. Jan Ziff, a top Mideast correspondent for the BBC, remembers being offered the prestigious job of Deputy Foreign editor several years ago when she was between jobs. "The money was fabulous, just fabulous," she said, "and I was practically out of money. It was very, very tempting but the more I thought about it, I just couldn't work for the Moonies."

In July 1984, founding editor James Whelan discovered that he could no longer work for the Moonies either. "The rule was that there had to be a wall separating the paper and the Church," says Whelan, "and they were constantly challenging it." He objected to Moon's newsroom visits and he said he felt harassed by complaints from Bo Hi Pak—the reverend's right-hand man—about the paper's reporting on Church matters.

Until quite recently, all coverage of the Church and/or Moon was conducted via the wire services to avoid charges of conflict of interest. Church officials, says Whelan, were especially miffed by the lack of a positive write-up on Moon's mass wedding of 2,075 couples at Madison Square Garden in 1982, an event that included seventy-five staffers. Then there was the paper's reliance on AP reporting when Moon appeared before a Senate subcommittee concerning charges of tax evasion and perjury filed against him in 1982 by federal prosecutors. "We might as well give our money to the *Washington Post!*" Pak hollered at Whelan.

"I have blood on my hands," Whelan says of his tenure at the *Times*. Lately, he has made something of a career out of Moon-bashing. He says that the newspaper's owners agreed they would never use the *Times*'s building for any Church-sponsored business. "A week after my leaving, they broke that rule," alleges Whelan, who complained that the building has since become a veritable dance hall for social functions for the Church's hundreds of front organizations. "Another rule was that we would not have any Moonie officials at any of our tables at any events such as White House Correspondents' Dinners," says Whelan. "There is almost a bidding war to see which news organizations can seat the greatest number of heavy hitters at their tables. Well, a year after I left, that rule went out the window and a very startled Donald Regan, then chief of staff, found himself seated next to Bo Hi Pak." Ronald Godwin, the current president of the *Times*, disputes all of Whelan's charges, adding that "Whelan was asked to leave."

After a brief stint as editor by Smith Hempstone, Whelan's shoes were filled by Arnaud de Borchgrave, who says he has read "a confidential file," and concluded that Whelan was simply "very greedy. He was asking for a limo around the clock, a driver on standby. He thought this was an endless source of welfare for himself. And it's very convenient when people don't get what they want to shout 'the Moonies have taken over.' " Though de Borchgrave was not the first or even fourth choice for the job, he proved to be a match of, well, divine inspiration.

A veteran of *Newsweek,* the indefatigable de Borchgrave was a legend of sorts, having covered a dozen wars, including seven tours of Vietnam where he was twice wounded. But in 1980, he was fired for politicizing his reporting with his fervent anti-communism. Born in Belgium and educated in English public schools, he has been nicknamed "the short Count" for his eccentricities and upper-class drawl. Famous for his year round tan, the George Hamilton of the Beltway has been said to go into combat zones carrying a sun reflector. Although an irrepressible name dropper, he is nonetheless regarded with bemused affection by most staffers. "Arnaud has no hidden agenda," says Mary Belcher, "he wears everything on his sleeve."

I caught up with the jet setting journalist at his father-in-law's condo in Los Angeles, a pit stop on his return from a vacation in Acapulco. "I've never worked for Moon in my life," he began, clinging to the notion that businesses owned by the Church, such as the *Washington Times,* are not Moon-controlled.

"If it was owned by Reverend Moon," he adds, "I wouldn't have been there. I've never known such freedom in my forty-five-year career. I fired twenty-five people who were members of the Unification Church without ever knowing they were members and I never got a phone call saying you can't fire so-and-so."

De Borchgrave literally lived at the newspaper for much of the first three years of his watch. "I installed a bed in my office and worked around the clock," he says proudly, "to turn this damn thing around and put it on the map." In addition to revamping the newspaper, plastering the newsroom with his personal memos known as "Arnaudgrams," he started the weekly magazine *Insight*.

As one of the capital's marathon partygoers, de Borchgrave's social connections opened significant political doors for the newspaper. Republican luminaries, including the Reagans, former CIA chief Bill Casey and Senator Bob Dole, became frequent dinner guests at the de Borchgrave Georgetown home.

Though de Borchgrave's first year at the helm coincided with Reverend Moon's time in federal prison, de Borchgrave says he was untroubled by the matter. "I investigated through the Justice Department exactly what led to his conviction," he says, "and five assistant attorney generals recommended against pursuing the case. He can barely speak English. Obviously, he is not filling out his own tax returns. He knows nothing about it. I don't fill out my own tax returns."

Convinced of Moon's innocence, de Borchgrave became one of the guru's most outspoken champions. In August 1985, following Moon's release from Danbury Federal Penitentiary, de Borchgrave gave a rousing speech for 1,700 of the Reverend's supporters at a welcome home bash. Months later, he published an open letter in the *Times,* arguing for a presidential pardon for Moon. De Borchgrave denies publishing the letter at Moon's behest but concedes that "a pardon is very important to him."

Asked whether the letter didn't make him a target for critics, de Borchgrave shoots back, "Let them take a shot at me. Who cares? I've survived much worse, including seventeen wars."

Indeed, de Borchgrave shrugged off the resignation of four editors in 1987 who accused him of being a "lackey" of the Church owners. William Cheshire, who was the paper's editorial page editor of three years, issued a statement that "it is no longer possible for the *Times* to maintain independence from the Unification Church under the editorship of Mr. de

Borchgrave." At stake was a planned editorial that criticized South Korean President Chun Do Hwan for a crackdown on human rights and a retreat from democracy. Cheshire, who became editor of the *Arizona Republic*, claims that after de Borchgrave made a visit upstairs to Sang Kook Han, the senior vice president of News World and longtime Moon pal, the editorial was rewritten "changing its essence 180 degrees."

De Borchgrave doesn't deny speaking with Han, who once served as the Korean Ambassador to Norway and Finland, but says he saw no impropriety about incorporating an owner's input. "It was a personality thing," says de Borchgrave, "Cheshire hated my guts. He felt he should have had my job."

As for the undiluted conservative slant of the paper's coverage, de Borchgrave makes no apology. "I'm not a right-wing fruitcake," he says. "I'm a Republican. Ben (Bradlee) says, 'I'm an independent.' Well, that's hogwash. Ben is a liberal Democrat. There's nothing wrong with that at all. What's wrong is to conceal where one is coming from."

De Borchgrave even wrote a passionate editorial denouncing the termination of U.S. financial aid to the Contras and ran it on the front page. Inserted at the end was an announcement that the *Times* owners were donating $100,000 to a newly created fund, the Nicaraguan Freedom Fighters, to keep the Contras armed. De Borchgrave denies reports that he was in cahoots with Oliver North, whom he claimed he barely knew at the time, explaining that he was simply "trying to raise money for the Contras. I had nothing to do with running the fund. I just had the idea for starting it." Nor did he see any ethical problem for a newspaper to solicit funds for a guerrilla group seeking to topple a government. When asked how he would have responded if Ben Bradlee had solicited $100,000 for the Sandinistas, de Borchgrave is uncharacteristically quiet.

The one blunder he admits to was running a page-one story under a banner headline during the 1988 election asserting that Democratic presidential candidate Michael Dukakis saw a psychiatrist after his brother's death. The story, attributed to the candidate's sister-in-law, turned out to be false, and prompted the resignation of reporter Gene Grabowski. "The Dukakis story was bogus," says conservative columnist Charles Krauthammer of the *Washington Post*, "and it really hurt their credibility."

"It was a deadline rush. I admitted I goofed and apologized," says de Borchgrave. "How many people admit they goof in this business?! No one!"

Unlike his predecessors, mixing newspaper functions with other Church businesses did not trouble de Borchgrave. "He's appeared at every Church picnic, conference, symposium, seminar, and clambake under the sun," says Whelan. De Borchgrave doesn't deny having socialized with Moon and Church officials, and admits that he flew to Seoul to attend Moon's seventieth birthday party. "The (editorial) wall was very important," suggests de Borchgrave, "but I didn't go out of my way to insult the owners, which is what Whelan did. I went out of my way to be diplomatic with them."

While de Borchgrave views the *Times* as just one of the many businesses owned by the Unification Church, many regard it as the crown jewel of Moon's empire. Moreover, says Whelan, it is the medium for Moon to garner the necessary respectability to accomplish his goals which, he adds, are nothing less than "the conquest of global power in order to establish a totalitarian theocracy headed by Moon!"

Reverend Sun Myung Moon is a man of no small ambition. He claims that Jesus Christ visited him on a North Korean hillside on Easter Sunday, 1936, when he was sixteen. According to

Moon's teachings, Jesus told him that he was to be sent on "an important mission to accomplish the fulfillment of God's providence." In 1990, Moon went even further, telling a stunned San Francisco audience that the world was in search of its "true parent, the Messiah. To fulfill this very purpose, I have been called upon by God."

To accomplish his destiny, Moon created his own religion, founding the Unification Church in 1954, a theological stew of Christianity, Taoism, and Oriental mysticism. For his anti-communist and religious activism, Moon says he did three stints in a North Korean jail, though the government of South Korea, where Moon found refuge in 1950, claimed his crime was draft evasion, a charge denied by the Church. A French journalist has also charged that the last arrest in 1955 was for adultery and bigamy, which Church officials contend is "absolutely untrue."

In 1960, the forty-year-old Moon remarried for the fourth and last time, to eighteen-year-old Hak Ja Han. They have thirteen children. In Church theology they are regarded as the "True Parents" of the entire human race and are addressed by their followers as "True Mother" and "True Father." Marriage is crucial to spiritual development according to Moon, whose teachings state that Christ failed in his mission by getting crucified and also by having never married. Moon has been reputed to speak for sixteen hours at a time, and, according to James Baughman, president of the American Unification Church, True Father is in contact with the spirit world. Asked to be more specific, Baughman claims that Moon has direct channels to Adam, Jonah, and Lucifer.

Unification missionaries first came to America in 1960 and laid the foundation for Moon's arrival in 1971. Followers were encouraged to call themselves "Moonies," and did so until quite recently when the term was abandoned because it had acquired a pejorative connotation. The Church's aggressive recruitment techniques created a public relations disaster, not unlike that of rival Scientology. Scores of parents claimed that their children had been kidnapped and brainwashed into evangelical robots spewing the miracles of Moon; travelers in the 1970s often had to dodge clusters of young Moonies at airports peddling flowers and handing out Church literature.

Then there were the mass weddings. In 1982, a total of nearly eleven thousand devotees who had never met each other, were paired off by Moon and married en masse at Madison Square Garden and in Seoul. Church officials claim that today their flock comprises more than three million members, with the great majority living in Japan and Korea. Although the Church says they have five thousand American members, congressional sources say the figure is less than three thousand.

In late 1982, the bubble burst for Moon when he was convicted on four counts of perjury and tax evasion. He eventually served eleven months of an eighteen-month sentence followed by two months in a halfway house.

Despite his criminal record, Moon decided that he wanted to be a world leader, not just an evangelist—and he was willing to pay for it. Some insiders say that the Unification Church was the number one contributor to conservative causes throughout the 1980s. In 1984, the Church gave $750,000 to the Conservative Alliance, a group spearheaded by the late Terry Dolan. It was a transaction riddled with irony: the Church fiercely condemns homosexuality and Dolan, a closeted gay man, was already sick with AIDS. Two years later, the Church bailed direct-mail king Richard Viguerie out of financial trouble by buying his Virginia office building for a whopping $10 million. Observers saw the transaction as a reward for a longtime friendship; Viguerie has handled the Church's direct-mail business since the late '60s. In 1988, the Church made a $50,000 contribution to President Bush's re-election campaign.

In pursuit of a presidential pardon, Moon spread even more money around. Paul Laxalt, Reagan's close friend and the former senator from Nevada, was put on a retainer of $50,000 a month plus expenses to lobby Reagan while Sen. Orrin Hatch became the point man for the "pardon team." Moon was said to be prepared to offer a half million dollars to anyone willing to guarantee him a pardon from Reagan. Rory O'Connor, who produced the *Frontline* documentary on Moon, said it was Nancy Reagan who terminated speculation about any such deal.

From the start, the *Times* PR team made sure everyone knew it was not the only church-owned paper around, citing the *Deseret Times* of Salt Lake City, funded by the Mormons, and the well-respected *Christian Science Monitor*. "I can't say that the Unification Church is much loopier than some of the tenets in the Mormon Church," noted *Times* critic Jack Shafer. "The difference between a cult and a religion seems to be about a hundred years."

However, while there are other Church-owned newspapers, the *Washington Times* is the only one that is also foreign financed. "To date, the *Times* has hidden behind freedom of press and freedom of religion," says Lars Erik Nelson, a *New York Daily News* reporter who has investigated Moon's finances, "but there's no excuse for them not registering under the Foreign Registration Act." That legislation, created in World War II to prevent the dissemination of German and Japanese propaganda, specifically states that any newspaper financed by a foreign principal must be registered with the State Department. Currently, such diverse organizations as the

British Information Services and the Japanese Auto Owners Association, which publishes sales bulletins, are registered. However, despite the fact that Church officials have admitted that most of the financing for the *Times* comes from Korea and Japan, the newspaper has never been required to register. Registration under the Act, which requires all entities to disclose the source and amounts of its financing, would demystify Moon's empire. Critics contend that the Reagan-Bush Justice Department turned a blind eye to the conservative newspaper's finances and possible violation of the law. Calls to the Justice Department were not returned.

Seeking to divine the source of the Church's vast wealth, I met with Ronald Godwin, senior vice president of the *Times* for the last six years, and Tony Webb, their new general manager. The interview was held in Godwin's third-floor office at the newspaper, a sparsely decorated room, save for an American flag standing next to Godwin's desk.

Godwin, who was sporting a Rolex and hunting boots, prefers being called "Doctor Godwin" in deference to a Ph.D. he earned at Florida State in planning and management. He is a wiry Southerner in his fifties who previously worked for Jerry Falwell and the Moral Majority. "I've made a career working for controversial religious leaders," he said, adding that he was recruited by Moon's top aide, Bo Hi Pak, also a supporter and generous contributor to Falwell.

Asked about reported frequent Moon sightings in the newsroom, Godwin dismissed them as rumor, and asserted that Moon has visited the paper "maybe ten times in ten years." Although Godwin said "there's been no lessening of commitment to the paper, it's fair to say that our owners are expecting an increase in revenue. I don't want to be a foundation publishing house."

Godwin, who described the *Frontline* documentary as "the

Geraldo show" and a "prostitution of the journalistic process," was particularly irked by the program's speculations concerning the Church's finances. Asked why the *Times*'s owners haven't revealed their funding to silence their critics, Godwin replies, "They regard it as a private business, which it is, and frankly it's none of anyone's business." In any event, said Godwin, it would be "an exercise in futility" to open up the *Times*'s books. "As Bill Clinton has learned, the questions would never stop." After viewing the *Frontline* segment, Webb said he wants to know "what the hell is wrong with democracy, the fight against communism, and supporting the troops and Desert Storm?"

Forty-five minutes into the interview, Webb asked, "What's the tone of your story? What's your angle?" Told that the story would focus on the future of the *Times*, Godwin's eyes narrowed. "I didn't fall off of a pumpkin wagon yesterday," he grumbled and signaled that the interview was over. All previously scheduled interviews with other staff members were suddenly canceled. The *Washington Times* was no longer available to answer questions.

In July 1991, de Borchgrave handed over the reins to managing editor Wesley Pruden and became the paper's editor-at-large. Although observers talked of feuding between the two very different men—the imperial de Borchgrave and the reclusive Pruden, a Baptist from Arkansas—de Borchgrave denied such reports. "I simply adore Wes," he said. Pruden, who has been in the trenches at the *Times* since its inception, is best known for his hands-on aggressive editing, known in the newsroom as "Prudenizing," a process that invariably ensures that stories have the correct conservative spin.

Jim Whelan says he hired Pruden at the urging of Smith Hempstone despite the fact that Pruden had been fired as a staff writer from the now defunct *National Observer* magazine, according to Whelan and others, for having "doctored" quotes (Pruden refused repeated requests for an interview). "He had been on the beach for almost five years," says Whelan. "I hired him and put him on probation for the first year." Eight years ago, he began a thrice weekly column, *Pruden on Politics,* which he continues to write in addition to running the paper. His reign began auspiciously enough with a lunch date on day one with President Bush and then chief of staff, John Sununu.

Directly under Pruden is deputy managing editor, Josette Shiner, perhaps the most enigmatic member of the *Times* family. Shiner, an attractive woman of thirty-seven, is frequently described as the "number one Moonie" at the paper. Some, in fact, regard her as the "de facto power," and one recently departed staffer says that "Josette runs the paper more than Wes." Following Whelan's departure in 1984, Shiner and another Church member, Ted Agres, were made assistant managing editors. While staffers are known to snicker over "the mindless cheerfulness" and "vacant eyes," of some Church colleagues, Shiner gets consistently top marks for her work, even from snipers who call her "the Ice Queen." Recently, she was invited to join the Council of Foreign Relations, nominated by de Borchgrave. "She simply breaks the mold," says Dawn Weyrich Ceol. "You would never know she's a Moonie."

In 1975, twenty-one-year old Josette made headlines when her distraught father, James Sheeran, then the New Jersey State Commissioner of Insurance, charged that he, his wife, and fourteen-year-old son had been beaten up by Moon followers when he tried to find Josette and her two sisters at the Church's two-hundred-acre compound in upstate New York. Sheeran, a decorated World War II paratrooper and former FBI agent, had been a two-term Republican mayor of West Orange, New Jersey, where he raised his large Irish Catholic family.

Following the lead of her older sister Jamie, Josette had dropped out of the University of Colorado in late 1974 and joined the Church. A third sister, Vicki, signed up when Josette did. "I have seen personality changes in my daughters," an anguished Sheeran said at the time. "They seem to think that there's a communist under every bush and they're seeing God all the time. I really love them, but Moon's got them selling peanuts and other stuff on the street while brainwashing them into thinking that no assault took place."

Two weeks after the assault, the three Sheeran girls, flanked by Bo Hi Pak and other Church officials, read a prepared statement at a press conference saying "we love our parents very much," but stating they had no intention of leaving the Church. They also denied being brainwashed. In 1982, Josette told the *Washington Post* that she "joined the church full well knowing it is something not yet understood by society. For me, it has an intellectual appeal."

Although the assault charges were later dropped, the publicity generated by the Sheeran family's distress galvanized state and federal investigations into Moon and his Church, culminating in Moon's eventual indictment for tax evasion in 1982.

Josette eventually returned to college. Upon graduation, she went to work in 1976 in the Washington bureau of the now defunct *News World*, a Moon-owned daily. She was one of the principal forces behind the *Washington Times*, and some staffers believe that the idea of starting the paper was hers. The Church, however attributes the paper's founding "to a vision of our Heavenly father," meaning Moon.

Famous for a cool, efficient demeanor, Josette is also a woman of considerable charm. According to staffers, she is the only Church member at the paper who regularly socializes with colleagues who do not belong to the Church. Nevertheless, no one doubts her devotion to Moon and the Church.

In October 1982, the Sheeran sisters were among those married off at the famous Madison Square Garden wedding ceremony to spouses selected for them by Moon. Vicki, who runs a struggling photo agency for the *Times*, was matched up with a maintenance man at the paper, and Josette was married to Whitney Shiner, who recently completed a doctorate in theology at Yale.

However, former *Times* staffer Lisa McCormack said that Whitney was not the first candidate proposed by Moon. According to another ex-staffer, "Josette was able to nix the first one because she had enough clout with the Church." The couple now have two daughters and, according to close friend de Borchgrave, "it's a terrific marriage."

Some staffers believe that the wall separating editorial from the Church owners has eroded considerably under Pruden's watch. He has abandoned the practice of relying on wire service copy to cover Church or Moon news, and has published columns and editorials flattering to Moon and his businesses. Pruden has taken a defensive stand on the subject, telling a *Post* reporter, "No one can find a single word of Church propaganda in this paper." However, in January, the paper ran a column celebrating the meeting of Moon and North Korean strongman, Kim Il Sung, and chastising the South Korean government for its irritation with Moon's visit.

But there was no explanation in the *Times* for the sudden fondness that Moon, the great Cold Warrior, now feels toward Kim, the world's most despotic communist dictator. Then there are Moon's other new pals, the Red Chinese, with whom he has invested $250,000 in a Panda car factory.

"Moon was willing to do whatever was necessary to suck up to the Chinese for business and evangelical reasons," says Andrew Ferguson, a speechwriter for President Bush and a former editor of the *American Spectator*, where he penned a tract critical of the conservatives' alliance with the Unification Church. "[Moon's] only credential as a conservative was being an anticommunist and now that's shot. It proves that, fundamentally, he's an opportunist." But the greatest embarrassment for Pruden came three months into his stewardship when Dawn Ceol quit.

Dawn Weyrich Ceol has the kind of fresh-faced, all-American blonde good looks featured in soap commercials. In 1988, she was hired by the *Times* at the age of twenty-four with very little experience. "After a year on Metro, they promoted me to the national desk," she said. "It was a tremendous opportunity. I knew I was doing something that people wait fifteen years to do."

Concerned about the baggage of being the daughter of conservative think-tank founder Paul Weyrich, she used her married name, Ceol, as her byline. "Because I'm Paul Weyrich's daughter, there's a kind of wariness about me," she said, "especially from liberals. I have been very careful and circumspect to have balance in my stories." For nearly three years, Ceol enjoyed smooth sailing in the newsroom—personally unaffected by office or Church politics. She had not even been "Prudenized"—not until she was assigned to cover the Clarence Thomas hearings.

Ceol got her first whiff of trouble after she filed a story about Anita Hill's initial appearance at Senate hearings. Late that night, remembers Ceol, she got a message from her line editor telling her she might want to check out her story. "I went into the computer and saw what had happened," says Ceol, "The story had been completely rewritten and had a new [headline] and lead. Next to the changed copy was Pruden's computer password. I had Anita Hill's testimony in the lead. After Wes rewrote the story, you didn't see her testimony until the eighth paragraph. It was all about Clarence Thomas."

Distressed, Ceol called her editor, Fran Coombs, at home who took a look at the revised story. "He told me, 'Dawn, you're really tired. You're working really long hours and you're overreacting. I think it's a good story,' " recalls Ceol. "So I thought to myself, 'Maybe he's right. I am real tired.' The next morning after a night's sleep I looked at it again and I knew *I* was right and I made a promise to myself that it would never happen again."

Days later, the panelists at the Senate hearings for both Anita Hill and Clarence Thomas testified. "I wrote another story and structured it like a tennis match, going back and forth between the two sides," said Ceol. "In the first edition, my copy went out untouched." The headline of the first edition was, THOMAS ACCUSER LAUDED, ASSAILED. Ceol began another story while watching the hearings. "John Doggett, that wacko, was testifying," she said, referring to the bombastic Thomas witness who characterized Hill as a woman who deluded herself that men, including himself, were romantically interested in her. "My impression was that Doggett was not a credible witness," said Ceol, with a roll of her eyes.

Wes Pruden felt otherwise. "My editor, Alan Bradford, called me saying, 'Wes told me that he thinks Doggett is a fantastic witness and he wants you to do a write thru for the second edition,' " remembered Ceol. "I said, 'I don't think so. I don't think he deserves more than a paragraph or two.' " Because Ceol was so busy, Bradford suggested that another reporter write up the Doggett paragraphs. Ceol said fine.

Sometime after midnight, Ceol decided to check on the story in her computer. "I saw a slug that said 'new Thomas head' and next to it was Wes's password," says Ceol. The headline was now MISS HILL PAINTED AS FANTASIZER, and the first eight paragraphs were devoted to Doggett. Ceol was furious. "There were also factual errors," says Ceol, "which really upset me because I'm a stickler on facts. Because of my last name, I feel I really have to do excellent work. I read the story and I was crazed. I called up Alan Bradford and said, 'If you don't get my byline off of this, I'm resigning.'" Bradford made some calls then got back to Ceol saying it was too late, the story had been plated. Ceol was furious. "When he told me it was too late. I started screaming, 'Then accept my resignation!'"

At two in the morning, she wrote and sent a two-line letter of resignation through the paper's computer. The following day, she sent another resignation letter, this time calmly citing her reasons. "The story in today's final edition not only gives an unbalanced impression of yesterday's testimony," wrote Ceol, "there is not one mention that four witnesses generally corroborated Miss Hill's statements. . . . In many ways, I believe this paper has gotten an unfair shake, but this kind of activity does not help dispel our reputation."

Ceol says she got more than fifty calls of support from colleagues at the *Times*, "from the copy desk to the editors—everybody but the glass offices. People were very upset because this was happening a lot. As a result, they wanted to start a union to protect the writers from exactly this."

The resignation of Ceol proved humiliating for the *Times*. There was no way to blame the mess on liberals. Not only was Ceol a blue-blooded conservative, she was also a known admirer of Clarence Thomas, having first met and interviewed him during his congressional hearings for the Court of Appeals.

Ceol was thrown a farewell party by her friend, Peter Baker, one of the few *Times* staffers to be hired away by the *Post*. "At the party, according to Ceol, "somebody put out some union literature, just as an afterthought." The following Sunday, Pruden took out a full-page "Message From the Editor" ad in the *Times* declaring as "FACT" that "a *Washington Post* reporter hosted a union organizing party for *Washington Times* employees," and accusing the rival paper of setting out "to destroy us from within."

Pruden informed staffers that Ceol's charges were "a total lie," and that her father, Paul Weyrich, had advised her not to quit and had tried to change her mind. That charge further infuriated Ceol. "My father gave me 100 percent support for what I did," she fumes.

The Ceol affair hardly helped boost morale that was already flagging from budget cuts. Austerity had finally hit the *Times*. A wage freeze was announced after more than eighty staffers had been fired in the previous year. Finally recognizing that *Insight* was never going to be *Time* and was losing many subscribers, the glossy magazine was downsized from eighty to thirty pages and turned into the paper's Sunday supplement. The unlimited expense accounts and lavish lunches are history. Even more chilling were the whispers that the Reverend, like so many tycoons of the '80s, may have hit the financial skids.

Few of Moon's American holdings have ever been regarded as big moneymakers. News World, which publishes the *Times* as well as several Hispanic and Korean language papers in the United States, and a seven-hundred-page monthly magazine called *The World and I*, has always required a massive subsidy. The Church's successful American businesses are believed to be fishing enterprises in Massachusetts and Alaska, extensive real estate holdings, and numerous video production companies in the D.C. area.

The bulk of Moon's wealth has always come from his businesses in Asia, principally Tong-Il Ltd., an extremely lucrative South Korean corporation that manufactures automobile parts, machinery, and military hardware. Additionally, Japanese church members are believed to have poured millions into Moon's coffers through the selling of religious relics and icons, a business which came under government scrutiny for its massive margins. It is also believed that many Moon devotees in Japan and Korea have turned over substantial assets to the Church.

One sure sign of unrest in the empire was the recall of Bo Hi Pak back to Korea to oversee Moon's businesses. Pak, once a lieutenant colonel in the Korean army, began his career in the Korean CIA, which some believe supplied money to Moon and the Church to aid his anticommunist crusade. Pak's devotion to Moon is seemingly boundless. In 1984, his daughter, Hoon Sook Pak, a ballerina with the Church-owned Washington Ballet, was married to the spirit of Moon's dead son who was killed in a car crash a month earlier.

This became somewhat problematic four years later, when the Reverend announced that his son's spirit had been reincarnated in the body of a visiting "black brother" from Zimbabwe. After it was clarified that the African was only the vessel of the son's spirit, it was decided that cohabitation would be unnecessary for the two.

The ever faithful Pak is said to be attending to such debacles as the loss of some $250 million in the Panda car company in China and the Church's diminished standing with the Korean government. There has even been some unusual infighting within the Church. In 1984, a high-ranking Japanese Church member, Yoshitazu Soejima, broke with the Church, telling a *Washington Post* reporter that Moon was no longer "working for the world, but for himself." Several months after leaving the Church, while preparing an article critical of Moon, Soejima was attacked outside his home and repeatedly stabbed. He survived the assault and the article was published in a Japanese newspaper.

"Business is bad for the Moonies," suggests Andrew Ferguson. "Col. Pak made numerous financial commitments to conservative causes that he couldn't fulfill." Lars Erik Nelson of the *Daily News*, who has tracked Moon's finances for years, agrees that "all of Moon's businesses, here and in Korea and Japan, are losing money." Still, no matter what perils Moon may be facing, it is unlikely that he will ever sell the *Times*. "The *Times* was the top priority of the Unification Church," said Soejima. He adds that Japanese Church members, responding to the exhortation of Moon, sent $2.5 million a month to the United States specifically earmarked for the newspaper.

Whatever misgivings they have regarding the Unification Church, even some of the *Times*'s detractors admit they would mourn the paper's demise. "Notwithstanding the reservations I have," acknowledges Ferguson, "it would be a disaster, just horrendous for Washington, if it died." If nothing else, he said, the *Times* has kept the *Post* awake at the wheel.

Most liberals disagree. "I'd hate to see any newspaper go out of business," said *Crossfire*'s resident lefty, Michael Kinsley, "but if I had to pick one, it would be the *Washington Times*." Not even the specter of the nation's capital being a "one-paper town," leavens the negatives of the *Times* for some. "If the choice is between a monopoly press or intellectually dishonest journalism," said Howell Raines, the *New York Times*'s Washington Bureau chief, "I'd go with the monopoly. It's more unhealthy for journalism to be financed by churches with a political agenda."

The Washington Times's impact on the city generates more raucous debate. One Bush administration staffer said that "everybody in the White House, in the media and all the players in town read the *Times*." Kinsley concedes that it has "a certain amount of influence," drolly adding, "plus the cachet of letting us peer into the conservative heart of darkness." Nevertheless, the *Post*'s Charles Krauthammer believes that while the *Times* "has largely transcended its origins and is now the town's conservative voice, it is not required reading like the *Post*, the *Wall Street Journal*, and the *New York Times*."

"It's a must read for people who want to be well informed," counters Jeanne Kirkpatrick, the conservative columnist and former U.S. ambassador to the United Nations under Reagan. "At one time, it had more foreign coverage than the *Post* . . . and it scoops the *Post* from time to time. Of course, the *Post* scoops the *Times* all the time but it's still a very good newspaper."

For Ferguson and many other conservatives the ideal solution would be for the Church to sell the paper. "Their primary purpose is to get legitimacy for the Church," said Ferguson. "They should realize they're never going to get it and sell the paper to some media megalomaniac like [Rupert] Murdoch." A sale would certainly be a relief for many fretful conservatives. "Are we really going to depend on South Korean philanthropy to fund a newspaper?" asks an incredulous William F. Buckley.

But the *Times* remains the most important weapon in Moon's public relations arsenal. "He needs it to impress the Koreans, Japanese, and Chinese governments that he's a serious player in the nation's capitol," Whelan points out. Without the *Times*, he adds, Moon would neither have been able to chat up former Soviet premier Mikhail Gorbachev in a private audience in 1990 nor have been a VIP guest at Ronald Reagan's inaugural ball.

For a pudgy Korean evangelist with a global dream in his heart, it seems that $830 million has been worth the price of admission.

Jesus Worms

By Tad Friend

Killed: *Vogue*, 1993

Ten years ago, during my annual lunch with Anna Wintour, the editor of Vogue, *I proposed an idea for a profile. I was a contributing editor to the magazine at the time and she had always given me wide latitude. This was partly, I think, because she liked me, and partly because the travel pieces and playwright profiles I wrote were so ancillary to the magazine's real business, fashion, that she couldn't get too worked up about it all.*

I told her I admired the British travel writer Redmond O'Hanlon and was eager to write about him; Anna said "Why not?" It soon became clear why not: the penis factor. If you write about O'Hanlon you have to mention his penis at least once, because he mentions it constantly. I thought it best to dispatch the matter quickly, in the first sentence. This was perhaps unwise. The line editor, who never commented on an article until Anna had read it, finally phoned to murmur a disconnected apologia to the effect of "unexpectedly graphic nature . . . a little too . . . I hope you know, of course . . ."

It wasn't that Vogue *was anti-penis. (Well, maybe it was. I never quite figured out the magazine's politics, beyond its unflagging support of the right of every American to buy a Kate Spade handbag.) It was probably more that anyone who would talk so much about his penis was not a* Vogue *sort of person. A* Vogue *sort of person would look coolly reflective in his Irving Penn portrait, or haughtily decadent when costumed in garter hose and a welder's mask by Helmut Newton. Redmond, by contrast, would simply have ended up looking cheerful and sweaty.*

Redmond O'Hanlon cares deeply about the safety of his penis. A notorious passage in his Amazonian narrative *In Trouble Again* concerns the *candiru,* a slim, spiny fish that O'Hanlon—on scant evidence—fears will swim into his urethra: "The pain, apparently, is spectacular. You must get to the hospital before your bladder bursts. You must ask a surgeon to cut off your penis." A variant of The Great Fear later comes to pass: "My penis had turned green. To the touch it felt like a hanging cluster of grapes. Swollen tapir ticks, as big as the tip of a thumb, were feeding all down its stem."

O'Hanlon makes his living writing about his travels to the remotest, jungliest, most penis-threatening parts of the world, but The Great Fear—and other, darker nightmares—surfaces even in the hedgecombed heart of England, as I discovered when he and I knocked around Wiltshire Downs for a few days.

"There's something lonely and soft and desolate about these Downs," O'Hanlon said, swigging from a bottle of red wine and staring across the quilt-work fields. "I used to come here as a child and sink into that terrible immediacy when you can only stare at one thistle. In the Downs you must lose touch with any idea of time continuing, reach that point of terror where any action seems pointless. If you're not verging on complete psychosis, the day has been a *waste.*"

We walked across oat and alfalfa fields to West Kennet Long Barrow, a five-thousand-year-old burial chamber. An alarmingly pale woman trailed us step for step, fifty yards behind. O'Hanlon looks safe to follow into the unknown: his gold spectacles, gray muttonchop sideburns, oxford-cloth shirt, and exuberant stride suggest an eccentric but basically sound veterinarian.

After poking through the musty stone burial chambers, we bestrode the invisible ley line, or force field, that runs from West Kennet to the prehistoric stone circle at Avebury Henge. In front of us a shaggy man arranged four aluminum saucepans across the ley line and flung himself to the ground, prostrate. It appeared that he was calling on Druidic forces to cook his food, as he hadn't matches, fuel, or a stove.

The pale woman came up and said disconnectedly, "Come get me if I don't come out. I'm going to Avebury, I'm going to Avebury, and I've got so much to do before I sleep."

"Yes, I can see that you do," O'Hanlon said politely. "Let's get out of here," he murmured as she ghosted off. "She may keep a mousetrap in her vagina."

I had heard about O'Hanlon a few years earlier from the poet James Fenton, who was then quite happy to be living in the Philippines, far from his sometime friend. The mandarin, impish Fenton was O'Hanlon's companion in his first adventure, *Into the Heart of Borneo*. The book sold sixty thousand copies in England and sixty thousand more in Holland—huge numbers for travel writing—and Eric Newby declared it "the funniest travel book I have ever read." (*In Trouble Again*, of which Martin Amis wrote, "Hallucinogenic, scrotum-tightening . . . the Great Travel Book," was just as popular.) But Fenton felt his portrayal as a bald aesthete was undignified, and had grown tired of being best known as O'Hanlon's sidekick. When asked to sign copies of O'Hanlon's book, he'd scrawl "Don't believe a word of it."

"He's very smart and charming," Fenton had said about O'Hanlon—then burst out, "but he's quite *fat,* you know, and he's a tremendous alcoholic, and he's *basically . . . utterly . . . mad.*"

"I had also behaved badly at that point," O'Hanlon told me later. "I brought Bruce Chatwin to meet James, and Chatwin was dropping names in an incredible way, out-Jamesing James with 'Pablo' and 'Braque' and 'Jean Renoir' and how he'd nearly been raped by Somerset Maugham, so James jealously put his feet up and pretended to fall asleep and, as he'd downed a bottle of whiskey, did fall asleep. I stole upstairs to James's study and found his journals in his desk, right where anyone would look. And I thought, I'll crack the window open and go read them and then sneak back through the window before he wakes up. So I lugged this chest off to the car. But Belinda"—O'Hanlon's wife—"took a moral line, I'm afraid, and made me return them immediately. Unfortunately, someone had locked the window, so I had to ring the bell and give the chest to James. He took it amiss. He took it about two-thousand percent amiss."

Three years later, the coolness long passed, Fenton was the first of four guests to arrive for a dinner party at Pelican House, O'Hanlon's ramshackle cottage outside Oxford. As his blond children, Puffin and Galen, gripped his legs like climbing roses, O'Hanlon showed Fenton his new garden. Fenton's eye was drawn from the scraggly buddleia and sedums—plants meant to attract butterflies, and not succeeding—to a group of bones dangling from a tree. "What's that?" he asked.

"Oh, some lamb bones for the woodpeckers." Fenton's gaze shifted to a pile of bloody chicken flesh piled on a wooden platform. "I meant to hang that as a birdfeeder," O'Hanlon said, "but just now it's a rat feeder."

Fenton considered his surroundings. "Redmond," he said at last, gravely, "your garden is rather . . . unsunny."

Pelican House is in similar Addams Family disarray. There are socks in the bookshelves, books in the sock drawer, stuffed caimans and great white pelicans scattered about, and various skulls grinning here and there. O'Hanlon's study, which appears to have been decorated by a tornado, houses—somewhere—his half-completed manuscript describing his latest trip, to Congo, written in a nineteenth-century-style longhand. Strewn about also are his bird's eggs, his toy tanks, and, in a Maxwell House jar, part of the charred foot of O'Hanlon's friend Douglas Winchester, who burned himself alive.

"We don't get many visitors," O'Hanlon's wife Belinda had told me before the party. "An old bat from the village came round when we'd just moved in and Redmond met her at the door with an axe and a strange gleam in his eye. She asked—what did she ask?"

"She asked if I was chopping wood," O'Hanlon recalled, "and I said 'No!' " He cackled wildly.

"It's easy to see a crazed buffoon, the Benny Hill thing that makes him such fun to be with," Lary Shaffer, who accompanied O'Hanlon to Congo, told me later. "He seems like a big teddy bear, bounding around dispensing scotch. I wish more people could see the shrewd, thoughtful side."

O'Hanlon's writing is shrewdly alive to the peculiarities of animal behavior, particularly his own. Rather than hiding behind the explorer's traditional stiff-lipped omnicompetence, O'Hanlon bares his quivering bowels and cockups. In Borneo, O'Hanlon thought to inquire about the spaghetti-like food prepared by his Iban guide Leon only after taking a few suspiciously rubbery bites.

"They the little snakes that live in the fish. How you say it."

"Jesus!" I said, "worms."

"Jesus worms," said Leon, "very good."

But O'Hanlon's Falstaffian pose of glorying in his bumptiousness, and of calling himself "fatso" or "fat fuck" though he's only moderately overtummied, is distraction behavior akin to a mother bird dragging a "broken" wing to lead a predator away from her nest. The eggs in O'Hanlon's nest are a faith in his nightmares, a Conrad-lover's belief in the jungle's power to drive men insane, a childish curiosity about what lies around the next bend in the river, and a fascination with sex. To these interests he applies descriptive powers worthy of his naturalist heroes Richard Spruce, Alfred Russel Wallace, and Charles Darwin. In the Congo manuscript he writes of the hammerkop:

> The bird was known to throw some spectacularly open-minded parties. Eight to ten hammerkops would be invited, some unattached, some married, some divorced . . . They ran in circles side by side until an orgy of (technically speaking) false mounting took place . . . males mounted females, females mounted males, males mounted males, and only lesbians were disadvantaged.

The discussion during O'Hanlon's dinner party was blithe and chiefly concerned with the mounting, and the mounting appendages. "Greek sculptures of their young men were perfectly proportioned, because they didn't like large penises," Fenton declared. "The old men are shown with these . . . hung . . . *wangs.*"

O'Hanlon topped everyone's glasses with whiskey and Medoc—"Watch how he makes everyone drink," Fenton murmured, "It's protection"—and turned the conversation to circumcisions performed in parts of the Arab world. "You flay the skin of the penis in a band up to the tummy button and then down the thigh," he explained. "Then the young man is cauterized over a fire and if he screams or wails at any point, no woman will look at him again." Belinda smiled at the wincing men and offered some Stilton cheese, a gift from Julian Barnes, who, like Martin Amis and Ian McEwan, is a regular visitor. "It's quite stinky and nice," she said. O'Hanlon dispensed cognac into our snifters as if he were watering a row of geraniums.

Sometime later we were all on our knees staring with boozy fascination into a tiny pond O'Hanlon recently built beside his other backyard construction, a distinctly breastlike ancestral mound. O'Hanlon shone his flashlight through the duckweed. "Each female water flea produces thirty thousand babies without a single chap in sight," he announced. "Look there, a newt pretending he's invisible, hanging like a weed stalk. You're staring down the butthole of a newt!"

After everyone tottered, off, O'Hanlon and I drank more Cognac and smoked Cuban cigars and felt rather splendid until 3:00 AM. At 3:01 I crawled into the guest room, whimpering like a basset hound, and passed out.

"My, that was a good talk we had last night," O'Hanlon said. He's been up since 7:00 AM.

"Oh, yes!" I couldn't remember a word of it. As my thunderous hangover receded, our conversation filtered back in queasy, cognac-tinged vignettes. "Even in the worst situation," O'Hanlon had said, "you're thinking 'This will make a great chapter.' The cheat of the writing is that I look so enthusiastic, but it's utterly false—I'm only enthusiastic to get out of the hammock and go upriver because I'm writing a book. As a journalist you're always protected; you're in it for the story."

I had noted that his companions regarded the trips somewhat differently, and that both Fenton and Simon Stockton, O'Hanlon's photographer in the Amazon, had answered that they would not travel with him again. (Stockton, in fact, had a breakdown and wound up screaming "Where's my tomato ketchup?" into a million miles of jungle.)

"I was attracted to the added drama of people who were suicidal, and I wanted to give them that extra push," O'Hanlon had replied, unapologetically. "If you're depressive yourself you unload it on the person who's obviously more depressed."

Even Lary Shaffer, O'Hanlon's photographer in Congo, who *would* travel with him again, told me that once O'Hanlon leaves civilization behind, he can become maddeningly self-centered. "In one small village a local power figure got threatening," Shaffer recalled. "He said we weren't leaving in the morning. We said we were. We crawled into bed at the local schoolhouse, and these extraordinarily hostile, ominous drums started pounding, and we could hear people screaming and getting whipped up, and a dog was growling like someone was creeping around. Marcellin, our Congolese guide, barricaded the door and began sweating heavily. I'm a mild-mannered psychology professor, and here I'd landed in this Indiana Jones movie. I was convinced our lives were over. Redmond was *asleep*. I woke him up several times to convey to him my view that our lives were over. And he'd just fall back *asleep*."

And so O'Hanlon and I set out across the Wiltshire Downs in his Renault; I protected by the story, O'Hanlon by his awareness of the story and by just being Redmond. He packed his knapsack with binoculars, birding books, camouflage pants ("In case we're fired upon"), an enormous hunting knife, and, to my dismay, several bottles of red wine. We stopped first at Fenton's house in Cumnor to drink white wine and view his exquisite classical French gardens. Between his imitations of a yellowhammer and a green finch, O'Hanlon kept pointing to flowers and asked pipingly "What's this, what's this?" like a child at the zoo. Fenton, who often treats O'Hanlon as a boisterous younger brother (though O'Hanlon is a year older), responded with the Latin names for flax, lilies, violets, anchusa, roses, and laburnum. Finally, Redmond asked about a short pinnate-leaved plant.

"That, Redmond," Fenton replied majestically, "is what we gardeners call a weed."

Then we looked at Fenton's turbid fish pond, where the carp were belly-up dead, and his equally lifeless frog pond. Fenton asked about oxygenating the ponds, and O'Hanlon advised, "Canadian duckweed, and lots of it." When Fenton muttered that his ducks would eat it all, O'Hanlon lifted an eyebrow and fell silent.

"Fenton's ordered gardens are the ego, and my tangled one is the id," O'Hanlon told me that evening over two bottles of white wine at an Italian restaurant in Salisbury. "It's all Freudian. Ponds are the vagina, and he has these two great vaginas which are clouded, green, and impenetrable. And he *wants* it that way, he doesn't want them cleaned up and fertile. When I realized that, I stopped pressing him."

O'Hanlon continued his psycho-topographic theorizing the following morning as we walked along the slender Avon River, observing a family of coots. We were still in Salisbury because our plan to (illegally) raid Stonehenge late the previous evening had fallen afoul of one of the local customs that so often confound travelers: by the time we tipsily emerged from dinner clutching napkins covered with lists of our favorite authors, the parking lot containing O'Hanlon's Renault had locked up for the night.

The parent coots, whose white face shields gave them the villainous look of hockey goalies, were pulling sticks from an old nest to build a new one several yards away. The problem was that their chicks were still *in* the old nest. As the chicks got wetter and wetter, they took it amiss. They took it about 2,000 percent amiss: indignant cries filled the air. "How extraordinary," O'Hanlon said, utterly focused. "I've never seen or read about such behavior. That must be part of where the expression 'queer as a coot' comes from. Reminds me rather of my mother talking about the vicarage, where I'd felt like minor nobility rattling around this big house." He put on a reedy mother's voice: "Redsy, all we own is the furniture, we could be thrown out at any minute!" Then he shifted to a reedy child's voice that was indistinguishable from the reedy mother's voice: "Waah!"

That seemed the moment to ask him the source of his remark in *In Trouble Again* that Marcel Proust "loved his mother so much that after a hard night's work he'd unroll a giant photograph of her head across the floor and shit on it," a scenario that struck me as owing more to O'Hanlon's imagination than Proust's distress. "Well, if I did make it up," he said cheerily, "I'm rather pleased to have released that sort of information to the public." (Later, back at Pelican House, O'Hanlon discovered that his supposed source, George D. Painter's Proust biography, was actually silent on the subject. "It seems a *logical* thing to do to one's mother," he said. "Perhaps I've compressed things and shown the inner truth, as usual.")

We walked on downstream, escorted by moorhens, wagtails, mallards, and one glistening swan. "Have you ever seen a woman gazing deeply into a pond or a river, or fishing all weekend?" O'Hanlon asked. "This also ties into my theory—which provokes only embarrassed silence or rabid disagreement—that homosexuals like dry arid places like deserts, and heteros like warm, hot, swampy places."

"Hmmm . . ." I said, after the silence had become embarrassing.

"God, I'm sweating," O'Hanlon said. "I'm clammy in the armpits." We were sitting in the pews of St. Mary, the twelfth-century parish church where his father was the vicar. "It really does smell the same, that mustiness. Christ! My father used to pull out his handkerchief, scratch his chest, and deliver an absentminded sermon about his lawnmower. God! He was perfect for this place." We walked through Calne's unprepossessing streets to O'Hanlon's old home. "Everyone since [William] Cobbett has agreed Calne was the ugliest town in Wiltshire," O'Hanlon said by way of apology as we pulled up in front of the large, ivy-covered vicarage. It looked like a perfect place to curl up in a window bay and dream of faraway lands.

"My mother would moan when the doorbell rang," O'Hanlon recalled. "She'd say:"—he put on his reedy mother's voice—" 'I'm living in a pig sty, no peace, what horrible person is at the door,' and then she'd clank down the stairs and you'd hear, 'Do come in, we were just talking about you!' and in would come some poor ravaged butcher with a marital problem. It took me years to realize that when people said, 'Do come in, it's good to see you,' they meant it."

As we drove past Marlborough College, O'Hanlon's prep school, he slowed and gave the grounds a dour glance. "Forty to a dormitory and no comfortable chairs and mass buggery," he said. "Actually, it was just general pulling of each other's penises. Off to my first prep school at seven, with the morning cold-water plunge and the beatings with a special flat board. It leaves you with that characteristic emotional hole—you learn to mask your feeling, and you can't respond to others' pain. It also gave me a real horror of the English middle class—I detest all that cricket and enforced bonhomie." Prep school looms large in the British psyche, but particularly so in the glory of British travel writing. Those determined expeditions to the farthest and hottest parts of the world, an impulse sent up in the Noël Coward song "Mad Dogs and Englishmen," are as much flight from as travel toward.

"My image of the jungle—vast trees and tremendous peacefulness—was formed here in picnics with my family on school holidays," O'Hanlon said as we walked through the old, dim beech and elm groves in nearby Savernake Forest. "The pleasure of the jungle is a gift from that childhood memory. Our backyard pond is there, at least 25 percent, to seed the future for Puffin and Galen—years from now perhaps they'll see a newt and discover a purpose in life."

I mentioned that Savernake reminded me of the Wild Wood in Kenneth Grahame's *The Wind in the Willows*. "Yes, yes," O'Hanlon said excitedly. "It occurs to me now, thinking about it, perhaps I've been looking for the Wild Wood all my life, shortsightedly peering about like the mole, running ahead and getting lost in no time at all."

Coming home through the Cotswolds, we drove past long fields full of poppies lit up by the late afternoon sun. "The ripening corn really softens everything," O'Hanlon said, with mingled pleasure and distress. "It's not right—it's not as I remember from childhood. I'm afraid this isn't the right time of year for feeling desolate. As far as pain goes, the trip has been a failure, really."

The Stranger-than-Truth Story of The Body Shop

By Jon Entine

Killed: *Vanity Fair,* 1994

Ever wonder why the British press routinely bashes the Royal Family but does not produce the kind of investigative reports on corporate corruption so common to the United States? How, for example, did Robert Maxwell, the right-wing British media tycoon infamous for pillaging his company's pension funds manage to avoid an exposé even though his misdeeds were well known among journalists?

Welcome to the stifling reality of investigative reporting in Britain, where corporations exploit Commonwealth libel law to ensure unpalatable truths remain concealed. In contrast to the legal protections of the First Amendment and The New York Times vs. Sullivan *(1964), in British courts the burden of proof is on the defendant to prove beyond a doubt the truth of any allegations. Even when journalists get all the facts right, they often lose. Only after Maxwell died in 1991 did Fleet Street admit they had been aware of his improprieties, but had refrained from reporting on them for fear of prosecution.*

The Body Shop hired Maxwell's former legal SWAT team, Lovell White Durrant, to squelch critical stories. "As you will no doubt be aware of by now," an editor at The Daily Telegraph *wrote me in April 1994 explaining why the paper had abandoned an investigation of Anita Roddick, the company's founder, "our libel law is much more restrictive than yours. The truth in certain circumstances is an insufficient defense."*

Vanity Fair *faced a similar legal onslaught from Lovell White Durrant. The legal advisors to the magazine, which prints a British edition, reluctantly concluded that publishing this story, no matter how accurate, was too financially risky.*

As disturbing as the self-censorship, however, was the wimpy reaction of so-called progressives to evidence of The Body Shop's ethical transgressions. While researching the story, I encountered an unexpected circle-the-wagons mentality from many journalists and activists, who knew about the gap between Roddick's rhetoric and The Body Shop's practices. Eager for a feminist superstar, they had willfully overlooked the hypocrisy—and the fact that The Body Shop's name, some of its products and its marketing concept were stolen from a predecessor chain of the same name—not out of fear of a lawsuit, but because they believed her message of "social justice" was inspiring and that someone with a progressive reputation was entitled to a 'get out of jail free' card.

In the years following my investigation, The Body Shop paid out more than $200 million to settle franchise disputes and to cover endless corporate reorganizations. Its stock dropped by three quarters before recovering slightly, stripping investors, peak to trough, of $700 million. In 2001, Roddick herself tacitly acknowledged the depths of the company's problems, deriding her creation as a "dysfunctional coffin," then putting it on the block. Only bottom feeders bid on it, and the company remains in her control.

Don't cry for Anita Roddick; she's still worth hundreds of millions. However, the "green" movement has paid a high price for this brazen exploitation of idealism. Following the trail Roddick blazed in cynical "cause related marketing," corporations now use green symbols to peddle everything from tobacco to industrial chemicals. Progressives love to create heroes and unmask hypocrites; with Roddick, they hit the Daily Double. Let's hope we've learned a lesson. If reformers and critical journalists don't have the guts to demand integrity and honesty from someone who poses as a social reformer, they stand for nothing at all.

xmiquilpan is a dusty town in the Mezquital Valley, four hours north by bus from Mexico City. It's mid-morning on this mid-September day in 1992 and the concrete shacks lining the road are broiling. Waves of heat shimmer off the corrugated scrap metal roofs. Everyone is outside.

Young Nañhu Indian boys play a game with a stick and string, careful not to dirty their white shirts and navy blue pants normally worn for church. A few older men look on languidly. The healthy men have taken off to Texas or to Mexico City in search of better wages. The girls and their mothers, their hair tied with colorful barrettes, gather in the town square. They are dressed in hand-embroidered shirts and skirts decorated with flowers. The women, the elderly, and the infirm eke out a living mainly hawking cheap scrub mitts made from maguey, a local plant resembling a giant aloe vera with huge fronds. The few pesos each one brings offer some relief from the grinding poverty that is sucking the life and the men out of the valley

As a half dozen vans pull up, a mariachi band strikes up a welcoming tune. Out bounds Anita Roddick, the founder of The Body Shop. The company, based in Britain, has mushroomed from a back-alley hippie shop in 1976 selling incense and hand-cut soaps into a multinational cosmetics empire with more than a thousand shops in forty-five countries. And Roddick has succeeded with a unique formula: While traditional cosmetic firms peddle beauty in a bottle, The Body Shop packages idealism and hope for a better world.

Anita—everyone calls her by her first name—hugs the women and rustles the hair of the boys. Her face is well lined and handsome, framed by her distinctive, frizzy, raven-colored hair. Although she doesn't speak Spanish, she chatters excitedly. The women understand little but they giggle shyly at the white princess with the hands that fly like birds. There is a magnetic force about her. Charisma. Presence.

Anita wades into the friendly crowd, enveloped by a small army of cameramen carrying boom mikes and reflectors. This is a made-for-TV event. The year before, American Express had contacted Roddick about making a commercial for its "Don't leave home without it" campaign. Although she had long boasted she would never stoop so low as to advertise—"crass capitalism," she says with disgust in her addresses at business schools—Roddick jumped at the promotional opportunity.

For the Nañhu, a lot more was at stake than an ad. The local women earn a profit of a peso (seventeen cents) per scrub mitt. If the impoverished laborers could get Roddick to increase her payments per piece, and if they could land a decent-sized order, there might be enough money to build a school or repair some houses.

With Roddick's arrival, remote and ramshackle Ixmiquilpan was transformed into a Hollywood set. There were two camera crews; Amex sent a film team of more than twenty and The Body Shop dispatched its own cameramen to film a promotional video.

It was a bizarre scene," recalls Alison Rockett a young Canadian, hired by Roddick to help organize the filming.

"Port-o-johns with flush toilets were hauled in from Mexico City. A chef was hired to prepare a smorgasbord and fettuccine Alfredo."

On the first day of shooting, Roddick corralled a cameraman and dragged him over to a crowd of Indians. "I want you to film my favorite people," she told him, and then turned to the ecstatic villagers. "I will be getting money for this filming, and I want to give it to you. What do you need?"

Rockett squirmed. Weeks before, she had sent Roddick a detailed report on the local culture, warning her not to make too many promises. "I don't know if she ever read it," says Rockett. "If she did, she certainly didn't absorb it."

With the camera rolling, one woman said the village needed a tortilla machine. Anita promised they'd get it. A teacher asked for a library. "Anita just kept saying 'uh huh, uh huh,' jotting down their requests on this little notepad," says Rockett. Anita ultimately pledged to donate $25,000. Word of her promises spread through nearby towns. People traveled for hours on foot to meet the woman who was going to lift them out of poverty.

"One village wanted a truck," says Rockett. "Another asked for a tractor. Anita was so enthusiastic they thought she was going to buy them everything they needed. It was all done so spontaneously but really so thoughtlessly. I'm not sure she remembered what she promised them. But they sure did."

Peter Winkel, the Dutch anthropologist who heads Xochipilli, the nonprofit that set up the scrub mitt project, sighs as he recalls the scene. "Roddick has no understanding of what it's like working with precapitalist cultures," he says. When after three years of ravaging inflation, he suggested a small raise in the price she pays for the mitts, Roddick wouldn't budge. "They told me they could get similar mitts cheaper in India, so I dropped it."

"She's dynamic but very contradictory," Winkel says.

Does she have a good heart? I ask.

"I'm not sure." He pauses. "Too many faces. I see too many faces of Anita."

Anita Roddick's public face is The Body Shop's trademark. Her stores display life-size images of the self-proclaimed "Queen of Green": there's Anita with impoverished Indian boys turning out Body Shop foot rollers; bare-breasted Amazon natives looking on as Anita smears a mysterious goop on her face; Anita in Siberia visiting former Soviet engineers happily making cheap wooden combs.

Roddick first gained notoriety for her outspoken attacks on the mostly male club of beauty barons. They "lie, cheat and exploit women" by selling "garbage," she raged in her autobiography, *Body and Soul*. By the late 1980s, by then a beauty baroness herself, she had morphed into a renowned gadfly, promoting the latest politically correct cause: saving the whale, ending animal testing, rescuing the rainforest, encouraging recycling, funding AIDS awareness. "I think you can trade ethically, be committed to social responsibility, empower your employees," she wrote. "I think you can rewrite the book on business."

Roddick is credited for creating the green consumer wave and riding it into the hearts and malls of the world. "Anita is the most progressive business person I know," enthuses Ralph Nader. "If someone says 'Let's do that,' Anita says 'Let's do it yesterday.'"

USA Today headlined one story THE MOTHER TERESA OF CAPITALISM. She was awarded an Order of the British Empire and the Audubon Society bestowed on her its top environmental honor. Baby boomers and their preadolescent daughters idolize her for promoting a new feminist business ethic based on "love" and "care" and "intuition"—and they snap up her not-tested-on-animals Brazil nut hair conditioner.

Shortly after Roddick's visit to Mexico, I had a chance to interview her for the first and only time. She was opening a new franchise in the glitzy Stoneridge Mall, just outside Walnut Creek, California. The scent of patchouli filled the store, but the crowd was more Bloomingdale's than bohemian. Girls in designer jeans stood painted nails-to-painted nails beside moms with Gucci bags.

Roddick launched into her familiar attack on Big Business. Corporate executives? "Robber barons," she hissed. Investment bankers, who floated her stock in 1984 and made her a multimillionaire? "Blood-sucking dinosaurs." Rough words but delivered with sincerity. "I'd rather promote human rights, environmental concerns, indigenous rights, whatever, than promote a bubble bath," she gushed. A shelffull of bath bubble gels framed Roddick almost perfectly.

Here was a harbinger of the New Age, weaned on can-do chutzpah and do-right rhetoric. There was no mention of her Georgian estate in southern England, a flat in London, the castle in Scotland, or her husband's collection of polo ponies that he flies around the world in leased 747s.

After the talk, Roddick allowed me just enough time for one question. She had just returned from a meeting of the International Chamber of Commerce, in Cancun, where she had excoriated delegates for not boycotting trade with China. "The new corporate responsibility is as simple as just saying 'no' to dealing with torturers and despots," she had said. She had titled the lecture: "Corporate Responsibility: Good Works Not Good Words."

Works versus words. "Anita," I asked, "how do you square your call for a boycott when The Body Shop sources dozens of products from China including all of your gift baskets?" I ticked off the names of The Body Shop's Chinese suppliers: "Willow Specialties, American Chens, Coe and Dru. . . ." Roddick looked at me with the eyes of a mother confronting a wayward child. "Jon, you just don't understand, do you? I was talking about what business *should* do, not what we *actually* do. My job is to inspire. But we do have a bloody business to run, after all."

Anita Roddick has built an enormously profitable business. But in recent years, her fabulous rags-to-riches-to–Robin Hood success story has begun to fray. Profits and margins are eroding. Some franchisees are losing money and charging fraud. Animal rights groups complain about misleading claims. Prominent Amazon activists say The Body Shop's trade initiatives are gimmicks. Its "natural" products have been pulled off shelves because of chemical contamination. Still, for the most part, the criticisms are below the public radar. To most of the media and to her cult of customers, Roddick remains a nonpareil.

I happened upon the real story of The Body Shop by accident. I was at my office at *PrimeTime Live* at ABC News in July 1993 where I was a producer, when my phone rang. A woman identified herself only as Erica. "My sister and I are franchisees of The Body Shop in Chicago," she said anxiously. "We were hoping you would consider doing a report on the company."

The idea of doing yet another puff piece sent my eyes rolling back in my head. "Not interested," I told Erica.

"But you don't understand," she persisted. "The Body Shop is built on lies. Anita runs a mean-spirited company that contradicts everything she claims to be about. I can put you in touch with other franchisees, suppliers, its former treasurer, even people who are still working there."

Journalists often get far-fetched pitches and this sounded like one. I had read glowing profiles of Roddick. I had purchased gifts for friends at The Body Shop. What Erica alleged, though startling and red meat for an investigative reporter if it was true, didn't add up. "What you're saying sounds too fantastic. If you have hard evidence, send it along. Otherwise, please don't bother me." I never expected to hear from her again.

Three days later, another call came into *PrimeTime* that would change my thinking. As is the practice, callers pitching stories are transferred randomly to a producer, in this case, serendipitously, me. "My name is Tiffany Haworth. I do the graphics for The Body Shop out of their headquarters in New Jersey and design the catalogues." Her voice was determined. "I was forced to print things that weren't true. I've never seen a company treat its employees so badly. I've worked with Anita Roddick. It's an ugly story."

I was stunned. Two unrelated calls in less than a week attacking a supernova of the New Age. Haworth sketched a remarkable story over lunch a few days later, backing it up with documents. Roddick fictionalized claims about the company's recycling projects. Employee benefits stunk. The allegations went on and on. "Check out her charitable contributions," she said. "I think you'll find out some interesting things."

With a bit of research, I found a flurry of quotes by Roddick proclaiming The Body Shop's generosity. "I don't care a bloody thing about money," she told one interviewer. "We give most of our profits away," she bragged to another. One brochure claimed the company gives "an inordinately high percentage of pre-tax profits to often controversial charitable campaigns." That was an easy claim to check. I contacted the English Charity Commission. As I read the documents that spitted out of the fax from London, I almost fell off my chair. I reviewed the company's annual reports and its charitable contributions going back to its founding in 1976. Over the first eleven years of business, it made zero charitable contributions—not once pence. Through the most recent fiscal year, 1993, it never once contributed the estimated average for U.S. companies, 1.5 percent of pre-tax profits.

The next week Erica called back, joined on the line by her twin sister Andrea. "We can't supply you with any more information," they said, palpably distressed. "We are negotiating to sell back our franchise and The Body Shop is threatening us if we should talk. They're well known for suing people who complain or talk to the press. They put a gag clause in our buyout agreement. But we believe this story should be told. Here's what we propose. There is a network of Body Shop franchisees and employees from around the world that know what's going on. You'll hear from them."

Indeed I did. Over the next two weeks, each morning when I arrived for work, there would be angry or distraught messages on my voicemail—franchisees, employees, activists.

"Hello, my name is Keith Knudsen. I was The Body Shop's first franchisee in France. This is a truly evil company, a wonderfully orchestrated scheme. Please call."

One employee, upset that the company was replacing many of its permanent staff with part-time workers who were paid less and received far fewer benefits, seethed: "There are only two types of Body Shop workers: those who are leaving and those sending out their résumés."

"It's a lot worse," said one former manager in its product quality division, "when you find out the robber who's been stealing from you is the local cop."

While most employees were disillusioned, more than one described their time at The Body Shop—some were still employed there—as the worst experience of their professional lives. One made a play on the company's recycling slogan, "Reuse, Refill, Recycle." Its true motto, she said, should be "use, abuse, and refuse." Another broke down in tears. "It's a sweat-shop," product manager Marilyn Gettinger told me. "Benefits are average, at best. Pay is 75 percent of what other cosmetic companies offer and we work sixty to eighty hours a week. Workers are fired on Anita's whims and get no severance."

Lisa Herling, a manager in The Body Shop's New Jersey public relations office, smuggled out an internal video exposé produced on the sly by some frustrated employees to educate executives about the breadth of the disenchantment. It was designed to look like a *60 Minutes* investigation, complete with the ticking stopwatch and a grim-looking Mike Wallace. Called "An Inside Look at The Body Shop in America," it portrayed a company that overworks its employees, denies workers federal holidays off, and offers no childcare pro-grams, despite championing movements that support these causes. "The company doesn't provide day care on site . . . or subsidize care in the community . . . or allow employees to pay for day care with pretax dollars," said the narrator. "Basically, the company does nothing in terms of day care."

The seriousness of the allegations was remarkable, espe-cially considering The Body Shop's pristine reputation. These disturbing stories contrasted with the glowing articles then appearing regularly in the press. In 1990, Roddick was famously featured on the cover of *Inc.*, with a blazing head-line: THIS WOMAN HAS CHANGED BUSINESS FOREVER. In light of the calls I was receiving, I found the sub-headline particularly ironic: "How Anita Roddick of The Body Shop has customers and employees clamoring for her brand of business."

What had gone so terribly awry and why have so many journalists neglected to write balanced stories about The Body Shop?

To answer those questions, one has to know Anita Roddick. She is, even casual acquaintances learn, a true believer in her mission. But what is her mission? Perhaps the last line of her autobiography offers a clue. "Make no mistake about it," she writes in bold type. "I'm doing this for me."

Anita Lucia Perella was always a showgirl. Born in 1942, one of four children of first generation Italian immigrants, she grew up in Littlehampton, a working-class town on England's south coast. According to her account in *Body and Soul*, life was a struggle. By day, she chafed under her strict Catholic schooling. On nights and weekends, she worked in her mother's cafe. Her most distinct memories were of being an outsider, desperate to be noticed in a society where social status is indelibly imprinted at birth. "We were different from English families," she writes. "We were noisy, always screaming and shouting, we played music loudly, ate pasta, and smelled of garlic."

As a teenager, she was fascinated by James Dean and constantly courted trouble. In her twenties, after graduating college, she tried her hand at teaching, but the hippie life beckoned. She left home for Israel. While living on a kibbutz, she orchestrated a stunt that had her boyfriend pretending he could walk on water as if it was the second coming of Jesus Christ. Kibbutz leaders were not amused. After being kicked out, she trekked through Africa and Greece and eventually landed in Geneva, where she worked as a secretary at the United Nations. She quit and rode steamers from Tahiti to South Africa. She settled in Johannesburg until she was deported, she says, for patronizing black nightclubs.

Exhausted from her travels and with only a few pounds to her name, Anita returned home in 1968. Her mother introduced her to a tall, thin Scotsman, Gordon Roddick. Though trained as a farmer, he had a love of travel and a passion for horseback riding. Anita fell for him. Gordon regaled her with his stories of his adventures: tin mining in Africa, floating down the Amazon, sheep farming in Australia. "The moment I set eyes on Gordon," she writes, "I wanted him to be the father of my children."

A year into their relationship, their first baby was born. Then wanderlust returned. In the fall of 1970, Gordon and Anita, pregnant again, set off for San Francisco. They stayed with his best friend, David Edward, and Edward's wife Alma Dunstan. One weekend, they visited Lake Tahoe, making a quick detour to the Silver Horseshoes Wedding Chapel in Reno. "My wedding outfit comprised a pair of tattered corduroys bulging at the waist and a red rain slicker, worn with sneakers and a howling baby in a harness on my back," she writes.

It was during this visit that Roddick says she got the first inspiration for her cosmetic empire to be. While in the United Staes, the Roddicks discussed and discarded one entrepreneurial idea after another, trying to figure what might transplant well in England. As she relates the story, she thought it amusing that car repair shops were named "body shops." The memory, she writes, would pop into her head when she decided six years later to open a beauty store in Brighton, a faded resort town near Littlehampton.

Fast forward to 1976. After years of running a spaghetti restaurant and other failed ventures, Anita and Gordon revisited the idea that had so intrigued them years before. Within months, and with the help of a £4,000 bank loan, Anita opened a small cosmetics shop on a down-at-the-heels, one-block alley near a funeral parlor, an organic food market, a vegetarian restaurant, and a secondhand bookstore. As Roddick delights in telling the story, when she put up The Body Shop sign, the mortician across the street demanded that she change the name, anxious it would confuse his customers. Roddick rang up the local paper, *The Evening Argus,* and landed a sympathetic column about an idealistic woman entrepreneur under siege.

It's an endearing tale, but according to friends and colleagues, it's a tall one. There was no threat from the mortician. The understaffed paper ran with it without checking. Much to everyone's surprise, The Body Shop's cash register rang madly. It was a lesson in media manipulation that Roddick would never forget.

The Brighton store offered a range of products rarely seen before in England. Roddick stacked her shelves with exotic-sounding potions in small plastic bottles with handwritten labels. Her early success was almost entirely her own. Gordon had skipped the country. According to many accounts, the Roddicks' marriage was volatile, and after one particularly ugly confrontation, Gordon took off for Argentina to travel with David Edward. How long would he be gone? He didn't know. Maybe two years.

Roddick marketed her products as "100 percent pure" and "natural" but they never really were. Although customers claim they want natural products, they want to keep their cosmetics for months without spoiling. Mark Constantine, who Roddick soon hired to develop products, added preservatives. They dyed the cosmetics to look pretty and added artificial fragrances so they smelled like their natural-sounding names, all to create the "fun" atmosphere that became so much a part of The Body Shop's image. "The use of all the chemicals . . . you have to understand that it was a lot more innocent than it appears today," Constantine told me. "We didn't know much better then and Roddick couldn't care less about ingredients. It never even entered into her consciousness."

Gordon returned far earlier than expected and reconciled with Anita. The Body Shop became a family adventure. They were never closer. Sales boomed. "It was very, very exciting," recalls Constantine. "Anita and Gordon were just so enthusiastic. They didn't concern themselves with the fact that my bedroom was full of product and I had stuff in the shed. You have to understand . . . .They are entrepreneurs. Everything was 'go, go, go.'"

Friends and strangers began inquiring about buying a shop of their own. It soon dawned on Gordon that they could make a lot more money at far less risk by selling products as a wholesaler rather than running stores themselves. One of England's first franchise businesses was born.

In early 1979, the Roddicks contracted with Janis Raven, who ran a public relations company in London, to handle the press. While Mark developed the cosmetics, Gordon remained in the background to oversee expansion plans. Anita was the public face and behind-the-scenes taskmaster, opening one new shop after another, drumming up newspaper stories, and attending road shows.

When Raven signed on, The Body Shop had only eight branches and was regarded as the choice of the "brown rice and incense" crowd.

"Anita was lovable in the beginning," she says. "The way we actually promoted the company was we made Anita Roddick very accessible. Unlike the Revlons and Max Factors of this world . . . she was touchable, she was reachable, she would talk to the press personally. Her general overall enthusiasm worked wonders." Shops multiplied.

Mark, Janis, and Anita became the merry mythmakers, concocting elaborate fables about some of their bestselling natural-sounding cosmetics: cocoa butter inspired by Hawaiian natives; peppermint foot lotion mixed on request of the London Marathon; eye gel developed for a computer firm concerned about worker eye strain. Not quite.

"What we were looking for was unusual ingredients," Raven recalls. The pineapple facial wash . . . we talked about Anita going to Sri Lanka and seeing the women rubbing pineapples over them. You know, that kind of nonsense."

Why was it nonsense?

"Because it wasn't true. That was Mark's information, and we just decided to make it a bit more romantic."

"I certainly never talked about how she came up with any of those things," Constantine insists. "If she said something, then I just kept quiet."

None of the original members of The Body Shop team thought of what they were doing as deception. It was fun. "We had a great time," remembers Constantine. The press, meanwhile, wrote adoring profiles of Roddick. The furious growth infused everyone with a sense of purpose.

The Body Shop thrived on the idealism of young women like Anne Downer, a British expat living in Singapore. On a visit home in 1981, Downer wandered into the Covent Garden shop and fell in love. "I thought Anita was quite a maverick. I liked her wacky sense of 'let's do it differently.'" The twenty-two-year-old hopped a train to The Body Shop's headquarters in Brighton, eventually coming away with rights to eight Asian countries for a few hundred pounds. It was so loosely run that "a shop design was a photograph and a splotch of paint on a piece of paper," she remembers.

When The Body Shop went public in 1984, its shares almost doubled on the first day. Overnight, Anita and Gordon were multimillionaires. More accolades rolled in. In 1985, Roddick was named UK Businesswoman of the Year.

Roddick's trademark passion for social issues didn't emerge until after the company went public. "Mark is the one who actually got her fired up about 'green things,'" Raven recalls. Roddick not only knew little about cosmetics, she was oblivious to the debate over animal testing.

"She and I used to have arguments over whether 'not tested

on animals' should be on the bloody bottle," Constantine says. "She couldn't see the point. It was just a few vegetarians and ex-hippies."

The Body Shop's campaigns for progressive causes began in 1986 as the company faced its first serious challenge to its natural marketing niche from Revlon and Marks & Spencer. Looking for a way to promote her products made with jojoba oil, which The Body Shop claimed was a substitute for whale spermaceti—it isn't—Roddick hooked up with Greenpeace UK, printing fundraising posters to "save the whale."

Raven, who shortly thereafter would leave the company in a dispute over her salary, created a brilliant media campaign. "The link with Greenpeace signals a change in corporate attitude at The Body Shop," Raven reads from her scrapbook. This marks a "serious public commitment to protecting the natural world." She looks up and laughs. "That is a real serious sort of nonsense statement, isn't it? And I wrote it."

But it worked. It generated another blizzard of publicity and a new wave of socially conscious customers. Emboldened by her PR coup, Roddick threw herself behind one cause after another. "We are great campaigners," she boasted. She transformed herself from a quirky entrepreneur into a leading spokesperson for progressive capitalism. The Body Shop's "two-for-one" sale had idealistic girls agog: buy a bottle of lotion and get social justice for free. Sales skyrocketed.

By 1987, a commercial magic had enveloped The Body Shop. Roddick was an international star. Many franchisees made out like bandits. The stock became known as "the shares that defy gravity." That's when the Roddicks made a fateful expansion decision: they decided to move into the world's most lucrative but most competitive market: the United States. But before they could open, they had to deal with a nagging problem.

One of the foundations of the Anita Roddick myth is that she invented The Body Shop concept. In fact, the company's origins began not in Brighton in 1976 but in the Bay Area in 1970, when Anita Perella and Gordon Roddick stayed with David Edward and Alma Dunstan.

A few weeks into my inquiry, I was put in contact with David Brostoff, an executive with Body Time, a chain of five natural cosmetic stores in the San Francisco area. Body Time's stores look remarkably similar to The Body Shop's. The product names are nearly the same. Both stores have a distinctive green color scheme. There is that all too familiar "breakthrough" recycling policy in which customers can bring in empty bottles for refills. In fact, almost everyone who visits Body Time is certain that it is a rip-off of Roddick's Body Shop. That irks the company's founders, Peggy Short and Jane Saunders, to no end.

Brostoff was blunt: "Anita Roddick is a fraud. And I have the documents to prove it." Over dinner in Anaheim, Brostoff handed over a folder filled with copies of the original Body Shop's old brochures and pricing sheets. One had a hand-drawn picture of a woman pouring cosmetics into small plastic bottles and surrounded by a cornucopia of natural products with The Body Shop sign above her. "As to quality," it read, "all biodegradable, our products are made to our specifications by our pharmaceutical chemist in his developmental laboratory. . . . As to prices: While requiring the highest quality, we have kept prices at a reasonable level by avoiding expensive gimmicky advertising, and by presenting products in modest but attractive packages. . . . Also, you might bring an empty bottle (a Body Shop first), for a price reduction for lotion, shampoo, or whatever."

It looked just like one of Roddick's early brochures—until I looked at the bottom of the first page. "Telegraph Avenue, Berkeley; Spring, 1973." That was three years before Roddick opened what she has long claimed was the "original" Body

Shop, complete with biodegradable products, pledges of no gimmicky advertising, and her "innovative" idea of offering a refill cosmetic bar.

During their visit to the Bay Area in 1970, Anita and Gordon visited a tiny hippie shop along Telegraph Avenue. Peggy Short and Jane Saunders, sisters by marriage, stacked their shelves high with round plastic bottles filled with shampoos and lotions. They sold an array of natural-sounding creams made with avocado, cocoa butter, and cucumber. They cut and wrapped freshly made glycerin soaps scented with strawberry and lemon and poured perfume oil redolent of gardenia, woody sandalwood, and honeysuckle. It was a fun place, known for its concern for the environment. It was housed in C.J.'s, an auto repair garage converted into a bazaar. The two Berkeley founders cleverly named it "The Body Shop." ("That was *the* place to buy shampoo and body cream," I was later told by the Roddicks' host Alma Dunstan. She recalls Anita going on a buying binge after a visit to the then-Body Shop's store on Union Square in San Francisco. Anita, she said, walked out with armfuls of hand-cut soaps, loofahs, and cosmetics in small plastic bottles with handwritten labels.)

As I compared these brochures with Roddick's copycat versions, I was startled at her brazenness. A blurb noted: "All of our products are Biodegradable & made to our specifications . . . Bottles 20¢ or bring your own." Roddick's later version: "All our products are biologically soft and made to our specifications . . . Bottles 12p, or bring your own." The original Body Shop offered Four O'Clock Astringent Lotion. Roddick's store sold Five O'Clock Astringent Lotion. A particularly telling knockoff is a facial scrub made from ground adzuki beans. Roddick called it "Japanese Washing Grains." She came across the wash, she has written, on a visit to Japan. The truth is more prosaic. In its original incarnation, offered years before, the Berkeley shop called this unique product, "Korean Washing Grains." The Korean woman who made the kimonos sold by Short and Saunders had developed it based on her family's secret recipe.

According to Constantine, whenever ideas for new products flagged, there was always the California Body Shop to secretly turn to for inspiration. Roddick would pick-and-choose from the catalogues sent by Gordon's pal David Edward.

The original Body Shop stores remained a major source of friction for the Roddicks, preventing them from entering the world's largest market. Shortly after returning from a trip to San Francisco in 1982, Gordon suggested opening in the United States under a new name, but Anita, worried that the move would raise suspicions, threw a fit. "She went absolutely crazy," Constantine says Gordon told him.

The Roddicks strived to suppress the real story of The Body Shop. When the British magazine *International Management* interviewed Gordon in 1986 about the alleged rip-off, he heatedly denied "any knowledge" of the Berkeley shops. "We have a different approach," Gordon said. *International Management's* former editor, Mark Johnson recalls that "Gordon was very threatening on the phone. Then I got a very aggressive letter." Fearing a lawsuit litigated under British libel statutes, Johnson deleted key facts. "It's a gangsterish operation beneath its kindly exterior," he says now.

The Roddicks finally resolved to settle the issue in 1987. Gordon struck a deal with Short and Saunders, who were unaware at the time of the brazen heist. The Roddicks paid the pair $3.5 million for the rights to The Body Shop name; all the Berkeley Body Shop had to do was to agree to change its company name to "Body Time."

Still, the issue wouldn't go away. In 1991, after *The Daily Mail* stumbled across evidence of The Body Shop's origins, the Roddicks sicced their solicitors on the paper. Lovell

White Durrant had cut its eyeteeth as defenders of corrupt corporate barons by shielding media magnate, Robert Maxwell, from investigative journalists. "There is no truth whatsoever in any allegation that Anita Roddick stole the idea for The Body Shop from someone else," the lawyers wrote the newspaper, threatening libel. *The Daily Mail*'s pulled their story.

The Roddicks steadfastly deny the original sin, brandishing a quote from Short and Saunders that Roddick "didn't rip us off." But "that letter was sent before we found out the truth," explains Brostoff, "before we happened across the copycat brochures." Over the years, these otherwise mild-mannered women in Berkeley became resentful when customers accused *them* of stealing Roddick's concept, showing them comparison copies of the brochures. "What really got them angry was the ongoing deception," he says. "Anita's constant lie that she originated the idea, the green color scheme, the products, all the things that gave the company its unique identity. Never in our wildest imagination did we think that Roddick, with all her claims about being so honest, would keep this fabrication going."

In one sense, the fib is understandable. Few retail ideas are original, certainly not selling faux natural cosmetics. Who would have predicted that a handful of New Age shops would ever become an international juggernaut? But a juggernaut it became. Thinking that the Berkeley situation was behind them, the Roddicks opened a company-owned store in Manhattan in 1988 that did blockbuster business. More than five thousand franchisee applications poured in.

Although they realized it was a long shot, Erica and Andrea, the twins from Chicago, launched a two-year campaign to win over Roddick. They believed they were a perfect fit. They were activists. Their mom, a journalist, contributed to *Mother Jones*. They wrote Roddick more than fifty letters during 1989 and

1990. They flew around the country to her speaking engagements to convince her that they had the "right values" for a franchise. Eventually, their aggressiveness paid off and they were awarded the first franchise in Chicago. "We were told we are now a part of 'the most honest corporation in the world,' " says Andrea. "I felt like I had died and gone to heaven."

There were problems from the start. The containers buckled and leaked because the company would not pay for product compatibility tests. Some products turned rancid. In almost every case, they say, The Body Shop gave them a hard time about taking back tainted products. Sales lagged far behind the projections given to prospective franchisees by The Body Shop's executives.

Their relationship with The Body Shop deteriorated month by month. At their first franchise meeting, the twins realized they were not alone. Few of the newer franchisees were making money. Franchising, once a cash cow, was turning into the company's Achilles' heel. Many franchise owners contend that The Body Shop has made overly optimistic verbal and written representations, then turned on the owners viciously when they raised questions about supply problems, tainted products, and a dubious business model. After writing Roddick about their dissatisfaction, the twins ultimately hired a lawyer and informed The Body Shop that they were prepared to sue to get out from under their franchise.

While new franchises struggled and formerly successful shops saw sales drop, the company itself, which by the late 1980s was raking in millions of dollars in franchise-related fees, initially felt little pain. As the parent company grew, it set tighter specifications on store design, lease terms, and a myriad of other things to maintain uniform expectations among customers. But just as the costs and risks of starting a franchise escalated, The Body Shop began facing more competition. The Limited's Bath and Body Works, one of many copycats, took off like gangbusters, with similar quality but lower prices. The Body Shop's once-massive margins began collapsing.

"This was going to be a dream," says Stacy Benes, who owned a franchise in Charlottesville, Virginia. "I don't usually use this kind of language but there's no other way to say it: They fuck over their franchisees. Less than a third are making any money and most of them are barely making it." Benes recently sold back her franchise after an eighteen-month legal battle.

Franchisee revolts have flared around the world. In Singapore, Anne Downer and The Body Shop are locked in a vicious multimillion dollar dispute. I fielded calls from frustrated franchisees in Norway, Scotland, Great Britain, France, and Spain. At the suggestion of several sources, I rang up Dean Sagar, a senior economist for the House Small Business Committee, which oversees franchise legislation. "Yes," he says, he has gotten numerous calls from desperate franchisees. He reviewed their franchise-offering document and found it troubling. It's "the lowest common denominator" in an already sleazy business, he fretted. Sagar decided to discuss The Body Shop situation with the Federal Trade Commission, which initiated a formal fraud investigation in September of 1993.

The Body Shop's mounting financial woes are compounded by a host of other problems, from questionable fair trade programs to Environmental Protection Agency probes of the company's environmental practices to criticism of The Body Shop's signature animal testing policies. The Body Shop's brochures are careful—some say clever—to state that it will not use ingredients tested for *cosmetic* purposes. That leaves a Swiss-cheese opening to use ingredients originally tested for *pharmaceutical* use, and The Body Shop takes full advantage. For example, it uses vitamin E acetate, which has recently been tested on animals, in numerous products. In 1989, the German government successfully sued The Body Shop for falsely advertising that it did not test on animals. In fact, almost all cosmetic companies have phased out animal tests on products; The Body Shop, like many firms, uses *ingredients* tested on animals. As the German ruling came down, The Body Shop changed its slogan from "Not Tested on Animals" to "Against Animal Testing." It claims the change was long in the works and is less confusing to customers.

The Body Shop positions itself as a model of "green" practices. It has published two environmental reviews it calls "Green Books." But in a familiar story, The Body Shop's reputation does not offer an accurate picture of its problematic operating practices.

One of the first calls I received in the earliest days of my investigation came from David Brook, The Body Shop's former U.S. director of environmental affairs and previously a lawyer with the EPA. "I can tell you their environmental programs are just window dressing," says Brook, who now works for the New Jersey attorney general. For years, he says, employees working with corrosive chemicals were not provided with protective gear. Brook also went head-to-head with management for flushing nonbiodegradable chemicals into the sewers at their former manufacturing facility in Hanover, New Jersey, a direct violation of state law. And he was incensed about the company's nonexistent, but widely praised, recycling policy. "The Body Shop couldn't even give away its plastic bottles because the synthetic fragrances we used permeated the plastic and recyclers don't want it. We'd send it out to landfills. Roddick knows all this."

Operational disarray contributed to repeated product quality screw-ups, employees of The Body Shop contend. "The summer has created its own problems, not the least of these being the significant levels of microbiological contamination we have experienced in our Manufacturing and Production operations," a technical manager wrote in a typical in-house memo in 1992. "Bacteria problems showed up all the time and they were regularly ignored," says Barry Hudson, a production supervisor who recently quit The Body Shop. "We were told to treat [tainted cosmetics] with radiation or dilute it with more product and hope it would not test too high. It was disgusting."

"Call Scott Tackach," Hudson told me. "He's in quality control and still works there. He'll give you an ear- and eyeful."

Tackach ended up ringing me on his own initiative, calling me one evening from The Body Shop's new manufacturing center in Raleigh. "If you don't believe us, come for a visit. I'll show you," he offered.

A few weeks later, I flew to North Carolina and drove to The Body Shop's relocated headquarters. Within an hour of touching down, I was locked in the trunk of Tackach's Toyota.

"Are you okay in there?" he asked.

I rapped on the side panel.

"Let's go."

Tackach drove past the twenty-four-hour guard and parked in the rear, well out of view, where I was let out. He pointed out a yellow sign emblazoned with a skull and crossbones and the word DANGER in black letters. "The Body Shop chose this spot for its plant." he said. "This used to be a fire-extinguisher manufacturing company. Walter Kidde. It's contaminated land. But I understand they got it for a good price."

Inside, Tackach switched on the lights. "That drain connects to the sewage system," he said, motioning underneath a machine. "We flush chemicals all the time, toxic chemicals, too. Surfactants, the stuff that makes soap suds and we use to clean equipment. It spills into a nearby creek."

"See these spray jets," he said, pointing to a mechanical filler. "This shoots product into bottles. We're supposed to clean it two or three times a day. But that slowed things down so the executive staff ordered us to skip the tests, do it once a week. Sure, it went faster, but now we're shipping out contaminated product."

Tackach ushered me into his office and opened a file cabinet. The folder marked "incidents" told a stomach-turning tale of rancid products. Roddick, he charged, overruled managers and ordered products shipped even though they were infested with bacteria.

"This is the worst," he said, reaching into a cardboard box and pulling out a container of Banana Shampoo. I squinted at the label: 239N. "That's the batch number. Now look at this." He brandished a lab report dated September 3, 1993, with the same number. "We were running behind schedule, months behind, so they opted to ship products the day of bottling, rather than waiting for the test results. It was Russian roulette. This batch was already on store shelves when we got the results. Look at this," he said. "It tested 1,000 percent above industry max."

For what?

"For *e coli, pseudenoma,* and *enterobacter gergoviae.*"

What does that mean?

"That's like washing your hair with water from a toilet bowl."

The Body Shop did not recall or destroy the product as is required by the federal government until they got word that the Food and Drug Administration planned an inspection. Franchisees, told nothing, innocently sold more than 150 bottles of the contaminated bottles. After being contacted by Tackach, the FDA visited the plant three times in five weeks. According to documents obtained through the Freedom of Information Act, FDA inspectors found evidence of high levels of bacteria on filling machines, improper bacteria sampling procedures, and skipped microbial testing on numerous occasions. The Body Shop had shipped and sold a variety of spoiled products.

Another top-selling product, Elderflower Under Eye Gel, has also received FDA scrutiny. In 1992, the agency noted "a high frequency of complaints for allergic reactions after use of this product." The gel contains two different volatile alcohols that release potentially dangerous fumes that can irritate the eye. And franchisees have long complained about another problem with the gel: mold in the container. According to a November 1990 company memo to Singapore franchisee Anne Downer: "We . . . confirm molds are present. However, we have also tested the product and found that it has not been affected by the mold that is present on the cap. All we can say at this stage is that the product remains unaffected and is therefore safe for use."

A recent *Consumer Reports* analysis of The Body Shop's eye shadow made fun of the company's use of "silk powder." The magazine found that "in the unromantic environment of the lab, silk powder falls into a category of chemicals known as powdered polymers." The independent German consumer magazine *Öko-Test* (Green Test) slammed The Body Shop after detecting formaldehyde, which has caused cancer in rats, in the Vitamin E cream, Self-Tanning Lotion, Carrot Moisture Cream, and Mama Toto Baby Cream, which is often used by breastfeeding moms. German scientist Dieter Wundram, who conducted the tests, says he believes the formaldehyde is a by-product of using large quantities of preservatives to mask bacteria problems. Says Wundram: "Their products are filled with bugs."

I asked Mark Constantine what he observed during his decade with the company. "I think they felt they couldn't afford [to pull contaminated products] so they definitely tried to reformulate them, or add preservatives, or do whatever they can. But like the Banana Shampoo and the Pumice Foot Scrub, those things are regularly contaminated. They still are, even Pumice Foot Scrub probably, I mean, Anita was quite aware when she rolled it out that it was . . . contaminated. They decided to do it anyway. . . ."

How could they do that?

"Because I would say that is very normal cosmetic company procedure."

That's not true for the natural products industry, however. Rishi Schweig, president of FeatherRiver, which distributes personal care products to health food stores, says of Roddick's cosmetics: "If you take The Body Shop name off the products and put 'Payless Drug Store' on the label, you get an idea of the products' quality."

Even The Body Shop's own suppliers are critical, and in one case, went on the record with its opinion. Lipo Chemical vice president Steven Greenberg dismissed The Body Shop's products for using "outdated formulations." "They claim all these wonderful things about their products that just aren't true," he said. "It's all marketing . . . their products are average at best."

According to suppliers and consultants, The Body Shop turned to cheap, off-the-shelf recipes after Mark Constantine left the company in the mid-1980s and took many formulations with him. For this article, I arranged for a chemist, an organic products expert, and a consumer activist who has published more than ten books on beauty care to review a cross section of The Body Shop's products. They found several "natural" products lacking natural ingredients. For example, the "full disclosure" manual on display in stores claims that The Body Shop's popular Hair Gel is based on an ancient custom: "Girls from Hamar in South Ethiopia traditionally styled their hair with ochre, butter, and acacia gum." The assessment from the trio of experts was not nearly so exotic. It's made up mostly of water. Its primary active ingredient, PVP/VA copolymer, has been found to cause tumors in rats when injected, and can be toxic when inhaled. The Body Shop's Hair Gel is based on southern Ethiopian ingredients in the same way nylon is inspired by silk.

The Body Shop has staked much of its reputation on what it calls "Trade Not Aid" ventures: no handouts; trade with natives and economically disadvantaged workers; let capitalism work for everybody. "First-world wages for third-world goods," Roddick proclaims at every opportunity.

The villagers in Ixmiquilpan, Mexico, are still waiting for their "first-world wages." After the video crews had wrapped and the American Express commercial was in the can, the Nañhu women organized a big celebration to fete Roddick. They cobbled together a choir of local children who entertained with songs and dances. Roddick watched for a while but could not get over how stiff everyone seemed. "This is wonderful," she whispered to Alison Rockett, the young location scout, "but no one is dancing."

"They are too shy," Rockett whispered back. Roddick was undeterred. "She winked at me. She wanted to rev things up so she dragged me out into the middle of this basketball court and started to dance."

One of the bands played norteña music, a mixture of Tex-Mex and Mexican mariachi. Anita and Alison had no clue how to dance to it so they improvised, wiggling their bodies, and making faces. After a few minutes, they dragged the women onto the court to form a conga line. "They all had their special shoes on, and she got them all in this line behind her and I had to tell them what to do. She would do all these funny movements and they had to imitate. She had great charm and charisma." It was a spontaneous and loving moment.

After the party, the caterers packed away their omelet pans and white tablecloths and Roddick and her entourage took off.

But in the months that followed, neither the money, nor the gifts, nor the increased orders for scrub mitts materialized. Roddick had raised expectations to the sky and now Alison Rockett and anthropologist Peter Winkel had to bring them back down to earth.

"I felt like I was running a fire brigade," remembers Winkel.

"Anita broke every rule in Anthropology 101," Rockett adds. "In the days after she left, people were abuzz with talk of presents that this white goddess was going to send them. People get so angry, but never with Anita. They blame the rest of us. We are the bad guys for not delivering on her promises. Months after she left, people were still saying 'Where's my tortilleria?' "

Roddick apparently does not grasp how erratic her behavior appears to the Nañhu.

"I always have to ask for permission to go into a market," she solemnly told a group of business students and faculty at Stanford University recently. "And asking for permission means I spend a year or so in that country working with indigenous groups. It's almost like I have to earn my right of passage. That's what we did in Mexico." She said this with no trace of hypocrisy, no recognition that it was a fabrication. The audience applauded wildly. The American Express commercial made during her visit to the Nañhu ran for months and brought Roddick even more praise.

"Anita is a mythomaniac," says Mara Amats, a fair trade expert who set up another of Roddick's celebrated initiatives, a papermaking venture in Nepal. In brochures, The Body Shop claims that it has "revived" the ancient craft of papermaking in the Kathmandu Valley by commissioning a range of handmade paper products. In fact, says Amats, The Body Shop rejected the chance to work with UNICEF to make higher quality paper using *lokta* (popularly known as rice paper) harvested in an environmentally sensitive manner and instead buys cheaper paper. "She never committed herself to the project. They just made symbolic purchases. Don't take anything she says at face value. Anita instinctively understands the facile nature of the press and just plays to it. She has her head in the clouds and her feet in shit."

Consider The Body Shop's much-hyped Amazon rainforest initiative. Mostly on Gordon's initiative, the company has set up a Trade Not Aid project with the Kayapo Indians, who crush Brazil nuts for hair conditioner. While it is innovative and idealistic in theory, Amazon experts say it's been a disappointment. The project employs only about seventy-five Kayapo on a part-time basis out of thousands in the villages. They each make $500 to $800 a year—not exactly the "first-world wages" The Body Shop trumpets.

"It's more like United Fruit," says University of Chicago anthropologist Terry Turner, an expert on the Kayapo. "Don't be fooled by The Body Shop's benevolent exterior. Their project has been very disruptive for the Kayapo." Turner judges the initiative a gimmick. "It amounts to aid by developing peoples to The Body Shop with no real trade in return."

"Anita is very clever," notes Richard Adams without a trace of admiration in his voice. The former founder and managing director of Traidcraft, a for-profit British-based fair trade company, Adams now runs New Consumer, a progressive research organization that promotes "green" business. Roddick wrote the introduction to one of his books, but their relationship soured when Adams began examining The Body Shop's practices. In an analysis of The Body Shop's fair trade initiatives for 1993, Adams calculated that payments made to producers constituted *one sixth of one percent* of customer purchases—an infinitesimally small amount.

"Many of us in the environmental and development

movements in Europe are embarrassed," Adams admits. "We've been attracted to the success and high profile of The Body Shop but got our wings burned. It has a vampire-like attitude toward social responsibility. If we don't watch out, the public will find out about The Body Shop's record and become profoundly skeptical about business with high-flying ethical claims, and we'll be partly responsible by not calling the company to account earlier."

Adams met with the Roddicks numerous times in the last two years in hopes of encouraging them to be more honest and more cooperative with fair trade groups. He got nowhere. "It was like plea bargaining," he says. "They're saying, 'We plead guilty to the minor charge of making small mistakes or being overenthusiastic or perhaps telling the odd fib or two, but in exchange they are asking you not to go into detail about fair trade [or] about how The Body Shop started."

To contain the public relations fallout from its fading reputation among activists, The Body Shop has adopted a good cop–bad cop strategy. Last fall, after years of the corporate cold shoulder, fair trade groups were suddenly being courted. Traidcraft, which couldn't even get its phone calls returned, was dangled possible new projects. "By the way," one of its managers said they were asked, "did you happen to get a call from an American journalist named Jon Entine?"

Last January, The Body Shop finally released the $25,000 Roddick had promised more than a year before to the Nañhu for helping with the film shoot. "They definitely feel the heat from you," says Pauline Tiffen, of the London-based NGO Twin Trading, which helped bring the bath mitt project to Roddick's attention. On her recommendation, Gordon hired a respected trade expert to overhaul its relations with third-world suppliers. Meanwhile, Anita has announced plans to fund a business school in Bath, England, that will specialize in "socially responsible business."

But the bare-knuckled side of The Body Shop is also apparent. The Body Shop retained Hill & Knowlton, the public relations agency known for its advocacy on behalf of the tobacco industry. The Body Shop's solicitors sent a barrage of letters threatening *Vanity Fair* with an expensive lawsuit that would be filed in England, where libel laws are heavily tilted toward protecting corporate plaintiffs rather than the press. Their lawyers also verbally threatened Adams with libel action for discussing his concerns.

Perhaps if The Body Shop had not spent its entire history promoting itself as a model ethical business it would not be such a target. "They would be just another company with a few interesting programs and lots of contradictions," says Adams. But like a rebellious, adolescent teenager, it seems to want it all—unqualified love and the freedom to do whatever it wants without scrutiny or criticism.

"I was the first person who would have remained loyal, along with Mark," says Janis Raven, one of dozens of the Roddicks' former friends and employees who bemoan what The Body Shop has become. "It was a company we all built together. But Anita Roddick has no loyalty to anybody. Everybody is a slave; a new slave of the month comes around and you get dumped in favor of them."

"You know," Raven adds, "Anita's gone a bit over the top. She just disappeared up her own backside. She started to believe her own publicity.

Even with all the problems, no one can take away Roddick's remarkable success. She turned one shop in England into an international cosmetics empire. She has amassed a fortune. But when the history books are written, she is not likely to be remembered as the world's most socially responsible entrepreneur. Even if The Body Shop manages to retool its ethics, it is a company built on the shaky financial prospects of franchisees and the betrayed expectations of its idealistic employees and customers. Anita Roddick never could decide whether she wanted to practice her social vision or merely exploit it. She is one more beauty baroness who created her own myth to make her dream come true.

"She stands full square between Estée Lauder and Elizabeth Arden," says Mark Constantine. "They all wrote their own stories."

Body of Work

By Gerald Hannon

Killed: *Saturday Night,* 1994

I began this piece in the early 1990s, after I'd been hustling for about five years. Most of what I'd read about male prostitution focused on the sensational or the lurid, and though I can enjoy that, I thought I might offer a more nuanced view, from the inside, than one usually gets. I was well enough regarded as a journalist by that time to have the story commissioned by Saturday Night, *then one of Canada's most influential magazines. The article earned praise from my editors, but as it was being readied for print the magazine's editor-in-chief was fired. Conrad Black,* Saturday Night's *right-wing owner installed Ken Whyte, a smart, young, conservative at the magazine's helm.*

Whyte immediately killed my article. I wasn't surprised—he had previously worked for the virulently homophobic magazine, Alberta Report. *That gay might be good, that sex work might be worth serious exploration—these would be novel concepts years before homos had become mainstream TV fare on shows like* Will & Grace *and* Queer Eye for the Straight Guy. *Whyte did have a business eye though. A few years later, when I was caught up in a juicy scandal arising from the fact that I worked both as a prostitute and as a journalism professor, he tried to buy the article back. I named a price he couldn't afford. End of deal. But not quite the end of the story.*

think Baby Geoffrey did it. I mean, after Baby Geoffrey I knew for sure.

This is what happened.

It's a Sunday afternoon, and I'm standing in a hotel hallway, knocking on this door and a voice says "come on in" and I turn the handle and it's not locked so I go in. Across the room, there's a man sitting on the bed. His legs are stretched out in front of him, and he's resting his back against the headboard. He looks about forty, and he's a big man—six-foot-two maybe, and a good two hundred pounds. He's wearing white cotton diapers, and a cute little shirt with fire trucks all over it. The safety pins on the diapers have yellow plastic duck heads on the clasps and as I get closer I can see that the shoes, which are white, are monogrammed with a fancy capital "G" (which is how I knew it was Geoffrey with a "G"). There is a large, economy-sized can of baby powder on the bedside table. The man smiles at me and says, "Baby Geoffwey glad to see Daddy."

I want you to know that I didn't miss a beat. I just said, "And Daddy's really glad to see Baby Geoffrey, too."

I didn't giggle.

I didn't giggle until I'd left that room, forty minutes later and sixty bucks richer. I didn't giggle because I knew that Baby Geoffrey didn't want to be laughed at. He'd called me up because he'd wanted his diaper changed and his hiney oiled and he wanted Daddy to tell him about how we were going to go shopping and how strict Daddy would have to be if Geoffrey cried and the nice things Daddy would do if Geoffrey was a good boy. Geoffrey was a *very* good boy. So Daddy oiled more than Geoffrey's hiney.

I didn't laugh at Baby Geoffrey, and I think that's when I knew I couldn't pretend anymore that I was just dabbling in this for a few extra bucks. Fact is, I had become a prostitute. A whore. I had—I have—sex with men for money.

A few correctives, now. I am not sixteen years old, fresh off the bus, jobless, working the streets, hating myself and my johns, seeking oblivion in drugs. I am not, on the other hand, a sculpted, well-hung, muscular hunk who spends half the day at the gym and the other half leafing through magazines, waiting for the phone to ring.

And, because I know you're wondering: I'm not getting rich at this. And I have yet to do it with a Supreme Court judge.

This is what I am: forty-nine years old (though I'll claim thirty-eight if there are dimmer switches), with a plain face that can look alternately dopey and intelligent. I have a better body than most forty-nine-year-olds, though it is far from magazine material. It's quite a hairy body—a real turn-on for many men—though I shave my shoulders, back, and balls in the belief that the overall look is more pleasing. I have a great ass and a smallish cock. Excellent social skills—I know how to make men feel comfortable from the moment they arrive. I take pride in my work. I think a lot about what I do, and try to do a good job.

I'm also a frequently published journalist who has won two National Magazine Awards.

Perhaps there is nothing new under the sun, but I feel part of a new social phenomenon: whores with attitude, men and women who *choose* this profession, men and women who have perfected that most ingratiating of personality traits—shamelessness. But it is a shamelessness untarnished by insolence, by the bravado of those who suspect they are in fact quite as trashy as everyone thinks they are. It is a sunny shamelessness. I think you'll like it. I think you'll like us.

Enough about me (for just a moment). A bit about you. You're fascinated by whores. You see us along the streets at night, wide awake, authoritative, lithe. You imagine we know everything there is to know about dark and the city. You see our ads and find something funny about their calculated lubriciousness. You've been to the movies so you know our lives are a little empty, a little sad, a little loveless. We have hearts of gold sometimes—you know that, too.

Perhaps you don't know that your marriages depend on us. Or—and here I'm becoming just a little grand—that the proper business of any prostitute is to become a saint.

I sold my body for the first time at five o'clock in the afternoon on August 29, 1987. I did it for that most mundane of reasons—I was out of work, and I was broke. The decision did not strike me as the first step in a spiral of degradation. I had never had any theoretical objections to the selling of sex. It seemed not much different from selling my editorial skills. I had just never thought that anyone would pay good money to have sex with *me*. Like most people, I thought hustlers had to be young, hung, and full of come—or at least *one* of the three. But a friend who is youngish and hungish—and was the one real live whore I actually knew—explained that, in the skin trade as anywhere else, there is such a thing as niche marketing. "Sell your muscles," he told me. "Sell the fact that you're hairy. Sell your age—not everybody's attracted to young guys."

I put an ad in *Now* magazine, an alternative weekly and another in *Xtra,* a gay paper. "Massage Plus," it read. "Trust your body to this muscular, hairy guy. Relaxation and sensual pleasure."

I have become rather resourceful about refining that niche-marketing strategy. I have advertised the opportunity to "do it with a muscular, hairy, prize-winning journalist" (though I lived in terror for a while that "dates"—whore talk for clients—would arrive at the door hoping to have their short stories and poems massaged. Bloated bodies I can handle. Bloated prose is quite another matter). I've even flirted with humor: "Massage Plus," my next ad read, "I work my fingers to your bone." That works well, though not, I think, because men are amused by the rather sophomoric joke. Sex is not a laughing matter for most people, and this ad seems to attract a very particular group—the young, and married first-timers. Novices seem to find exactly the right degree of titillation in it—anything more explicit would make them all too vividly aware of what they're getting into. A year from now they may be wandering the demimonde in a harness and nipple-clamps but, for the moment, the vocabulary of the school yard is exciting enough.

I became a whore.

I have not kept it a secret. In fact, given the need for a constant stream of clients, it cannot be too widely advertised.

I want to give you a clear-eyed look at this one small part of my life. I need your trust—few professions have attracted so much romantic nonsense, and I'm going to ask you to forget the hearts of gold, the longing for a real relationship, the drugs, the emptiness, the hope.

I'm going to earn your trust. I'm going to have you join me on a date.

The phone rings. Perhaps six times out of ten the caller will turn out to be a married man (I've become so much more benign about heterosexual men since becoming a prostitute. For one thing, there seems to be so few of them). If he is very nervous, or very new to this, he will book a massage (my ads always mention massage for just that reason) and tell me how he strained his back/neck/legs/whatever and exactly where it's sore. I make sympathetic noises, and we settle on a time. The charge is fifty dollars for an in-call; sixty dollars if I have to go out.

If he's not so new to this, he'll ask for a physical description. I'm reasonably accurate (after all, we're going to meet), though I usually subtract ten years from my age and add ten pounds to my weight. If he's going to hang up on me (and many do), this is when it happens. If he's interested and the price is right, we book a time though I don't, except with regulars, book for more than an hour or two in advance. (I *will* negotiate. I also have a thirty-dollar student/senior rate. Many have asked for—and paid—the student rate. No one has ever asked for the senior special.) The no-show rate increases dramatically for each hour of advance booking.

If he does arrive (and I'd say three out of four do), he'll arrive right on time. Like Jim, this afternoon. Arrived at the door promptly at one. Jim is twenty-six, good-looking, has a tattoo on one shoulder, comes from Brampton, a bedroom community north of Toronto. This was his first time with me, and only his second (he said) homosexual experience. Jim doesn't like to want what he wants so badly. He told me on the phone I'd have to tie him up and blindfold him to make him do anything, and that he wouldn't kiss (I gather they don't much like fags in Brampton, and I don't think Jim likes them very much, either). For some people, bondage is an exciting, highly developed, highly theatrical scene. For Jim, it's just a way of saying the whole thing wasn't his fault.

He undressed as soon as he got into my room. And this is where the veil is usually drawn. You are just to imagine what I, a masterly pro steeped in the arcane knowledge of the erotic arts, could do to bring this young man wave after wave of the most intense sensual pleasure. Etc.

Let's lift the veil. This is what happened: I blindfolded him. Made him undress me. Tied his hands behind his back. Made him suck. I forced him to kiss me (in this case, *no* meant *maybe*. I understand the current pieties on this issue, but I sometimes think that only someone who has never read a book—or, for that matter, had a life—could actually believe that *no* always means *no*. Or, for that matter, that *yes* always means *yes*). He finally came, by masturbating himself. He got dressed, thanked me, paid me, and went home. We were together for about half an hour.

It had all the banality, all the ordinary magic, of almost any sexual encounter anywhere. What is dazzling—what I find almost humbling—about that scene and the thousands like it has nothing to do with my management of fairly predictable combinations of body parts. I am in awe before the extent, the power, the range of human need. Need is a seething presence beneath the polite fictions of our everyday lives. If need were a force field, the city would glow at night. You could hover above it and see the lines of light reaching out and crossing and missing and connecting, everyone pretending there is no light at all, everyone making their dinners, reading their books, watching their televisions. But I see it. I feel, on some nights, when I am doing an out-call and sweeping across the city on my bicycle, that I am tracking the current of human need, a current visible only to me and to other whores, a current that will draw me to Baby Geoffrey, or to the seventeen-year-old high school student who hasn't figured out any other way of meeting people, or to the Italian grandfather who's finally getting what he wants, or to the man who does nothing but tickle my feet and tape record my laughter. There can be needs so sudden, so urgent, that I am called from shopping malls, from bars, from the lobbies of cinemas. There are needs so ordinary they can be satisfied simply by an orgasm in the presence of another warm, receptive body. And needs of quite Byzantine complexity. (I have given philosophy lectures in the nude. Had sex with someone who could be excited only by touching the fillings in my teeth. Been videotaped in a wrestling scene by a gentleman who brought along both the wrestling outfits and my opponent.) There are the occasional calls from women. There are the endless needs of married men—gay men who married back when they felt they had to, who love their children, who want the marriage to continue. Straight men who just seem to want to be on the bottom once in their lives.

And there is always, always, the need for my shamelessness.

The best marriages would be shameless, too—sunny and clear-eyed in the face of infidelities and sexual extravagance. Many are not. Men go to whores to save their marriages and, on the whole, I think that is a service we provide (though I have been responsible, I know, for the dissolution of at least one). Our shamelessness acknowledges, welcomes needs. And we have no needs of our own.

That is because the proper business of any prostitute is to become a saint. I don't mean piety here. I'm not expecting a call from the Vatican. I mean that I'm working, in my professional life at least, to obliterate, or at least subjugate, my own needs.

The thing that struck me about saints when I was growing up a devout Catholic boy was not so much that they did good things. Some of them, in fact, did very weird things indeed. No, what impressed me was that they had their needs and desires so carefully tamed, so managed—though they usually chose a life of denial as a way of making this happen. I've found that a life of excess works equally well.

I noticed it the first time I saw hustlers at work in groups. The boys often worked the baths (many years ago I was a frequent patron), and what struck me most, as they sat and smoked and talked and laughed together, was that they didn't *look*. Everyone else was acutely aware of every finely calibrated change in body language; everyone else was *looking*. But these boys, these talking, laughing, smoking boys, floated above desire, empty of need, loose and clumsy and drunk sometimes, but promising to be anything I or anyone else could want. I don't think I'm romanticizing them. Because I know now how they got that way.

Something changes when you've had sex with hundreds of men (I suppose, in my case, it's now thousands), particularly when you do not choose your partner. You discover, eventually, that there isn't much difference between having sex with someone you find very attractive and someone you think is ugly (though I should add that it remains difficult to have sex with someone I don't *like*). This is a revelation—particularly in a culture as image-obsessed as ours. When it starts to happen, it means you are witnessing the beginnings of the slow erosion of the power of need.

Need is always an engagement with the particular—a certain body type, the way hair falls across the forehead, the fullness or thinness of lips. When you discover that particulars are losing their power, when one set of particulars might just as well substitute for any other, you have taken the first steps toward a version of sainthood that only prostitutes can know. And you will be a better whore. Freed from the demands of your own needs, you will do a much better job catering to the needs of others.

I think I work harder at this than some whores. Tim is a friend of mine, an out-of-work engineer in his twenties who began hustling last year. (I take some pride in having been a bit of an inspiration for Tim. Without my example, he says, he might have ended up with a series of dreary temp jobs. It's always a pleasure—though an increasingly rare one these days—to corrupt the young.) He concedes that he has had surprisingly erotic encounters with men he has found quite unattractive, but he continues to cruise the baths regularly, intent on finding the particulars that still resonate for him. He's young, though, and still hooked on romance, that sticky need to see yourself as you imagine yourself in the eyes of another person. But I have hopes for Tim. That engineering professionalism is bound to carry over.

Prostitution has been the splendid discovery of my middle years. I don't know how long it will continue—even given the refinements of niche marketing, the pool of those men attracted to the fifty-plus age group must be rather small. I will never, though, lose my vision of a city luminous with need, my pleasure in its endless variety, my sense of self transformed by needlessness. I will always be a prostitute at heart.

I owe Baby Geoffrey a lot.

Chills and Spills for Children of All Ages

By Jan Pottker

Killed: *Mirabella*, 1994

How did a freelance journalist become the target of a dirty tricks campaign overseen by the former chief of "black ops" for the CIA?

In 1990, Regardie's *magazine in Washington, D.C., pub-lished my story, "The Family Circus," which chronicled the inhumane treatment by Ringling Brothers and Barnum & Bailey Circus of its workers. The article also explored the con-troversial life of the late Irvin Feld, who had bought the circus from John Ringling North in 1967 and built the company into an entertainment empire.*

In 1993, Ringling opened a show featuring child per-formers; I knew I had a new slant for a story: If the Circus treated its adult performers badly, how would it handle chil-dren as young as six? Ringling tried to cut off my access to its show, but I continued my reporting. My agent sold the article to Mirabella *magazine in December 1993. I received full payment for the thoroughly fact-checked article in spring 1994—then* Mirabella *abruptly killed it. I knew a Ringling publicist had disparaged me to the editor. I sus-pected, but could not prove, that the Ringling pressure had proven successful.*

Fascinated by the subterranean wrigglings my research had

revealed, I also shopped two proposals for books on the circus to no avail, chalking it all up initially to bad luck.

In late 1998, my thinking changed. A private investigator rang my doorbell one morning and informed me that a former Ringling executive wanted to meet with me—that afternoon.

At a local restaurant, I sat down with Charles Smith, Ringling's former CFO, who was in litigation with his former company over the value of his Circus shares. As part of his suit, Smith had charged Kenneth Feld with wasting corporate assets by using funds to carry out a personal vendetta against me. Over coffee, Smith detailed Feld's decade-long efforts to destroy my professional and personal life in retaliation for my 1990 exposé. He pointed me to an affidavit by Clair George— the disgraced former head of covert operations for the CIA (George had been found guilty in 1992 of two counts of lying to Congress in connection with the Iran-Contra affair; he was pardoned by President George H. W. Bush before he could be sentenced). In depositions, George admitted that he supervised a secret Ringling plot to divert my attention from the Circus called "Project Pre-empt."

To my horror, in an Alexandria, Virginia, courthouse where Smith had sued Feld and Ringling, I found years worth of surveillance reports on me. "Pottker intends to use her Mirabella article as a platform from which to research a book proposal," said one. "Pottker is departing to Florida for a family vacation (3/27) and is returning next week (4/3)," said another. The reports also revealed how Robert Eringer was paid to inveigle himself into my life under the pretext of being my business partner while actually reporting to George and Feld on my activities.

In 1999, my husband and I retained the firm of Gordon and Simmons to sue Feld, Ringling, and others involved in Project Pre-empt. In a deposition, Robert Eringer admitted, under oath, to duping me into believing he was working on my behalf while *he was actually on the payroll of Feld's companies. The discovery period is not yet over at the time of this writing.*

Recently, Johnnie L. Cochran, Jr., agreed to serve as our lead attorney. After endless delaying maneuvers by the defendants and their many lawyers, a trial is scheduled for September 2004.

Since the first American circus performed in Philadelphia in 1793, children have blustered to their parents, "I'm going to run away and join the circus." In its latest extravaganza, entitled "Children of the Rainbow," Ringling Bros. and Barnum & Bailey, the country's largest circus, is showing just what kids really find when they join the three rings.

The focus of "Children of the Rainbow" is on performers as young as six. Although children have often been part of circus performances, this particular show represents the largest assembly of youngsters in Ringling Bros.' history. From its opening in early 1993 until it ends in November 1994, the stunts performed by "Children of the Rainbow" are expected to draw an audience of more than eleven million people. As the circus's Red Unit travels more than thirty thousand miles from its home base in Sarasota, Florida, to ninety-seven cities, annual revenue is estimated at as much as $100 million.

The forty-five Rainbow Children include "human juggling balls," contortionists, and acrobats. Some of them are trained to ride a buffalo weighing nearly a ton through a hoop of fire; others are thrown about ten feet above the ground to be caught by an adult performer. By the time a concerned fan might wonder about the children's safety, the circus has likely moved on to the next town.

Circus promotions hype the "normal" life of circus young-sters. Ringling's videotape promoting "Children of the Rainbow" assures viewers that circus kids have "plenty of time to have fun."

But anyone who sees the Ringling work and travel schedule might question how much fun could be had by the children of the circus. Young people ages six to sixteen years work Feld's show for two years, performing nearly every day except when they travel on the Circus-owned train to a different city. They are usually under the spotlight at least once a day, and often twice, for a two and one-half hour show. Out of the ring, they may perform additional work, such as animal care. Some weekends mean "six packs": three shows on Saturday, followed by three shows on Sunday. The children receive two extended breaks; a sixteen-day summer layover in May, and five weeks at the end of the year. Kids must keep up their practice schedules, however, during these intermissions.

In large cities like New York, the children labor as many as fourteen days in a row with no day off. Sometimes, Ringling schedules performances in two large cities consecutively. Between the first Baltimore appearance on March 16 of this year, for example, and the last show in Washington, D.C., on April 11, the children will work twenty-six days with only one day off. This schedule gives new meaning to Ringling's traditional end-of-show farewell: "May all your days be circus days!"

And the hours are long. "On a three-show day, "we would get to the arena at nine in the morning and not leave until 10:30 or 11:00 at night," recalls Kristopher Antekeier, author of *Ringmaster: My Year on the Road with "The Greatest Show on Earth."*

A nationally recognized expert on child performers, Bennett Leventhal, M.D., chairman of the department of psychiatry at the University of Chicago reviewed the Ringling show itinerary.

He comments, "I have never seen a child who has worked at this level of intensity or at a schedule that is this grueling. It is a grueling schedule for an adult, let alone a child. This is a time when developing peer relationships, and having time to play is so important but these kids are on the road all the time. I could see this schedule—for kids who really wanted to do it—for two months. But two years is a large piece of their life, even for those who travel with their family."

Dr. Leventhal continued: "If we were talking about children of migrant workers, you'd say, 'My God, this is outrageous. We need to protect these children.' But because it's the circus, and the circus is 'fun,' we look at it differently. And I don't see that this is terribly different."

Kenneth Feld, forty-five, owner of Ringling Bros., has gone into places like Chicago's Cabrini housing project to pluck out impoverished kids and dangle circus glamour before them. But the Greatest Show on Earth may be as risky as street life for the "Chicago Kidz," as Feld dubs the children from Cabrini, one of the country's most notorious housing projects. Taking a running leap to bounce off a springboard, these African-American boys ages twelve to seventeen catapult over the bodies of as many as fifteen other children lined up on their hands and knees on a mat laid on the cement floor.

Feld, who refused to be interviewed for this article, needs a constant supply of fresh talent for his company, the largest live-entertainment business in the world. He owns 82 percent of Irvin Feld and Kenneth Feld Productions, Inc., which has yearly revenues conservatively estimated at $300 million.

Feld inherited Ringling Bros. in 1984 from his late father, Irvin. The two men were as close as Chang and Eng Bunker, Ringling's original Siamese twins. Irvin was the music impresario who moved the circus out of canvas tents and into air-conditioned arenas. He also eliminated the circus sideshow of people with gross physical deformities, saying, "I can't make money out of human misery." Kenneth Feld has used the years since Irvin's death to strengthen the entertainment empire. Besides two touring Ringling circuses, Feld's company owns George Lucas' Super Live Adventure Show and six Walt Disney World on Ice shows. He also produces Las Vegas's top illusionists, Siegfried & Roy. With 2,500 employees, there is a Feld-owned show performing somewhere in the world every hour of each day.

Irvin's success promoting singers and refocusing the circus preempted any family life he might have enjoyed. In addition, the man who coined the term "family entertainment" was bisexual. Partly because she could not understand her husband's sexuality, his thirty-one-year-old wife committed suicide in 1958 when their children, Kenneth and Karen, were still in elementary school. The children were raised by an aunt and uncle while Irvin traveled the world in search of brand-new circus acts.

Even urban America's teeming housing projects won't be able to sate the Circus' hunger for acts, so Kenneth Feld, like his father before him, travels throughout the world seeking foreign blood for Ringling. For this year's show, a number of Feld-hired foreign children perform, some with their families and some with a trainer who also serves as their guardian during the two-year run.

The Children of Cherepovets are Russian boys and girls ages nine to seventeen who perform stunts with each other and with the Chicago Kidz. A young girl, for example, is twirled by one extremity over the floor as a clown jumps over her. Another typical trick is for the boys to jump rope with another child sitting on their shoulders. This stunt worries medical experts.

"It concerns me to see a boy jumping up and down, holding

a younger child on his shoulders," says Dr. Jerome McAndrews, vice president for professional affairs at the American Chiropractic Association. "You can see the terrible force on the boy's legs and knees when he accelerates upward and then lands with a weight on his shoulders."

Several children are repeatedly thrown up in the air. Twelve-year-old Youlia, also from Russia, must fly high above her trainer's head, somersault, then fall—headfirst—into a handstand on his upstretched arms. This act, as well as others, troubles John T. Langloh, M.D., a prominent pediatric orthopedic surgeon in Arlington, Virginia: "The biggest problem with all the Ringling acts was if the children weren't caught correctly after they were thrown in the air, they could land incorrectly, on their head or upper neck. They could fracture their necks or backs, or break an arm or leg."

Though Dr. Langloh notes that the kids on the Circus promotional video seemed in good physical shape, he points out "they could be predisposed to injuries to the lower back."

Gabe Mirkin, M.D., a sports physician near Washington, D.C., says that circus performers compare closely to gymnasts, on whom there is solid medical research. "There is a very, very high incidence of injuries among young gymnasts," he says. "A wrong move or a tenseness when you should be relaxing can result in a bad injury."

Dr. Mirkin adds that circus children could have a chance of developing *spondylolysis*, a stress fracture in one of the vertebrae.

Aside from the physical risks, the pressures of circus life could cause less obvious injuries. "These children can't draw on any experiences outside the circus," says David Scott May, M.D., a Los Angeles child psychiatrist who is an expert on young performers. "There is no counterbalance to their parents. The Ringling schedule is so consuming that one's identity *is* the circus.

There can be no attachment to anyone else; they are insulated from other children and adults.

"It's like being in a cult," he concludes.

Ringling hires tutors for the young performers, but both formal schooling and social interaction may be difficult because the children speak a number of languages. According to Antekeier, when he was ringmaster, eighteen- and nineteen-year-old showgirls with no education credentials doubled as tutors. Antekeier, who now serves as dialogue coach to the children on ABC's television series *Boy Meets World*, says Hollywood's television studios set dramatically higher educational standards than the Circus, where only the more prosperous families could afford to hire a private tutor. Ringling's star animal trainer Gunther Gebel-Williams, for example, employed a credentialed teacher for his own children when they were young. Others are not so lucky. Feld personally negotiates each performer's contract and has a reputation, as *Forbes* reported last fall, of being "arguably one of the tightest men in show business."

"Feld is a brilliant, shrewd businessman and I respect him for that," says Antekeier, but one who pays clowns, for example, approximately $250 a week, or $20 per performance. To make ends meet, some of Ringling's performers moonlight for the circus in a second job, like the showgirls who tutor.

In a 1988 interview with this reporter, Feld talked about how much he pays his performers. "They can't be doing it for the money," he said. "They do it for their ability and to stretch their limits to the utmost, for the perfection, for the applause. That's not a bunch of crap. That's real."

Feld may be right when he says the performers can't be doing it for the money. Besides Ringling's low salaries, there are also fees to be kicked back to the company. In 1986,

Antekeier was charged a porter fee of ten dollars a week for his room on the circus train. "What's ten dollars to a man who's as rich as Feld?" asks Antekeier.

Performers must also pay a quarter each time they take Ringling's shuttle bus to the arena. Feld, on the other hand, has a personal worth estimated at $300 million. He lives on his Potomac, Maryland estate, replete with a swimming pool and a Rolls Royce in the garage. His three daughters, who are the ages of Ringling's young performers, have an entire floor of the mansion for themselves and their nanny. They attend private schools.

Advocates for children fret the circus does not adequately prepare young performers with the skills to thrive after their show business career ends. "What happens to the Chicago Kidz when the circus no longer wants them?" asks Linda Golodner of the Child Labor Coalition. "What will they do with their acrobatic skills when they reach adulthood?"

One former television star who made a rocky transition to adulthood is Paul Petersen, who starred in *The Donna Reed Show* as a child and went on to write several books. Petersen is founder and president of A Minor Consideration, an advocacy and support group for former and current child performers. "You break away from the circus and what are your skills?" wonders Petersen. "You're double-jointed? That doesn't get you far as an adult."

Ringling abruptly cancelled my scheduled interviews with their child performers, but whatever comments the kids might have had about their intensive work schedule and their future prospects may be irrelevant. They are just too young to be capable of giving informed consent, say the experts. "What seven- or eight-year-old is in a position to say no to their parents?" asks Dr. Leventhal. "Especially if their work may be a critical part of the family's income?"

He adds, "And that's why this country enacted child labor laws."

"These kids are definitely working illegally," charges Linda Golodner of the Child Labor Coalition. Indeed, the U.S. Department of Labor's spokesman Bill Gross explains that federal regulations prohibit work for children under fourteen years of age, unless the children fall under special exemptions, which, he indicates, circus kids do not.

To hire children fourteen years and older, employers must meet specific rules regarding number of hours and time of day that is worked. The rules vary by the children's age: for example, a fourteen- or fifteen-year-old is prohibited from working more than three hours on a school day. In contrast, the running time for each Ringling performance is two and one-half hours, and there are regularly two shows on weekdays. The government also forbids young people this age to work more than fifteen hours a week, or to work later than 7:00 PM. There are usually thirteen Ringling shows a week and evening performances start at 7:30 PM.

"I don't know how the Department of Labor allows such a public violation of the child labor laws," says Dr. McAndrews. "This is beyond the pale. It should be stopped."

Petersen, the former child actor, concurs. He characterizes Ringling's employment of children as "medieval," likening it to "serfdom."

According to spokesperson Bill Gross, the Department of Labor has not challenged Ringling's employment of children. The department tends to focus on industries where minors are most often employed, such as fast-food restaurants. Since many child labor complaints come from parents, it does not surprise Golodner that understaffed child labor offices have not scrutinized Ringling. "Circus children fall through the cracks . . . There's no cop on the beat."

In states such as New York and California, which have stricter requirements than the federal government regarding child employment, the circus is obliged to follow local laws and regulations. Although New York, unlike the federal government, grants circus children a theatrical exemption, it still requires stringent adherence to safety and education standards. Nevertheless, crazy-quilt enforcement remains a problem: Child employment permits are issued to Ringling by the mayor or chief executive of each city where Ringling performs. Rarely, if ever, is there interested staff with time to make a site visit to the circus. And because Ringling brings many thousands of tax dollars to each city where it stops, conflict of interest is also a possibility.

When it comes to protecting children, Rep. Tom Lantos (D-CA) is one of the most proactive members of the U.S. Congress. "The Ringling circus is boasting of a shocking exploitation of young children in its current show," says Lantos. "Clearly, this is a violation of the federal child labor law if the Department of Labor has taken no action." Lantos goes on. "The jobs performed by youngsters from Arkansas, Chicago, Russia, and China are extremely hazardous. Whether they are 'defying gravity' or leading mountain lions and buffalos, these juveniles are at serious risk and our government should act promptly to protect their welfare."

When asked about child performers, Jerry Sowalsky, general counsel and senior vice president (and minority shareowner) of Ringling, replies that various states give circus children theatrical exemptions. Told that the federal government does not grant an exemption, he responds, "I'm not sure which rules you're specifically referring to. I'll have to go back into our files. Before we did this show, we did a lot of research into what the requirements were. Obviously, we have a huge investment. . . ."

A promised return call never materialized.

Feld claims that the circus is simply in his performers' blood and that they take risks for love of a challenge. He explained his negotiating philosophy in an earlier interview: "I say, 'Look. I can't pay you what your life is worth, so this is what I can pay you. You either want to do it or you don't.'"

It was said of Kenneth's father Irvin that he left the arena at the start of a high-wire act. He couldn't stand to watch young people take such risks. Kenneth Feld seems to have no such qualms.

Mascots Reign at Fall Show

By Neil Steinberg

Killed: *Granta,* 1995

Writing has a way of falling into patterns, and breaking those forms can jar all those involved. I wrote the following short story as a parody of the trade publications I sometimes worked for, building it around the enormous annual restaurant show held in Chicago.

It was originally written for National Lampoon, where I was a contributing editor. But the Lampoon folded before they could publish it. So I sent it to Granta, the British journal. They had published an essay of mine on the National Spelling Bee, and were using my name in ads—Günter Grass on this, Martin Amis on that, Neil Steinberg on spelling bees. I figured it meant they liked me.

Nevertheless, I was surprised when Granta's deputy editor called me from London with good news.

"It's perfect for our food issue," she said.

"Then you're accepting it?" I said. "I can officially be excited?"

"Yes," she said.

"Because," I said, adding something I'll regret to my grave, "I've never had a piece of fiction published before."

There was a long silence.

"Wot, it's fiction?" she said. "It's not true?"

"Of course it's not true," I told her. "The Jolly Green Giant is a character in it, lying on a chaise like a Thai Buddha. How could it be true?"

"Well," she said. "We thought that was a journalistic conceit."

They should have published it anyway—Granta runs fiction. But what greater compliment for a work of fantasy fiction than for somebody to think it was true. Though for the life of me, I can't imagine how, a sentiment I think you'll soon share.

Big Boy is in the ready room, having his pompadour teased and airing out his crotch. He slouches in the stylist's chair, legs apart, naked from the waist down. His famous red-and-white checkered overalls are draped across a ratty couch. Near the couch sits a tray piled with dozens of Big Boy Burgers, cold and untouched, sent over by a local franchisee. Each burger is wrapped in grease-soaked yellow paper, the paper spangled with little running Big Boys, hefting their namesake burgers overhead and smiling happily at the world.

The genuine article grimaces and roughly slaps wide swaths of talc powder over his giant, hairless belly and flame red thighs. He is a tad over eight feet tall, according to his bio sheet, but has the genitalia of a five-year-old—a fact not mentioned in the press material, but readily apparent.

"If McDonald's would've put an extra dime into their Big Mac we'd have sunk fifteen years ago," he says, his voice thick and phlegmy. He turns his massive head toward a visitor, slowly, lest the torque snap his neck.

"Off the record," he adds quickly, and winks.

Once a pair of stylists in white tunics finish applying hair goo to Big Boy's upswept, Reaganesque coif, he grips the chair's armrests, hard, and with enormous effort, plus help from the stylists, hauls himself to his feet. When he turns to accept the overalls, he flashes a glimpse of his aluminum neck brace, de rigueur for someone whose head constitutes a third of his body weight.

He dresses, slowly, as if underwater. By the time he has finished, his forehead is beaded with sweat. Big Boy sticks out an arm to brace himself against a squirming stylist—sitting back down would be too much trouble. His face goes blank.

"I hate this," he says, in a slurry whisper.

"It's four o'clock, Mr. Boy," murmurs a nervous woman clutching a clipboard. Big Boy comes alive, smearing his hands over his face as if to wipe it clean. He scratches himself vigorously about the privates, then grins largely and plunges through a metal door into the chaos of the Forty-fourth Annual International Food and Restaurant Convention.

Tens of thousands of people mill past booths in Chicago's gigantic McCormick Place. So much to look at, the eye dances over the jarring graphics, waving flags, pulsating signs, flashing, rotating displays, dancing models, and walking food containers. All manner of sounds fill the air—the gargling flap of a multitude of voices, punctuated occasionally by the oddly familiar shriek, copyrighted maniacal laugh, or trademark whoop, not to mention the competing blare of electronic music, trumpets, gongs, sirens, and bells. Somewhere a calliope plays the circus theme: "brup-pup-puddah-duddah brup-pup puh duh . . ."

A small blimp, powered by electric motors, drifts overhead and stops. "Hey down there!" a canned voice calls. "Have you been to the Kraft Cheese-o-rama? Booth twelve on the Main

Floor. Kraft Cheese-o-rama. Get going! See the big cheese show. Cheese cheese cheese cheese!" Then the blimp moves off. Ten yards away, it stops and repeats the spiel. High above the crowded hall, half a dozen other blimps float gently in the distance.

The blimps can be viewed at eye level by those in the corporate suites ringing the main floor. In Suite 304A, a pair of men in baggy suits sit, their backs to the window, side by side at a table, taking notes. A moment passes.

"That will be all," says the older man, briskly. "Thank you." The clown gathers up his balls, a bit wearily, and, uttering little gratitudes, bows backward out of the room. A female secretary at the door sees him out, then looks, questioningly at the men, who shuffle their papers. It is utterly quiet—no noise from the hall seeps through the thick windows. The older man turns to the younger.

"Well?" he says.

"It's after four," says the younger, gesturing to his watch. "We're supposed to be down on the floor."

"Are we finished?" asks the older.

The younger consults a clipboard. "Three more."

"Let's get this over with," says the older.

"We'll miss him doing it," says the younger. "He's expecting us."

"So we miss it," replies the older. "He'll cope, and if he doesn't . . ." The man shrugs, then nods to the woman at the door. "Bring in the next one."

She opens the door and steps back. The Gouda Baby is brought in, pushed in a wheelchair by a small, middle-aged lady with an anxious expression.

The two men sit straighter in their chairs and gaze intently at the Gouda Baby. One of the rash of dysplastic infants, the Gouda Baby is actually not a baby at all, but a twenty-three-year-old who, despite his age, has the appearance of a four-month-old infant, albeit one that weighs 110 pounds and is three feet tall. "Gouda" was originally a description of his disconcertingly large, round, reddish cheeks, but for the past three years has also been his professional name.

"Good afternoon," says the younger man, standing up and reaching far over the desk, extending a hand. "We've admired your work with Hickory Farms." The older man looks down, fidgeting with an enamel pin on his lapel.

The anxious woman pushes the Gouda Baby's wheelchair as close to the table as possible. The Gouda Baby, who up to this point has seemed asleep, abruptly thrusts a pudgy hand in the general vicinity of the younger man, the elbow receiving a bit of guidance by the woman behind him, who introduces herself as the Gouda Baby's assistant but whom the two men assume, correctly, is actually his mother. The younger man snags the Gouda Baby's hand and shakes it, the baby's fleshy arm wangling loosely behind as he does.

Weighing as much as a compact car and with a head the size of a garbage can, Big Boy immediately draws attention. People in the convention hall freeze, gaping. Some wave or call out his name. Others whip out pocket cameras and snap pictures.

Moving slowly on his stubby legs, at the center of a flying wedge formed by the Big Boy Burger Boys—six solid young men in identical checked overalls—Big Boy hooks his thumbs in his overall straps. Towering above his entourage, he smiles and nods, slowly, his head like a boulder teetering on a ledge.

A teenage girl slips through the phalanx of security and thrusts a pen and a pad of paper at Big Boy. His bloated fingers can't grip the pen, however, and it clatters to the floor. The girl is swept aside, dejected, looking for her pen on the ground.

Big Boy arrives at the Big Boy Zone and representatives wearing his face on discreet enameled lapel pins jostle each other, lining up to greet him. The crowd thickens. Far away, across the huge hall, people notice what's going on, drop what they're doing and instinctively head in Big Boy's direction, some at a trot. Tony the Tiger shows up at every strip mall, it seems, but a Big Boy appearance is rare. The Marriott Corporation, owner of the Big Boy chain, is said to be in horror over the possibility of an incident. They prefer to use college kids in paper mache heads whenever possible and keep the actual Boy himself under wraps, sequestered in his custom-built home on an abandoned oil rig platform twenty-five miles off the coast of Florida.

But Big Boy is on his best behavior, so far. He extends a hand to anyone in front of him, and people strain over each other to take it, although most end up shaking just the tip of one finger, as if grabbing the fat end of a baseball bat.

"Hiya, hiya," Big Boy mumbles. "Nice to know ya, nice to blow ya!" His voice is such a low, moist slobbering, as if his mouth were filled with cole slaw, that nobody catches his words. Nevertheless, every time his lips move, the nervous woman with the clipboard flinches.

Public enthusiasm is important—trends in the industry are immediately registered at the fall show. Futurism was in a few years back, as the bedrock of American business rushed to update their suddenly-fusty images. The Consolidated American Tea & Food Company, founded in 1837, changed its name to CATFO, and the etching of a Yankee clipper at full sail that had long adorned its products was etiolated into a pair of blue triangles. That year, there was hardly a mascot to be seen.

No longer. A quick glance at the displays of the major companies in the main hall announces that nostalgia is back, even if it is nostalgia for 1969, when Quaker Oats introduced Quisp and Quake, both of whom are here and looking fit. A dense line of people forms around the refrigerated semi-trailer where the Jolly Green Giant is kept, lying on his side on a chaise, like a Thai Buddha. He exchanges a friendly word or two with his admirers as they file by. A boiled spinach smell hangs in the humid air.

The tone is more subdued at Kentucky Fried Chicken. Attendees shuffle, heads bowed, past Colonel Sanders, embalmed in his glass coffin. At Pillsbury, Poppin' Fresh signs autographs for a long procession of fans. He is perched on a stack of phone books, making small talk, laughing that particular tee-hee-hee giggle of his and rolling his cow eyes. A miniature pen is stuck in his fluffy stump of a hand, and he keeps leaving traces of himself over the "I Met the Doughboy at Food/Rest/Con '95" notepaper he is signing. A closer look reveals that his skin has the tendency to collect dirt—grit, chips of glass, a stray black pubic hair, even a paperclip—pressed into the soiled dough.

The sound of thunder and heavy rain nearby draws attention to a circular stage shrouded in a silver curtain. Lights flash and speakers boom, and the curtain flies up to reveal the Morton Salt Girl.

There have been perhaps twenty Morton Salt girls—they replace them every few years. This one is a pistol. Maybe eighteen, with bobbed black hair. Big dark eyes, a full, pouting mouth. She wears a short, yellow, baby-doll dress and black patent leather shoes. With the slightest motion the dress flies up and she flashes a pair of tiny yellow panties. Dozens of businessmen cluster around the edge of the platform.

The foul weather sound effects subside, and the Salt Girl, twirling her enormous umbrella, skips her way once around the stage, pouring a trail of pure white salt from the drum-sized blue canister under her arm.

"Morton Salt welcomes you to the 1995 Food/Rest/Con!" she says, cheerily. "This is the forty-fourth year of the show and the forty-fourth year that Morton Salt has been a part of it. Salt is a vital nutrient and basic dietary building block—deprive the body of salt and life is impossible. Salt is mentioned forty-seven times in the Bible, and was so precious in ancient days that the Romans paid their soldiers with salt. Our word 'salary' comes from the Latin word for 'salt.'"

She says all this in a childish singsong, accenting every noun. Only the first row or two of spectators realize she is lip-synching. Her speech continues for a while, punctuated with broad, pinwheeling arm motions. It ends:

> . . . whether adding zest to the most expensive French meal, or spicing up a bag of French fries, salt is the world's most popular seasoning and Morton Iodized Salt is the world's most popular salt. Customers who know you serve or use Morton Salt know that you maintain the highest standards possible. Turn to Morton Salt—"The Salt of the Earth." Thank you and enjoy your day!

She executes a valedictory twirl. The audience gets a parting shot of her yellow panties. The men around the stage disperse, after each grabs a handful of free salt packets from huge barrels designed to resemble Morton canisters. Everyone carries plastic shopping bags, loading them up with samples and brochures and books and magazines and coasters and branded change purses. The Big Boy organization hands out key chains—a tiny plastic Boy, in his classic running pose, burger held high. Soon the crowd strips the tables clean of the key chains, and another crate of freebies is called up from storage.

The main floor is mobbed, but only a relative handful of stragglers find their way downstairs, to McCormick Place's lower level—where the third-rate exhibitors are scattered amidst piles of cardboard boxes, splintery wooden pallets, and great gray dumpsters of garbage waiting to be hauled away. Here the glitter of the main hall quickly fades into forlorn displays of odd culinary devices and obscure foodstuffs—spiced apple rings, marshmallow fluff, Indian curry, egg timers, those multicolored candy dots on strips of waxy paper.

Straining on tiptoe to catch the gaze of the occasional passerby, a dwarf dressed as a pear hands out bags proclaiming ENJOY SYNTHETIC FRUIT! and urges conventioneers to fill them up from a cornucopia of realistic-looking NewApples™, NewOranges™ and NewPears™ ("Half the calories; twice the taste!") Behind him, a large, gleaming machine with quivering rubber hoses injects more NewFruit™ into steaming molds.

Bosco Bear, who arrived at McCormick hours before his call time, has wandered down the lower level. He extends a paw to accept a NewApple™ from the dwarf and, nibbling distractedly, strolls slowly down the nearly empty aisles. From the corner of his eye, Bosco notices Pop, sitting by himself, ignored, half-hidden by a cart piled high with folding chairs. Bosco's heart swells—ever since he was a cub he has loved Pop. Staring somberly at the dingy linoleum floor, Pop does not see the bear. Above him is a frayed banner reading RICE KRISPIES! A tattered, grimy sign on an easel proclaims HERE TODAY! LIVE IN PERSON! SNAP! CRACKLE! POP! Someone has taken a red pen and drawn a line through "Snap" and "Crackle."

Pop looks terrible—dry and wizened and trembling with some kind of palsy. His pointed ears stand out at right angles to his yellowish, shrunken skull. He can't weigh more than foryt-five pounds.

"I love your cereal," Bosco says, hesitantly, afraid of embarrassing himself. Pop scribbles what could be "Best wishes—Pop" on a cereal box and pushes it across the table, never looking up. "Sorry about Crackle," Bosco says, dropping the box into his plastic shopping bag. Pop gazes up at last, revealing dull, cloudy eyes.

"Yeah," he says, flatly.

Bosco lingers a moment, then he turns away, saddened. But he can't afford to be down, he thinks to himself. He needs to be up. Dynamic. Bosco looks at the clock. Only fifteen minutes left, he realizes. Better hurry.

Bosco tries to purge his mind of the awkward encounter with Pop. Now that Snap and Crackle are gone, few people expect Kellogg's to let a lone, fading Pop represent Rice Krispies. Supposedly, they offered to shift Pop over to Cocoa Krispies, but he refused to work with the monkey. Now the rumor is that a trio of giant, rapping rice kernels dubbed "R. K. Snap" is being groomed for Pop's job.

Ducking into the scummy, unmaintained men's room—there is only one, apparently, serving the entire lower level—Bosco turns his head to the left and notices another bear using the adjacent urinal. His face brightens with recognition.

"Hey, Sugar Bear," Bosco says, cheerily, finishing up. "Bosco Bear. We were at Denver two years ago. Remember: 'Drink Your Bosco Every Day; Bosco, Bosco, It's Okay!' He extends his paw, holds it out for a moment, then lets it drop, unshaken.

The other bear seems pained. "It's *Golden* Bear now," he says, sheepishly, running his finger over a purple sash across his chest that, indeed, reads "Golden Bear."

They wash their paws in silence. Both bears' fur soaks and remains wet even after using a half dozen paper towels.

"That's right, I'd heard that, sorry," Bosco finally says. "How did that happen?"

Golden Bear shoots Bosco a hard look. "Here's a joke," he says. "What's white and sweet and granular and goes in coffee?"

"I . . . I don't know," Bosco says, trying to play along. "What *is* white and sweet and granular and goes in coffee?"

"I don't know either," Golden Bear says, turning and walking away.

Bosco hurries after him, but he's gone. No time anyway. He rushes toward the "Up" escalators.

The Gouda Baby would give his eyeteeth, if he had teeth, for a cereal gig—sugar, golden, or otherwise. But he couldn't even get himself onto the Kellogg's short list. Too pudgy—try Campbell's, they said. He had nearly resigned himself to the idea of spending the rest of his life handing out cubes of smoked cheese at shopping malls. Then Marriott called.

The Gouda Baby had only a few weeks to practice, but everything goes splendidly. A plaster of Paris burger prop carefully constructed at home is set on the coffee table and the Gouda Baby is placed next to it. On a whispered command from his mother, he snaps from his usual narcoleptic near-stupor into an expression of amazement—eyes goggling, hands thrown back in surprise and delight, fingers splayed—that would look exaggerated in a silent movie. But the two executives seem pleased. The younger man asks if the Gouda Baby can do "the loft" and the baby spastically sticks out a chubby arm. He nearly topples forward as his mother places the heavy plaster burger on his hand, but then steadies himself. The men nod and whisper, and the older man hurries around the table to walk the Gouda Baby and his mother to the door. In the hall, a tiny elephant nervously probes the carpet for crumbs with this trunk.

"You were marvelous," coos the mother, stroking one of the

Gouda Baby's pillowish cheeks, as she rolls him toward the elevators. The Gouda Baby, already asleep, emits a snurgling sound.

Downstairs, in the pandemonium of the main hall, things are heating up at the Big Boy booth. The Burger Boys push the eager crowd back. It is obvious something is about to happen.

Big Boy is helped onto a circular platform, two feet high and maybe four feet in diameter. Next to the platform is a giant chair—more like a throne. Big Boy sets his legs wide, as if bracing himself. One hand creeps hesitantly across his hip, and the nervous woman with the clipboard, watching from below, goes pale. Big Boy's face darkens with concentration and anxiety. Two Burger Boys bring a gigantic plate holding a burger the size of a stack of automobile tires. The burger isn't real, but appears to be made out of fiberglass; the bread, beef patties, and cheese are secured by a barely visible bolt through the center. The Burger Boys grab his hand and slide it through a strap hidden under the plate. Big Boy gazes around.

"Where are they?" he asks, drool cascading out of his mouth when he opens it.

"They must have been detained," says the nervous woman with a clipboard.

A Burger Boy quickly dabs Big Boy off with a sponge mop and then everybody steps back as a fanfare of trumpets and French horns explodes from a hidden sound system, a blast worthy of the entrance of a Bourbon king. Air hisses. The platform shudders, then rises about five feet off the ground. There is an anticipatory flutter among the dozen or so press photographers and TV cameramen. The clatter in the great hall subsides. Even salesmen closing deals nearby pause and turn toward the Boy.

From Big Boy's great height, he takes a moment to survey the hall and the crowd in front of him. His face is calm now. Catching the eye of the nervous woman, he makes a quick, feinting motion with his free hand, then winks. Concentrating hard, he takes a breath, then *raises* the plate over his head, tilting forward slightly, the other arm trailing back, as if running. He seems to lose his balance for a moment, but then he catches and sets himself, like a weightlifter bracing for the count. There is a collective intake of breath from the onlookers and a smattering of applause.

Big Boy holds "the loft" position for three, maybe four seconds, then slowly lets out his breath and sags. His hands drop to his sides. The hamburger does not fall off the plate, even when vertical. The platform quickly descends with a hydraulic sigh and two Burger Boys rush to guide Big Boy into the waiting throne while another slips the plate off his limp hand. Big Boy turns to draw deeply from an oxygen bottle. Someone mops his head again, and a bald man with a small black bag places a stethoscope against Big Boy's heaving chest. The cameramen, putting on their lens caps and spooling up their cable, record none of this. The crowd disperses.

After a few minutes, Big Boy is coaxed to his feet. He makes his way slowly across the hall, leaning heavily on a pair of Burger Boys toward a side exit, where a specially equipped van waits to take him to his four-star hotel.

A green blimp, vaguely shaped like a pickle, follows the entourage, hovering above, haranguing them about the allure of sweet gherkins. Big Boy and his handlers leave quickly through a metal door. The blimp butts itself gently against the cinderblock wall above the doorway, hesitates for a moment as if puzzled, then makes a forty-five-degree turn, its little electric motors whining, and heads off in another direction.

"Hey, you!" it screams. "Hey hey hey. Howsabout a sweet gherkin to go with that? Wouldn't a nice gherkin taste good right about now . . ."

The Lay-Z-Boy Position

By Erik Hedegaard

Killed: *Details*, 1996

When I heard, in 1995, that singer John Mellencamp was still smoking cigarettes despite doctors' orders and a heart attack suffered the previous year, I immediately thought to myself, this is gold, pure gold! In short order, I got on the phone to my editor at Details, explained the situation, and said, "Hey, how about I go see this Mellencamp nut and spend a day smoking cigarettes with him? My editor, being no dummy, thought it was a genius concept. Shortly thereafter, I flew to Indiana, puffed up a storm with the rock star, returned home, wrote the story, submitted it to the magazine, was greatly pleased to hear that the editors loved it, and was subsequently horrified to learn that it'd been sent upstairs to the advertising department for a quick look-see. The ad department had only one thing to say: that the story would never, under any circumstances, ever see the light of day in the pages of Details. Its tobacco advertisers would lose their minds, pull their ads, and a boatload of money would be lost. My editor reported this news to me with a sigh, and right then I knew that the days of separation between editorial and advertising were truly over. And this was proved to me time and again over the next several weeks, as I sent the piece out to several *other major magazines who each had the same thing to say: love the piece, it'll never run. But it finally did find a home, in a small, ad-free literary publication called* Open City. *My payment for the story: two copies of a magazine with a circulation of about seventeen, which at that point was as good as pure gold to me.*

t's just this simple. If I don't quit smoking, I'm going to have another heart attack and that'll be it," John Mellencamp said the other day. He leaned forward in his chair, inside his recording studio. "I've got Monday as my target date to stop, but I've had fifty days like that. What a fucking idiot. I've got a wife, a one-year-old son, and a new kid on the way. I've got a twenty-three-year-old daughter, a fourteen-year-old daughter, and a nine-year-old daughter. I've got all these people depending on me, and I'm still smoking. I'm a fucking asshole. I'm a big fucking asshole."

Slipping a pack of Trues out of my coat pocket, I said, "Mind if I smoke?"

John checked out the brand. A Marlboro man since forever, he said, "Those are girl cigarettes. But lemme have one, man. Lemme have one."

He took the cigarette and placed it between his lips and fired it up with a lighter the size of a Sherman tank. He was down to eight cigarettes a day now (give or take a half-dozen) but during the height of his smoking career, which ended with his heart attack last year, he could put away 80 cigarettes a day, 560 cigarettes a week, 29,200 cigarettes per annum. He was a regular sideshow wonder. "Nobody could smoke like me," he said. "That's all I did was smoke. Cigarette after cigarette. After cigarette."

John took the True out of his mouth and held it in front of his eyes. Smoke corkscrewed up into the atmosphere and spread out and covered us all. He took another hit. "I just love to fuckin' smoke," he said.

"The difference between you smoking and me smoking?" John said later. "I woke up in the night to smoke. I mean if my eyes opened in the night, I'd smoke. I used to smoke in the shower and just throw the fucking cigarette butts down the drain. My wife Elaine would come in and go, 'John, quit ashing in the shower. And quit ashing on your plate at dinner. And quit smoking in bed. You're going to burn us up.' Yeah. I smoked all the time. When I was fourteen, I'd smoke before school, at lunch break, and after school. I got kicked off the track team for smoking. I got kicked off the football team for smoking—and I was the fastest guy on the fucking team. Now, I'm in Rome, it's 1981. I'm just a fucking kid with a black leather jacket, tattoos, and earrings, and I'm walking around this big fucking place, the Vatican. I pulled out a cigarette and started smoking. This guard came up to me. 'You can't smoke here.' I thought to myself, 'Oh yeah, I guess not. This is where Jesus lives.'

"I smoked on stage. I smoked while I was eating. I'm smoking in every picture ever taken of me. I smoked on David Letterman, although my publicist and managers said it just wasn't cool, like I give a shit."

At the time of his heart attack, John was forty-two years old, no longer young but not really old. He'd been in the music business for twenty years. When he looked in the mirror, he saw a pasty-white, cross-eyed guy with a big fat gut hanging off him. He thought nothing of it. What was there to think about? Then, one night, he woke from his nighttime slumbers feeling like hell. His hands were shaking. He roused Elaine and said, "Man, I'm fucking going to pass out."

Elaine pondered this and said, "You woke up to figure out you're going to pass out?"

Nonetheless, she helped him to the shower, where he smoked the life out of a cigarette and began to feel better. He thought maybe it was the flu. But a few weeks later, while getting a pretour physical, his doctor told him the god-awful truth. John didn't believe him at first, calling him a crazy stupid motherfucker; finally, he accepted it and said, "If we're going to continue this conversation, I'm going to smoke. I've got to smoke. If I can't smoke, I'll leave." With one artery closed, he smoked a cigarette in the doctor's office, later checked into a hospital, and continued to smoke there.

When he left the hospital, he left knowing he'd lost 8 percent of his heart forever. He left knowing a few other things, too, which he shared with me during our cigarette-smoking time together.

"If you have coronary heart disease like I've got," John was saying, "every time you have a cigarette, it puffs up the cells inside your blood system, as if it was rice or popcorn puffing up. So, if I light up, and I happen to be passing a blood clot, a *big* blood clot, I could go from being 45 percent blocked to a heart attack just like that."

He snapped his fingers.

"Boom!" he said.

"Jesus," I said, lighting up a smoke.

"Yeah," John said, "I could have a heart attack right now."

He maneuvered my True with certain silky grace, not holding it down toward the knuckles, as some smokers do, but somewhere near the tips of his fingers. When the cigarette went into his mouth, it stayed there as the smoke emptied out around his head, occluding it in a kind of ghastly haze.

"Have your various wives and girlfriends been smokers?" I asked him.

He twitched in his seat. "What do you mean various wives and girlfriends? What the fuck does that mean?" Then he relaxed a little. "Well, oddly enough, none of them smoked until they got married to me, then they all smoked. It was like, if you can't beat 'em, join 'em. And I never ran out. If you were in my house or in my studio, there were these boxes set around all over, literally hundreds of them, and every one of them had forty cigarettes in it and a lighter. It was a very sophisticated way of smoking, but Elaine doesn't smoke now and the boxes are gone."

John had driven a silver BMW 3251 convertible to the studio today. He wore blue jeans, a black sweatshirt, white socks, and dark, wraparound shades. He was four songs into the recording of a new album. On some of the walls in the building were awards indicating how his albums had done in the past. They had gone single, double, triple, and quadruple, and quintuple platinum. Because of his success, he's easily been able to find people to take care of his needs. He never has to carry a thing. No paper money or loose change weigh down his front pants pockets, and no wallet bulges from his back pocket. It's all carried for him. "If you and I was to go out to lunch," he likes to say, "you'd have to buy it."

It's a little different for John now. He's in need of the kind of help that's harder to find. Not long ago, in his quest for freedom from the smoke, he went to see a shrink. Right off the bat, the shrink wanted to know if John had ever had any homosexual experiences. He also wanted to know when John had last masturbated.

John hightailed it right out of there.

While we were talking, John said. "To be honest, I've always thought I was Superman. I've done what I wanted and never questioned myself. If I felt like doing it, I did it. I've lived like a force of nature. I'm the baddest motherfucker around. But now I'm afraid to walk out of the house, afraid I'm going to run into a cigarette somewhere."

He laughed (bitterly), shook his head, stood up, circled around to the coffee table, and plucked one of my Trues from its package. From the way he talked about smoking, I doubted he'd quit any time soon. It seemed too big a part of him, too much like an animal urge.

"What about sex?" I asked. "I bet you enjoyed a good smoke after sex."

Tipping some ashes into the ash tray, John snorted. "After," he said, "and during."

"Don't tell me!" I said.

"Yeah, fuck yeah," he said, coolly. "The best thing in the world was getting into the Lay-Z-Boy position and smoking, Puff, puff, puff. Yeah, head straight for the Lay-Z-Boy and smoke. I even used to smoke while I ejaculated. Girls didn't like it much but girls that knew me just knew that I was going to smoke. 'You want to have sex? I'll be smoking.' "

John chuckled, thinking about all his years as a smoker. So far, there'd been twenty-nine of them.

"Man," he said, shivering with some kind of pride. "World class."

The Hype Geist

By Larry Doyle

Killed: *Us*, 1997

Back before it became a supermarket find, Us would occasionally try to be a magazine. This would typically involve hiring an editor, who would attempt various improvements, and then get fired. In 1997, the mandate was to distinguish Us from rival People by making it fresher, hipper, edgier, and other adjectives of that ilk. Naturally, this involved imitating Spy magazine, which had been so hip, fresh, and edgy it was defunct.

The new Us editors called around to surviving Spy contributors, and I answered my phone. A few months earlier, I had done a faux celebrity profile of Beavis and Butt-Head for Rolling Stone, which unlike much current journalism, was known to be fake when it was published. I suppose Us thought it would be fun to do something like that again, only this time slightly different. I can't remember if the idea of doing a faux celebrity-style profile of a publicist was theirs or mine. In any case, I submitted an outline and was told it "reeks of potential."

A short while later, I handed in a fleshed-out outline/draft and received in return a detailed, insightful critique by the assigning editor. None of the suggested changes violated any of my civil rights. *The closest hint that trouble might be brewing, perhaps, was this:*

> *Our reading of the story—as outlined—is that it's a very arch, dark satire (at least by the end). We're concerned—and I'm not sure exactly how to put this—that you don't forget to have . . . fun. I mean, publicists can be psycho bitches from hell but their endeavors largely do not involve matters of life and death. In fact, that's what's laughable: they treat all this celebrity stuff like matters of life and death. The point is, the piece shouldn't read like one long dark note. Maybe the mini-dramas—is that my word?—should be thought of as mini-comedies.*

I set to work having fun, but before I could complete the revision—hence the Last Tycoon-*like italicized notes at the end of the piece—I was told the story was being killed. I have heard rumors that some higher-ups were concerned that the piece would damage their relationships with publicists and thus hurt their access to celebrity treasure. Ironic, if true, given that* Us *finally achieved its profitable distinction by ignoring publicists altogether, along with all standards of decency.*

Of course you've never heard of Petra Geist. But if it wasn't for her, you might not have heard of anybody.

Tis is her time.

Five am, when she is awoken by her trainer Danyel, until 8:30, when she hops in her black Mercedes 280z convertible and zips up the Santa Monica freeway to her Century City offices, is the one part of the day that Petra Geist can devote completely to herself—and to the East Coast.

"Tina! How are you, love?" Geist steps from her bathroom at 6:45, buried in a white Armani bathrobe, the omnipresent cell phone headset stretched around her towel-swaddled head. "I talked to Sly, and he *loves The New Yorker.* So it's a go. But we must talk about the writer, I'm afraid."

Geist walks into the second bedroom, recently converted into a cedar closet, and returns a moment later with a short black dress, which she lays across the bed. ". . . I *know* it was years ago, but Sly is an absolutely elephantine about these things. Besides, Sly feels, and I have to agree, that male writers tend to develop testosterone issues around him."

"*Tee*-na!" Geist exclaims, picking the hanger up off the bed and walking back to her closet. She returns with a seemingly identical short black dress.

"Tina, what if *you* did the piece? Wouldn't that be brilliant? *Copland* is Sly's return to his dramatic roots and your story will be your return to your journalistic roots; could be very essayish. . . . *Do* think about it." Geist looks at the second dress, puckering her lips critically. "Think a little longer than *that*, Tina."

"Now can we talk about a cover?" she says disappearing into the closet again. She reappears with a third small black dress. "I know you don't do celebrities usually . . . not *ever*, Tina, you did one for Malcolm X."

Geist listens, crinkling her nose.

"No, no, no. I am not suggesting that Sylvester Stallone is as *important* as Malcolm X," she says. "Never. But I'll wager he *sells* better. Sly is going to give you stuff nobody else has, Tina, the whole dark night of the soul and all that.

"All right, but do let me know soon. I can't keep not returning Graydon's calls. Love to Harry."

Geist taps the side of her headset, redirecting her attention to the most recent little black dress. She makes a soft clicking sound with her tongue, and shucks her robe to the floor. For several seconds she is completely, and astonishingly, naked.

As she steps into the dress, I cough involuntarily; Geist looks up, eyebrow arched.

"Sorry," Geist says, turning away casually. "I completely forgot you were here."

As the first golden haze soft-lights Los Angeles, Petra Geist is putting on her public face, the trademark cinnabar she applies in thick waves to her overstuffed sofa of a mouth. Her hair, a wet tangle of jet black prematurely spiced white, will dry naturally into an amazing wild bob that Beverly Hills's best stylists have yet to replicate. The ebony brows and walnut eyes consummate the look: here is the face of the most famous unknown in show business.

Geist finds that terribly amusing.

"I just don't know where that idea came from, publicists 'controlling' everything," she says, "From a publicist, I'll wager."

She has a high, disarming giggle.

"I'm like this mirror," Geist explains, giving her lips another glossing. "I'm a two-way mirror, with the media on one side and the clients on the other. I let the media see through on their side, but all the clients see is their own reflections. Ideally. That's all there is to it, really."

Few in the media would agree with that disingenuous assessment. "Pet Geist is the most important publicist in

Hollywood," says gossip grande dame Liz Smith. "That makes her the most important publicist in the world." But though widely acknowledged within the industry as the smartest and toughest of the new breed of female superflacks (which includes Pat Kingsley and Leslee Dart, both at PMK, and Peggy Siegal, the New York party planner), the thirty-five-year-old Geist is all but invisible outside show business; even so, she controls much of what the public reads or hears about celebrities, meaning much of what the public reads or hears.

"Pet has the power to tell you who you can write about, when, what pictures you're going to use and a lot of times, what the headline is going to be," says the editor of one large circulation magazine that covers entertainment on a weekly basis. "She has changed the way magazine journalism works; I won't say in a good or a bad way, but in a profound way. Don't use my name."

Geist is rubbing a glop of red lipstick off an incisor when her head begins to purr. "Call," she says, reaching to her ear. "Mira, love! How are you? Oh, yes, I know. The Internet is horrid. It's all just little boys, you know." I gather from the context that Geist is talking to the actress Mira Sorvino, who recently had the misfortune of being photographed falling out of her dress at a Geist-organized benefit for Orphans with AIDS; while Geist managed to persuade *Movieline* not to publish the shot as part of a photo essay on ingénue décolletage, the image made its way unto the Web, where it quickly superseded Alicia Silverstone's Batgirl as the download of choice.

"Excuse me," Geist says, gently pushing me out of the bathroom. "I must pee."

I eavesdrop; Geist is talking faster, lower, considerably less sweet. "I promise you this, Mira. The little bastard who took that picture will never so much as *see* another celebrity . . . I don't know there is any more I *can* do, love; I can't bloody well shut down the Internet . . . I wouldn't know where to start; I'll have a look into it . . . Mira, love, it's not that bad; you do have very nice knockers, and it's not like nobody's ever seen them . . . Mira, let's talk a bit later, when you've calmed down."

Geist strolls out of the bathroom, betraying nothing. "Do you know anything about the Internet?"

I begin to answer and she puts her hand up: another call.

"Yes . . . yes . . .

"Oh, dear.

"Tell me, is he? . . .

"Oh, hell . . .

"Yes, I will."

Geist takes a deep breath and exhales. "Well," she says, "this day has turned to shit." She then looks at me with a huge, theatrical smile. "Gone?" she asks.

I haven't the slightest idea what the question is.

"Lipstick," she says through bared teeth. "Is it gone?"

The offices of The Geist Company are extremely white, as is, not surprisingly, the personnel. The employees are also, without exception, female (they are known as "Pet's pets" within the industry). Geist is in no mood for introductions this morning, though, and blows by one junior publicist after another. They know the drill; none utters a word and more than a couple stare down at their desks rather than make eye contact.

Geist bangs open the door to her corner office with the heel of her palm. Behind a glass desk in the anteroom, a young thing in a black jumper looks up and flinches, cowering like a frightened animal.

Geist stands silent for a moment, collecting herself, and then in a dead voice: "Becky, did you get that folder over to Kyle?"

"I've got it right here," Becky responds. "I'm going to run it over at lunch."

"I thought I told you," Geist says, measuring her words. "I'm *sure* I told you, that I wanted it delivered to his apartment first thing this morning, before seven."

"I got caught up—"

"You got caught up screwing your boyfriend!" Geist screams, quite a bit louder than anything I've ever heard coming out of a human.

Becky leaps up, gathering up papers in her arms. "I can go over right now."

"Why don't you," Geist says, calm again. "They need somebody to ID the body."

Becky has no idea what she's talking about; neither, frankly, do I.

"He's dead. Kyle is dead. So I guess there's no rush on that folder."

Becky begins to cry. "I'm sorry. I—"

"What are you waiting for? Get over there and ID the goddamn body!" she screams again, and adds, cool again. "Before it decomposes too badly, love. And let's see if we can keep the *Globe* from getting a shot, shall we?"

The poor woman staggers out of the office.

"Stupid twat." Geist mumbles to herself. She turns and seems surprised to see me standing there.

"Listen, love," she says. "If you're going to be under my feet, we need to talk about what's on and off the record."

> A young documentary filmmaker whose award-winning debut feature chronicled his struggle to find a reason not to kill himself was found dead in his Silverlake apartment Wednesday of an apparent suicide. A preliminary investigation suggests that Kyle Baker, thirty-one, died of a drug overdose but police say they are continuing to look into the matter.

"No case is open and shut," said Sgt. Mike Scully. "Even a slam dunk like this one."

Scully said authorities had not found a suicide note, though Baker's film One Reason "might lead one to suspect that this individual was contemplating such an act."

One Reason follows Baker as he visits friends and relatives, asking them to give him "one reason" to keep living. This past February the film was awarded the Golden Cojones Award at Damndance, the film festival that was established in 1996 as a reaction to Slamdance, itself an alternative to Sundance, Robert Redford's well-established independent film festival.

Despite being heralded as "a dark It's a Wonderful Life for the '90s" by the syndicated critic Susan Granger, One Reason nevertheless failed to secure a U.S. distributor and was recently panned in Film Threat, which likened it to a "Sherman's March without the laughs."

Friends nevertheless seemed incredulous that Baker would actually kill himself.

"Kyle had a great career ahead of him; he was talking to people at the highest," said Petra Geist, a longtime acquaintance. "They saw his genius; it's a shame that the general public will only be able to glimpse that genius in One Reason."

One Reason will soon have a limited run at the Nu Art theater in Santa Monica, Geist said.

A black Richard Tyler suit today. She is in mourning. "Yes, Kyle is a client, was a client," she is saying. "But he was also a friend, a dear, dear friend."

Geist puts a finger up; she'll be off this call in a minute. "No, *One Reason* still hasn't found a distributor; that's what makes this a real tragedy. . . . Yes, I know you'll handle this the right way; thank you ever so, Liz."

The publicist touches a computer screen built into the top of her chalk white Philip Starck desk. "Becky? No more calls about Kyle this morning; too upset making. And see if we can't lasso Alicia on the phone."

She looks up and her pupils noticeably dilate. "Oh, this isn't what you came for at all, is it? Not the wacky flack-to-the-stars at all, I'm afraid. It shows you, though, behind the glitter, real human beings who cry real tears and grieve for their friends, who were so very talented and had so much to give. I went through this so many times in the eighties, lost so many dear talented friends. And now Kyle."

How long had you known Kyle?

"Only a couple of months, but we became so close . . . oh, hold on. Alicia?

"Put her on." Geist swivels away. "Alicia, *how* are you? . . . So Alicia, I've been seeing quite a few shots in the tabloids of you out and about without a stitch of makeup on. You must not do that, love. . . . I know, Alicia, but they take Sharon Stone seriously and you never see her walking around with no face. Listen to me, Alicia and this time next year, we'll have you on the cover of *People*'s 50 Most Beautiful and *Premiere*'s 100 Most Powerful. . . . Only *Premiere* then; *Forbes* if you like. Now, Alicia, how are we on this MTV thing? . . . You go in, introduce your favorite videos and say *Excess Baggage* just as many times as you possibly can. . . . You don't have to pick the videos, dear; they're pre-picked. . . . We know they're your favorites because they're all from the movie, love. . . . I'll see you there."

Talk about how Geist has a reputation of being tough. Some examples. Reporter interjects a gratuitous personal note: Last year Geist prevented him from doing a profile of Andie McDowell for Allure. He asks her why, if she wouldn't let him profile a client of hers, she'd let me profile her. She explains that she knows a little something about handling problem reporters, and laughs.

She's getting a lot of requests re Kyle Baker. She is setting up interviews with his parents, and booking co-stars on E.T., and the like. She discovers that Baker left behind a videotaped suicide note. Geist fails to hide her excitement.

Passage of how Geist rose to the position she was in, how she is "the woman who invented AIDS,"—from a public awareness point of view. (Geist demurs that AIDS was, in fact, a disease that didn't need any publicity, but whatever she could do to help, etc.)

Various other dealings with Geist. Perhaps we are at a big event she is throwing and having to deal with all these people being interested in Baker: producers wanting to know if he had any unproduced scripts, for example.

"He worked spontaneously," Geist explains. "He used to say, 'it's in the vapor, not on paper.' "

"That's too bad," the producer says.

The reporter watches One Reason. It sucks.

Back with Geist. A major distributor has agreed to pick up One Reason, which now will have the video suicide note appended to the end.

Geist is already whipping up Oscar talk.

Becky is fired in a particularly humiliating way.

Reporter tries to talk to Geist's clients, and finds no one will talk to him; instead they refer all the press inquiries to Geist herself. Geist chides the reporter for going around her, and sets up the interviews. The celebrities come off as sounding like Stepford celebrities.

A section of Geist wanting to keep her private life private, then giving up all sorts of tragic details of her early childhood.

The reporter receives a call from Becky. They meet. The assistant tells the reporter that "much of what Pet Geist says about herself is not true." That's not her name, and she's got to be in her forties. Also, she hints darkly after a couple of drinks, she *thinks—based on a discussion she overheard on the phone—that maybe the Baker suicide was a set-up. Becky was supposed to go over there and discover Baker before it was too late.*

Geist laughs this off, and paints Becky as a desperate ex-employee. Suggests that the real reason she fired Becky is she discovered she was stealing money from petty cash to give to her physically abusive, heroin-addicted boyfriend. The reporter sort of buys this.

End on triumphant premiere of One Reason.

Money Changes Everything: Coming to Terms with Father's Day

By Ted Rall

Killed: *The New York Times Magazine,* 1997

Some years ago, the New York Times Magazine *began running "Lives," a column on its last page. Ordinary readers were invited to submit essays about events that changed them, but I noticed that, in practice, many of the pieces that appeared in the section were by professional writers like me.*

I called a hip young Times *editor to pitch "Lives," which posited that my generation's resentment of its elders (Baby Boomers and other assorted codgers) stemmed from their penchant for irresponsible behavior. I thought that dissing my dad in a piece that ran on Father's Day would make an amusing counterpoint to the litany of "aren't fathers just the best?" pap that usually gets published on that Hallmark holiday. And I hoped that it would communicate to other children of divorce that they weren't alone.*

After I filed, my editor called with good news: the Magazine's editorial committee had signed off on the piece, which was scheduled for publication in June as I had suggested.

Weeks passed. Finally my editor called to say they were killing the piece. I heard that it had made some influential people on West Forty-third Street feel "uncomfortable."

As a writer I've often been surprised by what topics editors consider too hot to handle. We live in a nation with a 50 percent divorce rate, yet the media still ferociously defends the sacred myth of the rock-solid nuclear family. When I called one of my collections of essays "Kill Your Parents Before They Kill You," buyers for major chains that carried books about bestiality and terrorism refused to stock it unless I agreed to change its title. (I did.)

The Census Bureau reports that 27 percent of all American children live in single-parent households. They're more likely to grow up poor, become criminals, and get divorced themselves. Divorce is a major issue, but the mainstream media seems scared to admit that Leave It To Beaver is dead. At least during the '90s publications occasionally referenced children of divorce as part of pieces about Generation X (remember them?). Now they almost never do. You read more editorials and features about the problems of children in Afghanistan and Iraq than you do about those right here in the United States.

When I was a kid, I always dreaded the week before the third Sunday in June.

The Hallmark store in our local shopping center was larger than Kettering, Ohio, deserved, but I could never find the right Father's Day card for the man I saw during court-ordered visits.

Nevertheless, my mother insisted that our shattered-rump family attempt to maintain appearances, to retain a vestige of normality despite the facts. That meant dropping a few dollars on a card for "Dad."

Money and my father had been symbiotic words as long as I could remember. Mom and I didn't have and couldn't get it.

Dad had more than he knew what to do with but wouldn't part with any.

I was two when my parents split up. Dad moved to a high-rise apartment in downtown Dayton with abstract art on the walls and a pool on the roof. Mom found a job teaching high-school French. In a ritual familiar to tens of millions of Americans, a county family court judge ordered my mom to turn me over to my father on alternating Saturdays and Sundays, 1:00 to 7:00 PM, plus two consecutive weeks in August. Dad stuck to the judge's schedule with the pinpoint precision that he'd picked up at MIT, cutting his latest new car—he was partial to Pontiacs— into our driveway at the exact moment that the news on his radio came on at the top of the hour. We spent most of the ensuing six hours at the mall, watching action-adventure films, feeding quarters into pinball machines, and shopping for (his) stereo equipment. He never held my hand, put his arm around my shoulder or referred to me by name. "Son," he'd say, "don't ever wear your heart on your sleeve." It was good advice.

The stuff of day-to-day parenting—school assemblies, Boy Scouts—fell to mom. She taught me how to swim, worried about bullies, and unraveled the mysteries of fractions, angles, and logarithms. Dad didn't exist during the week. He never called. Dad was like James Garner in *The Rockford Files*. Both came on every weekend; neither felt real.

Dad, an aeronautical engineer, had been working on a supersonic bomber project for the Air Force when he left my mom. Only four prototypes were built, yet it turned out to be his biggest triumph. He invented the plane's movable nose, a feature later incorporated into the Concorde. I think about him whenever I see it.

He bought furniture and more art as he did better at work. Every time I saw his new stuff on those alternating Saturdays and Sundays, I hated him a little more.

One morning, Dad broke routine. He appeared with the principal of my elementary school at the door of my classroom. "You're going with your dad," the principal said. My first thought was that mom had died. As we left, Dad broke into a rare grin. "How about box seats to the World Series?" he asked, waving two tickets. It was a magical afternoon. The Reds beat the Sox. Reds shortstop David Concepcion signed my ball. For half a day, I forgot that Dad was usually late with the child support. ("Thank God it's too little to matter," my mom joked.) I nearly felt something like love for my father.

A few months later, Dad remarried.

Dad bought a sprawling new split-level to house the five stepchildren he'd acquired through Mrs. Rall II. Every alternating Saturday and Sunday he exposed me to the lavish upper-middle-class lifestyle that might have been mine if not for my parents' divorce. Dad and his new wife merged her children's photos with mine on the wall of the new house's family room, but my picture appeared on the bottom right-hand corner of the arrangement.

After the remarriage mom and I spent many weekdays downtown in family court, trying to force Dad to honor the divorce decree he'd signed back in 1968. First he refused to pay for my braces, an expense he had agreed to bear. Knowing that he didn't stand a chance in court, he showed up at my orthodontist's office a day before the hearing. He slammed fifteen hundred-dollar bills on the receptionist's desk and stormed out.

Although we never discussed money when we were together, I couldn't ignore Dad's latest rancid court maneuvers during visitations. I'd come home incensed at nothing in particular, unable to articulate my rage, my head throbbing for hours as I stared at the patterns in the paint on the ceiling.

After I got my first job, bagging groceries in a supermarket, I asked my boss to schedule me for as many weekend afternoon shifts as possible. I saw my father less frequently. Oddly, I felt guilty that I didn't miss him. Mom and I fought the battles of my rebellious teens, with others and against each other. She was always there, providing the moral grounding that my irresponsible father couldn't or wouldn't give.

In the divorce decree, Dad had promised to pay my tuition at the college of my choice. He didn't indicate that he planned to welch until the last minute. As I was packing to leave for Columbia, Dad called Mom's lawyer to say he refused to pay more than the equivalent of in-state tuition at Ohio State. I went to Columbia anyway. I paid $850 a month in student loans for ten years.

At age twenty-nine, I was still seething at my dad. I mailed him a nine-page letter listing my complaints. For the first time, he called. At his suggestion we met for a bizarre weekend summit at an Embassy Suites on the I-270 loop outside Columbus, Ohio. During the course of two day-long sessions, Dad admitted that he had never felt emotional responses. Love, hate, fear, regrets—they were all strangers. He blamed his own distant, Methodist parents for his coldness. Great: my dad, the sociopath.

His take on his cheapness was: "I can't do anything about it. That's all in the past now."

"You *could* pay off my student loans," I suggested, knowing full well that he would never try to repent for his neglect. And he didn't. Upon my return to New York I found a newsy letter from Dad in the letterbox. He obviously believed that we were friends now, that we could start afresh without revisiting the past. I haven't spoken to him since, nor have I thought about sending him a Father's Day card.

But I've reconsidered that holiday lately. Just because my dad wasn't a father doesn't mean I didn't have a father. This year on Father's Day, I'm calling my *real* dad. I'm calling Mom.

Living Well Is the Best Revenge

By T. D. Allman

Killed: *GQ*, 1999

Being in Tiananmen Square during the demonstrations of May and June 1989 was one of the great experiences of my life as well as of my career as a foreign correspondent.

Ten years later, it seemed time to go back to Tiananmen Square, and find out what had happened to China. GQ was enthusiastic about a story involving an exotic locale and telling what had become of three heroic young men, so I flew to Beijing in December 1998, and spent more than a month traveling all around China. After returning to the United States in January 1999, I visited New Jersey, Chicago, and California in order take up the threads of the lives of the three young Chinese students I had come to know best during those tumultuous days. A big layout was planned. The magazine hired an expensive photographer, and the students involved were flown to New York at the magazine's expense. One torrentially chilly morning we all stood for hours in the rain under the Statue of Liberty in New York Harbor. At moments, it seemed pneumonia might do to us now what bullets and tanks had failed to do a decade earlier.

I was very proud of this story. I felt I was doing justice to three lives, and through them, showing America what had happened in the intervening decade to a nation of more than a billion people. The day after the magazine went to press, I received a two-paragraph e-mail stating that the story had been pulled at the last moment. There was no explanation. I was devastated, but took solace from the fact that everyone had warned me a tidal wave of trivialization was sweeping U.S. magazine publishing. It was true that most American magazines were running far less foreign news than they had during the first Gulf War and, before that, the period when the Berlin Wall fell. There was also talk that serious journalism had gone out of fashion. I supposed my masterpiece had been replaced with page after page of bathing beauties or rap artists.

When the magazine reached the newsstands, I bought a copy—and found my humiliation to be complete. Sex symbols or fashion plates I could have understood, but it turned out that my story of three young men from Tiananmen Square, and how they fitted into the destinies of China and America, had been replaced by an article on the loopy multimillionaire Steve Forbes who had declared himself to be a candidate for president of the United States and, since he was rich enough, was taken seriously, at least until people got to vote.

To this day I am astonished that such an editorial decision could be made—that the narcissistic quest of the mediocre millionaire for political office could have been considered more worthy of publication than the life dramas of three young men whose lives intersected with so many of the great changes of our time.

My Chinese friend Steve figures knowing me has cost him $20 million.

"That's how much I'd have now if I'd stayed in China after Tiananmen Square, instead of going to America," Steve says one night in Beijing, as we watch TV in my hotel room while waiting for his brother to show up for dinner.

Steve—then known as Honghai—and I first met ten years ago in the crowded lobby of the Beijing Hotel during the very day the Goddess of Democracy raised her torch of freedom over Tiananmen Square. I was a foreign correspondent; I'd rushed to China from Libya to cover the world's biggest breaking story. Tiananmen Square was a cauldron of shared excitement, bubbling hope, and spontaneous human encounters. Within hours, I'd met three young Chinese, including Steve, who now ten years later, all live in the United States and whose lives are still interwoven with mine.

On that day in May 1989, Steve and I immediately started discussing the interrelationship in China of economics and sociology as the crowds ebbed and surged around us like currents in an ocean. Since then, our conversation has never stopped.

At the time, he was doing graduate work at Beijing University. But after the Tiananmen demonstrations were crushed, he came to America. For more than eight years, he's lived in Chicago, at first alone as a graduate student, more recently with his wife and their infant son. Gradually—whenever we'd meet in New York or Chicago, or converse by phone or e-mail—Steve and I would agree: We must return to Tiananmen Square together someday. Now, after more than a year of planning, we're sitting in my room in the Beijing Hotel, watching Chinese TV.

With its gurgling samovar and high ceilings, the room harks back to the days before Beijing got indoor ice-skating, Internet chat rooms, frontal nudity on the daytime soaps, and a new consumer class to go with it all. The TV announcer gestures at the on-screen graphics as though they're weather maps, but—sign of how China has changed—they're actually digitalized displays of the highs and lows making financial weather at China's stock exchanges. Ten years ago everyone in China talked about freedom; now everyone talks about money, and it's not just talk. When I tell Steve I'm short of cash, he says: "No problem. My brother will lend you a thousand." He doesn't mean a thousand renmenbi; he means dollars. Sure enough, at dinner, his brother, who's a partner at one of Beijing's glossy new law firms, pulls out ten hundred-dollar bills and slips them to me. A decade ago, when I stumbled into Tiananmen Square, jet-lagged out of my mind, the idea of a young Chinese lending me a thousand dollars was absurd. Today, a lot of those students can buy me and sell me.

Recently, Steve's brother bought his first car, as have many other Chinese who, back during the demonstrations, couldn't afford a bowl of cabbage soup with meat in it. People are driving Peugeots and Audis who, a year ago, didn't know how to drive at all because in China, just like in America back in the fifties, buying a car is now what's expected when you start making money. "What the Chinese want next is better, bigger housing—condos, town houses, gated communities," Steve says, as we go out on the balcony to look at the Beijing's new American-style skyline.

Ten years ago, from my balcony in this same hotel, overlooking Chang-An Avenue, the great boulevard that leads into Tiananmen Square, I watched the Man stop the Tank. I saw the statue go up and then, in darkness, heard the tanks crush the Goddess of Democracy. It was noisy when all that happened, but the noise was never so unrelenting as it is now—all the Chinese in their new cars which they've bought with their new money zooming around Beijing chasing more money. Ten years ago, cars were rare in Beijing: Tiananmen Square was a bicycle revolution. The students would ride out onto the wide flat boulevards by the hundreds of thousands every day, converging on the square. Even the different parts of the Goddess of Democracy—her torso, arms and torch, her head—were carted into the square on bicycle-lorries, and assembled there. Ten years later, bikes have almost disappeared from central Beijing, crowded out by cars. Bikes are now banned from Tiananmen Square—for traffic, not political reasons.

Since we returned to Beijing, I've noticed that Steve, too, looks more and more American—his body gestures faster, his speech patterns choppier—than the Chinese who live in China. Steve's teeth also set him apart. He's wearing braces. Since going to America, not only has Steve's accent gotten more American, his smile has become Americanized too.

For all his regrets about missing out on China's economic boom, Steve is not doing so badly in the U.S. Back in Chicago he's writing his doctorate in economics and paying his way through school by working in real estate. He started by scraping up the down payments on a few little houses by borrowing on credit cards. Now he owns or manages more than twenty investments. Since we got here, Steve has been meeting with young Chinese who are interested in buying real estate in America, but it's clear that what he'd really like is to develop some real estate for himself in China. Standing on the balcony overlooking the city, Steve is fascinated by the sight of all the new skyscrapers, and the lives and money that went into creating them; he loves analyzing why one project's profitable, why another has failed. But as I look out from the balcony, I'm fascinated by the many things I cannot see, because they no longer are there.

For instance the spy cameras once mounted on the tall street lamps lining Chang-an, and surrounding Tiananmen Square, have disappeared. All during the demonstrations the spy cameras kept taking pictures. Afterward, the secret police retrieved the videocassettes, and used them to pinpoint demonstrators for arrests and beatings. But the secret police didn't get all the videotapes, because even after the student demonstrations were thwarted, the hooligans—the criminal street gangs of Beijing— still roamed the shadows at night, climbing the lampposts and smashing the cameras. I liked the hooligans, and used to go out with them after the Goddess of Democracy had been destroyed, and the area around Tiananmen Square turned into a dead city. They called me "The Last Man in the Beijing Hotel" since I refused to leave after almost everyone else had cleared out to avoid the gunfire. By then, I was like those people who, the morning after the Goddess of Democracy was crushed, kept trying to march back into Tiananmen Square, straight into the rifle sights of the soldiers. I hadn't forgot bullets killed, but how could I leave when the story wasn't over, while the hooligans were still resisting?

Every night in my hotel room I'd pile mattresses up against the windows and the glass door to the balcony as a precaution against flying glass. Then I'd lie on the floor behind the bed, next to the phone, waiting in the dark for reports from my sources. Of these, Steve was the most faithful. Every night he'd call from a different phone; then one night, he did not call.

"Well, he's dead," I said to myself. But the next night, precisely on time, the phone rang. It was Steve. "So much happened," he began, "launching into a description of all he's seen and heard over the past twenty-four hours." "For Chrissake," I exploded. "You could have called." The night before, it had seemed normal. Steve was dead. Now my feelings were hurt because he hadn't phoned. Looking back, I think that was the moment our acquaintance became friendship.

I had figured Bao and Ke Feng—the other two demonstrators who I had befriended—were probably dead too, though they weren't. Bao, who now calls himself Jeffrey and sells photocopy machines for a living in Los Angeles, was one of the builders of the Goddess of Democracy. Of all the demonstrators I knew, Bao was the gentlest, the bravest, and most faithful to the cause. Of my three Tiananmen friends, Bao also has been the most cheerful in the face of adversity. Unlike Steve and Ke Feng, Bao stayed in the square until the very end.

The police later picked up Bao, and imprisoned him for four months. He was tortured once—hung by his wrists in handcuffs in the prison courtyard from a tree branch, in the cold, over night.

Bao was the last of the three to make it out of China, long after Ke Feng and Steve did. His fidelity to the cause cost him the most, financially as well as emotionally. While Steve and Ke Feng got support from institutions and individuals, including me, Bao paid his own way. He had to bribe Party officials to get his passport. Officials and lawyers rooked him out of thousands more dollars, which he earned working as a freelance graphic designer in southern China after he fled Beijing. "That first night in prison I wanted to die," he told me recently, while we ate lunch at a Mexican restaurant in Los Angeles. "Then I resolved to live. I learned happiness is not outside you. You must make yourself happy, every day, whatever your situation."

As anyone who was there knows, the "Tiananmen Square Massacre" is a myth. No one was killed inside the square that famous night of June third to fourth, 1989. Instead, when the troops reached the entrance to the plaza, the armored column paused. Following negotiations with the military, most of the hundreds of thousands of people in Tiananmen Square left in an orderly, self-disciplined fashion. But some people felt they had to stay, Bao among them. It's because there was no massacre that Bao, like Steve, is still alive.

"We gathered around the monument in the middle of the square," Bao said "The tanks kept coming closer, but they left space between them, hoping we would lose heart and flee. Finally the soldiers hit us with the ends of their rifles so we had to leave." Bao still has scars on his back and shoulders from the rifle butts.

No one was killed right in the square, though from my balcony I saw dozens killed on Chang-Ang Avenue when demonstrators attempted to reenter Tiananmen Square the next day. It was also on my balcony that I got shot. While I was looking down at the tanks that I felt the sting on the left side of my neck. I touched the spot and saw the blood on my fingers and went to put some hydrogen peroxide on it. Later I found the twisted bullet on the balcony, and decided to have it gold-plated and put the bill on my expense account. But the jeweler said the bullet was made of a special alloy; it couldn't be plated.

This gave rise to one of several aphorisms I use to sum up lessons I learned in Tiananmen Square. This one concerns the fact that, sometimes, just getting out alive is sufficient. It is: *"Don't Try to Gild the Bullet."*

Journalism truly is the rough draft of history. Ten years ago, the meaning of the Tiananmen crackdown seemed clear. But over the past ten years, contrary to all expectations, the Tiananmen crackdown has been followed by a deep-running liberalization of Chinese society.

The recurring crises in China-U.S. relations make the

biggest headlines. The reports you read about Chinese government repression are true. But something else is true: More people in China are living better, freer lives than ever before, and the change isn't limited to the big cities of coastal China, as I saw when I traveled around the country. Even in distant regions like Yunnan province, the computer screens were blinking, and the cell phones were ringing along with the cash registers. Today, China has 260 million TVs, basically one for every family. And a transportation revolution has taken hold. Ten years ago it took twenty-four hours to go from Shanghai to Beijing. Today it takes half that time. Now, even faster high-speed rail lines are being built to link all of China's major cities. Freeways are now penetrating remote provinces. New airports are everywhere, packed with travelers who ten years ago had neither the money nor freedom to fly.

China has become an information supermarket, too. One weekend afternoon, I visited a state-owned bookstore, a skyscraper full of volumes, which was thronged with thousands of customers. In the past decade, a vast corpus of the latest foreign literary and scientific thinking has been translated into Chinese, and made available to the public.

This gigantic, well-run emporium of information had benches for casual reading, and micromanagement at the computerized checkout link. You could find nearly anything you wanted to read here, even the works of Chairman Mao if you searched hard enough.

This afternoon, walking back from Tiananmen Square, I passed a *hutong*, an alley leading into the Forbidden City. There I encountered the personification of the past ten years' change in the form of a Chinese man in his early thirties. Ten years ago had he been in that *hutong*, he would have been running for his life. Today, he was withdrawing money from an ATM, while talking on his mobile phone.

When I get back to the hotel, and Steve and I take our places on the balcony, I say, "I remember the night I thought you were dead," which causes Steve to ask: "Is this the same balcony where you got shot?"

"No," I answer. "I checked. There's no ricochet mark on the wall. It was another room."

Steve and I stand here, looking out over two different Beijings. We planned this trip together. But ever since we got here, it's been clear we're on separate journeys.

I'm out to recapture the past, but Steve's searching for his future, which brings us to the biggest change in his life. Steve, like everyone else in Tiananmen Square, wanted something better. He also had a personal motive for protesting. "I scored the highest from my province on my exams," he told me, "so I applied for a Ford Foundation grant, and won it. But I wasn't allowed to go to America. The grant was given to the son of a party official." Once the only thing Steve wanted was to get out of China—which he did. Now what he wants, more than anything, is to find a way back.

Ke Feng, in contrast, is tempestuous, a great dramatizer—you might even say he's desperate to return. Though to say "Ke Feng is desperate," given his nature, is almost tautological—as self-evident as saying, "Ke Feng has wavy black hair and almond-shaped eyes, and if you're ever foolish enough to leave that manipulative little taker alone with your telephone, he'll run up a thousand bucks in calls to China before you can say: 'Get out of here, Ke Feng. I never want to see your face again.' " Of course, I always do see his face again; our lives, first tangled in Tiananmen Square, became more entwined when he escaped to America, and found freedom on my living room couch.

There Kevin, as he now styled himself, proceeded to make international phone calls and eat me out of house and home until I kicked him out. Or, to put it more accurately, I refused Ke Feng further access to what formerly had been my life, but which now, like Tiananmen Square before it, had become another cluttered stage set in the ongoing Epic Drama of Ke Feng.

It was Ke Feng who had the idea of erecting a Chinese Statue of Liberty in Tiananmen Square—Ke Feng, too, who pestered, manipulated and inspired people into actually building it. Few people I've met are as good at conceiving a visionary project as he is, or as relentless at exacting work and money from people to make it happen. It's no wonder, in my opinion, that after leaving China, Ke Feng announced he was a film director, and then actually became one.

Telephone Ke Feng and ask him for dinner, and before you know it, he's picking the locale and the restaurant. Meet him at a cocktail party, and soon he'll be a permanent presence on your answering machine, asking you to finance his latest project.

The same qualities that, in America, make Ke Feng such a pest, in Tiananmen Square helped him become the moving fingertip of history. How had he come to play this extraordinary role? Ke Feng's from Shanghai, where he was active in student demonstrations. He might never have come to Tiananmen Square at all, but the Chinese authorities, miscalculating as usual, decreed at the height of the crisis that all students could travel free on China's railroads. They hoped this would end the demonstrations by unleashing an exodus *out* of Beijing. Instead millions of young people, including Ke Feng, jumped on trains, and headed for Tiananmen Square. There hadn't been such an uncontrolled, mass movement of impetuous youth across China since the Cultural Revolution of the 1960s, but they weren't the only ones converging on Beijing.

Stealthfully, methodically, the Chinese military was moving soldiers and weapons toward Tiananmen Square. In Shanghai,

Ke Feng and some others already had built a copy of the American Statue of Liberty. "The original idea was to bring our statue to Beijing, but they wouldn't let us take it on the train," he told me the first time we met, in a tent in Tiananmen Square. So he arrived in Beijing alone, with only an idea, but what an idea!

I've never forgotten my first encounter with him. In the midst of all that tumult, he was calm; he was engaging rather than charismatic. He spoke very softly, directing his kid-brother eyes straight at you, which made you listen harder. When you first meet him, Ke Feng has a way of making his hopes your own, and that day when I asked him how long he thought the Goddess of Democracy would endure, he answered: "I hope she stands here forever."

Imagine one kid and one idea swirling into Tiananmen Square, right off the train from Shanghai. Then imagine hundreds swirling with the same idea, then thousands. Imagine a tidal surge enthralling hundreds of thousands of people with the idea: "We're going to build the statue!"

Ke Feng strode from the Beijing railroad station to Tiananmen Square and started spreading his idea, but also interrogating people, asking the same questions he asks now, when he directs a film: Who has the money? Who has the connections? And where are they?

To build the statue required money, organization, and technical skill, not just romantic vision. That's where Bao enters the story. Bao acted as liaison among many different groups of students, ranging from painters to architects, whose organizations were represented in the square. Bao was a very competent organizer, but his most vital skill, it turned out, was his ability to listen—with his mind as well as his ears—to a total stranger.

Bao immediately grasped the grandeur of Ke Feng's concept; and also the technical challenge of turning it into reality.

He quickly started raising money to build the statue, and enlisting the commitment of artists and engineers who had the technical skills to design and construct it.

For weeks, Bao and Beijing-based students like him were the ones who kept the demonstrations going.

Ke Feng epitomized the kids from the provinces, lured to Beijing by the glamour and adventure of what was happening in Tiananmen Square. As for Steve, he personified another kind of participant—a member of China's future elite who saw the demonstrations as a chance to push China further in the direction of better management, freer markets, freer speech.

The night they built the statue, the students seemed like children on a gigantic jungle gym as they swung about on the scaffolding, maneuvering the different parts of the Goddess into place while those of us watching them sat cross-legged on the brick pavement, looking up. It took the dawn to reveal the wondrousness of what they had created. There she was, fragile yet immense, both universal and idiosyncratically Chinese. Billions of people around the world watched, enthralled and aghast, as the beautiful, white willowy Goddess of Democracy faced squat, dark, metallic buglike tanks. The ensuing battle was an epochal confrontation of freedom versus repression, of youth versus age, and of lightweight construction materials versus boiler plate, both military and ideological.

Most of all it was a confrontation between an age that was dying and one being born.

The tanks converging on Tiananmen Square were propelled by the notion that history is made from the top down—that ideology, the nation-state, and authoritarian hierarchies would dictate the shape of the future in China, and around the world.

The Goddess of Democracy prefigured a different future, a

new interactive age in which the kid who crashes on your living room couch can influence history more than armies.

All this didn't occur in a void. In 1986 the supposedly docile Filipinos had toppled the Marcos dictatorship. After Tiananmen Square, the Berlin Wall and all the communist regimes of Eastern Europe would fall like dominos. Within the next seven months this extraordinary span of events was the real end of the twentieth century, the real beginning of the new millennium.

Bao argues that the Goddess of Democracy would never have happened without Ke Feng.

But while Bao and others were risking their lives, Ke Feng skipped out of Tiananmen Square as soon as the Goddess of Democracy was built. Having met the girl of his dreams in the days leading up to the showdown, he decided to make love not revolution. Politics provided the international headlines, but sex was a subtext in Tiananmen Square.

The girl Ke Feng met in Beijing told him that she too had come to fight for democracy. Actually, she was a spy for State Security, assigned to befriend, then rat on, democracy activists. But Ke Feng's extraordinary personal magnetism worked its magic on her too. Instead of subverting him, she fell in love and resolved to give up her career in state espionage.

I learned about their subsequent history earlier this year. Just before leaving for Beinjing with Steve, I took the train from New York to Hoboken, New Jersey, where Ke Feng and his girlfriend currently live.

Following the crackdown, their romance had as many twists and turns as a Beijing soap opera. Ke Feng had little trouble escaping to America: The Chinese government was delighted to get rid of student protestors by giving them passports, and Ke Feng went to work immediately, peppering universities in America and people like me with requests for help. Things were different for his girlfriend. It was one thing for the Chinese government to let an obscure student dash off to America, quite another to let a state security princess (both her parents worked for the state security as well) disgrace herself by running after him. As Ke Feng fleshed out the scenario over dinner in Hoboken, the plot line involves the usual accouterments of a Chinese family melodrama, including infusions of guilt, torrents of public shame, and, at crucial moments, cash under the table.

"It was two years before they even let her resign from state security," he tells me. However unsmoothly, the course of true love nonetheless eventually flowed to New Jersey, where Ke Feng's girlfriend now works as a telemarketer.

As one might imagine, Ke Feng landed on his feet in America. After I kicked him out of my apartment, he made a film in Canada that won a prize. He's much prouder of *The Final Account,* a melodrama he managed to shoot in the United States about the Tiananmen Square crackdown that nevertheless looks like a low-budget film made entirely in China. *The Final Account* has also attracted honors, winning Ke Feng a nomination for a prize for best Asian film maker from the Directors Guild of America. He and his girlfriend own the condo where they live, which has a big-screen VCR he uses in his work, along with some tastefully arranged reproductions of Chinese antiques; the complex, as Ke Feng likes to point out, has secure parking.

For most Chinese lucky enough to get to America, all that would be an accomplishment. Yet for the progenitor of the Goddess of Democracy, his film work in America is only a stepping stone. To what? Ke Feng aspires to do nothing less than portray China's entire transformation. "There's no other way. The Cultural Revolution was the story of your generation," he tells me. "Tiananmen Square is the story of my generation."

But to do that, he needs to return to China. He could just get on a plane, of course, but as in Steve's case, that's increasingly only a theoretical option. There are the mortgage payments on the condo, and his girlfriend will only return to China for one reason, to get married. Would he be arrested? It's not impossible, given the Chinese government's strategy of cracking down on troublesome individuals while according more freedom to society as a whole.

Then there's the really big question, the one haunting every film maker: Money. The answer can only be found by checking things out, on the spot, in China. As dinner in Hoboken progresses, I once again find myself being cast in a supporting role.

He lists the people I should contact on his behalf when I get to Beijing: the head of the Beijing Film Studio, faculty members at the Central Academy of Fine Arts. He writes down the subject matter he wants me to raise with them on an index card: "Re: return of an exile foreign-trained film director."

Bao's route to America was much more arduous than Ke Feng's. When he continued agitating publicly for democratic rights, he was forced to leave his academy. After being imprisoned he suffered a kind of internal exile, lying low in his wife's home province until he could get travel documents.

And when Bao finally did get to America a lesson in the perils of freedom awaited him.

Within three months of arriving in Los Angeles, his car was stolen and his wife left him. Bao still has hopes of being the technical wizard behind multimillion-dollar films some day, just as he was the organizational leader behind the building of the Goddess of Democracy. But the reality is that he has to sell photocopy machines to survive, and he lives alone in a single room he rents out from an immigrant family in El Hambra.

Despite his new-found conviction that happiness comes from within, Bao has not given up his belief in the destiny of the

Tiananmen Generation to reshape China and so change the world. Like Ke Feng he dreams of doing it cinematically—by becoming the technical wizard behind multi-million dollar films.

For Steve, the levers of change are all financial. "It's not just the money," Steve tells me one night in Beijing. "In China you can make a difference. In America I'm just like everybody else." Yet if a web of bourgeois obligations now tie Ke Feng to Hoboken, a whole shroud of responsibilities wraps itself around Steve in Chicago.

You can't just abandon twenty houses, including the lovely Victorian he and his wife are restoring for themselves. And how can he go back to China without finishing his doctorate?

This doesn't stop either of them from hoping, and believing. "I could be the Bill Gates of China," Steve says. Ke Feng sees himself as beyond metaphor. He doesn't want to be China's Bertolucci; he wants to be the Ke Feng of China. For he, more than anyone else who was in Tiananmen Square, has held history in his hands. He knows what beautiful things you can create out of it.

Both Steve and Ke Feng still look so young. They seem so innocent—until you hear them talk about all the megabucks and megamovies it's their destiny to make. Hearing them talk, someone might think they're crazy. But I know they're not crazy. I know their ambitions are rational because, when I go to China, I see with my own eyes how, in the ten years since it seemed that all its hopes had been crushed, the Tiananmen Generation has turned out to be full of winners.

After Ke Feng and Steve left China, some of their friends were thrown into prison. Others became millionaires. What's revelatory about Steve's best friend in Beijing, whom I meet my first night back in Beijing, is that both things happened. First he was thrown into prison. Then he became a millionaire.

"Prison taught me to be patient, to be strong. It helped me make big business decisions later," he tells me. He says prison also helped him keep his weight down. Unlike Steve, this ex-demonstrator and new multi-millionaire has never adopted a American name, and never considered moving to the United States. He's having too much fun in China making money and eating gourmet food. He also has fun with his computers, his cars, and his collection of Cultural Revolution kitsch.

Ten years ago, he was an economics researcher like Steve. After the Tiananmen crackdown, he was arrested, and held for one year. "The government forced me to become a millionaire," he told me, laughing at the joke destiny had played on him. "My research institute had been closed down, and I couldn't get a job in a state enterprise, so I had no choice but to go out and make money."

Because of his training in macroeconomics, Steve's friend had extensive knowledge of financial markets. By analyzing the markets he could foresee changes in interest rates and when the government allowed trading of bonds for first time, he made his fortune. He started with less than $10,000, and is certainly worth at least $10 million now. Besides Beijing offices and apartments, he owns a villa outside town he bought for $500,000. He's married, with one son, and has four cars: a Volvo, Honda Civic, two VWs.

Prisoners who become millionaires never are typical, but Chairman Mao would recognize such people immediately. These young rich Chinese are the present-day equivalents of what, under Maoism, were called the "vanguard of the revolution." "We were the best and brightest," Steve's old friend tells me another time, in the apartment where he sleeps when he doesn't go home to the villa. He's one of those young millionaires who prefers the graduate student style of interior decor. Leftover pizza sits in a grease-stained delivery box. An untended computer screen blinks, waiting for its master to log on with his latest big idea.

Far from ending, the protests that began in Tiananmen Square have radiated into the countryside, along with the PCs, TVs, and cell phones. "Farmers and workers are protesting every day," one Beijing-based journalist told me. "But it only gets reported if someone gets killed."

Another Tiananmen alumnus told me why there won't be another Tiananmen Square: "Ten years ago, we tried to stop the tanks, but couldn't, because all we had were bikes. Today we could stop them easily by blocking the streets with our cars, but who wants his car smashed by a tank?

"In 1989, we had nothing to lose except dead-end jobs in state enterprises, Now we have everything to lose—computers, cars, apartments."

Life in America offers many satisfactions, but it can't offer the sense that fills the lives of many of Steve's friends who did not leave China—that, every day, they're on the cutting edge of history. This belief that they're helping to shape a new China imparts verve to their lives.

So when another of Steve's friends says, "Those who fled to America, their situation is not as good as ours here," the comment stings him.

"It's all your fault," Steve complains to me later, and in a way he's right. After finally leaving Tiananmen Square, I felt I never wanted to come back to Beijing again. But within five months, in November 1989, I was back in the Beijing Hotel, working on a completely different story, about Cambodia.

As it turned out, I had no trouble at all finding Steve and Bao. (Ke Feng, moving fast, already had made it to the States.) Times were tough just after Tiananmen; spies were everywhere. Also the United States was beginning to lose its enthusiasm for issuing visas. One November morning I played the tourist,

Steve played the tour guide, and we drove up to the Great Wall in a car with a driver we'd made sure didn't understand English so that we could talk freely about Steve's future. Ke Feng would have outlined his plan immediately, telling me what I was expected to do; Bao would have freely shared his visions for the future. But it took some time to pry out of Steve his great dream. Ever since he'd been denied his Ford Foundation grant, he'd badly wanted to get his doctorate in economics at the University of Chicago, the most respected such department in the world.

Steve amply merited admission, and a letter of recommendation from me, a journalist who actually had been in Tiananmen Square, was something no admissions committee could ignore back then. The only hard part came, after he was admitted, when the clever economists at Chicago demanded half my life savings up front, as a guarantee for Steve's academic fees. He paid everything back within a year.

These days in Chicago, Steve is eyeing his biggest real estate project yet, a 125-unit building near Lake Michigan. His wife is doing well in her accounting business. Steve is certainly not as rich as he might have become in China. But he's already made more money than most Chinese, and many Americans, make in a lifetime. You'd almost describe Steve as an American success story, except he doesn't want to be an American success story, even though he senses his life and himself becoming more and more American every day, whether he wants it or not.

It's not just Steve's teeth that have become Americanized. In fact late one night he does something so American it stuns me. We're driving around in Steve's brother's car, and come to the Temple of Heaven. Steve wants to see the Temple even though it's closed, so he offers the guard twenty dollars to unlock the gate. The guard can't figure out why this tourist wants to see the temple in the middle of the night, let alone violate the rules forbidding it. And Steve can't figure out why the guard won't let him do whatever wants, regardless of the hour, so long as he pays for it.

On our last night in Beijing Steve suggests a new restaurant. "Why not Chairman Mao's place? You haven't been there yet." At the restaurant, there's a shrine at the entrance dedicated to Chairman Mao. But instead of displaying hydroelectric projects and agricultural communes, this one displays examples of Mao's native Hunanese cuisine.

The Chinese characters above Mao's portrait proclaim: "Taste Mao's Dishes and Remember Chairman Mao Forever." Of all the role reversals in post-Tiananmen China, this surely is the most surreal: the Great Helmsmen metamorphosed into a Hunanese Colonel Sanders.

Even though it's Monday night, the Tiananmen Generation is out in force. The talk can't drown out the mobile phones buzzing. Another sign of the times: Once no Chinese would have brought home leftovers. It would have been considered demeaning. Now doggie bags are chic, especially since so many working wives don't have time to cook anymore, and Chinese leftovers warm up so nicely in the new microwaves. The waiters and waitresses wear shiny gold-colored Mao buttons. When I ask our waitresses if I can have one, she scoops dozens of them into a bag. "Give them to your friends," she says. "Tell them about our restaurant."

The restaurant was opened on Mao's birthday, and drew a crowd that included Mao's mistress, Mao's daughter, Mao's grandson, and Mao's personal chef. Why did these people lend themselves to such a trivialization of Chairman Mao's legacy?

"Everyone is looking for money," the manager says, as a

wriggling tortoise is displayed for our edification before being eviscerated and plunged into the soup kettle, "so naturally Mao's relatives came to our opening."

Some of the people eating here tonight were tortured and imprisoned. The lives of them all have been shaped by the decades of foreign war, civil war, and social and economic upheaval that accompanied Mao's rise to power, his rule, and the aftermath of his domination of the country. Yet, no Chinese seems offended that Chairman Mao's effigy now presides over a for-profit enterprise catering to the Beijing bourgeoisie.

Looking around, you see Mao is good for a chuckle, but not much more, as people use this bustling restaurant to help make up for all the years when merely enjoying a night out with the family was deemed "counterrevolutionary." How to sum up this sense, which you encounter all over China, that life is now to be enjoyed precisely because joy so often was a crime in the past? Tonight, as we watch everyone partaking of the good life, Chinese-style, in the restaurant that preserves Mao's memory by mocking it, I recall another aphorism. It is: *"Living well is the best revenge."*

After returning to Chicago, Steve has an epiphany: "If I'm really going back to China, I'll have to finish my thesis." Yet when I drive out to the Midwest for a visit, I find it's his latest real estate venture—the 125-unit apartment building—that, as usual engrosses him most. It will be his biggest deal yet. "If I develop this one right," Steve tells me, "it will guarantee my son a bright future." He and his wife already accept the boy will be American, though they hope he'll grow up speaking Chinese as well as English.

It occurs to me as we celebrate his son's first birthday with balloons, cake, and ice cream, that there are no indoctrination classes in America, the way there once were indoctrination classes in China, but America indoctrinates you all the same. In the park in front of their Victorian home, there's a baseball diamond where, sooner than seems possible, the boy will be throwing a ball around. Across the park is a school. If I had to bet, now, I'd bet that in another ten years Steve will still be in America.

Back in New York, Ke Feng comes over for dinner. We laugh about the old days when he camped out in my living room. Then he announces: "I'm becoming a U.S. citizen." I'm less stunned than I once would have been. After all, what Ke Feng always does is grab the opportunity—whether it's an historic event, a free place to crash, or a privileged travel document. He rationalizes his decision as follows: "When I go back to China with a U.S. passport it will be safer when I express democratic opinions."

His girlfriend's parents are planning a big wedding, he adds. I smile at the idea of the guy behind the Goddess of Democracy having a wedding banquet hosted by his State Security parents-in-law.

Of the students I met in Tiananmen Square who made it to America, Bao has had the least fortunate experience. Coming here cost him money, a car, and his wife. But when I fly out to California to see Bao—or rather Jeffrey, which is the name his answering machine gives—it seems his luck has started to change.

Bao loves the used Lexus he bought after his first car was stolen. "My final payment is next month," he tells me. "It's a powerful car, which can take me everywhere."

Bao was never the intellectual theorizer like Steve, or the master director like Ke Feng. But he, too, retains the vast horizons of the Tiananmen Generation. "Why don't we drive across the country?" he says. "I'd love to see the Grand Canyon, and New York." At his mention of New York, I realize Bao still hasn't seen the original Statue of Liberty, even though the idea of it has shaped his life.

Though Bao still sells photocopy machines to pay the rent, there is finally some very good news. He's been admitted to a college program in digital media art design. He's received grants and scholarships and is going to learn high-tech filmmaking, and become an expert in all those computerized wonders that increasingly make conventional special effects obsolete.

"When I graduate, I'll open my own film business here," he vows. "When that's profitable, I'll open branches in China, where there will be a tremendous market for high technology in the movie business."

Time and America have begun to change Bao's personal life, too. "My wife wants to come back to me," he says. "But I've told her I think we should defer a decision like that until after she gets her degree in fashion design.

"Besides," he confides, "I'm beginning to think, maybe now I should live for myself." Bao would like to date, though he's still too shy to ask an American girl out. An unexpected possibility suggests itself to me: that Bao, not Honghai or Ke Feng, will wind up being the one who most successfully harmonizes his Chinese identity and his American reality—the one who best combines the pursuit of happiness with the happy ending. I imagine him with film studios in America and China; I also imagine him with an American wife.

Bao enjoys his Mexican lunch. "Two and a half years in California," he says, "and this is my first taco!"

For him, too, character has turned into destiny.

Pledge Allegiance

By Rich Cohen

Killed: *Talk* Magazine, 2001

Maybe Tina Brown killed my story about my life in a fraternity because it was too racy or too ugly. Maybe she looked at it in the way I have come to expect from many people of the (slightly) older generation, the last generation built on the old model of ambition wrapped in a right-seeming idealism—that is, appearing to do the right thing, while, at the same time getting ahead. For my own generation, at least for the kids I grew up with on Bluff Road in Glencoe, Illinois, I think the drive is toward experience for experience, undisguised, with no message or goal.

Which is to say, there is no message in this story, no larger quest or grail, and even now I feel no need to apologize for the asshole or schmuck I was then because I am sure, though I am trying hard not to be, I am an asshole and schmuck now. It was, as Homer Simpson put it, just a bunch of stuff that happened, only it happened to a lot of us, and it seemed significant, like most things do, for a good five minutes after it was over. I did get to give Sam Donaldson the secret fraternity handshake, though. It was the summer after initiation. I was working as an intern for a TV show in Washington and old Vulcan-eyebrowed Sam was a guest. I greeted him in the lobby. When I got him alone in the elevator, I gave him the shake—and all the shaking was on my side of the deal. I shook him like you shake a pear tree. He smiled vaguely, as if, for a moment, he recalled an ancient memory. And then, when the shaking was over, and Sam had straightened his cuffs and stepped out of the elevator, I felt deeply ashamed.

In August of 1986, I arrived in New Orleans, the strangest city in America. I was eighteen years old, an incoming freshman at Tulane University. I grew up near Chicago, a city of crisp autumns and straight lines, a gray, sober, Germanic city. All at once, I found myself in a drunken, weedy, greenhouse of a town. New Orleans looks like a capital in the French Antilles, a port backed by swamps. Tulane is in the English quarter of the city, and the houses are ramshackle and Victorian. The leaves cast spiky shadows and vines run up the carports, which glisten in the drenching tropical rain. Each afternoon, I would climb up to the roof of my dorm, where I could look out over the neat greens of the campus to the twisting coil of the Mississippi River, tugboats heading for the Gulf of Mexico. In the evening, the sun dropped through bands of dust and the sky passed through the colors of a mood ring—placid, agitated, angry.

At night, I followed the other kids in my dorm to the parties that raged on fraternity row. I knew almost nothing about fraternities—only what I had picked up from the big brothers of my neighborhood. There had been talk of drinking and strippers and hazing. Freshmen were forced to clean, drink, and eat things that, on other occasions, they would refuse to clean or drink or eat. In high school, I had reacted to such stories, and to everything else grouped under the loose heading "Greek Life," with contempt. Closing my eyes, I pictured preppies swallowing goldfish as they were paddled in the ass by beefy jugheads. I considered myself clued in, cool. Of the many things I planned to do with my life—hitch to Mexico, make love to twins—joining a fraternity was not among them. So why, during the first week of college, did I go to the fraternity parties? Because that's where the girls were going.

On these occasions, I was usually with the few freshmen that had also graduated from my high school. It was a sort of melancholy association, a rough alliance that we knew would not last more than a few days. There was a kid named Randy, who, in high school, anxious to lose his virginity, had visited a prostitute. Before Randy had sex with her, the prostitute asked if he wanted to do anything else. He said he wanted to "try that sixty-nine thing." As a result, Randy had to rush home, feeling ill, still very much a virgin. There was Danny, who later became a bartender at a local dive called the Boot and who always gave me free drinks. There was Jeff, who I had known since the second grade. Early in the week, Jeff became fixated on the idea of joining ZBT, the Jewish fraternity. This fixation caused him to drink a lot, and do a lot of backslapping and high-fiving. Jeff did not get into a fraternity, and he was destroyed. By the time classes started, his father had taken him out school. When I went home for Thanksgiving, friends told me Jeff had dropped out of Tulane for medical reasons; they said he had smoked pot soaked in formaldehyde and that it had made him go insane.

At Tulane, the fraternities are scattered along Broadway, a street that skirts the campus. When you imagine fraternity row, you might picture an Ivy League school in the Northeast, brick mansions set amid manicured lawns, a pledge raking leaves as upperclassmen toss a football. Well, get that picture out of your head right now! The streets around Tulane are dilapidated, and the fraternity houses—each a different color—are narrow wooden shotgun shacks. Wandering along Broadway, we walked into and out of a dozen houses; they were like restaurants at a mall food court, each with a slightly different theme but offering the same basic meal: there were the Sky Caps, who took drugs, played Ultimate Frisbee, and loved bandana-wearing dogs; there were the Pikes, who owned a fire truck, which they parked on their front lawn, who got drunk and rang the bell and dated girls that looked just like them; there were the Sigma Nus, jocks and would-be jocks, who, during pledgeship, rolled around naked on the floor; there were the Kappa Alphas, creepy Southern throwbacks who, for their formal, wore the dress grays of the Confederate army; there were the ZBTs, kids mostly from Long Island who wore their hair long and curly in back and who spoke in three tenses: "I was so fucked up." "I am so fucked up." "I'm gonna get so fucked up." There were the SAEs, who sported backwards baseball caps, chinos, pink shirts and white bucks, and who called everyone, "Son." "All right, Son, let's go get ugly!" There were the Alpha Sigmas, who were rundown and burned-out and funny and fallen.

Like a great religious festival, the party-hopping went for seven days. It was Rush Week, and there were no classes. During this time, about 60 percent of the student body would pledge a fraternity or sorority. Since the drinking age in New Orleans was just eighteen, Rush became a school-sanctioned spree. My memory of the week is as gap-filled as a home movie: I am at the Sigma Chi house, drinking beer from a funnel; I am in front of the Boot, trying to ignore Jeff, who holds out his hand and shouts, "Give me the skin!"; I am in the yard of the Alpha Sigma house, drinking 151 Diesel. Each night, I wind up back at Alpha Sigma. Of all the frat boys in the bars, the Alpha Sigmas seemed the most self-aware. Of course, just beneath the surface—and often right on the surface—they were working me like a sucker at a used car lot, promising a new life. *I see you in this Impala. You owe it to yourself.* One fool—I think he was in his late twenties—said, "Don't join this fraternity if you don't want friends who will last the rest of your life, and if you can't fuck all night, 'cause the girls who hit on us, man, they're heavy-duty."

By the time Rush Week ended, I had shed my disdain for Greek life. Fraternities throughout America—and this is even truer today—were under attack and were caricatured as dangerous and reactionary and incorrect. For a kid from a liberal home like mine, joining a fraternity therefore had an air of rebellion. It seemed the surest way to a new experience, to life outside the right-thinking path. I wanted to join for the same reason I wanted to drink a bottle of tequila and swallow the worm. I was out for the complete experience, the secret meetings and private parties, late-night excursions into the real South. More than anything, I did not want to spend four years in New Orleans with kids just like me (suburban, Jewish) from Highland Park or Scarsdale or Shaker Heights. The members of Alpha Sigma were from Louisiana and Mississippi and Alabama and Texas, the prep schools, and small towns of the New South. Even Jewish kids in the fraternity seemed exotic. One night, Bourbon, a drifter, was in the house, bitching about, "the Jews." A kid from Savannah, Georgia, interrupted him, saying, "Bourbon, I am Jewish." Bourbon leaned back on his heels, and said, "You Jewish? No, sir. You black."

One afternoon, after I had been asked to join Alpha Sigma, I called my father for advice. My father is a champion of the solo expedition. He believes any form of groupthink, even if it results in a charity drive or a trip to a nursing home, is a hop, skip, and jump from evil. As he spoke, I could hear his office chair creak and the scene arranged itself in my head: Sitting at his desk on the second floor of our house, in a bathrobe and leather boots custom made for his extra-wide feet, looking at the backyard, the leaves red with the autumn. He said, "Our family descends directly from Aaron, the brother of Moses. When Aaron was your age, he was asked to join the Royal Order of the Third Eye. Do you know what Aaron said? Aaron said, 'I don't do clubs. I am not a follower. Thank you. No.' That has been a tradition in our family ever since. If you join, you will be the first family member to break a tradition that is over three thousand years old."

The next night, I joined.

While he is a pledge, even the best-looking, sharpest-tongued, most determinedly romantic boy cannot get a date. Why? Because when you are a pledge, you have been trained to see yourself as the lowest creature on earth, half-realized, of no use. And you are convinced that is how the world sees you, too. In fact, as the weeks go by, the brightness of the outside world dims, until the girls on campus, the guys in the dorms, the teachers in the classes, all of it, becomes as pale as a shadow. Only the *House*, and the people in the *House*, exist. Even the mama's boys have to be reminded to call home. In this manner, the fraternity operates like a cult or the army, separating you from your old life. By the time you realize the size of the commitment you've made, you deduce, by an arithmetic known to every pledge, that you are just a few weeks away from initiation. It would be such a shame to quit now, so close to the end. So, you pour in more troops and more troops, until you are too deep to withdraw. As you might have guessed, I am hacking my way toward a Vietnam analogy. And here it is: Pledging the fraternity was, for me, Vietnam; a bloody ground war, the results of which, positive or negative, are still being debated.

I had gotten myself into a situation where my behavior was running head first into my beliefs—cognitive dissonance is what they call it out in the big world; the more effort you expend the greater the value of the prize. Was it worth it? Well, I walked through a legion of shit to get it, so it damn well better be. On the afternoon TV shows they throw up their hands and say, "I just don't like *me* anymore." When you find yourself, for whatever reason, behaving in a way that clashes with your beliefs, you either change your beliefs or you change your behavior. What usually gives way are your beliefs. This, is why so many institutions—college fraternities, street gangs, religious cults—impose discomforts on initiates: Those who stick with it often become passionately committed to the very institution that was responsible for their discomfort. "I suffered for it so it *must* be worth it." Did this happen to me? I'm still trying to figure that out.

Of course, it started slowly. In the first few weeks, being a pledge meant little more than wearing a small, shiny pin, going to parties, having a new way to explain yourself to girls. Every night, we went to dinner at Alpha Sigma, the last house on fraternity row, a few yards from St. Charles Avenue and the shriek of the streetcar. It was ugly, a two-story building shaped like a matchbox, with an upstairs balcony, barred windows, a small driveway and a ratty lawn. Most often, we entered through the side door, which had a combination lock. Like most things in the fraternity, the code to the combination was geared for the simpleminded. Press 1-2-3-4 and the door opened on a cement-floored dining room and kitchen, where food rotted in buckets. Most nights, dinner was red beans and rice.

The pledges sat at a table in back. There were a dozen guys in my pledge class and when I looked at them, I could not help thinking of the rotted food in the buckets; you would not describe them as thoroughbreds. There was Joe Smith, a red-haired kid from Fort Worth, who was nothing until he was drunk, and then he was as stubborn and belligerent as a hobo in a silent movie. There was Magna Para, a Samoan from Little Rock, his face as simple and convincing as that of a cartoon character, black little eyes and two holes denoting a nose; he drove a black Pontiac Fiero. There was Ezekiel "Zeke" Rizzo, from Jackson, Mississippi, an awkward, neurotic kid with huge ears, fleshy as hams. If ridiculed, he would say, "In the Far East, big ears are a sign of virility." As he said this, his eyes filled with confusion. In these first weeks, the pledges were told to get to know each other and I remember nights spent passing a bottle, telling stories. I talked about the time my dog Lazlo disappeared and was found three days later, behind the washing machine in our basement, chewing gum; Zeke talked about running away from home; Joe Smith claimed that he had slept with over a hundred women, mostly during family vacations; Magna Para told us that, in high school, no one liked him until senior year, when his father bought him the Fiero. "After that," he said, "people liked me a lot."

In front of the dining room, there was a small platform, five wooden steps that left off mid-climb. The number of steps—five—was said to have great significance. Now and then, as the members of the fraternity ate dinner, a pledge was told to stand on the top step and tell a joke, or answer questions. One night, as Zeke stood on the stairs, legs quaking, he was badgered by a junior named Paul Fairly. Paul, with shoulder-length dark hair and a twitchy mouth, resembled Sonny Bono. Yet, Paul had nothing of the cheerful disposition that so swiftly guided Sonny Bono through life. Paul was a short, squat, pigeon-toed bully. "C'mon," he asked Zeke. "Tell me something about your pledge brother, Magna Para."

Zeke stammered, then said, "Magna Para was not popular

in high school until he got a Pontiac Fiero and then people liked him."

Paul wheeled on Magna Para. "I hate guys like you," he said. "You buy your friends. Bastard. Up on the stairs." For the next four months, Paul Fairly, and a lot of other members of the fraternity, were after Magna Para day and night, driving his personality, or whatever part of it had survived high school, underground. Magna Para was forced to run errands, clean trash, and humiliate himself; he was kidnapped, snatched from his dorm, forced to drink entire bottles of Mad Dog, yelled at, abused. On one occasion, he was left on the Causeway, the longest bridge in the world, which skims Lake Pontchartrain. The Causeway is actually two bridges separated by fifty yards of water. Magna Para was dropped in the middle of the bridge heading away from New Orleans. He had to hitchhike ten miles across the lake, turn around, and hitchhike back.

Why did Magna Para put up with it? Why did any of us? Speaking for myself, I had come to accept this new life, so far removed from my high school idea of college. Busy with the fraternity, I rarely went to class. If I did, I was the kid dozing in back. I almost never spoke to my parents. I heard from hometown friends only in ranting letters that ended: "Have you forgotten me?" In a few weeks, I had been successfully cut off. With each step, I told myself, "A little further. You're too far to turn back." In return, I was getting one of the great lessons of my life, a course in human nature. Each night, I watched as seemingly normal people, given power over other normal people, became sadists. If not stopped, some of these people, often those who appeared the nicest, would bully or beat or, I am convinced, even kill a pledge. Sometimes, when I was being hazed, I felt worse for the person abusing me than I did for myself. It was like seeing someone afflicted with a disease.

The biggest abusers were often those people who, as pledges, had been the most abused. Maybe the tormentor recognized something in the tormented, a spark of his own malady. I would have lost all hope if not for those few people, often guys with throwaway nicknames like Sparky, who did their best to protect the pledges simply because it was a decent way to behave.

A few weeks after we accepted our bids, each of us was given a green pledge book with his name inscribed on the inside cover. We were told to carry the books everywhere, and, cutting across the wide fields of campus, we would pass kids holding pledge books for other fraternities, like ships flying foreign flags. Two nights a week, we met with our pledge trainer, a short, fat, gray-haired senior named Planet, who, trying to scare the life out of me, said, "I looked just like you when I was a freshman."

Planet lived in a tumbledown wreck and we would sit in his living room, taking notes as he led us, chapter by chapter, through the pledge book. It told the history of Alpha Sigma, a fanciful bit of mysticism that traced the roots of the fraternity to an ancient city in Italy, a citadel protected by five towers. There was mention of the University of Virginia, where the first American chapter of Alpha Sigma had been organized, and a picture of old Tom Jefferson, the founder of that university. There were instructions on how a gentleman should wear his cuffs, answer an invitation, tie knots: Windsor knot, half-knot. There was the credo every brother was to live by, which included the words, *zeal, humility, courage.* There was a list of Alpha Sigs who had gone on to fame—Hoagy Carmichael, Sam Donaldson, Robert Redford. Hearing this, Zeke said, "I can't wait to slip Bob Redford the secret handshake."

At the end of each meeting, Planet gave us a test. We had to list the names of every member of the fraternity, write out the credo, and an essay on the meaning of zeal. As the weeks passed, we spent ever more time studying the fraternity—neglecting, or simply abandoning, our actual schoolwork. Actives boasted of the House's low GPA, which hovered just above a D+ average. Of the twenty kids who pledged the fraternity my freshman year, only six graduated from Tulane.

In October, we were told to pick a big brother, someone in the fraternity to guide us through the last weeks of pledgeship. Magna Para chose a junior named Vince Pelt, who had a glass eye. Now and then, Vince dropped his eye into a beer, chugged the beer, and caught the eye in his teeth. Everyone called him Cyclops. Zeke chose Boyd George, a senior who spent his junior year in Japan; for this reason, Zeke believed Boyd would not mock his tremendous ears. Boyd George had been the Magna Para of his pledge class. Zeke never again had to tell a joke at dinner. An Active would ask, "Who is your big brother?"

Zeke would say, "Boyd George."

The room would break into hysterics.

I chose Mike Mozambi, a junior who everyone called Mozambique. He was tall and dark with long lashes and saloon singer eyes. If Mike was drunk, he would say, "If you can talk you can sing, if you can walk you can dance—a saying from Mozambique." He grew up in Minnesota and there was insanity in his family. At night, he used to go to bars, order a beer, find a quiet corner, and stand facing a wall, his nose brushing the brick. Sometimes, facing the wall, he would laugh and say, "Why yes, yes, of course." He often locked himself out of his apartment. Rather than hire a locksmith, he slept at the houses of friends until kicked out. To solve the problem, someone bought him a key chain that beeped when you clapped three times. A few nights later, as I was sitting in my living room, my front door flew open and in walked

Mozambique. I had not seen him in several weeks. He clapped three times. Nothing. He walked into the bathroom and clapped three times. I heard several beeps, and Mozambique left with his keys.

By my senior year, Mozambique, who had spent seven years at Tulane, stopped going to class. He worked at Domino's. One night, instead of delivering a large order, he broke into the homes of eight friends and left a pizza on each kitchen table. When I woke in the morning and saw the box, I said to myself, "A saying from Mozambique." I would run into him most often at the bars. He told me he had been drinking too much and so had cut back to three cocktails a night—a pitcher of beer, a sixty-four-ounce daiquiri, a double bourbon. The last time I saw him was on the back patio of the Rendon Inn. He said he was leaving New Orleans and wanted a farewell drink "something terrible." I ordered a Gorilla Fart. Mozambique drank it down and walked out the door. Years later, a friend told me that Mozambique was living with a migrant family in California, picking grapes.

After I chose Mozambique as my big brother, we spent a lot of time together, driving in his car, talking. He was a great friend. Once, as we walked through campus, under a canopy of mossy trees, a putrid wind blowing in from the river, he told me about pledgeship, how difficult it would get. "Here is what you must remember," he said. "The object of this thing is to break you down and turn you into nothing and make you fall to pieces."

I said, "No one will break me."

Mozambique said, "You will break like a twig, and cry like a little girl."

One night in November, we met at the House after dinner. I asked why we were there and someone said, "Pledge Court."

We were seated in a room upstairs and told to study our pledge books. One at a time, the pledges were led downstairs. Waiting upstairs, I could hear shouting and breaking glass. I asked to use the bathroom. I was escorted in the manner of a convict. I was then marched to the living room and pushed to my knees, before a table with a candle and a skull. Flickering in and out of the light was the president of the fraternity, a roly-poly kid from Brazil called Rocky Top. He looked at me and said, "Never take your eyes from my eyes."

He asked a question, some trivia about fraternity history.

I could feel the entire fraternity behind me in the dark. The room filled with shouts, broken bottles, a blast of noise. My heart turned over. Someone yelled out another question, then another. Each question was followed by a riot of noise. Much later, I was pushed out the side door and found myself sweating on the street. I walked past shuttered stores and dark houses. I spoke to myself in a loud crazy voice. "What the fuck is wrong with you? No, that's not the thing? What is the thing? Don't you get it? There is no thing!" A man out walking his dog turned and hurried the other way.

This was the moment when my last shred of dignity fell away. I decided to quit. All at once, a parallel destiny seemed to glide up alongside my own, a train running on the next track, lights on, people talking quietly inside. Through the windows, I could see myself sprawled in a cushioned seat, my head in the lap of a beautiful young girl. But then I began to think of myself as someone who had not made it through—a quitter. I argued the case for pledgeship. In my life, what hardship had there been? I had grown up in an age without depression or war, when a young man had no way to test himself. I was now passing through a trial. If I survived, I would be stronger. More than anything, I thought of my pledge brothers. If I quit, they would be blamed. "No,"

I decided. "I cannot quit." And then the train on the next track ghosted off into the dark.

Everything was different after Pledge Court. In high school, I had often pictured myself at college, rushing off to courses in wine tasting and jazz appreciation, dazzling professors with midwestern wit, taking study breaks with coeds. I now saw in myself a lowly creature, far from home, lost to my parents and friends. It was not exactly what I had planned. And yet, there was a kind of mindless stability in my new life, the certainty of knowing just where to be and how to behave. I suppose it was a flight from freedom, every move plotted and planned. Two or three times each week, my pledge brothers and I were told to come by the House at night. In a group, we walked the gloomy paths of campus, past security guards and the studious glow of the library. We ducked into the House and hustled to the second floor, where the members of the fraternity were waiting. We were told to line up, shoulder to shoulder, in the narrow hall, keeping our eyes in the corner. Paul Fairly, or one of the other Actives, would ask, "Where is the corner?" In unison, we would shout, "Where the wall meets the ceiling." If anyone in the dorm asked how we had spent the night, we were to say, "Smoking and drinking at the House."

These proceedings were called lineups. At a lineup, which might run anywhere from one to four hours, you were shouted at and quizzed. Now and then, you were ordered to "Think," which meant you stretched out on the floor, supporting yourself only with the tips of your toes and your elbows, head resting on your palms. You stayed in this position until your elbows burned. If someone said, "Ponder," you drummed your fingers on your face and said, "Oh no, I wonder why I am so stupid." If someone said, "Think high," you scrambled up the walls and, using your feet and hands, suspended yourself near the ceiling. One night, Zeke came to a lineup wearing Japanese shoes with small suction cups on the soles. Another night, he invented his own move, a back-flip landing his body in the Think position. He named it, "The Funky Think." If, for some reason, a pledge irritated an Active, he might be told to do one hundred push-ups. As the pledge did the push-ups, another Active would say, "You let your pledge brother do push-ups alone?" As you dropped to the floor, someone else said, "Who the fuck told you to do push-ups?"

At three or four in the morning, you were dismissed. As you walked to the door, you were jumped. A fight ensued—twelve pledges trading blows with a hundred Actives. Ducking your shoulder, you charged through a shower of fists. At last, you were outside. You caught your breath, checked for blood, looked around: Someone missing. Magna Para. You tried to get back in; the door was locked. This was a symbol of failed brotherhood: You left a soldier on the beach. You went to the dorm and waited. At 4:00 AM, the phone rings. You take down directions and then drive to a gas station out on the Bayou. The sun is rising. Fishermen steer their boats through the weeds. You find Magna Para stretched out in a field. You carry him home.

A few days later, on a Friday night after Thanksgiving vacation, in a line up at the House, we were told the coming week would be Hello week or Help week or Helen week; anything but Hell week, which the school had outlawed. During Hello week, there would be lineups every day, sometimes at midnight and again at 3:00 AM, tests, errands; we would also have to collect the signatures, in our pledge books, of every fraternity member, which would stand for a blessing. Though I was nervous, I was also elated that the dreaded week was here at last. "No matter what else happens," I told myself, "It will all be over in five days."

For me, the memories of Hello week are faded, and there

are not many of them. Why? Because, during Hello week, I did not get more than two hours of sleep at a time, because I did not have any food to eat, because I did not shower or shave or change clothes or have a moment to think, because, when I did get something to drink, it was usually Cuervo or Jägermeister, or some combination, because, on several occasions, I found myself in fights with Actives that left me bruised and woozy and exhilarated.

Closing my eyes and concentrating, here is all that I remember: Magna Para and me cleaning up Paul Fairly's room. I get Paul's signature. A kid we'll call Harrison making us line up in the dorm before he will give Zeke his signature. Harrison was a pool shark and a college drunk. A few years later, he told me he was kicked out of a bar managed by a friend of mine. "Because I was making out with a girl," said Harrison. When I told my friend, he said, "First of all, I didn't kick him out. Secondly, he wasn't making out with a girl, he was making out with a guy." Harrison was nothing to me and I did not want to line up for him but Zeke insisted. Then Harrison insulted Zeke until I saw a vein bulge in Zeke's neck and I thought, "Uh oh," and Zeke attacked Harrison and would have hurt him if we did not pull him off. Zeke got the signature. I also remember Zeke jumping from a roof, reaching up for a flag, missing it, and falling ten feet into bushes and coming up in prickers. In these hours, there were no sudden epiphanies, no moments of clarity—or if there were, I was not yet trained to see them. And still, there were moments when the color of the sky and the shape of the trees came together in such a way that, for an instant, I could glimpse a memory being formed, a process as mysterious as the birth of a star. At such times, Zeke would put his hand on my shoulder and say, "Don't drift on me. We have just a little further to go."

By Friday, we had our signatures and the week behind us.

Each pledge breathed a sigh of relief. That night, there would be a party to celebrate our impending initiation. We were told to wear our best clothes. Before the party, we had an hour to ourselves and so we went, in our suits, to Burger King for the first meal we had eaten in seven days. It was a brisk fall afternoon and we sat in a booth, watching it get dark as the lights came on in the Camellia Grill, the streetcar screeching around the bend from St. Charles to Carrollton. It was a wonderful interlude. We talked about how it would be when we were Actives; we would be good and kind; no pledge would suffer at our hands. "I will treat them only as I would want to be treated myself," vowed Magna Para.

For the last four months, I had spent little time with anyone but my pledge brothers, and, as a result, I often resented them. After all, I had not selected these friends. They had been assigned to me. I had been ordered to look after each of them, to shoulder each weakness and pathology. But then I thought of my friends from home, the kids I had grown up with in Northern Illinois, of Raymond, who was simpleminded and easy to fool; of Cochise, who tried to steal my girlfriends—and I realized that these friends, too, had been assigned to me—by the school district my parents chose, by the sports I had played. My true friends, who I would find in a natural and beautiful way, who would know me and understand me and love me, I had yet to meet. Until then, these friends would do fine. Until then, these were my best friends. We spent a long time over our Whoppers, talking and laughing. It was one of the great meals of my life.

Then we walked to the pledge party, which I figured would be some kind of celebration with a buffet table maybe, or a waiter in a tuxedo serving vodka in heavy glasses. The party, thrown in a ratty clapboard house a few blocks from campus, was anything but. Actives waited for us in T-shirts and jeans with bottles of grain alcohol. We were welcomed with a round of tequila shots followed by more tequila, beer, and more shots. It was a nightmare dressed up in pleasantries, in congratulations and niceties remembered from high school graduations. Before each shot, someone offered a toast. "Here is to the pledges! May they discover the true beauty of brotherhood!"

As we got drunk, the Actives started mixing disgusting cocktails. At one point, I was standing in the kitchen, swilling 151 Diesel mixed with Chocolate Quik. "It's good for you," someone said. "Chocolate coats your stomach." At another point, as an Active held my drink, I leaned on a fence and puked. Even then, this struck me as symbolic: I was giving back the only meal I had eaten in a week. When I stood up, the Active filled my glass and told me to drink. I swallowed it, leaned over and puked. He filled another glass. This went on— a carnival of faces coming in and out of the light, grease paint and smiles, sad country music on the radio. With each drink, the faces seemed to fade until only the smiles remained, big, slick smiles floating through hallways, in and out of rooms, across the lawn. In the yard, I saw Zeke throw Paul Fairly to the ground and shout, "That's it bastard, tonight you die." Then everything got shaky.

The next thing I remember, someone was kicking me in the stomach. Here is how drunk I was—between each kick, I fell back asleep, the way you doze between bursts of an alarm clock. At last, in great pain, I looked up to see who was kicking me. An old man with waxy white hair. "Get up," he shouted. "Get up and get out or I will call the goddamn cops. I mean it. Get out." He kicked me again. I got to my feet and looked around. I was in an ordinary American living room—stuffy couch, fake Oriental rug, TV tray. I stumbled out the door, down two flights of stairs, and into the street. To this day, I am not sure exactly how I wound up in the old man's living room, but I have come up with an explanation that has let me move on with my life: Drunk and senseless, I wandered down the street, looking for shelter. When I discovered an open door, I went in and climbed the stairs until I discovered another open door.

I was awakened by banging on my door, an Active shouting for me to get out of bed. He took me to the House, where the other pledges were waiting. Tequila shots were followed by a series of errands. In the afternoon, we were sent back to the dorms for our suits. When we returned to the House, the windows had been covered in tin foil, like something in a CIA training film. The doors were locked behind us. The outside world ceased to exist. We were lined up in the dining room. It was Senior Hour and, for one hour, we were hazed by seniors. Near the end of the hour, Paul Fairly turned to Zeke and said, "Tell me something about your pledge brother, Magna Para."

Zeke again said, "In high school, Magna Para had no friends until his father bought him a Pontiac Fiero, and then everyone liked him a lot."

Someone stood behind me and wound an Ace bandage around my eyes. I was thrown to the floor. A voice said, "Pledge Olympics." A substance with the texture of cookie dough hit me in the back of the head. Something else hit my neck and went down my shirt. I reached for my blindfold. My hands were pushed away. Hot liquid scalded my face. Someone said, "I am pissing on you." Then, all at once, I was pounded from every side by what, I later learned, was beer and water and rotten food, which mixed on the floor into a rank batter. When I tried to stand, I slid and fell. Someone rolled on top of me. A voice said, "Magna Para, stop trying to fuck your pledge brother."

When it was over, we were marched to the bathroom. Our blindfolds were removed. Over the urinal, someone had driven a nail through a cockroach and written, "He died for your sins." We were each given fifteen seconds in a cold shower and then told to put our dirty clothes back on. For the next several hours, whenever I moved, chunky grime would fall down my back.

Before sunrise, we gathered for Redneck Hour, during which, the most backwoods, good old boys in the fraternity led us through a country sing-along, grooving in their cowboy boots. We danced to "I'll Fix Your Flat Tire Merle," by the Pure Prairie League, to "All My Rowdy Friends," by Hank Williams, Jr., to "White Lightning," by George Jones. At one point, as I stumbled along, a senior put his arm around me and said, "I've been outside and I can promise you that time is passing. This will be over. And, for the rest of your life, you will look back and say, 'I made it through that, I can make it through anything.' "

In the morning, we were led to the kitchen, where Planet, our pledge trainer, was waiting. He looked like an undertaker, his gray hair brushed in a side part, his bulk crowded into a dark suit. He shuffled a stack of papers. "Your pledge tests," he said. "Pass them, and you will be initiated." The test was twenty pages long; multiple-choice, fill-in-the-blank, essay. My hand cramped as I wrote, and my eyes blurred and my head fell back and I was dreaming. Planet, setting down his newspaper, nudged me awake.

When three hours had gone by, he said, "Turn over your papers and pass them forward."

"While the tests are graded, you will be asked to wait upstairs," said Planet. "As you wait, we ask you to think of five reasons why you want to be an Alpha Sigma. You will present these reasons at the initiation ceremony, so they are important. Without them, you cannot be initiated."

Someone wound a blindfold around my eyes. Planet was now just a voice, saying, "After all you have been through, thinking up these reasons will be easy, and should take you no more than ten minutes."

We were then brought upstairs and each led to a different room. Walking in and out of the rooms, Actives would ask how you were doing with your reasons. You would recite what you had come up with and an Active would say, "Keep trying." Or, "Is that really what you mean?" A music tape kept returning to "All I Want for Christmas Is My Two Front Teeth" by Alvin and the Chipmunks. As the hours crawled by, you could feel your mind begin to reel. Saturday afternoon I was still in a room going over my reasons, seated next to my big brother. "Those are good reasons," said Mozambique, dropping a strand of Mardi Gras beads over my head. Another voice said, "That's all he has? Those are bullshit reasons. I'm blackballing this fucker."

Someone said, "Defend yourself."

When I tried to talk, the words got caught in my throat and I choked and I pulled at the beads around my neck and the strand broke and the beads raced across the floor and hot tears rushed to the corner of my eyes.

"That's it," said Paul Fairly. "This fucker is gone."

"You blackball him, I'm gone, too," said Mozambique.

"You deserve to go," said Fairly.

Fairly grabbed my arm and pulled me toward the stairs. I searched my mind for the moment everything had gone wrong.

"Where are you taking me?" I asked.

"Through the blackball ceremony," said Fairly.

We stepped into the downstairs living room. I heard the president of the fraternity, Rocky Top, say, "You are now entering an ancient city in Italy." Paul Fairly took my hand, his grasp wet and warm, and led me across the floor, the president narrating: "You are now passing through the gate of the old city; you are now walking beneath one of the city's medieval towers; you are now crossing a footbridge over a swift river." Straining against my blindfold, I could almost see the cobbled streets of the city, towers backed by a clear Tuscan sky. When I reached the center of the city, Rocky Top asked me a series of questions, and then had me repeat a phrase. When I did so, a cheer went up and my blindfold was pulled away. I was surrounded by the graduates of the fraternity. Everything glittered. Mozambique hugged me and said, "You're in buddy. You made it."

A few hours later, when Zeke was initiated, Jason Flash, an Active with a lightning bolt tattooed on each fist, took him aside and said, "There were no reasons. It was all bullshit. None of it meant anything." Rocky Top overheard Jason Flash, and he was angry. To say that none of it meant anything was wrong, explained Rocky Top. The meaning of pledgeship is just not something that can be summed up in five reasons; the meaning is in the struggling to come up with the reasons. In other words, the meaning is not at the end of the trial, it is in the trial itself. It is in the suffering that binds you with your pledge brothers. "When you walk in this place, you feel a charge," said Rocky Top. "And that's what I'm talking about. Yes, the House is a rundown wreck, but it is ground made hallow by your struggle."

In the coming years, the fraternity became a home to me, the first and last stop of every evening out. In one way or another, pledgeship brought me close to everyone in the House. We thought of ourselves as soldiers who had seen each other through a battle; we swore to never let each other down. In extreme situations—the middle of a binge, the end of a Mardi Gras—I turned to my fraternity brothers for the kind of help one might expect from close relatives, and I was never disappointed. Score one big for cognitive dissonance. And yet . . . I never lived in the House and I never hazed a pledge. During lineups, I stayed away. I cannot stand to see a person confused or humiliated. By senior year, I had become a "satellite," one of those fraternity members who drift in and out of view, only half-connected to the House. But by then, I was already focused on life beyond college, a world where the stories of pledgeship would seem as strange and inexplicable as the initiation rituals of the chthonic religious cults of ancient Greece. In the end, the fraternity was less something I wanted to do, than something I wanted to have done.

Mein Doll

By Jamie Malanowski

Killed: *The New Yorker*, 2001

The following piece was eagerly commissioned by The New Yorker *in the summer of 2001, enthusiastically accepted when it was turned in, and slotted for a late September publication. But before the story ran, the September 11 attacks took place. Suddenly readers wanted to know more about terrorism and Afghanistan and anthrax than an admittedly creepy figure like Mike Fosella.*

But it was more than interest in suddenly compelling secret organizations that governed the public mood (and the editorial mood, as well). Vanity Fair *editor Graydon Carter famously observed that this event marked "the end of irony"; a few weeks later, he backtracked, and quipped that he meant to say "the end of ironing." But I'm not sure he was wrong. Black-and-white linear thinking took hold after 9/11, and it hasn't entirely let go.*

Mike Fosella is forty-three, a tall, gaunt man with half-mast eyelids who lives with his mother and five dogs and some goats and pot-bellied pigs at the end of a secluded cul-de-sac in Pound Ridge, New York. Fosella owns and operates R.F.T.G. Inc.—it stands for Resin from the Grave—a company that in the tradition of the old Aurora Plastics produces and sells by mail order mostly movie monster models. Among his larger successes have been Frankenstein, the Werewolf of London, and the fat guy from *Plan 9 from Outer Space*, but he also recently sold five hundred copies of a Betty Boop in the classic slipping towel pose at $140 a piece. However, we've come to this leafy Westchester suburb to talk about Fosella's latest product: a limited edition, twelve-inch, G.I. Joe–sized doll of Josef Mengele.

"I'm not trying to endorse Nazism," says Mr. Fosella in his kitchen, where the foot-high Mengele sits on the table. "I'm not a skinhead. I know this is not for everybody's stomach. This is for the serious collector."

Fosella started R.F.T.G. about fifteen years ago, and over the years discovered that while his Werewolves and Betty Boops have found an audience (Michael Jackson, Eddie Van Halen, and Kurt Hammond of Metallica have been customers), the pieces could easily be ripped off. "There was a lot of recasting," he says, "so I began to look into dolls." A couple of years ago he began fashioning his line of Nazis. "Mengele's first," he says, "but I'm going to do all of them— Himmler, Bormann, Goering. Goebbels will be at a podium with a microphone. Eichmann's going to be in a glass booth." The Hitler doll, in which he's shown wearing a trench coat leaving Landsburg prison in 1924, has been sold out in pre-orders, but Fosella plans four or five *führers*. "I'm going to do one of him at the Berchtesgarten, wearing *lederhosen*, with a hat on," says Fosella. "That'll be a nice piece, man. All my customers are saying 'Put me down for that one!' "

Amazingly, however, Fosella isn't the only one who has had this Nazi doll brainstorm. Drastic Plastic, of Hollywood, is putting out a mini-Hitler as part of a Leaders of World War II series; the others, as you might guess, are Roosevelt, Churchill, Stalin, Mussolini, and Hirohito. David Reeves, part owner of Drastic, says he's doing it in part to promote a knowledge of history. "We've always had lots of kids playing with the toys around here," says Reeves, whose other products appear, among other places, with Burger King meals. "When the kids played with the World War II stuff, they always knew the Americans were the good guys and the Germans were the bad guys, but they never knew why. Kids twelve, thirteen, fourteen—not one knew who Hitler was!" Drastic decided to bridge the gap with this series. The company will make up to 25,000 of each, priced at $59.99.

"I don't think they should be mass produced," argues Fosella. "They shouldn't be for kids. How many kids are going to get a Hitler doll and know how much he went through, all he went through? How he built the Autobahn, how if he didn't invade Russia and didn't do Auschwitz and those other terrible things, we'd think he was one of the greatest statesmen ever?" Fosella's dolls will appear in far more limited editions—fifty Mengeles, twenty Eichmanns—and will cost between $170 and $200.

Like Reeves, Fosella sees himself spreading historical knowledge. This he accomplishes with a devotion to detail, which he attains with the assistance of platoon of artists. "There's a guy in Erie, Pennsylvania, who makes the hats and batons, and an artist in the New York area does all the painting. I have an Indian woman, eighty-five years old, who makes the coats. She can't do more than one or two a day. There's a guy who does the boots and the SS insignia. I can't tell you who, he's already been contacted by the Jewish Defense League. The medals are made by a person in Chappaqua who shall remain nameless. It's a touchy subject."

Touchy indeed, but the results can't be dismissed. Unlike blank-faced G.I. Joes, with their stiff, ill-cut clothing, Fosella's Mengele, with its strong facial likeness and realistic clothing and accessories, looks like a figure from a museum diorama. "Everything is completely authentic," says Fosella, "Look at the *Totenkopf* on the cap, the piping on the brim, the gloss on the visor. He's wearing a gray uniform, not black; the SS changed to field gray in 1942. We show him smoking, because he smoked five packs a day, and he's holding a baton, because when he was doing selections on the dock, who would live and who would die, he would hit people with his baton. And look at the lab coat—" Fosella opens the white coat with its SS marking on the breast—"it has an inside pocket, just like the original."

Obligingly, we ask the obvious follow-up, how he knows that detail. Fosella leaves the room and returns in an instant with a white garment over his arm. He unfurls it. There, under a shelf full of his mother's ceramic chickens, in front of butter softening on the sideboard, now slightly yellowing, is Mengele's lab coat—with the big insignia, the inside pocket, the faded inkstamp on a hem that says it was make in Auschwitz, the large stain on the back whose yellow-gray outline looks like a map of the Balkans, which Fosella says came from a U.S. Army Ranger who urinated on it.

"Don't ask me how I got it," says Fosella, who, as it turns out, has a large collection of Nazi artifacts. He declines to say how many pieces he's amassed ("Oh, a lot!" says his mother, with an exasperated eye roll), but among them are a gold-plated Walther P-38 Hitler gave Otto Skorzeny, the SS pilot who rescued Mussolini when he was being held by Italian soldiers in 1943, and the signed copy of *Mein Kampf* Hitler gave Goebbels. "I used to have a Nuremberg Rally flag," he says. "Eight by ten, pockmarked, some mold, not brittle, really nice. I sold it to a guy for $3,500 cash. He burned the damn thing in my driveway! I said 'What the hell are you doing that for? That's a piece of history!' But he paid for it, he could do what he wanted. He was a rabbi."

Such experiences have evidently given Fosella at least some perspective on his toy making. "Look, I'm not a nutcase," he says, trying to position himself. "If I offend someone, I'm sorry. I don't have Nazi flags on my wall. I have lots of friends who are Jewish. And I'm not trying to make a million bucks— I'm making fifty of these figures, and I could easily sell five hundred. Five thousand! Making them is just a personal thing. To put these pieces out, as authentic as they are—"

He gropes, then settles on a phrase. "It gives me a chubby."

My Man Vinny

By Julian Rubinstein

Killed: *The New York Times Magazine*, 2001

Writing about drugs, which I've done, can be a tricky proposition. Writing about drugs which I've done proved even trickier. When I proposed this story to my editor, she had just one question: "Are you sure you want to write about this?" I was, after all, admitting to a crime. "Yes," I said, without checking the statute of limitations or sentencing guidelines, "I'm sure."

Of course, the piece ended up—unlike me, an admitted user—dead on the newsroom floor. Another victim of the war on drugs? Perhaps. For any publication that strives to be seen as objective, the impossible but worthy challenge is to achieve the subjective goal of balanced coverage. This doesn't just mean balance within a story. The best publications recognize that the strict he-said, she-said objectivity model often cheats readers out of the depth or insight a more "one-sided" piece can provide. So, often magazine stories in particular are permitted to have an opinion— so long as tabs are kept internally for the next time the same politically charged subject comes up. Like the equal time doctrine that television news stations adhere to when covering political candidates, these publications apply their own fairness standards in an attempt to give all sides equal space.

To its credit, the New York Times Magazine *is one of the publications that often chooses to navigate the booby-trapped terrain of point-of-view journalism. And not long before the magazine assigned this essay, it happened to run a first-person cover story entitled "Experiencing Ecstasy" that critics complained was excessively pro-drug. When my rather pro-drug story reached the final approval stages, the editorial rudder was likely pointing in the other direction.*

T hings between Vinny and me began on the rocks: misunderstandings, jealousy, tension; the usual. But over the course of time—seven years, now—our relationship had become, I thought, among the most reliable and trusting I'd ever had. We were simpatico, or so it seemed, until the incident a few months back shattered my notions of everything we ever had. Strangely—or not, as I guess is the point—I'm not sure he's noticed, as our rendezvous routine still remains the same.

"You called," he says, responding to my page.

"Yeah," I say. "I'm on [X Street] and [Y Avenue]."

"Who's this?" he asks.

"John," I used to answer, and once "June," deciding midsyllable that I should try to retain whatever anonymity can be had when buying reefer from someone to whom you've already given your address and phone number.

"Who?" he always asks, no matter what I say.

You get the picture. The lines are all scripted. They always were. But given the way our relationship started, I guess I should just be happy to be saying them at all.

I'd arrived in New York like a blunderbuss. In my first

conversation with Vinny, years ago, I'd asked "How much?"— a question that I soon realized suggested an impending sting operation. Vinny immediately hung up and I was left atoning like a nonpracticing Jew on Yom Kippur: starving, sad, and suddenly so goddamn sorry. It was months before I beeped Vinny again. Of course, he didn't call back. But then another time on another evening, Vinny unexpectedly offered me his forgiveness, phoning back and stoically fulfilling my order. I tried not to wonder how much his change of heart had to do with the fact that I'd moved to another apartment and was dialing from a new number.

In any case, the awkward tension that had defined our early days melted away and Vinny and I entered a time that now feels so distant. We shared that exquisite bliss derived from the perfect blend of blind trust and the flouting of jail time.

Of course, it had dawned on me one day, as I deliberated not taking my wallet to an early-lunch rendezvous, that Vinny was actually his ragamuffiny cast of deliverymen: twenty-something immigrants with battered bikes and dying cars who were available at any hour. But somehow I was too smitten make a real distinction. Just look at them—they were as wary and afraid of me as I was of them. As easily as they could have been knife-wielding maniacs, I might have been a cop, a narc, a thief, a Republican!

Oh, my man Vinny! I could see right through the curt phone manner, the emotionless speech patterns: clear self-defense mechanisms. He needed me as I did him. In fact, in some ways, I came to think of myself as *his* provider. I gave the financial support. It was charity work. But he was exceptionally low-maintenance. Comfort in Vinny's world was all about minimalism. Most questions or gestures, even a pat on the back, could be perceived as threatening. But I began to let the bike deliverymen up to the apartment, offering a sweaty

Swedish guy in a helmet water; I chatted with an Ecuadorian in Spanish about the Mets while sitting in a smelly coupe with no A/C; and with the others, the warm weather, or, alternatively, the cold.

Surely Vinny would appreciate my thoughtfulness. Or so I imagined, until that rainy afternoon a few months ago when I made my call and got what I had coming.

Like always, Vinny called back in about twenty minutes—it was never more than an hour, anyway—and muttered in his endearing monotone the make and color of the vehicle currently double-parked on the block outside my building. (In bad weather, I'd noticed, he never made his carriers travel by bike.) I hung up, went downstairs, and picked my way down the street, trying to make eye contact with parked drivers. I could never remember if Vinny said a blue Cutlass, a gray Mercury, or what other wreck no one would look at twice. But halfway down the block, a young Hispanic guy in a pocked-up Something returned my glance with a nod. I strode over and got in.

"Hey," I said. "What do you got?"

He lifted off a fake veneer of a stereo and pulled out several plastic bags of green bud in two sizes. "This one really good," he said with a thick accent. I ducked down to smell and fondle a few before settling on one of the small ones. "Forty," he said. "Prices change?" I asked. "No," he said. "Oh," I said, handing over two twenties, putting the stuff in my pocket, and telling him, "Thanks, man, stay dry." I headed back to my apartment where the phone was ringing, and my answering machine was blinking with three new messages. I picked up.

"Where are you?" demanded Vinny in a tone I'd never heard from him before.

"What do you mean," I asked, my heart jumping.

"He's waiting outside," Vinny said.

"I just got back," I told him.

"I'll call you back," Vinny said. Just as the phone rang again it hit me.

"What car did you get in?" Vinny screamed when I picked up.

As revelations go, I wouldn't have expected that discovering Vinny's outfit to be one of perhaps hundreds of similar operations carpeting New York City to be anything but a story he and I would one day tell our children. Why should he be jealous? I was happy with him. I didn't need anyone else. We were just having a moment.

But as Vinny's verbal assault hit its stride, I began to get the idea that, at least for him, the thrill was gone.

The conversation, and, in effect, our "relationship" ended a few minutes later almost the way it all began: with an ominous hang up, leaving me to worry if Vinny would be sending someone over to get me. He didn't. In fact, Vinny still takes my calls as if the whole thing never occurred. ("Who?" he says, half-convincingly.) But it's made me think about something I didn't want to consider before. Vinny may be my man, but as it turns out, I actually am just a John.

Unfortunate Con

By Mark Schone

Killed: *Rolling Stone*, 2002

Even by the standards of a book called Killed, *the story behind this story is morbid.*

In 1999, a publishing house killed a controversial biography of George W. Bush, and two years later the author of the bio killed himself. In 2001, Rolling Stone *asked me to find out why the writer had committed suicide—and if it really was suicide—but then killed my piece about the dead author and the dead book. The Oxford American ran a shorter version of my article in the summer of 2003, only to become a casualty itself within weeks when it ceased publication because of a lack of advertising.*

"Unfortunate Con" is the saga of James H. Hatfield, an obscure writer from Arkansas who for a few days seemed to have landed the biggest scoop of the 2000 presidential campaign. According to Hatfield's book Fortunate Son, *three secret sources had confirmed that in 1972 a friendly judge had covered up George W. Bush's arrest for cocaine possession. When reporters learned that Hatfield himself was hiding a criminal past, St. Martin's Press pulled the book off the shelves and Hatfield fled home to Arkansas.*

For the next two years, Hatfield continued to insist that the coke bust and his highly placed sources were real. Then, in the summer of 2002, as part of the relaunch of Fortunate Son *by a different publisher, he finally revealed the names of his alleged informants, including his "Deep Throat." Hatfield was found dead six weeks later. Some on the left still wonder whether President Bush had a hand in his death.*

Given the well-known political leanings of Rolling Stone *boss Jann Wenner, some of my colleagues have suggested that he lost interest in this story when I didn't dig up proof of GOP perfidy. That's not an unreasonable suspicion, but it's probably unfounded. After some preliminary research I made very sure my editor knew which way the chads were hanging before I ever boarded a plane.*

The real reason for the article's death probably has more to do with the magazine business as a whole than with any one editor's political leanings. After four months of reporting, I handed in a dense, complicated parable about self-invention and self-deception. When Rolling Stone *nixed it as too long and too "depressing," I was less than surprised by the rejection. In an era when "hot" lists are feature articles, and Hollywood publicists pick cover shots, there just aren't that many major magazines around that will assign a story like this one, much less publish it.*

When he was fifty yards from his target, Bruce Gabbard dropped to his knees and began to crawl through the high grass until he reached the treeline at the edge of the field. It was nearly midnight on a hot July night. Rising to a crouch, he peered through binoculars across a chain-link fence and a lawn and into the window of a wood-and-brick house. In a square of light stood his friend Jim's wife and a few other women. Between Gabbard and the light, at the edge of the lawn, lay a hot tub and a gray shed that held the metal safe he intended to steal.

That afternoon, J. H. "Jim" Hatfield had been found dead in a hotel room, an apparent suicide. Just seven weeks earlier, Hatfield had told Gabbard, "If anything ever happens to me, I want you to make the safe in my backyard office disappears. It holds my secrets. I don't want them to fall into the wrong hands." Hatfield had hinted that those secrets might have something to do with the CIA and President George W. Bush. So ten years after his military service in the Gulf War, forty-year-old Bruce Gabbard found himself on a stealth mission behind a ranch house in Bentonville, Arkansas.

He scaled the fence and crept behind the shed. The latch of the little building's rear window had been left open. Gabbard climbed through.

The office was tidy, as it had always been. Paperback thrillers and file folders, the orderly rubble of Hatfield's controversial career as a writer, lined the shelves. Gabbard jerked the hundred-pound safe from its hiding place beneath a custom-built desk and lifted it through the window.

He humped the weight a sweaty half-mile through pastures and woods. It was a heavier load than he'd ever carried in the military, and it took him almost an hour to reach the field where he had parked his Jeep.

For hours Gabbard listened to his police scanner and drove the silent streets, the metal box in the back. He was afraid. Hatfield had intimated that powerful forces wanted to silence him, and now Hatfield was dead. Gabbard's own wife waited at home with the lights on and a pistol nearby. He was reluctant to call her because he didn't know who'd be listening.

Finally, right before the sun came up, when he was certain he wasn't being followed, Gabbard drove home. Later that morning, he met with his attorney, then drove to a storage complex and moved the safe into a locker. Jim Hatfield's secrets were secure.

Two years before, on the afternoon of Tuesday, October 19, 1999, Jim Hatfield was sitting in his editor's office at St. Martin's Press eating sushi. Though he longed to be home in Arkansas with his six-day-old daughter, he was excited to be in New York instead, in a corner office on the seventeenth floor of the Flatiron Building, waiting for reporters to call. It was the official release date of the book that was going to make him famous.

The editors and publicists of St. Martin's, meanwhile, were happy to finally meet their new star. Until a few days earlier, Hatfield had been no more than an upbeat drawl on the phone. In person, he turned out to be a balding, high-strung forty-one-year-old with a nervous yen for other people's cigarettes, and a striking likeness to Billy Bob Thornton.

When Hatfield signed a contract for a biography of Bush in September 1998, he was a midlist author of science-fiction trivia guides. He told St. Martin's that he had freelanced for alternative papers in Texas and had won the Isaac Asimov Foundation Literary Award for his biography of Star Trek actor Patrick Stewart. He hardly seemed the best choice to profile the leading GOP presidential contender, but editor Barry Neville, who'd hired him for a quickie bio of Ewan McGregor for the Berkeley Publishing Group, had moved to St. Martin's, and when Hatfield sent him a proposal, Neville vouched for his professionalism. St. Martin's, a reputable but second-tier publishing house, was only paying a $25,000 advance anyway, and didn't expect much more than a repackaging of previously published material. Hatfield's editors were pleasantly surprised in June when he handed in a polished manuscript that listed more than one hundred people as interview subjects.

They were floored when he called them on September 2 and told them that he urgently needed to add an afterword to the book, because he now had a scoop that would make Fortunate Son a bestseller. "We contracted for a bland, nice clip job," said one of the editors, "not a bombshell."

According to Hatfield, three unnamed sources from the Bush camp had informed him that in 1972 Bush had been arrested for cocaine possession, and that the arrest had been covered up with the help of a Houston judge. One of the sources had noted that the judge was a Republican. In the now infamous afterword, Hatfield explained that he'd read an article on *Salon.com* about a rumor that Bush had been sent to work at the Martin Luther King, Jr., Community Center in Houston as part of a deal to hide a coke bust. The *Salon* reporter had quoted the director of the center denying that Bush had spent any time there. Since, at the elder Bush's request, George W. had in fact logged several months at a different Houston community center called P.U.L.L., Hatfield had decided to investigate whether P.U.L.L. might hold the key to the coke rumor instead:

> To confirm my suspicions regarding Bush's community service, I chose three confidential sources who had been extremely helpful with other sections of the book. . . . If I was going to get any one of them to talk . . . a poker game was certainly in order. With each of them I would have to claim that I had numerous sources who were confirming the allegations "on the record". . . . Basically. I would tell them I was holding a royal flush, when in reality I would be sitting at the table with nothing at all.

Hatfield said his first source, a Yale classmate of W.'s and longtime friend of the Bush clan, yielded to the faux flush with surprising ease. "I was wondering when someone was going to get around to uncovering the truth," Hatfield quoted him as saying. Hatfield said that the second source, an "unofficial political advisor," also confirmed the rumor.

The last of Hatfield's alleged confidantes, a man who had supposedly described himself as a "close associate" of Bush's, was the most important. The man had called him out of the blue months earlier, Hatfield said, to see how his book was coming along, and to make sure he was getting his facts straight. Hatfield reported that he told the man he'd already turned in a manuscript, but the source suggested they meet anyway because Hatfield could always revise the galleys. According to Hatfield, the pair decided to rendezvous at an enormous man-made lake south of Tulsa called Eufaula. The purported meeting made Hatfield's wife, Nancy, so nervous that she begged him to take a gun.

For three days in late June, claimed Hatfield, he and his mystery date fished and talked, after which Hatfield was told not to contact him again unless it was an emergency. A few months later on September 2, Hatfield said he phoned his Lake Eufaula connection again. Hatfield reported that his man said, "I wish you hadn't called me," then cursed him for using a cordless phone. He did, however, agree to call Hatfield back. Hatfield asserted that thirty minutes later the Lake Eufaula connection confirmed the P.U.L.L. story, and closed with a warning—"watch your back"—and a slap at his boss: "You know what makes me sick about all this shit?" said the source. "It's Bush's hypocrisy. . . . I've known George for several years and he has never accepted youth and irresponsibility as legitimate excuses for illegal behavior—except when it comes to himself."

Hatfield declined to tell anyone at St. Martin's the name of the Lake Eufaula man. When publicist John Murphy challenged Hatfield to tell him how someone with no national reporting experience could beat the media elite to the story of the year, Hatfield explained that he had access through his Texas-bred wife to Bush pals in Houston. "I'm a good old boy," he said, " I know how to talk to these people."

With the biggest scoop of the 2000 race in the bag, St. Martin's gave *Fortunate Son* a code name: M.J., as in Michael Jordan, as in the Franchise. They raised the print run from 20,000 to 100,000, and pushed the publication date up to October 19.

Murphy sent more than two hundred advance copies to newspapers, magazines, and television stations, and awaited a barrage of phone calls.

By M.J. Day, though, it was apparent that something was amiss. After a day of investigating Hatfield's claims, the *New York Times* declined to run a piece about the book. "They couldn't get confirmation," says Murphy. "They had three different reporters working on it."All the networks ignored the Hatfield story as well, and the CBS Evening News shelved a pretaped interview with Hatfield because of concerns about his credibility. A reporter from the *New York Post* challenged Hatfield on his facts: A GOP judge couldn't have buried Bush's cocaine charges, because there were no GOP judges in Harris County, Texas, in 1972.

By the time Hatfield ordered sushi on October 19, John Murphy was worried, but he was still thinking bestseller. That's when the publicity department fielded a call from a Dallas Morning News reporter named Pete Slover. Slover said that someone named James Howard Hatfield had been convicted of soliciting murder in Dallas in 1988. "I got a mug shot of this guy," Slover said, "and I think it's your guy."

Hatfield looked Murphy in the eye and swore the charge

wasn't true. Then Hatfield got on the phone with Slover and tried to turn suspicion onto the Bush campaign. "Doesn't it seem a little bit weird to you," he said, "that all of a sudden, the guy that's accusing potentially the next president of the United States of having a criminal record expunged, all of a sudden miraculously has a record himself in the state of Texas? . . . If I've got a secret past, I'm damn sure not going to be going all over the country plastering myself all over the newspapers or TV."

He repeated his denials to the whole St. Martin's team. He threatened Pete Slover with a lawsuit. Then he left the building and went back to the Inter-Continental Hotel. "We were trying to get him the next morning at his room," says Murphy, "and he had disappeared."

Hatfield *was* the guy in the picture. On October 20, the *Dallas Morning News* ran a prominent story revealing Hatfield's criminal record. When Hatfield was exposed as a felon, the mainstream press interpreted this revelation as evidence that he was lying about the coke tale, too. On the 22nd, St. Martin's pulled *Fortunate Son* out of circulation; a company spokeswoman described it as "furnace fodder." Before it became a collector's item, however, the controversy pushed *Son* to number 30 on the *New York Times* bestseller list.

In the weeks that followed, the media ripped the book apart. Hatfield claimed in his source notes to have interviewed hundreds of people. Reporters at *Texas Monthly* and *Brill's Content* contacted twenty-seven of Hatfield's purported interview subjects and not one recalled speaking to him.

As for the sensational afterword, most observers rejected it outright. Texas reporters had been hearing stories about W.'s party-boy days since his first gubernatorial run in 1994. In a half dozen years of digging, they'd never found anything but smoke. Then some hick burst out of Arkansas with three unnamed sources and a fish story. The mainstream press took Hatfield's felonious past and feeble cover-up of same as proof he was P.U.L.L.ing their legs about the coke tale, too. The media wolf pack scattered without investigating Hatfield's scoop and without asking why: True or not, why would a closeted ex-con tell such a radioactive yarn?

Bentonville, Arkansas, had no stoplights when Hatfield was a boy. Today it's a boomtown famous for being the world headquarters of Wal-Mart. There are few people still around who remember that "Tammy Stewart" was ever married to Jim Hatfield. Actually, even Stewart's teenage kids from a later marriage don't know, and she prefers to keep it that way. She won't meet a reporter in person, or let her real name be used, but she agrees to chat on the phone about her first marriage and Hatfield's first trip to New York to meet with a publisher.

In 1976, Stewart, a pale, insecure majorette at tiny Bentonville High, fell in love with Hatfield, who drove her school bus. She was a sixteen-year-old sophomore; he was an eighteen-year-old Bentonville grad who had dropped out of college and come home to work. They exchanged vows as soon as the school year ended. "I was young and dumb," says Stewart, who was married to Hatfield for about a year and a half, "and no man had really paid attention to me before."

Stewart says Hatfield seemed to have been overindulged by his mother, Pearl. His only sibling, Ray, was fifteen years older, and his father, Ralph, a county worker, was distant. Pearl, however, still packed her youngest son's lunch every day—with detailed instructions on which items to eat first. Stewart would later learn that Hatfield's mother had told his father, "You ruined the first one. This one's mine."

But Hatfield captivated Stewart with his bright blue eyes and his compliments. Most of all, he enchanted her with his ambition to be a famous writer, a goal he'd had since childhood, when Ian Fleming, author of the James Bond novels, became his hero. For his twelfth birthday Hatfield had requested an electric typewriter. At Bentonville High, Hatfield was vice president of the Library Club. He was so single-minded about writing that at sixteen he arranged a meeting with a local author of horror novels named Ruby Jean Jensen.

Hatfield's new bride helped him edit his first novel, a thriller about giant mutant serpents gone berserk called *Year of the Snake*. In lieu of a honeymoon, the couple flew to New York to pitch his book to publishers. Stewart waited nervously in a hotel room while Hatfield hit the pavement, manuscript in briefcase. He'd vowed to knock on every door in Manhattan till he found a publisher. Recalls Stewart, "He came back just a few hours later and said. 'They bought it! I got an advance!' " When they returned to Bentonville, Hatfield wrote a check for a new Ford LTD and put a $50,000 down payment on a suburban mansion.

Though Hatfield wanted to be a famous writer, the patience needed to earn success the plodding, orthodox, workaday way was, apparently, beyond him.

The checks bounced. Hatfield had printed them up on a copier. There was no huge advance. There hadn't even been any meetings with publishers. "He flat chickened out," says Stewart. "I think he went to one place, and he realized how hard it was going to be."

Hatfield was arrested. But his behavior was so delusional that instead of sending him to prison, the judge shipped him to the state mental hospital in Little Rock for a month of observation.

Fewer than six months later, in April 1978, Hatfield was in trouble again. After his release from the hospital, he had continued to tell people that he'd sold *Year of the Snake* for a fortune. He began breaking into houses and snatching art and potted plants. The things he stole were props for his fantasy of success. Arrested on five counts of burglary and three counts of theft, he was sentenced to five years in prison. "He had some great dreams," says Stewart. "I just didn't think he had the guts to achieve them by legal means." After less than a year, Hatfield was paroled.

By 1981, Hatfield was in Dallas. Larry Burk, president of a real-estate firm there called Credit Finance Corporation, instructed Kay Burrow, his vice president, to hire a thin, well-dressed twenty-three-year-old transplant from Arkansas as her personal assistant. Two years earlier, Hatfield had rented an apartment at the Leigh Ann, one of Burk's federally subsidized housing complexes in the south Dallas suburbs. The manager of the low-income low-rise had noticed the bright, friendly country boy and given him a job. Burk was ordering Burrow to promote him to the main office in the Cotton Exchange building downtown.

Though Burrow and Burk have since moved to a different Dallas skyscraper, they still work together, as they have for thirty-five years. Side by side at a long oak table in a conference room, they bicker good-naturedly about Burrow's former assistant.

"The first time I met Hatfield, the hair stood up on my neck," says Burrow. She gives her boss an accusing smile. "But Larry was so naive about him. He was charmed."

Burk concedes the point. "He seemed like a decent young kid from Arkansas who was interested in literature."

"He was good with the baloney," Burrow says.

Most of the women working at CFC's headquarters liked Hatfield's ready smile, his curly brown hair, and his flirtatious manner. And they were impressed when he told them that he wrote books in his spare time, including a thin volume of love poetry called *New Beginnings*. They learned that the height of Hatfield's ambition was to write a James Bond book.

Several years into his tenure at CFC, Hatfield announced that he'd won a license to continue the Bond series in a contest sponsored by the estate of the late Ian Fleming. Hatfield said that his first 007 book would be titled *The Killing Zone*, and would feature a curvy, blond killer named Lotta Head and a gay Nazi drug lord. "Bond's narrow eyes squinted with a hint of anger," read one passage. " 'Who is this bastard Klaus Doberman?' "

Hatfield shared the most intimate details of his ambitions with his best friend, Norma Rodriguez, a receptionist at CFC. Rodriguez was a stocky, brassy Mexican-American a dozen years his senior. She and Hatfield became so close they vacationed together. Much like Hatfield's first wife, Rodriguez tells a story of waiting in a Manhattan hotel room while Hatfield pretended to take a morning meeting with his "publisher." At the CFC offices, he would often tell Rodriguez that he was expecting to hear from his other publisher in London about the Bond book. "Every time I went to the bathroom," says Rodriguez, "this guy would call. Jim would say, 'You *just* missed it!' "

Rodriguez glimpsed a side of Hatfield that he hid from everyone else at CFC. "He always said he wanted to be rich," she says. "He always said he would make a lot of money before he reached the age of thirty-five." The only obstacle, as Hatfield saw it, was his immediate superior, Kay Burrow. Says Rodriguez, "He wanted her gone so he could be Mr. Burk's right-hand man."

In 1986, after five years at CFC, Hatfield invited both Rodriguez and Burrow for a weekend in Mexico. On a pleasure boat in Puerto Vallarta's harbor, Hatfield asked Rodriguez to lure Burrow to the front of the boat, where he could push her over the side. "He showed me how the propellers would rip her apart," says Rodriguez, still amazed. "He was very serious."

Rodriguez didn't fetch Burrow, but she didn't tell her to fly home either. By that evening, the unlikely threesome was drinking margaritas together at the bar of a cavernous night-club, watching Mexicans dance to salsa. Hatfield was getting drunk and morose. "C'mon, Jimmy," Burrow said. "Get out there and dance." He refused. She kept insisting, until finally Hatfield exploded and kicked a chair across the room.

"I said I didn't want to!" he shouted, then stormed out of the bar. Burrow and Rodriguez returned to the hotel suite, rifled through Hatfield's bags until they found their airline tickets, and flew home.

After the Puerto Vallarta trip, Rodriguez tried to keep her distance from Hatfield. He'd begun to lapse into unprovoked table-pounding temper tantrums about Burrow. Rodriguez finally decided to warn her. Recalls Burrow, "That's when Norma said, 'He's not your friend. Don't ever believe he is.' "

Realizing that her initial distrust of Hatfield had been justi-fied, Burrow contacted the Ian Fleming estate in England and learned that the executor had never heard of Hatfield. Burrow didn't confront Hatfield with her discovery, but she let others in the office know. When Hatfield presented his office mates with self-published copies of The Killing Zone, Burrow probably wasn't the only one who snickered at the hand-drawn bullet holes on the front cover and the typo on the back: "Bond has his hands full as he battles a lucious [sic] lady assassin."

Then, in January 1987, Burrow figured out how Hatfield could afford to have The Killing Zone printed. A year before, Larry Burk had made Hatfield responsible for paying vendors who worked on CFC's two dozen HUD-subsidized properties. By inspecting Hatfield's checks for irregularities, Burrow noticed that a vendor's name had been slightly altered. When she flipped the check over, she saw that the firm's account number had changed, too. As federal agents would later discover, Hatfield had talked an elderly female teller into letting him open several accounts without proper identification. Each phony business had a name very similar to a CFC vendor. Before Burrow caught him, he'd funneled $100,000 into these look-alike accounts. On advice of counsel, Burk says he decided to forego prosecution and simply have Hatfield fired.

A few weeks later, at 9:45 AM on February 9, 1987, Burrow slid into the driver's seat of her blue Buick in the Cotton Exchange parking garage. Her new assistant, Gordon Jennings—Hatfield's replacement—got in beside her. Burrow turned the key in the ignition and put the car in reverse. An explosion lifted the front of the big sedan about a foot in the air. Flames billowed from under the crumpled hood, but other than shaken nerves and bruised knees, Burrow and Jennings were not injured. "Call the fire department. The battery blew up," said Jennings. "No," shot back Burrow, "call the police."

The bomb was ineptly constructed. The Buick had been parked over a mound of black powder primed with a blasting cap. Black powder is an unreliable explosive, and not all of it detonated. "That device could've killed fifteen people," says veteran ATF agent Gary Clifton, who handled the case. "But the net effect was about as powerful as if you ran over a culvert and hit the bottom of your car."

"I knew right away. I knew it was him," Burrow says. A week before the bombing, on his last day of work, Hatfield had walked Burrow out to her parking space and hugged her goodbye. "He said how much he loved me and how much he liked to work for me," Burrow marvels, "when he already knew he was going to try to kill me."

Though Hatfield had established an alibi by flying to Mexico before the bombing, Clifton agreed with Burrow about the prime suspect, especially after his first face-to-face encounter with Hatfield. Clifton's assessment is direct. "A shit-bag sociopath," he snaps. "A spineless, backstabbing son-of-a-bitch. Everything is always somebody else's fault. He was incapable of making a complete statement without part of it being untrue."

Eventually, Clifton squeezed a confession out of another suspect, a CFC maintenance man named Charles Crawford. Both Rodriguez and Hatfield knew him. Crawford said that Hatfield had hired him to kill Burrow. But it was Norma Rodriguez who became the prosecution's star witness. In front of a grand jury, she said that the night before the bombing Crawford had come to her apartment and admitted that Hatfield had paid him $5,000 to kill Burrow. He wanted her murdered with a knife or a gun, something "up-close and personal," as Rodriguez testified, but Crawford didn't have the guts. Instead, he'd checked a book on bombs out of the public library.

Hatfield copped a plea and got fifteen years in state prison. With good behavior, he would have been free in five. But not long after entering the Beto II penal facility in Palestine, Texas, Hatfield devised a scam that led to his third confinement. As FBI agent Larry Guerin puts it, "He was just intelligent enough to get himself into trouble, but not intelligent enough to stay out of trouble."

In 1990, while at Beto II, Hatfield wrote a letter to the Inspector General of the U.S. Department of Housing and Urban Development alleging that his old mentor, Larry Burk, was a crook. In secret meetings, claimed Hatfield, Burk had taught him how to bill the government for repairs to private property. HUD took Hatfield seriously enough to launch an audit of CFC.

Guerin and a HUD investigator visited Hatfield. The agents found him to be an arrogant grifter who talked fast and repeated himself. He bragged about the famous people he'd met, the books he'd written, the great things he'd done. He insisted he'd been an important vice president at CFC. Recalls the HUD agent, who wishes to remain anonymous: "He had delusions of grandeur."

But he also had what sounded like credible evidence against Burk—until, to establish believability, he confessed to some wrongdoing of his own. He admitted to the investigators that he'd embezzled money, and that he'd tried to kill Burrow because she caught him cooking the books. Hatfield had somehow convinced himself that he couldn't be charged for embezzlement if he was already doing time for the attempted murder.

The informant turned into a suspect. When Larry Burk's lawyer called HUD and told them that Hatfield had offered to withdraw his accusations if Burk paid him $25,000 upon his release from prison, the agents realized that Hatfield's actual goal had been to use them in an extortion scheme. The investigation of Burk ended; Hatfield was charged with one count of embezzlement and one count of making false statements. He cut a deal and pled guilty to the latter. When he was paroled from Beto II in April 1993, he was sent immediately to a federal facility in Oklahoma to serve time for his latest conviction.

When Hatfield finally got out of prison for good in December 1994, on federal probation and state parole, he had nowhere to go but home. He returned to Bentonville. His mother had died while he was in jail, and his brother had moved to Tulsa long before, but his seventy-two-year-old father was still there, scraping by on a meager pension. Hatfield moved in with him.

For eight months, Hatfield did things the hard way. He hefted boxes at a Wal-Mart warehouse, walking to his grunt-level job till he'd saved enough money to buy a used pickup. He hadn't listed his prison record on the application. "We tell them not to lie," shrugs his parole officer, Eddie Cobb. "But we also tell them they have to work. What are they going to do?" Hatfield began dating a coworker, and eventually told her about his years in prison. When their relationship fell apart, the woman retaliated by calling his boss at Wal-Mart and blowing the whistle. Hatfield was fired.

At that point many ex-cons would've packed it in. They would've closed the deal by doing crimes till they got locked up again for good. Instead, at the lowest point of his life, middle-aged, unemployed and living with his dad, Hatfield began making his childhood dreams come true.

At age sixty-two, George Burt is an ex-con success story. There are three limited-edition sports cars in the air-conditioned garage of his mansion on a golf course in the Dallas suburb of Plano. He's proud of what he's achieved since leaving Beto II. He's built a multimillion-dollar computer-consulting business with big-name clients. Seven years ago, he decided to share some of that success with his best friend from prison, Jim Hatfield. Burt, who was doing time for attempted murder, had bonded with Hatfield over a mutual interest in science fiction.

In August 1995, after Wal-Mart fired him, Hatfield called Burt and proposed a partnership. Hatfield would write science fiction books and Burt would handle the marketing and finances. When Burt's research convinced him there were thirty thousand hardcore fans who'd buy anything associated with the *Star Trek* franchise, he agreed to give the plan a shot.

"But I didn't do it for money," insists Burt. "I did it to help a friend realize a lifetime dream."

According to their agreement, Burt would pay Hatfield a monthly stipend of $2,500 plus $500 a month to lease a car. The men would share royalties and writing credit for any book they sold. They began with a couple of self-published quickies. Using the pen names Jake Dakota (Hatfield) and Scott Steele (Burt), they slapped together a trivia guide called *The Quotable X-Files* and a book of aphorisms called *The Teachings and Sayings of the Vulcan Surah*, and sold both books over the Internet. Hatfield then renewed the only real publishing contact he'd ever had, Ruby Jean Jensen, the same local author he'd schmoozed as a sixteen-year-old. She vouched for him with her publisher in New York, Kensington Books.

In 1996, Hatfield, who had written many books, held in his hands a copy of the first book he hadn't paid to have printed, *The Ultimate Star Trek Trivia Challenge*, published by Kensington. Within six months, Kensington released two more titles by Burt and Hatfield, including a biography of Patrick Stewart, Captain Picard of *Star Trek*.

With his career in motion, Hatfield turned to improving his personal life. He proposed to a twenty-seven-year-old transplant from Houston named Nancy Bledsoe. Like Tammy Stewart, Bledsoe is reluctant to talk about her marriage to Hatfield. She'll only answer, via e-mail, the most general questions about their relationship. "He was extremely outgoing and fun-loving," she explains. "He enjoyed life to the fullest, which made people want to be around him."

Hatfield captivated Bledsoe with his love for writing, as he'd done with Stewart, but he also claimed to have other, more earth-bound yearnings. He told her that he'd found big-city life in Dallas unsatisfying, and that he'd come home to Bentonville to settle down. Says Bledsoe, "He wanted a nice, quiet life with a house, children, friends, a wife, and a dog."

Through his wife's circle, and his own magnetism, Hatfield quickly made friends, including computer technician Bruce Gabbard and an emergency-room doctor named Mark Rubertus. Hatfield was unafraid to talk about religion and politics, and soon he was the center of attention among his new acquaintances.

His job gave him the freedom to sit in his backyard hot tub drinking beer at three in the morning. "I think one of the reasons we liked him so much," says Kitty Rubertus, Mark's wife, "is that we lived vicariously through him."

Kitty asserts that Hatfield was more than just a con artist. "You really couldn't say anything bad about him," she says. "The Jim who did that stuff in the past is not the Jim we knew." Mark agrees, and he understands why Hatfield could never bring himself to tell his new friends, or his own wife, the truth about his past. "He wanted himself to begin [in 1996]."

Hatfield soon had a happy, comfortable life. Bledsoe got pregnant; they had a BMW and a Durango and plans to buy a ranch-style house. And in a city without much of a literary scene, even a paperback writer enjoyed a limited celebrity. "Everywhere you went he knew somebody," says George Burt.

Hatfield told publishers he'd been a freelance writer in Texas. The day-to-day deceit was harder work. Embittered by the betrayal of his Wal-Mart girlfriend, Hatfield never admitted to his wife or his new friends that he'd ever been in prison. When they asked about his past, he would change the subject. Recalls Kitty, "He'd say, 'Oh, it's a long story.' We'd say, 'We've got time.' But he wouldn't tell us anything."

Burt realized Bledsoe was in the dark the first time he met her. "She made some comment about me and Jim being in the military together, the Special Forces." Hatfield also never told her about Burt's stipend.

Gradually, though, for the benefit of Bledsoe and his friends, Hatfield had to fill in the blanks. He suggested that while in Dallas, along with writing for newspapers, he'd worked for the CIA as an undercover profiler. Bledsoe got the most lively version of this fable. For example, the man who'd stopped by the house and introduced himself to Bledsoe as a "parole officer," Eddie Cobb, was, according to Hatfield, a CIA operative.

No matter how absurd his ruse seems in retrospect, it worked. His friends say there was nothing in Hatfield's demeanor that suggested he had anything sinister to conceal. There were none of the angry outbursts that had frightened Norma Rodriguez back in Dallas. And though he lied about his past, he was supporting his new life with honest labor. The delusional scammer had become a workaholic who pounded out a book every few months—real books, printed by a real publisher.

The hard facts of Hatfield's life and the long-nurtured fantasy of it were beginning to dovetail. By early 1999, he even had a baby daughter on the way. Then, as always, he overreached.

First, he wrote a biography for Penguin on the actor Ewan McGregor without telling his nominal co-author George Burt; the solo byline meant an increase in status, but Burt, miffed, stopped sending the monthly paychecks.

Then he took on the Bush biography, which was inspired by the same phone conversation with his literary agent, Richard Curtis, that had produced the McGregor book. Explains Curtis, "I said, 'Who do you think is going to become famous?' He said, 'The guy in *Star Wars* and George W. Bush.' I said, 'Write a campaign biography. Be the first one out of the gate.' "

Hatfield saw the Bush biography as a chance to leave the world of pulp paperbacks behind. *Fortunate Son* would be a hardbound tome on a serious subject, and for the first time he'd be doing real journalism. "That book was his lifeline," states his friend Mark Rubertus. "He really thought he'd hit the big time."

As much as he wanted fame, Hatfield recognized that the book meant an increased risk of exposure as an ex-felon. When he got the contract at St. Martin's, he asked if he could use a pen name, saying he didn't want to be mocked as a sci-fi hack who was out of his depth. But the publisher balked, and Hatfield dropped the issue. Still, he might have escaped detection if he hadn't received an e-mail from St. Martin's editor Barry Neville on August 31 telling him the book was postponed.

By then, it had been nine months since Hatfield had received a check from George Burt. A month's delay in the publication of "Son" would only exacerbate his financial problems. It also meant that Hatfield's chance of fulfilling his dream would be lost, since four other books on Bush were on the verge of publication. He began to search for something that would make St. Martin's reconsider. Two days later, on September 2, 1999, he found it, and he wrote the infamous afterword.

On October 19, as the reporter from Dallas prepared to fax a mug shot to St. Martin's, Hatfield realized he'd lost his bet. But once home in Arkansas, he began to fight back. He told people that Bush's father had forced St. Martin's to kill the book, and that the Bush camp had threatened reporters with total loss of access if they discussed the coke story. He complained to friends and associates of death threats on his answering machine and armed men in his yard. Richard Curtis recalls Hatfield warning him to check his telephone line for taps. "I really f—ing freaked." Curtis says. "He got me very creeped out about Bush, Jr., and Bush, Sr."

In reality, Hatfield had launched his own operation to suppress the truth. A month before the release of *Fortunate Son*, he'd mailed George Burt a multistep plan on what to do in case of emergency. If his past was revealed as a result of the bio, or if "something tragic" happened, Hatfield had instructed Nancy to call Burt immediately. "If you have received that call," he wrote Burt, "I need you to do the following: Call [my father] . . . and advise him that Nancy never knew the truth about me . . . I don't want Nancy or my child to think of me as an ex-con that lied to them repeatedly. If it is publicized that I have a criminal record . . . please explain to her that it is all planted . . . records can be created, etc., [as] part of a smear campaign."

As it happened, Hatfield was able to handle steps one and two himself. And two years later, when "something tragic" did happen, it was Bruce Gabbard who carried out step three, which begins, "Go to my office and the safe is in the far corner . . ."

By late 1999, the *Son* storm had blown apart Hatfield's carefully fabricated life. "There's not a day goes by," he lamented to filmmakers Michael Galinsky and Suki Hawley, who began shooting a documentary about him in November 1999, "that I don't regret [*Fortunate Son*]. I wish I'd never, ever, ever f—ing sent in a proposal."

He lost most of his friends. One couple turned on their heels when they saw the Hatfields in a restaurant. Two other couples canceled a planned camping trip. "It was like a death in the family," observes Bruce Gabbard. "What had died was Jim's reputation, and by extension Nancy's."

More importantly, he lost his career, modest as it may have been. Penguin Books and St. Martin's paid him $15,000 for two books they had contracted him to write, but told him not to bother turning in the manuscripts. He completed a children's book—*The Zoocairitas*—but even in the realm of children's literature he was a pariah. "I couldn't sell *Zoocairitas* under his real name," concedes Richard Curtis, "and it was too dangerous to sell it under a pseudonym."

To anyone else, this might have been a sign. But not to Hatfield. He could have disavowed *Fortunate Son*, moved to a new town, and taken a job flipping burgers. Instead, he tried to sustain the persona of an important writer, the Hatfield he'd created after leaving prison. With his wife and friends, Hatfield started boasting that he'd rebounded from the scandal with a six-figure contract from a major Hollywood studio for multiple screenplays. In fact, the only venue that ever published any new work by Hatfield after October 1999 was the leftie webzine *Online Journal*, which ran his increasingly vitriolic anti-Bush screeds. The only sure source of cash and glory, meanwhile, was a reissue of the book that had caused all the problems in the first place.

When *Fortunate Son* was killed, Hatfield's eager embrace of martyrdom had found a public. Unaware of the length of Hatfield's rapsheet, unimpressed by the corporate media's quibbles, a conspiracy minded slice of the left decided he'd been gagged for speaking truth to power. The very speed with which he was discredited and dispatched only strengthened that conviction. To Hatfield's defenders, *Fortunate Son* was an instant classic of suppressed literature.

A month after St. Martin's dumped the book, Hatfield had an offer from tiny Soft Skull Press to republish it. Run out of a basement on Manhattan's Lower East Side, Soft Skull specialized in offbeat, left-wing titles. It operated on a tiny budget, but founder and CEO Sander Hicks had scraped together $15,000 to entice Hatfield to let Soft Skull release *Fortunate Son*.

Hatfield accepted the offer. Hicks then urged him to write a new foreword and come clean about his past. But Hatfield couldn't. He still hadn't admitted to anyone in Bentonville that he was guilty of anything. When the media had revealed his stint in prison, he'd been able to persuade Bledsoe and some of his more gullible friends that he'd done the time as an undercover CIA assignment.

So instead of fessing up, Hatfield's brainstorm was to lie some more. He invented a new version of the Dallas Cotton Exchange bombing. In the first Soft Skull edition of *Fortunate Son*, 46,000 of which were printed, he wrote that Kay Burrow had been blackmailing Larry Burk, and Burk wanted her dead. Hatfield claimed he was a mere middleman who had hired a hitman because Burk put his arm around his shoulder and said, "Look, Jim. I need your help on this. You're like a son to me."

Now, in addition to the still-questionable afterword, *Son* had a libelous foreword. Larry Burk sued. Many months and many thousands of dollars in legal fees later, Hatfield signed an apology to both Burk and Burrow, and Hicks agreed to pull the foreword. By then, *Fortunate Son* had nearly killed Soft Skull. The company was $60,000 in debt and had lost its distribution deal.

Hatfield, meanwhile, owed a lawyer more than $100,000. Desperate for cash, unwilling to tell Nancy the truth about his dwindling bank account, on July 16, 2000, he resorted to blackmailing his best friend. It was his first financial crime in a decade.

A man calling himself R. J. Hendrickson and claiming to be an AP reporter Fed Exed George Burt a letter warning him that he was writing a 48,000-word feature article that would run in papers nationwide. The story, to be called *Fortunate Felon*, would expose Burt, the millionaire computer consultant, as an ex-con. For $18,000, however, Hendrickson would sell Burt the rights to the article. "Tomorrow is the deadline," wrote Hendrickson. "I hope you are overnighting the signed contract and fee . . . or life as you know it will change dramatically."

Burt hired a private detective, who quickly learned that the

Oklahoma mailbox to which Burt was supposed to send cash had been rented with a check signed by Jim Hatfield. Burt did not respond to any of "Hendrickson's" subsequent e-mails, and he changed his mind about his former best friend. "I decided that basically, mentally, this man is really a criminal."

In the spring of 2001, Hatfield got one last shot. With the Larry Burk libel suit settled, Soft Skull found a new distributor for its titles. Amazingly, Sander Hicks wanted to release yet another edition of *Son*.

Tall, muscular, and striking, the thirty-two-year-old Hicks started Soft Skull while working at a Manhattan Kinko's. Between running the press, writing plays, singing for a punk band, and working as a building superintendent, he decided to rescue *Fortunate Son*.

Explains Hicks, "I wanted to do my part as an American and as an independent media person to support freedom of the press, and to get the truth out about the Bushes." Counters Jim Fitzgerald, a former St. Martin's editor who helped Hicks prepare the book for reprinting: "[Hicks] hated Bush and he saw it as a political statement. Nothing else to it."

As Hicks now admits, he never bothered to look into Hatfield's past or investigate *Son*'s afterword because he was certain that St. Martin's had quashed the book for political reasons.

In January 2000, Hatfield and Hicks had been walking down Ludlow Street on the Lower East Side with two friends when Hatfield told Hicks that they needed to have a private chat. The two friends were waved on. "Jim was looking like Jack Nicholson in his navy peacoat," remembers Hicks. "It was me and him on the street corner." Hatfield leaned toward Hicks and divulged what he hadn't told anyone at St. Martin's, the name of the Lake Eufaula connection.

"My understanding," says Hicks, "was that I would take this information to my grave."

Because he believed in Hatfield, Hicks had stuck with him through the failure of the first Soft Skull edition of *Son* and the disastrous lawsuit. He kept the relationship going even though Hatfield, under stress, had reverted to the worst of his Dallas-era behavior. Hicks didn't know about Hatfield's attempt to blackmail George Burt, but he did have to weather tantrums. "Hatfield is a jerk," groused Hicks to the documentarians Galinsky and Hawley. "I'm coming to the conclusion he's a crisis magnet with a temper."

Hatfield had been especially prickly after Hicks informed him in April 2001 that he wanted to promote Soft Skull's second edition of *Son* by telling the world the secret they'd shared on a New York street corner the year before. They argued, but in the end Hatfield agreed to allow Hicks to write a publisher's foreword that revealed the names of his three confidential sources. He also agreed to accompany Hicks to the BookExpo America in Chicago, where on June 1 they would relaunch the book and drop their bomb on the media.

Before setting off for the BookExpo, Hatfield began to hint that something bad was about to happen to him, that he might be arrested or die or disappear. On Thursday, May 31, 2001, the day before he flew to Chicago, Hatfield asked Bruce Gabbard to meet him at a bar in Fayetteville, thirty minutes south of Bentonville. When Gabbard arrived, Hatfield was already many beers ahead of him.

Hatfield told Gabbard that the threat of a Writers Guild strike had put his multipicture screenplay deal on hold. To make money, he had to do two things, both of which threatened his personal safety. First, he had to out his sources in order to promote the new Soft Skull edition; second, he had to return to his old job at the CIA. He'd already been to Little

Rock, he informed Gabbard, for a security check and psychiatric evaluation.

Then, says Gabbard, Hatfield's mood shifted from resigned to cryptic. "He started talking in puzzles," recalls Gabbard. He mentioned James Bond and his birthdate and the safe in his backyard office. Hatfield told Gabbard that he'd once had an agreement with George Burt to dispose of his safe in case of an emergency, but that the CIA had told Burt to keep his distance. Now it was up to Gabbard. "If something happens," Hatfield said, "I know from your history you know how to make it disappear."

On the first day of June 2001, Hatfield met Hicks at the Book-Expo. Hicks had decorated Soft Skull's booth with airbrush paintings so that it resembled a graffitied New York subway car. He passed out wooden nickels stamped with W.'s face and fliers touting a Soft Skull press conference the next afternoon. Hatfield gamely signed books and shook hands.

At 4:00 PM on June 2, Hicks and Hatfield stood behind a podium in Room A of the McCormick Center, facing reporters from Reuters, the *Washington Post, USA Today,* and a half dozen other major media outlets. Hicks read off two of the names of Hatfield's sources: Clay Johnson, a lifelong Bush friend and campaign aide, and, sensationally, the Eufaula Connection: Karl Rove, Bush's chief political advisor. (The other reputed source, Jim Mayfield, the president's pastor, was not mentioned at the press conference.)

"We allege that this was a deliberate media disinformation campaign," concluded Hicks, and then handed the mic to Hatfield so he could take questions.

The reporters were stunned. Hatfield was claiming that his Deep Throat was the man so identified with W.'s rise that he's been called "Bush's Brain." Bob Minzesheimer of *USA Today* wanted to hear it from Hatfield's mouth. "Are you saying Karl Rove was your source on the cocaine arrest?"

"Yes, Karl Rove was one of my major sources," replied Hatfield. He said that Rove had given the scoop to him, a felon, so that no one would believe it.

For any reporters who were interested, Hicks had brought copies of a hotel bill that showed Hatfield had spent two nights on Lake Eufaula in June 1999, and phone records from September 2, 1999, that proved he'd dialed the numbers of all three men. An attached "phone chronology" explained each entry.

After the press conference, Hicks and Hatfield, with the documentarians Hawley and Galinsky in tow, rushed out of the convention hall and piled into a rental car, breathlessly congratulating each other. "We had a huge euphoric adrenaline rush," remembers Hicks. "Jim said, 'Can you imagine the White House press office right now? Their phones are probably ringing. Their fax machines are probably going. How are they going to spin this?' "

In fact. they didn't have to do any spinning. Only the *New York Post,* the *National Enquirer,* and *Inside.com* ever ran items on Hatfield's revelations, and *Inside*'s piece trashed him as "rambling and at times incoherent." They didn't believe his tale about Rove. They didn't think his hotel bill and "phone chronology" were even worth investigating.

Hatfield's writing career was finally over, and he knew it. When the high from the press conference abated, he dropped his happy salesman's mask. On the night of June 2, Hawley and Galinsky filmed him as he smoked a cigarette on a Chicago street.

In the footage, his eyes are tired, his face red and puffy, and there's brown Just for Men hair dye daubed into his goatee to hide the spreading gray. Backlit by the floodlights of a gas station, he looks into the camera and all but tells Hawley and Galinsky he's going to die, though he's ambiguous about who to blame.

First, he fingers the president. "The thing that scares me is now what the hell's going to happen? The first time we just pissed off the Bush campaign, and we saw what they did. This time it's the White House. . . . They could say we searched your home and found weed, and that's all it takes."

Then, tellingly, he blames himself. "I used to bitch and moan to [my wife] about those trivia books. . . . I've known guys in prison and the thing they always told me was that greed will get you every time. And maybe that's what got me on this. I wanted to make that big leap. I wanted to get off that midlist.

"If anything happens to me, you guys get this [documentary] sold, okay? Get it out in the press. Can you do that much?"

Seven weeks later, just after checkout time on July 18, 2001, the staff of the Days Inn in Springdale, Arkansas, found Hatfield in room 312, dead. The police ruled it a suicide. Within hours, an outpouring of conspiracy theories appeared on the Web. "Karl Rove killed the book," squawked one Web site. "God only knows who killed the author." His friends wondered, too.

"They got him," says Gabbard. "That's what went through my mind."

On behalf of all the true believers, Sander Hicks took a road trip to Arkansas to investigate Hatfield's death. In a back room of the Bentonville police department, Chief James Allen shoved a file across a table at Hicks and waited, hands clasped.

The file showed that on a single day in April, Hatfield had applied for five credit cards. He'd done it again on June 21. Several of the cards were taken out in George Burt's name.

They were supposed to be shipped to a Mailboxes Etc. in Bentonville. Hatfield had been caught when MBNA, a major credit card company, made a routine verification call to Burt in Texas. At 9:00 AM on July 17, Bentonville police officers arrived at Hatfield's house to arrest him. Hatfield let them in without protest, and sat calmly in the living room waiting for his lawyer. At 11:00 AM, with his lawyer present, Hatfield struck a deal with Detective Don Batchelder. He needed a few hours to settle his affairs, but he'd turn himself in at the station at 3:00 PM Batchelder agreed, and he and his partner left.

At fifteen minutes past noon, Hatfield filled prescriptions for Clonazepam (often prescribed for panic attacks) and Celexa (depression) at a Wal-Mart in Bentonville. He drove his BMW south to nearby Springdale. At 12:34, he purchased grapefruit juice and 1.75 liters of Gordon's Vodka at Last Chance Liquors. Paying $75.22 in cash, he checked into the local Days Inn. He parked his car behind the building, took the elevator up to his suite, and locked himself in.

The housekeeper and the manager found him just after noon the next day, his head propped up on three pillows. He was partly on top of the covers, his legs crossed, a watch on his right wrist. Underneath the body was a picture of Hatfield with his daughter Haley in his arms and his wife next to them, beaming. The booze was on the nightstand, three-quarters gone. Empty pill bottles had been shoved beneath the mattress. There was no sign of trauma.

Detective Batchelder's business card lay on a dark wood desk to the right of the TV. On the back, Hatfield had scrawled: "Don— Thanks for giving me some time. You were only doing your job."

There were multiple notes to Bledsoe. One told her where to hold the funeral and who to have as pallbearers: Gabbard, Rubertus, and a few others. Another, scratched on a hotel notepad, said, "Forgive me for screwing everything up."

The longest note was as close to a confession as Hatfield could get:

> I just tried to keep us afloat, at least until Zooks sold or FS made some $$. You'll be okay, my love. I wanted to grow old with you and walk my daughter down the aisle, but it's not going to happen. . . . I'd rather her grow up with no father than one she's afraid of, ashamed. . . . [T]here is no other way. Now, you can finally raise your head in this town and blame it all on me.
>
> I'm not going to complain or whine. I brought this all on myself. It's been all downhill since Oct. '99 and this day was my destiny. . . . I am complex, deceitful, and just remember, no matter what anyone tells you, I was a good man who got caught up in bad circumstances. But I'll meet my maker with the knowledge that I loved 2 great ladies . . . and tried my best to the very end.

Nowhere did Hatfield blame Karl Rove or the Bush team or the media or anyone else for his predicament. There was no reference to the tru
th or falsity of his big scoop. The truth Hatfield wanted to establish was one he left on a Fisher-Price Magna Doodle pad that he had borrowed from Haley. Above his lavish, swooping signature, he'd written in block letters: I LOVE MY FAMILY.

When Hicks finished reading the file, he ventured a mild protest: "There's still a small inkling of a chance that there might be some sort of involvement by people that are bigger than all of us."

Chief Allen disagreed. "Every single thread leads to Hatfield."

Sander Hicks wrote a "Suicide Diary" about his pilgrimage to Arkansas, and posted it on the Web. "Reading the suicide note is like colliding with a building," he wrote. "These days, I'm between my stubborn initial defensive posture about Jim and realizing that he was a scam artist, and not a good one. . . . I need to revisit all assumptions."

Hicks was convinced, however, that Hatfield told *one* truth in his life. "As a writer, as a researcher, I accept that he was not perfect," admitted Hicks, "but did he lie about the afterword? I don't think so."

It's a measure of the tenacity of Hicks's faith that he never fact-checked Hatfield's phone chronology or tried to account for Karl Rove's whereabouts in June and September 1999. He drove from New York to Arkansas to look at a police file, but he never spoke to any of Hatfield's supposed sources.

If he had, he'd have been very disappointed. He'd have learned that the "evidence" that Hatfield used to support the most dramatic scoop of the last presidential campaign was fiction. Setting aside the fact that Mayfield, Johnson, and Rove all denied they'd ever spoken with Hatfield—such denials mean nothing to conspiracy theorists—every entry in the phone chronology raises questions about Hatfield's competence and honesty.

At 12:49 PM on September 2, 1999, Hatfield called Democratic party headquarters in El Paso, Texas. The phone chronology claims that he spoke to his "frequent source, Robert Grijalva . . . to question him about the possibility that Bush had been arrested in 1972 for cocaine possession and had performed community service at Project P.U.L.L. in Houston." Grijalva, an obscure party volunteer who happened to be manning the phones that day, remembers the conversation. It was actually the first time he'd ever spoken to Hatfield, and Hatfield didn't ask him any questions about P.U.L.L. Instead, he went on and on about a timeworn rumor that George W. had impregnated his Mexican maid and hidden their offspring in a border town: "He said he'd come up with credible evidence . . . and that the bastard son was living over in Ojinaga. He needed a little extra information to confirm it."

It was an anecdote with a particular appeal to Hatfield. Twenty years earlier in Dallas, he was sitting at the Leigh Ann pool with his best friend Norma Rodriguez when he began talking about writing a bio of Lyndon Johnson. He had a sure-fire way to sell it. Explains Rodriguez, "He said, 'Everybody knows he liked Mexican women. I want you to go out to the media and we're going to spread this about how you were one of his mistresses. . . . They'll pay you for interviews! We'll go halves!' "

Twenty years later, faced with a delay in the printing of *Fortunate Son*, he reached for a similar fable about Bush as a fast way of getting St. Martin's attention. The questions he asked Grijalva explain why he started his supposed coke investigation on the far western edge of texas, close to the rumored love child but 750 miles and a time zone removed from Houston and P.U.L.L.

Grijalva knew nothing about any Mexican baby. The chat devolved into an all-purpose gossip session about the GOP front-runner. Grijalva happened to mention that Bush had changed his driver's license number when he became governor. Hatfield, who'd missed that nugget when it appeared on MSNBC.com, got excited. He wondered whether Bush had changed the number to hide a past arrest. Says Grijalva, "He started talking about this cocaine rumor. He was the one telling me about P.U.L.L., not the other way around."

After he got off the phone with Grijalva, Hatfield shifted his attention east. He did call Karl Rove. His cellular bill shows a two-minute call at 5:10 PM to Rove's residence west of Austin. Hatfield's story that he spoke to Rove, however, and that Rove phoned him back thirty minutes later, seems implausible. On the afternoon of September 2, Rove was in Los Angeles, sitting on a dais, watching Bush deliver a speech to the Latin Business Association. "I was sitting behind [Rove]," attests Ken Herman, reporter for the *Austin American-Statesman*. "I was staring at the back of his head." At best, Hatfield left a two-minute message on Rove's answering machine or spoke to whoever happened to pick up the phone.

The supposed evidence of the three-day Lake Eufaula meeting with Rove is no stronger. The LaDonna Inn registry shows that Jim Hatfield checked in at 2:15 PM on Saturday, June 26, and stayed two nights, checking out Monday. Bush had officially launched his presidential candidacy just two weeks before in Iowa, and Rove was constantly at his side. On Friday, June 25, Rove accompanied Bush on his first fundraising trip to Florida, flying back to Austin late that night after a cocktail party in Miami. On Monday, Bush held a reception in Austin, then flew to San Diego to start his first fundraising swing through California, with Rove in tow.

Rove must have been very tired (and sunburned) if, as Hatfield claims, he drove five hundred miles from Austin to Lake Eufaula, went fishing, then drove the five hundred miles back—all in time for the reception.

The registry at the LaDonna Inn says that Hatfield was alone.

Throughout his life, when reality wasn't good enough, Jim Hatfield invented fantastic encounters to fill in the missing pieces of a dream. He'd gotten Bledsoe and the St. Martin's editors to believe in a secret meeting with a secret source the same way he'd fooled his first wife Tammy Stewart and his best friend Norma Rodriguez into thinking he had appointments with publishers.

By writing George W. Bush into his private drama it was Hatfield, not Rove, who immunized the presidential candidate against drug rumors. The public lost interest in W.'s past and became suspicious of all accusations about it, legitimate or not. It can be argued that without *Fortunate Son*'s discredited afterword, the last-minute revelations of W.'s drunk-driving arrests might have swung the election to Gore.

Fortunate Son is now in its third edition with Soft Skull Press, and continues to sell reasonably well. The conspiracy theorists and the dead con man fill each other's needs—one to believe, the other to be believed. Hatfield's death means they can pursue their romance forever, free from the inconvenience of fact. They can close their eyes and see Hatfield and Rove adrift on Lake Eufaula. They can hear Rove groaning, when Hatfield confronts him with the P.U.L.L. scoop, "Ooh, you got me." If you can't prove Rove didn't answer his home phone on September 2, they reason, then he did—maybe he had it forwarded to his cell phone in Los Angeles. If you can't prove he never called Hatfield back, then he did. If you can't prove Rove wasn't Hatfield's Deep Throat, then he was.

After Hatfield's death, Bruce Gabbard gradually accepted that he'd been tricked into committing a burglary. Chastened, Gabbard returned the safe to Hatfield's widow. Together, they decided to open it.

Gabbard and Bledsoe walked the brick path past the hot tub to Hatfield's backyard office. There, on the left, on the shelf above his desk, right where he'd said it would be, was *The James Bond Trivia Quiz Book*. It was a guide to the spy novels Hatfield had loved since he was a child, and a model for the trivia books he himself had written in the days before *Fortunate Son*. As directed, Gabbard opened to page fifty-eight, the year of Hatfield's birth, and in the margin found a four-digit combination.

While Haley played in the yard, Gabbard opened the safe. Inside there were no CIA files, no audiotapes of Karl Rove, no contracts for screenplays. Instead there were only secrets he'd been keeping from Bledsoe, legal papers documenting that he had done time in Arkansas for burglary, in Texas for attempted murder, and in Oklahoma for making false statements. One file revealed that he would have been finished with parole in April 2003. Two more years and his wife and daughter would never have known. The reinvention of Jim Hatfield would have been complete.

Remember "the Whys"

By Robert Fisk

Killed: *Harper's*, 2002

When a Harper's *editor originally asked me to write this article, it was agreed that I would hit out hard at the double standards of journalism as well as the breakdown of serious journalism during the 2001 Afghanistan bombardment—the way, for example, in which American reporters donned military costumes and—in one notorious case—carried a gun. Several days after I submitted my article, the same editor called back. I knew something was wrong when she said that it was "very well written." That's always a bad start. Then she said that it didn't seem to be "exactly the article we had spoken about over the phone." She had expected more concentration on CNN's behavior in Afghanistan, she said, less on American journalism's failure to report on the Israeli–Palestinian conflict.*

I pointed out that we had both taken notes on our original telephone conversation—she had been in New York, I in Beirut—and that my notes showed that I had very clearly discussed the importance of American journalism's failure to report fairly on the Israeli–Palestinian conflict.

The Harper's *editor then presented a quite different argument; she said that a recent article in* Harper's *about the Israeli-Palestinian war had produced a lot of unfounded criticism, and*

that to print my article now might be "a little too close in time."
When I asked if she might wish to publish it a month or two
later, she said it might need substantial re-writing. I pointed
out that every claim and statement was substantially footnoted.
She said she knew that and repeated that it was "very well
written."

She suggested I might wish to re-write the article along dif-
ferent lines. I refused. I said that I had written about the very
journalistic issues which needed to be addressed in the Middle East
and was not going to change my words because Harper's had just
been attacked by pro-Israeli lobbyists—which was what she was
talking about—over an article which had nothing to do with me.
The Independent, *I said, would never buckle under in such cir-*
cumstances and would face any critics over my work. If Harper's
was not that brave, I said, this was Harper's problem. This was
the last contact I had with Harper's.

On December 8, 2001, I was attacked by a crowd of
Afghan refugees in a village called Kila Abdullah not far
from the Pakistan-Afghanistan border. My car had
broken down and the Afghans, many of whom had lost
relatives in the recent US bombing raids around Kandahar,
decided to take out their rage upon me. I was beaten on the
head with stones, kicked, and cut. Rescue came from a religious man—I recall he had a turban but I had so much blood
in my eyes that I could scarcely see him—who escorted me
to a Pakistani police van.

Sitting in the Red Cross ambulance on its way to Quetta, I
realized how carefully I was going to have to handle the frightening and very painful event that had just occurred and that I

knew would be reported by my fellow journalists. I did not wish to be the source of yet another Muslim-bashing story, the lone Briton savagely assaulted by an "angry mob" of Afghans. I hate the "what and where" stories that leave out the "why." Their fury had to be given some context, some reference to the fact that they had been most cruelly bereaved and that my sudden—very definitely Western—appearance in the village represented for them the face of those who had just destroyed their loved ones.

In every interview I gave, I therefore made this point. Indeed I said—and later wrote in my own newspaper, the *Independent*—that if I was one of those grief-stricken Afghan men, I too would have attacked Robert Fisk. Those who beat me, I wrote, were "truly innocent of any crime except that of being the victims of the world." Almost every published and televised report mentioned the reasons behind the assault except for the British *Mail on Sunday* which used an agency story, which deleted my explanation. In the *Mail*, a mob of "angry Afghans" attacked me, but apparently without reason. Readers might have been excused for thinking that Afghans are always "angry," primitive, generically violent, and thus prone to beat up foreigners on a whim—the classic Islamophobic response of anyone reading the *Mail* story.

Later reactions were even more interesting. Among a mass of letters that arrived from readers of the *Independent*, almost all of them expressing their horror at what had happened, came a few Christmas cards, all but one of them unsigned, expressing the writer's disappointment that the Afghans hadn't "finished the job." The *Wall Street Journal* carried an article which said more or less the same thing under the sub-head "A self-loathing multiculturalist gets his due." In it, Mark Steyn wrote of my reaction that "you'd have to have a heart of stone not to weep with laughter." The "Fisk Doctrine," he went on, "taken to its logical conclusion, absolves of responsibility not only the perpetrators of Sept. 11 but also Taliban supporters who attacked several of Mr. Fisk's fellow journalists in Afghanistan, all of whom, alas, died before being able to file a final column explaining why their murderers are blameless."

Quite apart from the fact that most of the journalists who died in Afghanistan were killed by thieves taking advantage of the Taliban's defeat, Steyn's article was interesting for two reasons. It insinuated that I in some way approved of the crimes against humanity on September 11—or, at the least, that I would absolve the mass murderers. More important, the article would not have been written had I not explained the context of the assault that was made on me, tiny though it was in the scale of suffering visited upon Afghanistan. Had I merely reported an attack by a mob, the story would have fit neatly into the general American media presentation of the Afghan war with no reference to civilian deaths from US B-52 bombers and no suggestion that the widespread casualties caused in the American raids would turn Afghans to fury against the West. We were, after all, supposed to be "liberating" these people, not killing their relatives. Of course, my crime—the *Journal* gave Steyn's column the headline "Hate-Me Crimes"—was to report the "why" as well as the "what and where."

I was crossing the Atlantic on September 11; my plane took off from Belgium just after the first reports of the attack on the World Trade Center and turned round off the coast of Ireland when the United States closed its airspace. I filed my first column to *The Independent* from my airline seat on the plane's satellite phone, without notes, dictating it to a copytaker, pointing out that there would be an attempt in the coming days to avoid asking the "why"question. I wrote about the history of deceit and lies in the Middle East, the growing Arab anger at the deaths of thousands of Iraqi children under UN sanctions, and the continued occupation of Palestinian land by Israel. I suggested bin Laden may have been responsible. I wrote that thousands of Muslims may soon die in Afghanistan or elsewhere as a result of the outrages in New York and Washington.

E-mails poured into *The Independent*, mostly in support of my article, a number demanding my resignation. The attacks on America were caused by "hate itself, of precisely the obsessive and dehumanizing kind that Fisk and bin Laden have been spreading" said one. According to the same message from Professor Judea Pearl of UCLA, I was "drooling venom," and was a professional "hate peddler." Another missive, signed Ellen Popper, announced that I was "in cahoots with the archterrorist" bin Laden. Mark Guon labeled me "a total nutcase." I was "psychotic," according to Lillie and Barry Weiss. Brandon Heller of San Diego informed me that "you are actually supporting evil itself . . ."

On an Irish radio show, a Harvard professor announced that I was a "liar" and a "dangerous man," and that "anti-Americanism," of which I was obviously guilty, was the same as anti-Semitism. The show's presenter eventually pulled the plug on the professor, but I got the point. Not only was it wicked to suggest that someone might have had reasons to commit the mass slaughter, but it was even more appalling to suggest what these reasons might be. To criticize the United States, or to be "anti-American"—whatever that is—was to be a Jew-hater, a racist, a Nazi. Merely to suggest that Washington's policies in the Middle East, its unconditional support for Israel, its support for Arab dictators, its approval of UN sanctions that have cost the lives of so many Iraqi children, might lay behind the venomous attacks on September 11, was an act of evil in itself. Oddly, the fact that the mass murderers were all Arabs—and that most came from Saudi Arabia—was not regarded as a problem by reporters or readers. This fell into the "where and what" slot. "Arab terrorists" are, after all, familiar characters in America. The sin was to connect the Arabs with the problems of the lands they came from, to ask the "why" question.

I've spent twenty-five years in the Middle East, trying to answer the "whys." And in no part of the world is reporting so flawed, so biased in favor of one country—Israel—and so consensual in its use of words. Indeed, the language of Middle East journalism has become so cowardly, so slippery, so deferential, so locked into the phrases used by the State Department, the President, the U.S. diplomats, and Israeli officials, that our reporting has in many cases become incomprehensible. For an American readership unfamiliar with Middle Eastern history or recent events—or for American viewers who may have no intrinsic interest in the region—our reporting has reached such poverty of expression as to render any real understanding of the conflict impossible.

Such is the bizarre nature of our profession in the region that any article like this has to follow a kind of mantra: Saddam Hussein is a wicked, cruel tyrant who invaded Iran and then Kuwait. He used poison gas on the Kurds. His Iranian war cost up to a million lives. He has a hangman on twenty-four-hour duty. Yassir Arafat is a corrupt and vain little despot, allowing his eleven—some say thirteen—secret services to beat, torture, and occasionally kill Palestinian opponents. (I should add that I never could see why Israel wanted to negotiate with him— unless they saw in him a weak militia ally who could police the West Bank and Gaza on their behalf.) Palestinian suicide bombings are a fearful, evil weapon. But we are nevertheless lying about the Middle East because we are distorting the truth, either because we are afraid of criticism from Israel and its supporters, or because we journalists prefer an easy life, unencumbered by hate mail and letters to the editor.

Take the pejorative use of the word "terrorist." The mass murders of September 11 may require a redefinition by those journalists, including myself, who normally abjure the word in Middle East reporting on the grounds that it is used exclusively about Arabs. But its overuse—almost as a punctuation mark in any discussion of the Arab-Israeli conflict—remains as poisonous as ever, perhaps racist. It is difficult to explain to Arabs, for example, why the New York and Washington massacre was an act of terrorism but why the massacre of up to 1,700 Palestinians in the Sabra and Shatila refugee camps in on September 16–18, 1982, has never been called an act of terrorism by journalists or governments. The death toll in Shatila, after all, was more than half that of the twin towers.

Was this strange omission of the word "terrorism" because the killers—members of the Christian Lebanese Phalangist militia—happened to be allied to Israel? Did it not qualify as an act of terrorism because most of the murderers were wearing Israeli Defence Force (IDF) uniforms (albeit with the acronym Tsahal's Hebrew for IDF painted out)? Or did it fail to meet the "terrorism" test because Israeli forces had surrounded the camp and Ariel Sharon, then Israel's defense minister, had sent the Phalange into the camps? Not once—ever—has a Western newspaper called the mass murderers of Sabra and Shatila "terrorists." Indeed, Israel's own Kahan commission of enquiry into the massacre, which held Ariel Sharon "personally responsible" for the killings, called the Phalangist killers "soldiers."

This is not an isolated example. When an Israeli reserve officer, Baruch Goldstein, massacred twenty-nine Palestinians in a Hebron mosque on February 25, 1994, he was not called a "terrorist." CNN referred to him as "deranged." Later, the

Israeli ambassador in London said that Goldstein was "deranged by fanaticism." Other reports spoke of Goldstein as an "extremist." Yet when Hamas took its inevitable—and wicked—revenge with a bus bomb in the Israeli town of Afula, CNN recovered its nerve. Reporter Bill Delaney told us it was an act of "Arab terrorism."

Palestinians are "terrorists." Arabs are "terrorists." Israelis are not. Could anything demean a people more than the constant association of the word with an ethnic or religious group? Like the Afghan "mob" that beat me in December, Palestinians as a people are reduced to the level of animals. Back in spring 1993, CNN covered the return of the Palestinian peace delegation to the West Bank and reported Palestinian anger on the streets. The footage that accompanied this report showed children throwing stones at Israeli troops in Gaza. By chance, I had just filmed the same kids throwing the same stones for a Discovery Channel documentary on Islam. But the real reason why they were protesting in Gaza was because the Israeli army had just destroyed the homes of more than a hundred civilians after finding a Hamas gunman in the area. The children on CNN were protesting the loss of their houses—they were not protesting about peace at all. When I took this up with then–CNN Jerusalem bureau chief, he remarked that the footage was used because it was "generic." I understood the implications immediately: that Palestinians throw stones at Israelis without reason (about peace, for heaven's sakes); that Palestinians are somehow "generically" violent.

Of far graver ethical significance was the cover of *Newsweek* magazine on February 19, 2003. "Terror Goes Global," the headline said, alluding to Osama bin Laden's "international network" of terror. Beneath these words was a photograph of a Palestinian in a *kuffiah* headdress that almost totally concealed his face, holding in his hand an automatic rifle. The reader might have supposed him to be part of the "terror network." Indeed, the reader was obviously meant to believe this. But I was puzzled by this cover picture. I had seen it before. It was taken by Ilkka Uimonen of the Gamma picture agency in Paris. Uimonen lives in New York, and when I called him, he confirmed the cover picture was his. "I took the picture in the West Bank," he told me. "It was a member of Tanzim at a Palestinian funeral."

Thus a Palestinian gunman, armed and attending the funeral of a fellow Palestinian killed by Israelis, had been turned into a representative of "global terror." Palestinians as a people—and the man on *Newsweek*'s cover was very definitely a Palestinian—had been effortlessly transformed into enemies of the world. It wasn't the photographer's fault. But *Newsweek*'s cover picture was a lie. The man whose face was covered by the *kuffiah*—dangerous though he would be to Israelis—had nothing to do with bin Laden or the lead story in the magazine.

If Palestinians can be falsely implicated in such a way—and Ariel Sharon, now Israel's prime minister, has been doing his best, though without much success, to link Yassir Arafat with bin Laden—journalists have gone out of their way to decontextualize Israel's role in the occupied territories. Indeed, once the State Department told its diplomats to stop using the word "occupied" in relation to the West Bank and Gaza, American journalists dutifully followed their example. Henceforth, the land would be called "disputed"—as in "Benjamin Netanyahu turns up the heat by okaying new houses in disputed territory" (a *New York Times* caption on March 10, 1997). "Disputed," of course, changes the reality. By deleting "occupation" from their lexicon, journalists erase the colonies illegally built—for Jews and Jews only—on Arab land. They erase the many Israeli checkpoints that covered—as they do today—the West Bank and Gaza. "Disputed" suggests an argument about land deeds—or "conflicting heritage claims" as CNN once memorably called them (failing to point out that the Palestinians have documents to prove land ownership while many Israeli settlers claim God gave them the land). The Associated Press has now gone one further. Anxious to avoid the word "occupied," the agency now refers to lands that were "war-won." This contorted expression places an almost victorious facade upon the illegality of occupation.

I have been searching, in vain, to find the first use of the words "settlements" and "settlers" in relation to Israel's occupation. In its Wild West context, I suppose it makes sense. For if the Israelis have taken this land less brutally than America's settlers took lands from America's native inhabitants, the word still obscures the reality. These Israeli settlements on occupied—yes, occupied—land are colonies, and their inhabitants are colonists, every bit as much as the French in Algeria. When I made this point in my own newspaper, the London *Independent*, a stream of letters accused me of deliberately trying to make a parallel between Palestinian "terrorism" and the FLN's ultimately successful 1954–62 war for independence against France. I was indeed making that parallel. Interestingly, Sharon himself has compared all of Israel to Algeria under French rule, revealing to the correspondent of the French magazine *L'Express* how he told President Chirac of France that "you've got to understand that we here, we are like you in Algeria. We have no other place to go. And besides, we have no intention of leaving." The French word for a settler is *colon*, accurately representing what the Israeli settlers in the West Bank and Gaza are doing.

But today, even that tame word "settlement" is disappearing. CNN, in one of its most recent contributions to journalism, sent out instructions to correspondents, telling them that Gilo—the Jewish settlement built on Arab land south of Jerusalem—is to change its definition. "We refer to Gilo as a Jewish neighborhood on the outskirts of Jerusalem, built on land occupied by Israel in 1967 . . . We don't refer to it as a settlement."

Now it happens that Gilo is a settlement (or a colony) built only for Jews on occupied Palestinian land—CNN at least got that bit right—which is partly owned by Palestinians in the village of Beit Jalla (*Gilo* is Hebrew for *Jalla*). It was constructed in violation of UN Security Council resolutions 242 and 338, and against international law. It has also been incorporated into the enlarged municipality of Jerusalem, in itself partly an illegal annexation. But CNN's little lie about "neighborhood" transforms this history. Cruel though it is for them to do so you can see why Palestinians choose to attack a settlement called Gilo, which they do (from Beit Jalla). But why on earth would they ever attack a cosy, friendly "neighborhood"? To fire guns at a neighborhood—like Brooklyn or Queens' or some small suburb of upstate New York—is an act of madmen (or terrorists). As the viewer is spared the reality of a settlement, so Palestinian violence against Gilo becomes inexplicable. Asked for a comment about the style instructions, a CNN spokesman told *The Independent* that "we really don't want to talk about this." I can see why.

The BBC has also recently advised its reporters in the Middle East to use the phrase "targeted killings" for the murder of Palestinians by Israeli death squads, preferring this to "assassinations," which—so thinks the BBC—might be reserved for more important folk than the suspected Palestinian gunmen and bombers on Israel's hit list. But it just so happens that "targeted killings" is Israel's own expression for its killing of select Palestinians—and I don't believe the BBC is unaware of this. As the growing list of totally innocent civilians killed during these attacks demonstrates—they include women and children—the word "targeted" is itself highly misleading.

When the Arab dead are self-evidently innocent, one sure way of spotting Israel's responsibility is the use of another of our journalistic copouts—"crossfire." After the Israeli massacre of 106 Lebanese civilians at the UN camp at Qana on April 18, 1996—which followed a Hezbollah mortar attack from the same village on a group of Israeli soldiers laying booby-trap bombs on a nearby hillside—*Time* magazine ran a photo of a dead Lebanese baby. The caption read: "Killed in crossfire." Of course, she had been killed, like all the other refugees crowded into the UN compound in Qana, by Israeli shellfire. Today, we regularly hear that Palestinians have been killed in "clashes"—rather than shot down by Israeli troops. "Clashes" has become another copout word, as if a "clash" is a natural phenomenon, like an earthquake or a flood, those responsible simply deleted from the story.

I was amazed to see a BBC advertisement for a television documentary about the end of the "peace process"—who, I wonder, invented the word "process" that we all parrot?—called *When Peace Died*. It began: "Two images captured the hatred that has destroyed the peace process in the Middle East. Mohammed, the boy from Gaza, shielded by his father but still dying under a hail of bullets and the brutal murder of two Israeli soldiers by a Palestinian mob."

Note how Mohammed al-Dura's death carries no attribution. Many Israelis and almost all the journalists who investigated the case—though not, of course, the Israeli army—concluded that Israeli troops killed the boy, although they may not have known they were shooting in his direction. So al-Dura's death was caused by "a hail of bullets"—a distant relation, I suspect, of "crossfire"—while the killing of the Israeli soldiers is firmly attributed, and rightly, to "a Palestinian mob."

Almost invariably, investigative reporting is rewarded with hate mail. When I got my hands on a UN-made videotape proving that the Israeli army had a pilotless "drone" reconnaissance aircraft over Qana at the time of the 1996 massacre—a drone with live-time picture capability that the Israelis originally said did not exist—the first item of mail to arrive on my desk from London began: "I do not like or admire anti-Semites. Hitler was one of the most famous in recent history . . . You are a disgrace to a profession that should report the news." I have over the years found a rhythm to this kind of correspondence. When Israel scores a military success, the level of hate mail drops. When Israeli troops lose what they believe is the moral high ground—following Sabra and Shatila, for example, or after their May 2000 retreat from southern Lebanon, the level of abuse rises, as if the reporter had somehow provoked the news that he reports.

The easiest way out of this problem for many journalists, I fear, is to distort the coverage so that the events that are unfavorable to Israel, however dramatic, are buried deep in the story. Just five days before the Qana slaughter, an Israeli pilot flying an American Apache helicopter fired an air-to-ground missile at an ambulance packed with women and children in southern Lebanon. The Israeli army claimed—wrongly—as I discovered after weeks of investigation—that a Hezbollah fighter (a "terrorist" in Israel's parlance, of course) was in the vehicle. I used the computer-coded markings on the exploded missile parts to trace its origin back to a Boeing factory in Duluth, Georgia. The story of the missile—which was initially sold to the U.S. Marines, taken to Saudi Arabia for use against the Iraqis in 1990, and subsequently given free of charge to the Israelis, along with another batch of the same rockets—was later reprinted by *Harper's*. Yet not a single American news outlet followed it up. The best attempt came from a radio station in Chicago whose reporter eventually told me he couldn't write about the missile "because the Defense Department won't confirm the story."

Far sadder was the American coverage of this little atrocity involving the ambulance. Like most other papers in Europe, *The Independent* front-paged the story. "In the latest and most terrible of Israeli attacks on civilians, an Israeli helicopter gunship yesterday fired a missile into an ambulance . . . killing four girls and two women on board," *The Independent* reported. This at least conformed to what they teach in journalism school—which American would-be reporters often attend, unlike their British opposite numbers. The most important part of the story goes in the first paragraph. Or so you'd think. For some strange reason, the *New York Times* didn't agree.

Serge Schmemann, writing for the *Times* on April 14, 1996, began his story like this: "Israeli gunboats blockaded Beirut and other Lebanese ports today and Israeli guns rained shells on southern Lebanon as Israel steadily raised the heat of its operation against Islamic guerrillas."

Paragraph two began: "Israeli commanders noted that the guerrillas of the Party of God, the Iranian-backed organization also known as Hezbollah, fired only a few Katyusha rockets into northern Israel today."

Where, you may ask, have the deaths of the four children and two women gone? Paragraph three began: "'They've been able to fire only a very small number of Katyushas,' an Israeli officer told reporters in northern Israel today."

And so it went on, with details of refugee figures and a Lebanese death toll of twenty-four. Only in paragraph six did Schmemann mention the rocket attack: "In the deadliest incident today, an Israeli helicopter fired a rocket at a Lebanese ambulance . . ."

There then followed a comment from an Israeli officer who claimed, wrongly, that the vehicle was being used to carry a Hezbollah guerilla. Schmemann devoted twice as much space to Israel's justification for this terrible attack as he did to describing the victims.

I still ask myself why the *Times* should have shown such a serious distortion in its news values as to relegate what by its own admission was the "deadliest incident" of the day to paragraph six. And I have to ask myself whether—if the situation had been reversed—if a Syrian helicopter had attacked an Israeli ambulance and killed four Israeli children and two Israeli women—Schmemann and the *Times* would have put this fact into the sixth paragraph. I have to say that I believe, had the victims been Israeli, Schmemann would have put the attack in the first paragraph. That's where the story should be. That's what they teach you in journalism school. So why did the Lebanese dead only merit paragraph six? Because the dead were Arabs? Or because they were slaughtered by Israelis? It reminds me of the *Newsweek* edition that was published two weeks after the Sabra and Shatila massacre. Its cover story, reflecting the mass demonstrations against the slaughter in Tel Aviv, was headlined "Israel in Torment" with a subhead that read "The Anguish of American Jews." I don't doubt the anguish, but anyone who followed the story might have more accurately concluded that it was the Palestinians who were in torment and that it was the survivors of Sabra and Shatila—not American Jews—who were the anguished in this case.

Now that Sharon, the man held "personally responsible" for the massacre by the Kahan judges, is besieging Yasser Arafat in his Ramallah office, it's worth examining just how hard we journalists have tried to avoid his bloody background. When he was Israeli foreign minister in 1998, Serge Schmemann of *The New York Times* reported on Sharon's role as mediator at the Maryland peace talks with just a casual reference to the "condemnation by some [*sic*] as the defense minister who did nothing to block a massacre in the Sabra and Shatila refugee camps by Phalangist Lebanese Christians." Elsewhere in Schmemann's story, Sharon was "a veteran of the Arab-Israeli frays" who arouses "ambivalent feelings," but who was "a tough pragmatist."

After Sharon became Israeli prime minister in 2001, the Sabra and Shatila connection began to disappear altogether from reports. Writing on relations between Sharon and the Bush Administration in March 2001, AP's Laurie Copans referred only to his "hard-line views and actions." Reporting from Amman a few days later, the *Times*'s Neil MacFarquhar would only go so far as to say that Sharon was "viewed in the Arab world as a killer for his long association with deadly attacks on Palestinians." On the same day, Deborah Sontag in the *Times* talked about Sharon's "old instincts as a warrior" and his new instincts "as a leader who strives to be pragmatic." Now I know Sharon called his biography *Warrior*, but does the *Times* think Sabra and Shatila fits into the "warrior" tradition?

Predictably, CNN was the first to massage Sharon's history after his February 2001 election. According to the CNN Website, Sharon was "a barrel-framed veteran general who has built a reputation for flattening obstacles and reshaping Israel's landscape." Flattening indeed. BBC World Television went lame on Sharon by referring only to his "checkered military career." Not long after his election as prime minister, I participated in a Los Angeles radio talk show on a panel including at least one rabbi and a professor from Hebrew University. I described my experience of walking into the Sabra and Shatila camps just before the massacre ended in 1982. The rabbi spoke eloquently and bravely of Israel's responsibility but the professor got the date of the massacre wrong and called it "worrisome." Worrisome? The murder of up to 1,700 civilians? The talk-show host let this go without comment.

It is ironic that among the exceptions to the grotesque and misleading journalism coming out of the Middle East are a few brave Israeli reporters who question the morality of Israel's actions with a ruthlessness that is rare in any European publication and almost totally absent in the United States. Among the most courageous and eloquent of these is the work of Gideon Levy and Amira Haas in *Ha'aretz*. Haas recently told me that she believes the duty of a journalist is "to monitor the centers of power"—as good a definition as I've heard for our profession—but it raises an important question. How can Amira Haas say things that her American counterparts shy away from? How can Amira Haas report on the cruelty of Jewish colonists and the immorality of Israel's shooting of child stone-throwers when far better paid and supposedly more powerful American journalists cannot—at least not without weasel words that immunize them from any criticism?

Needless to say, Haas not only puts us but Arab journalists to shame, as well. For out in the arid wastes of Arab journalism, there is as little interest in serious investigation of the Middle East's conflict as there is in the United States—as I know to my cost. Abused as a "liar" on Damascus radio in 1982 after describing at first hand Syria's bloody suppression of the Islamist uprising in Hama, I have been called a "black dog pecking at the corpses of Egypt" in the Cairo press for writing about Egypt's rigged elections; and I was cartooned as a rabid dog in a Bahraini newspaper for investigating the activities of a former British Special Branch officer running a torture center on the island. Rabid dogs, of course, have to be exterminated. The cartoon was not a joke.

In all the Middle East, however, nothing quite surpasses our journalistic desire to humor Turkey by obfuscating the reality of the twentieth century's first genocide: the deliberate killing of one and a half million Armenians, most of them slaughtered in 1915, by the Ottoman Turkish authorities. No serious academic—except those holding chairs funded from Turkey—disputes the facts, and anyone who doubts them should read the recently published *Encyclopedia of Genocide* by Israel's foremost Holocaust scholar, Israel Charney. Indeed, *The Independent* now refers to the Armenian Holocaust with a capital "H" as in the Jewish Holocaust. Much of Charney's horrifying documentation comes from 1915 editions of the *New York Times*. Recently, however, these appalling and bloody events have been almost universally referred to by journalists as "disputed" —like the "disputed" West Bank, I suppose—or as "controversial" claims. And most extraordinarily of all, the *Times*—the paper which eighty-six years ago did more to publicize the massacre than any other paper in the States—has done its bit to discredit the tragedy.

In March 1998, for example, the *Times*'s Stephen Kinzer wrote a report about the 70,000 Armenians who live in present-day Turkey. Here is a key paragraph from his report:

> Relations between Turks and Armenians were good during much of the Ottoman period, but they were deeply scarred by massacres of Armenians that pro-Ottoman forces in eastern Anatolia carried out in the spring of 1915. Details of what happened then are still hotly debated, but it is clear that vast numbers of Armenians were killed or left to die during forced marches in a burst of what is now called ethnic cleansing.

I still read this paragraph with a sense of shock. What did Kinzer mean by "deeply scarred"? Relations between Turks and

Armenians came to a virtual end in 1915, because tens of thousands of Armenians were no longer alive to have any kind of "relations" with anyone. And note the intriguing phrase "pro-Ottoman forces," which effectively avoids the use of the word "Turks" or "Turkish." Most incredible of all is Kinzer's assertion that the details are "hotly debated." Turkey may use its lobby groups to lie about the genocide, and the Turkish government still tries to cover up the massacres as the side effects of civil war, but for the *Times* to present the Armenian Holocaust as a subject of serious dispute is as insulting to Armenians as it is for Jews to hear the facts of their Holocaust disputed or denied.

Note, too, how Kinzer talks about "vast numbers" killed, thus avoiding the all-important and terrible figure of one and a half million. And how "ethnic cleansing" takes the place of genocide in the text. Another of Kinzer's articles, written from the Armenian capital of Yerevan, even carried the headline "Armenia Never Forgets. Maybe It Should." I find this as outrageous as I would if the Times had run a headline stating that the Jews should forget the hideous crimes committed against them. During the Pope's recent visit to Yerevan, scarcely a single agency report referring to the genocide ran without a Turkish government disclaimer. BBC World Television's coverage of the papal visit referred to more than a million Armenians killed "as the Ottoman empire broke up." Like the Palestinians who mysteriously die in "clashes," the BBC couldn't bring themselves to tell us who actually killed more than a million Armenians.

So I ask the same questions I did about our coverage of the 1992 Sabra and Shatila massacre. Why do we journalists try so hard to avoid the truth, to extenuate, to dissimulate, to cover up? Is it because Turkey is an important political and military ally of the United States? Because it is a valuable purchaser of

American weaponry? Because it is an ally of Israel? Because it has a powerful lobby group in Washington?

I know all about lobby groups. Back in 1993, I made a three-part documentary film for the Discovery Channel called Beirut to Bosnia, which attempted to find out why an increasing number of Muslims had come to hate the West. We filmed in Beirut, southern Lebanon, Israel, the occupied West Bank and Gaza, Egypt, Bosnia, and Croatia. Among many stories we filmed, we followed the last—and hopeless—attempts of a Palestinian farmer to hold onto his land. It was subsequently taken for a Jewish settlement. We also reported the aftermath of the 1982 Sabra and Shatila massacre. We visited the former Acre home of a Palestinian refugee in Beirut, now owned by an Israeli Jewish family, and we traveled to Poland to find the house of the elderly Israeli in the Acre house who had been driven from his own original home and whose parents were killed by the Nazis in 1939.

Shortly after the series aired on the Discovery Channel, a series of pro-Israeli lobby groups, including CAMERA (the "Camera Media Resources Center") bombarded the channel with complaints. Joseph Ungar wrote to complain that for me to say that Israel "confiscates" or "occupies" land and "builds huge Jewish settlements on Arab land"—all facts acknowledged by Israeli and international human rights groups as well as foreign correspondents for many years—was "twisted" history. To say that the Phalangist militia was sent into Sabra and Shatila by Israel (as Israel's Kahan commission clearly established) was "an egregious falsehood." Alex Safian of CAMERA wrote to Clark Bunting, senior vice president of the Discovery Channel, on June 9, 1994, claiming that a sequence in our film that showed the Israelis refusing to allow a Palestinian woman to go to hospital during a Gaza curfew "may have been staged for the camera." The claim was totally false; indeed, we found the woman still in her home. An Israeli officer, believing our camera had been turned off, lied to us by claiming that a car had already taken the woman to the hospital.

The Discovery Channel rang me in Beirut to say they were receiving "lots" of letters condemning the films from various groups. Then director Mike Dutfield and I heard that it had cancelled a re-broadcasting. In an imperishable letter to Dutfield, Bunting wrote that:

> given the reaction to the series upon its initial airing, we never scheduled a subsequent airing, so there is not really an issue as to any scheduled re-airing being cancelled.

When I read those words, I felt ashamed to be a foreign correspondent.

Interestingly, the condemnation and abuse I regularly receive—far outnumbered, I should add, by literally thousands of e-mails praising *The Independent*'s coverage of the Middle East—has increased significantly since *The Independent* became available, through its Web site (www.independent.co.uk), to Internet users throughout the world, especially America. Many American readers appear to lament their own "lobotomized" journalistic coverage, as one recent e-mail remarked. A number of letters of support also came from American Jewish readers. But the mailbag contains the usual vitriol. Last year, an American law student at a British university wrote to tell me that I was "an evil fucking man," a remark he withdrew when I called him at college and threatened to report his remarks to the police as a threatening letter (he had obligingly added his telephone number). Another letter, anonymous this time, began: "To Mr. Shit Fisk. You are what you are an evil, medieval anti-Semite . . . your judgment day will come." One of my most recent messages, again anonymous and thrown with disgust into the garbage bin, contained the accusation that my mother must have been "Eichmann's daughter." (My mother Peggy died in 1998 after a long battle with Parkinson's disease; in 1940, she was an RAF radio repair mechanic at the height of the Battle of Britain.)

In South Africa, where our sister paper *The Johannesburg Star* publishes my reports, a number of rabbis complained that I was helping the right-wing historian and Holocaust denier David Irving. I have never met David Irving. I don't want to. Denial of the Jewish Holocaust is a wicked act. The rabbis later withdrew their false allegation. Then the Israeli ambassador to Ireland used the platform of a question-and-answer session at a meeting of an Irish charity in Belfast to attack my reporting. I was given no right of reply, of course; it was a "closed" meeting and I only later heard what the ambassador had said. But I wrote about his remarks in the *Independent* and the ambassador subsequently complained that he had made his remarks "off the record." This was revealing. The Israeli ambassador to Ireland didn't want to be reported. He wanted his remarks to harm my work but he didn't want them on the record.

Can we journalists ignore the abuse and the lobby groups and the attempt to soft-pedal our reporting about the Middle East? White House spokesman Ari Fleischer's remark last October that "the press is asking a lot of questions that I suspect the American people would prefer not to be asked or answered" carried some ominous implications. And CNN boss Walter Isaacson's instructions to staff—that "it seems perverse to focus too much on the casualties or hardship in Afghanistan" because it runs the risk of helping the Taliban— was perhaps the most shameful journalistic remark ever to come from a media head.

But can we really go on depicting the tragedy of the Middle East through a distorted lens, where illegal colonies are settlements and then just "neighborhoods?" Where we pretend that occupied land is merely "disputed" or "war-won"? Where the Israeli siege of a Palestinian town becomes a "closure"? Where Arab victims are killed in a "crossfire"? Where a man held responsible for a massacre is called a "warrior" or a "pragmatist"? Where Lebanese prisoners held in Israeli jails to be exchanged for captured Israeli soldiers are not hostages but "bargaining chips"? Where uncomfortable atrocities are pushed into the sixth paragraph and a holocaust is downgraded to ethnic cleansing?

We journalists have to learn to suffer the sticks and stones. They can't be as painful as the stones that hit me in Kila Abdullah. All we have to do is risk the crossfire, remember the "whys," and tell the truth. Or, as in the old maxim, tell it how it is.

The Clinton Legacy and America

By Todd Gitlin

Killed: *London Review of Books,* 2003

In June 2003, Mary-Kay Wilmers, the editor of the London Review of Books, *asked if I would be interested in reviewing the two just-published memoirs, Hillary Rodham Clinton's* Living History *and Sidney Blumenthal's* The Clinton Wars. *I was pleased for three reasons: I had already read enough of the Blumenthal book to know that it was important; reviewers had already begun to overlook or play down its value; and knowing the* London Review *to be rather dismissive of any redemptive possibilities in American politics, I welcomed an invitation to address its readers with a point of view to which they were not normally exposed.*

I replied to the editor that Blumenthal and I were on friendly terms and that this relationship was neither an irrelevancy nor a disqualification. If the publication had no objection to an essay emphasizing the hammering that Blumenthal's book was getting from the very American journalists who had carried the foul water of the Right against Clinton, I was their boy. Like many American reviewers, Ms. Wilmers called Blumenthal's book "the work of a courtier" and said she felt "quite strongly that that needs to be pointed out." But she was willing to commission the piece nevertheless.

After filing my piece, Ms. Wilmers wrote me to say that my review had "many good things in it," but now she wanted me to convey "a sense of the appeal of Hilary [sic] Clinton." A few days after I sent her my revision, Ms. Wilmers responded: "I don't think it will work for us. It's not a question of disagreeing with anything you say: the problem is that it reads like a review in an American paper, rather than one written for a European audience."

If my review read like "a review in an American paper," it's curious that no American paper—or magazine, for that matter—ever ran a review anything like it; curious, too, that her earlier letter said nothing about any overabundance of Americanness in my first draft. (Meanwhile, it is perhaps of more than minor interest that when soliciting subscriptions, the London Review *likes to advertise that it reaches many American readers.) I surmise that, confronted with the prospect of running an article departing significantly from left-wing orthodoxy on Clinton's political achievement, the* London Review *succumbed to political jitters.*

America is at one of those tricky junctures when the forces of fierce reaction are wobbling and the forces of possible reform strain to find their footing. As the right reduces itself to fiery self-caricature and Bush's support subsides, some who would relieve us of the burden of his rule stir from their despair and think they see a green light to rush headlong leftward. It is, then, an appropriate time to review the political history that brought us Bush's version of Reaganism without Reagan.

To do so requires, among other things, reckoning with the only Democratic presidency to have succeeded in winning two terms since Franklin D. Roosevelt, that of William Jefferson Clinton.

Such a reckoning, in turn, requires an intellectual confrontation with the hatred that greeted and savaged Clinton, ruptured his reign, and escorted the Bush restoration into office. Indeed, American politics over the past decade are incomprehensible unless you grasp the intensity of Clinton-hatred, its motives, sources, and channels.

Two substantial new memoirs place Clinton-hatred at the center of the story and help decipher the frenzy—one, Senator Hillary Rodham Clinton's *Living History*, more or less inadvertently; the other, former Clinton advisor Sidney Blumenthal's *The Clinton Wars*, indispensably.

An Anatomy of Clintonophobia

In late May 1993, a calendar called "365 Reasons to Hate Bill Clinton" was already on sale in right-wing bookshops. Clinton had moved into the White House a bare four months before. Who had already divined 365 reasons to *hate* him, and why?

The claim that the scandals caused the hatred runs afoul of the fact that the hatred preceded most of the scandals. True, early in the 1992 campaign, scandal sheets funded by Clinton-hating fat cats had wound up the volume on charges that Clinton was not only the longtime lover of the lounge singer Gennifer Flowers, but a drug-smuggler, a serial adulterer, a rapist, and the father of a black baby.

More consequentially, the *New York Times* had jumped in with a front-page story implying a sleazy though barely penetrable real-estate partnership between the governor and a fast-talking investor whose building society, founded years later (a fact that the headline obscured), was subject to state regulation.

Whitewater allegations, implications, and offshoots cascaded through the respectable news, promoted by Clinton-hating Republicans in Congress and the special prosecutor's office. No spin-off charge was too petty—"Travelgate," "Filegate"—to be dubbed an auxiliary case of White House malfeasance.

When the relevant federal agency cleared the Clintons in 1995, major news organizations (including the *New York Times*) could barely be troubled to notice. It didn't seem to matter that, after years of grand juries and headlines, no one was ever convicted of any charge stemming from the Clintons' failed investment in Ozark real estate. As Sidney Blumenthal writes without exaggeration, "never before had a sitting president been so assiduously investigated about a matter that had occurred before his election."

By the second half of Clinton's first term from 1992–96, the incoming Republican Speaker, Newt Gingrich, was calling Clinton "the enemy of normal Americans" and forcing the government to a standstill. Slash-and-burn criminalization was all the rage on talk radio and in the bought-and-paid-for right-wing press. Establishment pundits relayed such charges with glee while prettying them up as "the character issue."

For the scorched-earth right, Bill Clinton was, if not the literal Antichrist, a close approximation: the perjurious, adulterous doper Slick Willie, admitted draft dodger and reputedly serial womanizer who had opposed the Vietnam war, visited Moscow, and married a card-carrying feminist who only belatedly took his name and was the first professional woman to take up First Ladyship. Clinton was, in their eyes, the 1960s incarnate, and worse: he won elections (five out of seven in Arkansas, including his last four in a row). He promised, now, to baste together the left and center of the Democratic Party.

The hard-right viewed such successes as infringements upon their God-given prerogatives. They did not mourn, they organized. The story of how they succeeded is the shank of recent American political history.

A Very American Autobiography

An American campaign autobiography is not so much a book as a ceremony of innocence. Senator Hillary Rodham Clinton's scrappy, earnest update of *The Pilgrim's Progress* is a superior example of an inferior genre—the tell-little advertisement for oneself. As in the stock celebrity interview, the idea is to (a) offer up unsurprising surprises, (b) defend oneself from a backlog of known charges, (c) demonstrate that one can overcome obstacles, (d) josh at oneself enough to certify that one is, after all, plain folks, all the while (e) stuffing one's résumé with proof that one is destined for higher things.

The résumé is impressive though sketchily delivered. So is her imperturbability. Perhaps this is the main news she delivers to her legions of admirers: that you can emerge from the meat grinder of political notoriety with your smile on. Certainly the ratio of surprises to pages is low. It's not exactly astonishing when Senator Clinton writes of her reaction to her husband's belated confession that he had lied to her about his extramarital adventures in the Oval Office:

> As his wife, I wanted to wring Bill's neck. But he was not only my husband, he was also my President, and I thought that, in spite of everything, Bill led America and the world in a way that I continued to support. No matter what he had done, I did not think any person deserved the abusive treatment he had received.

Nor is her travelogue of countless foreign visits astounding; though it has, in addition to snapshots, more gravitas than one might expect. Senator Clinton is, after all, a feminist lionized in much of the world, with policy interests and knowledge unmatched since the long reign of Eleanor Roosevelt.

Equally unsurprising is the sangfroid with which she states her innocence of the various "-gates," which, if it is not a careful walk through the countercharges, at least convinces that she *had* a defense. This is a fact kept from many television-watchers and newspaper-readers during the long years of her public trial for . . . something.

So is the list of thank-you's. The book is long on party favors dispensed for services rendered by staff and friends. It is slender on political and policy analysis—unfortunate lapses when it comes to understanding what went wrong with her first major foray into national politics, the ungainly health care plan of 1993.

Conceived in secrecy (in order to co-opt many contentious interests), awkwardly complicated (because conceptually original), besieged both by Democrats who wanted only a more ambitious plan and those who wanted none, its defeat broke the momentum of her husband's limited mandate for reform. Those who want to understand this failure will have to look elsewhere—though she is probably right that even a sleeker, more comprehensible plan, indeed any plan at all, would have doomed by the combination of insurance company lobbying and Democratic indiscipline.

Critics Always Hate a Blockbuster

It should not surprise that her book has been greeted with much the same acrimony that her White House tenure occasioned, in fact-challenging reviews (for example, that of the artfully snippy Maureen Dowd in the *New York Times Book Review*) that hold her to a standard of disclosure never deployed toward other tell-little memoirs—say, Nancy

Reagan's, or for that matter, George W. Bush's 2000 exercise in deceptive nondisclosure, generally understood to have been written by his airbrusher-in-chief, Karen Hughes.

Many pundits' assumption, now as during 1998, the Year of Lewinsky and Starr, is that Hillary Clinton *owes* us a detailed X-ray of her marriage. To her antagonists, she can never be done beating her husband. But her many fans don't seem to mind that the banshees are again in full howl; if anything, they expect an uncomprehending chorus of stock villains to certify that she, and therefore they, are right to be beset by such enemies.

Still, the book's astounding commercial success requires some mulling of its own. What accounts for the biggest news surrounding it, namely, its opening numbers? As in the case of a blockbuster movie, *Living History* arrived with a gigantic pull-out-all-stops publicity roll-out, and is said to have sold 200,000 copies during its first two days on sale, and more than a million to date in the United States alone.

Outside a Manhattan bookstore, a queue started to form the night before Hillary Clinton came to sign copies. What with gigantic foreign sales, even after an $8 million advance paid by Simon & Schuster, the book should prove a triumph of globalization. The enthusiasm of many buyers, one senses, rises above celebrity-worship to the territory of true admiration. As in all door-stopper book purchases, buyers are buying not only a read but a totem—a faith-rewarding item that rubs off on them. What do they think they are buying?

The only other recent political memoir to have grazed such staggering numbers is General Colin Powell's 1995 venture, *My American Journey*—which immediately gives us a clue. The general's memoir doubled as a place-card for a possible presidential run. (His triumphal book tour concluded, he proceeded to take himself out of the Republican race.)

Some of those who want a ticket for a quick tour through Hillary Clinton's past are buying a piece of her future—voting with their fingers and credit cards. Given a Democratic field that has (as of yet) inspired little enthusiasm about the prospect of expelling George W. Bush from the White House, intimations that she is free to run in 2008 offer a hint of righteous (if belated) revenge.

Though her enemies only find new reason to hate her in her refusal to open the bedroom door wider than a crack, she is also deeply admired for her imperturbability during a marital crisis that was more closely scrutinized on more continents than the sum of all seasons of reality shows on earth.

To some of her public—not least middle-aged women— dignity matters, and dignity under fire from Ken Starr and Rupert Murdoch matters all the more. Her refusal to play either spurned woman or vengeful virago plays to her twinned strengths as moralist and survivor. It plays, not least, to public curiosity: Just how does one cope with modern marriage? For, if the results of current research on sexual experience is accurate, the private Bill Clinton is more typical of American males than not.

THE DOUBLE-VOICED UTTERANCE

There is a related attraction to *Living History*—precisely the decorum that offends the cut-throat critics. Long intertwining the roles of dutiful wife and professional woman, Hillary Clinton writes in both voices. Her duality, with which tens of millions of women identify, would not be possible if she abandoned sobriety; and sobriety requires discretion, which is twin to evasion.

Sometimes naïveté courts misunderstanding. When she writes about her changes of hairdo, this isn't triviality or braggadocio (of which she's been accused); she's taking account of how hard it is to stand in the media floodlight and uphold both roles. Look, she says, to be true on both scores, you have to observe the right social tone. Thus does the lady, unfit for burning, cope with duality. Remain staunch—indeed, stoical—and you can overcome.

Despite the consequent anodyne quality of the former First Lady's account, one element is frequently helpful for understanding the apparent helplessness with which the Clintons confronted the frenzy that overtook their White House years: her naïveté—which was, by extension, her husband's as well.

She recalls that after his first political campaign, for Congress in Arkansas in 1974, the phone rang at campaign headquarters long after midnight and "someone shouted . . . 'I'm so glad that nigger-loving Commie fag Bill Clinton lost,' and then hung up." She goes on to ask: "What could inspire such bile?"

It seems to have taken her twenty-five years to arrive at an answer: the "vast right-wing conspiracy" that she famously named just after the Lewinsky story broke—something that would better have been called a network of foundations, law firms, propagandists, and reactionary ne'er-do-wells who never ceased hurling mud until (thanks to Bill Clinton's zipper openness and Monica Lewinsky's audacity) they finally found some to stick.

What surprises is that, after close to two decades in and around the swamps of Arkansas politics, barely done with the era of murderous white supremacy, Hillary Clinton could arrive in Washington surprised to discover that the Clintons had many vicious enemies and that some of them would be well received by the press corps. Why should the frenzy have surprised her?

The answer she inadvertently offers is that she was a nice person who believed that she lived in a nice country, whose establishment wanted the country to grow nicer still. She was, to be precise, a Methodist by upbringing and inclination. Earnest, she expected earnestness in her adversaries. She couldn't imagine that Washington's establishment would consider the Clintons rank interlopers, she as a professional woman, Bill as a guy both too smart and too sloppy for his own good—both Arkansas and Oxford, catching them in a class pincer.

This version of moralism left little room for malevolence in the world. There were, after all, Republican wives in Hillary Clinton's prayer group. When she writes about enemies, her tone conveys a certain plaintiveness: *Can you believe grown-ups carrying on this way?* Hadn't the people spoken and elected her husband? (Well, yes, but with a mere 43 percent of the popular vote.)

So, whatever the bitterness of Arkansas politics, she thought matters would turn out differently once she got to the White House. After all, she had grown up a right-winger herself, the dutiful teenage Goldwaterite daughter of a Republican father, and if she had come to see the light, like her "closet Democrat" mother (though quietly), why couldn't anyone else? She had gone liberal at prim Wellesley College, a campus that on her account made it through the late 1960s with one student protest. She thought that, given the facts, even people in high places would give her the benefit of the doubt as she put together an unwieldy health care plan in secret and fended off a shower of pseudo-scandals.

Possibly, Hillary Clinton is disingenuous. More likely, what makes her account unsatisfying except to diehard devotees is precisely the quality that often stopped the Clinton administration from realizing what it was up against—innocence.

THE CLINTON WARS

Sidney Blumenthal's The Clinton Wars is a superb book of an altogether more serious order, though it would be hard to know this from many journalists' reviews, busy as they have been renewing their animus against the Clintons and presuming that only a sycophant would see Clinton as more sinned against than sinning.

Among other things, *The Clinton Wars* forcefully reconstructs the assaults on Clinton, from Newt Gingrich's 1994 seizure of congressional power to Whitewater, the various pseudo-gates and the *Götterdämmerung* year of Lewinsky and Kenneth W. Starr, yet without sinking to the staccato chat show "talking points" style that has run away with American political discourse.

Blumenthal has a fine talent for narrative, and punctuates his eight hundred pages with considerable wit at the expense of his enemies, as in his observation of his famously former friend Christopher Hitchens (who delighted the impeachers by filing an affidavit alleging that Blumenthal had denigrated Monica Lewinsky as a "stalker," a charge against which Blumenthal defends himself robustly) that "as a political writer, Christopher was a literary critic."

Trying to Repeal the 1960s

Reading the many polemical reviews that discern only a brief for the author and his employer, you would hardly know that Blumenthal makes a coherent argument. It is, in short, that Clinton was a Progressive president in the line that began with Andrew Jackson and continued through FDR, Kennedy, and Johnson; that reactionaries regarded all of them as intruders on their sacred ideological soil; and thus that, like his predecessors, he inspired wild and desperado hatred and a long-running campaign to bring him down and repeal the 1960s.

So a network of foundations, media, lawyers, politicians, and other operatives hijacked first the Republican Party and then the Republic. On this network, Blumenthal offers the most convincing description yet, naming names, dates, acts of bad faith, amounts of money transferred. Even if the claim about Clinton's Progressivism is discounted by half, the main argument remains. For that matter, discount Blumenthal's encomia to his former employer by three-quarters and you will still learn a great deal about the workings and energies of American politics—energies that now have the rest of the world quavering.

This is the moment where I should add that during much of Clinton's first term, I am one who frequently found occasion to criticize him for lukewarm centrism, forfeiting the long-delayed chance to recover from the residue of Reaganism and move the centre of gravity of American politics leftward. After the disastrous midterm election of 1994, I decided I had drastically underestimated the power of the right.

Given the sluggishness of American political culture, I came to appreciate some of Clinton's poverty-fighting initiatives, in particular the little-noticed Earned Income Tax Credit, as well as family and medical leave, childhood immunization, gun control, and funds for police. His failure on health care struck me as a blunder for which there was much responsibility to go around, not a political crime. I eased away from liberal orthodoxy on deficit cutting, coming to think that Clinton's budgetary caution freed funds for investment and helped send unemployment to record lows.

Moreover, I approved of Clinton's intervention in Bosnia, belated as it was, as well as in Haiti, and later his Kosovo action. After Blumenthal, whom I had a met a couple of times before, went to work in the White House in 1997 (and was instantly greeted by a libelous accusation by the Internet gossip Matt Drudge acting in behalf of other right-wing operatives), we became friendly. I mention this not only because honesty requires it but to attest that, in this case, friendship followed judgment and not vice versa. My respect for Blumenthal's acumen, and my continued dissent from Clinton's policy on some issues (for example, NAFTA and media consolidation) does not keep me from declaring my opinion that his book is cogent and, on the available evidence, convincing.

THE BLINDNESS OF THE COMMENTARIAT

If you like, discount *that* assessment by half and you are left straining to understand the many nasty reviews as anything other than payback, since no more than a handful of trivial factual errors have turned up. How could critics blind to the big story of the right-wing takeover of American government overlook the fetid forest for an occasional broken branch?

Many of the same journalists who snarled at Clinton while he was in the White House have reviewed *The Clinton Wars* as if it were nothing but the longest courtier's tribute in history. This is royally unfair. For one thing, the book is not uncritical. (For example, pages 121–122 are admirably scathing on Clinton's errors during his first two years.) For another, it is not irrelevant that many Washington reporters already despised Blumenthal before he went to work in the White House—for giving voice (at *The New Yorker*) to the highest-minded case that could be made for Clinton's policies, then for writing a hilarious radio play mocking the press corps, and, if that wasn't bad enough, for going to work for a president they loathed ("Sid Vicious," snarled Murdoch's *New York Post*).

Major newspapers and magazines (falsely, indeed hilariously designated "the liberal media" by right-wingers, some of whom are sincere about it and others are not) have mainly been scathing or mocking, or both. In the *New York Review of Books*, the *New York Times's* erstwhile (and for a while, thanks to the Jayson Blair scandal, acting) executive editor Joseph Lelyveld once again defended his paper's role in pumping up the Whitewater furies without troubling to address Blumenthal's main arguments and the immense and amply documented weaknesses in that paper's coverage.

The Washington Post's regular reviewer, Jonathan Yardley, declared, without any evidence and against Blumenthal's sworn denial that, as a matter of "plain fact," Sidney Blumenthal directed a "below-the-belt campaign" against Clinton's female accusers. In *The New Yorker*, former *TIME* managing editor Walter Isaacson sniffed about his "excesses of loyalty" while failing to refute any of Blumenthal's significant claims. In a typical disingenuous he's-right-but-he-can't-be-right-so-he's-credulous move, Isaacson confusingly added that Blumenthal's account of the "anti-Clinton cabal" is "true enough," also noting in a buried sentence that his is a "largely persuasive case that prosecutors and the press . . . became overly, even weirdly, obsessed with the Whitewater story."

Mainly, Isaacson blamed Blumenthal and Mrs. Clinton for having been "notably unsuccessful at focusing press attention" on the conspirators "rather than on the President's own misdeeds"—taking zero responsibility for the press's (not least his own) virulent gullibility on Whitewater and other pseudo-scandals. (Isaacson later, as head of CNN, wanted to hire the serial liar Rush Limbaugh for "balance"). Sooner than take account of Blumenthal's devastating account of the bumbling and law-breaking of Clinton's persecutors in Starr's office, the House of Representatives, and the press, most American reviewers changed the subject.

One of the few American journalists willing to defend Blumenthal publicly, Richard Cohen of the *Washington Post*, recently wrote that many of his critics "use the book to pick up where they left off. They have no second thoughts, no backward glance to see the mess they made or to wonder how investigative reporting and commentary went right off a cliff and into a sewer. . . . Blumenthal's book, describing what a madhouse Washington became back then, has for some reason been given to the inmates to review."

TWO FAILURES: JOURNALISM AND POLITICS

Blumenthal closes with a retelling of the saga of the 2000 Florida vote, wherein George W. Bush's dynastic team, with the help of some of the same journalists who had knocked Clinton around, proceeded to knock around the hapless Al Gore, making him look like a liar while letting Bush glide by on a useful reputation for folksy harmlessness. Since Bush got to Washington, most White House correspondents have tiptoed around, afraid that a tough question or two would earn them a slammed door the next time they dared knock. (It happened to the *Washington Post's* Dana Milbank, who called deceptions deceptions.)

No *Gotcha* team hammers Bush day after day on talk radio or cable news about his many years as a drunk, or the missing year during his draft-evading service in the Texas Air National Guard, or the mysterious windfall oil profits that came his way when other investors in his company were losing their shirts. Reporters have only recently begun to mar his triumphalist excuses for press conferences by asking pesky questions about Saddam Hussein's phantom nuclear deal with Niger, or his putative Al-Qaeda connections, or other untruths this administration has found useful. The Niger-uranium deception finally undermined Bush's amazing reputation for plain speaking, but on most issues he still escapes sustained scrutiny.

Today, as Richard Cohen writes, the ruthless Tom DeLay "and other Clinton-haters wander the streets of Washington, unscarred, uncensored but, nonetheless, unhinged." DeLay, who declared that what was at stake in Clinton's impeachment was nothing less than "relativism vs. absolute truth," is not some random crank with a weblog or any old former exterminator from Sugar Land, Texas, but the House majority leader, the most powerful man in the House of Representatives.

His fellow Texan know-nothing nationalists and oilmen rule not only Washington but as much of the known world as they can (barely) handle. Their vitriol, venom, and victories, Blumenthal knows, are the big story of American politics in the last generation. A journalism that does not know that it happened is clueless. A politics that fails to address it is helpless.

Experimental Programming

By Douglas Rushkoff

Killed: *Seed*, 2003

This piece was inspired by an episode of Joe Millionaire *in which I watched a young woman—who had, most likely, performed oral sex on a man she believed to be a millionaire—finally learn that he was just a low-paid construction worker. I'll admit, her face at that split second—the moment between the horrific revelation and her effort to mask her sense of shame—displayed more genuine pathos than a full season of* ER. *But this reality program, like so many that went before and after, derived its entertainment value from the humiliation of its real life subjects.*

It occurred to me as that reality TV scenarios are set up much in same way as now-forbidden psychology experiments. As luck would have it, a brand-new magazine called Seed *had just asked me to write a regular column about how mainstream media perverts or expresses science. So it seemed like the perfect match. I had a meeting with the editor who loved the idea. He pitched it to his publisher, who approved the topic. A month later, I was on my fifth rewrite.*

The editor seemed to think each revision would satisfy his publisher's concerns, but the pieces always came back to me with requests for more science. More Darwin. Something. Ultimately, the piece was canned. The publisher, I later learned, didn't consider psychology to be a science.

In some ways the magazine industry works like a science experiment or a reality TV show, too. It's not that editors hope to humiliate their writers. It's that each assignment is really just the testing of a hypothesis: can this subject/writer combination yield a piece that we'll want to publish months from now?

That's why contracts have clauses about "kill fees," and why magazines assign many more articles than they ever run. Editors might like the piece just fine—but it may not reflect whatever they have told their publisher or what the publisher has told their advertisers about the magazine's "direction." In fact, an increase in killed pieces is a good sign that a magazine has lost its way, or is desperately trying to find one.

Still, the net effect can feel as humiliating as if it were intentional. I like to remind myself at such moments that the editors handing down inconsistent, contradictory orders must feel pretty exposed and humiliated, too. They're the ones whose judgment has been overridden, not me. Plus, I've been paid, at least in part, for a piece I'm now free to place elsewhere. They're stuck at the scene of the crime.

An apparently random sample of average people is divided into two groups: teachers and students. Each student sits on one side of a wall trying to remember a sequence of words, while the teacher sits on the other and is instructed to deliver an electric shock at each wrong answer. The voltage is increased, until the student is writhing around on the floor and screaming in agony. How far will each teacher go? Will he or she deliver a lethal dose? Finally, it will be revealed to the teachers that their "students" are really actors, pretending to be painfully shocked. Won't they be embarrassed when we all see how easily they can be turned into sadists?

No, this is isn't one of next season's reality shows but a real psychology experiment carried out at Yale University in 1961 by Dr. Stanley Milgram. Participants were so anguished over their capacity to inflict pain on demand that the much-publicized saga led to new ethical guidelines for psychological experimentation.

No such restrictions appear to apply to reality television programs, where sustained sadism of this sort can be observed somewhere on the TV dial pretty much any night of the week. Just when it seems as though this genre, if we can call it that, has finally peaked, a new crop of shows even more outrageously cruel or dishonest with its participants than the last appears on the horizon. Welcome to the American mediaspace, where neither a psychology degree nor an ethics certificate is required for us to look in on psychological terrorism, just for the fun of it.

How did television fall to such new lows? The abuse of traditional storytelling techniques certainly had something to do with it. Ever since Aristotle intuited the "arc" of increasing tension and release that serves as the dramatic spine of any successful play, writers have been honing this formula down to its most crude and utilitarian essence: create characters we like, put them in danger, and give them an easily digestible solution before the end. It's led to a predictability in mainstream drama and comedy that's nauseatingly claustrophobic. Shows that aren't assembled through focus groups are written by committee, so that anything resembling nuance or meaning is ironed out before they reach the commercial airwaves.

Any real messages are reserved for the sponsors, who use the very same arc to program product preferences. We don't call the stuff on television "programming" for nothing. It's not the schedule or television being programmed; it's us. So, for about twenty seconds we are brought up the incline plane of increasing stakes—A yucky pimple? Fired from work? Carpet stains? Social anxiety?—and in the last ten seconds all is set right by the sponsor's product: a new cream, an investment, solvent, or pill. In ancient drama, these quick-fix solutions were called deus ex machina, in which a god would descend from the heavens to save the hero from an otherwise tragic circumstance. Now, a "miracle" product serves that same function. But relentless exposure to these mini-dramas has made television audiences cynical and difficult to please. Having seen the machinery of storytelling at its most manipulative, viewers have grown suspicious of narrative in general.

In such an environment, reality television was initially greeted as liberation from the captive spell of the programmer. By throwing a dozen real people (or, at worst, wannabe actors) in a house, on an island, or in a chateau, and forcing them to come up with their own dialogue, these unscripted shows seemed to release audiences from the predictability of crafted drama and to replace it with the spontaneity—and the stakes—of real life.

Unlike scripted shows, with their preprogrammed agenda, reality programs project an aura of fair play, not unlike live sporting events. This is a competition, the format seems to say, in which only the laws of natural selection will determine who is left on the island at the end of Survivor, or which of the handsome men will win the affections of the single Bachelorette.

As hardened media consumers, of course, we may wonder just how much the producers of such shows actually leave to chance. But in a world where everything from the job market to the stock market to national elections appears to be in some measure fixed, even the illusion of real-life competition on a level playing field can be appealing.

So instead of Darwin's Galapagos, we get the island of *Survivor*, where only the strongest and most cunning will make it to the end of their battle against the elements, insects, starvation and each other. And we, the viewing public, get to watch the participants, stripped of the artificial pretenses and conveniences of modern life, duke it out as humans were "meant" to.

On *Temptation Island*, real couples test the bounds of their socially constructed unions by mixing with buff and buxom singles in bathing suits who have no purpose but to seduce. Participants who actually had sexual intercourse with the tempters might be said to represent the triumph of "untamed" animal instincts over social and cultural "programming." On this rawest of narrative levels, reality shows seem to be about restoring what audiences conceive of as the natural order. Even the talent show *American Idol* means to replace—for one lucky winner, anyway—the insiderly, casting-couch-driven culture of the music industry with a fair, democratically chosen pop star.

But while such moments may seem to restore a sense of fair play to television, reality shows are anything but natural selection. They may not be scripted, but any connection between shows like *Survivor* or *Joe Millionaire* and real life is purely coincidental. In fact, they are fixed decks, where the preliminary conditions and choice of participants yield a predictable array of possible outcomes.

It's not just because the eight MTV veejay hopefuls on the *Real World* wouldn't normally find themselves living together in a fabulous loft in Seattle. Rather, it's because these totally crafted productions are based on premises as far removed from reality as TV's classic situation comedies were. Back in television's so-called "golden years," situation comedies were precisely that: situations. A guy's uncle is a Martian. My horse can talk. Your mother is a car. That's why they were called *situation* comedies—because the situation drove the comedy. Today's sitcoms have no situation to speak of: some friends drink coffee in the same place. An office where, uh, people work. One of our friends is gay.

While today's sitcoms more closely resemble real life, at least in their situational components, reality TV has staked its future on the absurdity of its setups. Far from focusing on ordinary human behavior, these shows are coming to resemble laboratory experiments (with poor controls) in which conditions are set up in a very particular way so that the most dramatic (read: painful or humiliating) results can emerge.

Like psych experiments, each show has an implicit assumption. What will happen if people are put on an island where they must depend on one another for survival? To forestall the "uninteresting" possibility that they might just learn to get along, what if we require that the group vote one person off every day? That should tip the balance toward down-and-dirty in the "survival of the fittest" maneuvering. What if a group of pretty women compete for the attention of a multimillionaire? Been there. Okay, what if he's not really a millionaire, but only pretending to be? That brings an undercurrent of humiliation to even the most innocent of encounters. Cool. What if we go Big Brother one better by putting a group of formerly famous people in a house together? What could be more pathetic than a houseful of one-time winners desperately trying to prove that they are not losers—and failing miserably.

It is immediately apparent that these shows aren't "reality" programs at all, but precisely constructed exercises in humiliation. We watch them not to enjoy the seemingly natural (but ultimately spurious) unscriptedness of these shows, but because we find the cruelty itself so compelling. Even a reality show as seemingly innocuous as *The Osbournes* finds its core entertainment value in the sad pathos of its drugged, mentally-ill protagonist and his dysfunctional family.

An all-too-human tendency to not only tolerate but even participate in the infliction of pain and suffering on others—especially on those who cannot fight back—was observed in another infamous psychology experiment that was later condemned for unethical treatment of unwitting test subjects. The Stanford Prison Experiment of 1971 split a random group of men into "prisoners" and "guards." Almost immediately, the guards took it upon themselves to develop increasingly humiliating tortures for their prisoners to endure. In fact, they were so successful at concocting demeaning situations that the experiment, planned for two weeks, was cut short after just six days.

Are we, the television audience, aligning ourselves with those "prison guards" when we take delight in the humiliation of reality show participants? What was it, after all, that compelled more Americans to tune in the final episode of *Joe Millionaire*—a show where women competed desperately for the hand of a fabulously wealthy hunk they had not yet learned was actually a construction worker of limited means—rather than watch Dan Rather's exclusive interview with Saddam Hussein? Wasn't it the chance to see, from a safe distance, the shock and humiliation on the face of a woman who had engaged in a sex act under false pretenses only to be rejected in the end by Joe, our avatar?

It's one thing to admit that the popularity of this kind of show exposes unpleasant truths about human nature. But can such cruel diversions actually turn us into crueler people? A study released recently by two psychologists at University of Michigan suggests just that. It found that men who had frequently watched violent programs as children were more likely to shove people than those who watched them less.

Other studies have concluded that after being shown violent TV programs, children are more inclined to behave violently toward their peers. And such links aren't limited to just physical behavior. In 2002 researchers at the National Institute on Media and the Family attempted to demonstrate that watching violent TV makes kids not just more physically violent, but "relationally violent"—in other words—meaner.

Such research is famously fraught with difficulties. For example, just because socially and physically violent people watch meaner, more violent programs doesn't mean that such shows *cause* mean and violent behavior. It might just be that people with an especially strong tendency to behave violently gravitate to TV shows that specialize in violence.

But even if TV cruelty only panders to existing tendencies in some of us, we engage in tele-sadism at our own risk. This is the real lesson to be learned from those psychological experiments of the past that look so much like today's reality programs. In the Milgram experiment at Yale, it was the "teachers"—the pain *givers*—who, confronted by their own capacity to mete out punishment, became wracked with guilt and shame. These were ordinary folks who discovered they were capable of great cruelty, as long as it was somehow "justified" by the situation. Either the infliction of pain was presented as being "good" for the recipients (the actors who pretended to suffer), or it was seen as a "natural" outcome of the social hierarchy set up in the experiment. So who was *ultimately* responsible for inflicting the real pain in these experiments? The researchers who devised the experiments in the first place! And like the pain givers who were merely "following orders," these researchers had elaborate justifications for their actions, based on the perceived value of their work to science and to society at large.

Indisputably, there's a harsh emotional price to be paid by

even passive observers of cruelty. The pleasure we take from watching cruelty also requires justification, some internal adjustment of attitude that blames the unwitting victim for being greedy or stupid or self-deluded or in some other sense "deserving" of his or her treatment.

In the great uncontrolled social experiment that is network TV, we, with remote controls in our hands, are the test group. The question is, how far will we go? How much cruelty on the part of the producers will we find "enjoyable"? Long ago, the limits of audience appetite were tested in this fashion, bringing us the death matches of the Coliseum in Imperial Rome—and we know what happened to the society that sponsored them. But unlike the Romans, this time we have no emperor to blame. By rewarding reality shows with high ratings we the audience are in fact responsible for their continued success—which means that we are ultimately responsible, in cahoots with the producers and the networks, for the pain and humiliation inflicted. Now *that's* interactive entertainment.

Review of *The Five People You Meet in Heaven*

By Carlo Wolff

Killed: *Detroit Free Press*, 2003

When the Detroit Free Press *spiked my review of a book by its star columnist, Mitch Albom, the newspaper damaged its brand and intellectually insulted its readers—and Albom as well.*

In late August of 2003, I was given the assignment because, I was told, a staff-written review of work by a Free Press *employee would smack of conflict of interest. Originally slated to run on September 21, two days before the book's publication, my piece first was postponed, an apologetic editor at the paper told me. He explained that Albom's "constituency" had gotten wind of my review and alerted management, which decided to hold it for a week so "buzz could build "for the book. Finally, executive editor Carole Leigh Hutton killed the story outright on September 23.*

I called my editor at the Sun-Sentinel in Fort Lauderdale, which subsequently published a news article about the controversy and later ran a version of my review. News of this clear case of self-censorship generated plenty of column fodder, angry letters in the Free Press, *and a Hutton column defending her decision. "I decided not to publish it" wrote Hutton, ". . . because I think all our employees should be protected from, as one colleague put it, 'the ethical dilemma and no-win position of passing critical judgment on a colleague's work.' "*

Hutton was within her rights as the paper's mother hen, but she blew it as its leader.

Her decision highlights a reflexive protectiveness all too common among made members of the journalistic Mafia. I suspect that the author of the megaselling Tuesdays with Morrie *is sufficiently thick of skin to weather criticism. Otherwise, he shouldn't be in the game. Apparently, I have more confidence in him than his own paper.*

How many ways can you define "superficial"? Mitch Albom's new book suggests quite a variety.

The Five People You Meet in Heaven attests to Albom's imagination and verbal dexterity, but his widescreen sentimental streak skewers his credibility. His imagination and linguistic facility carry a very short day in the follow-up to *Tuesdays with Morrie,* the self-aggrandizing 1997 bestseller Albom wrote about his former teacher, Brandeis University sociology professor Morrie Schwartz.

Readability is not an issue here. The issue is depth.

This is the story of Eddie, a schlub who fixes rides at an old-fashioned, seaside amusement park that evokes Coney Island. Eddie is way past his prime; war wounds, loneliness, and lack of pride hamper him. But "Eddie Maintenance" is proud of his work and, when he allows himself to consider more than its mechanics, he realizes it's ultimately about taking care of the kids who go on the rides.

On his eighty-third birthday, Eddie puts himself in harm's

way when he tries to save a little girl from being crushed by a cart falling off its track. Eddie doesn't know what hits him. He also doesn't know that in his final moments, he becomes enough of a hero to justify Albom's thin, mawkish story.

This is a book you can read in two hours. Albom conveniently makes it pocket size, appropriate for a story so downsized. Albom can write vividly, however—or, at least, cinematically:

> In those final moments, Eddie seemed to hear the whole world: distant screaming, waves, music, a rush of wind, a low, loud, ugly sound that he realized was his own voice blasting through his chest. The little girl raised her arms. Eddie lunged. His bad leg buckled. He half flew, half stumbled toward her, landing on the metal platform, which ripped through his shirt and split open his skin, just beneath the patch that read Eddie and Maintenance. He felt two hands in his own two small hands.
>
> A stunning impact.
> A blinding flash of light.
> And then nothing.

Well, not quite. After a brief flashback to Eddie's birth—Albom's peeks at the past are among the more winning aspects of this book—Eddie finds himself in a bizarre, sugary heaven. It seems to be a nice place. God knows he feels better there than he did on Earth, what with no more aches and pains.

From then on, this fable about What Binds Us All Together in Harmonious Afterlife takes place on the extraterrestrial plane, a field of dreams, and revelations in which Eddie finds himself no more freakish, or lonely, than the other heavenly residents. He also finds peace with himself and, in Albom's manipulative hands, brings facile closure for readers.

Where some attempt to write the Great American Novel, Albom seems content to write the Great American Postcard. Every so often, however, he suggests where he might have taken his story had he worked to raise it above greeting-card level.

He could have deepened his characters, given them flesh and blood instead of limiting them to symbols. He could have dug history more deeply to paint a painstaking, fascinating picture of the evolution of amusement parks (his occasional reference to the parks' evolution suggests he's done his homework). He could have explored the philosophical ramifications of some of his imagery, which can be evocative. This picture of Eddie, who is surprised to find himself feeling good, even frisky, in heaven, is not only gorgeous; it's thought provoking:

> He ran down the heart of the old midway, where the weight guessers, fortune-tellers, and dancing gypsies had once worked. He lowered his chin and held his arms out like a glider, and every few steps he would jump, the way children do, hoping running will turn to flying. It might have seemed ridiculous to anyone watching, this white-haired maintenance worker, all alone, making like an airplane. But the running boy is inside every man, no matter how old he gets.

For every tantalizing image, however, there's a treacly assertion that doesn't quite work: "Every life has one true-love snapshot," Albom writes, recalling Eddie's first glimpse of his wife-to-be. "For Eddie, it came on a warm September night after a thunderstorm, when the boardwalk was spongy with water. She wore a yellow cotton dress, with a pink barrette in her hair. Eddie didn't say much. He was so nervous he felt as if his tongue were glued to his teeth."

That "true-love snapshot" is simplistic. It rings false in light of our complicated lives.

After Eddie becomes acclimated to heaven, he meets the Five People Who Really Mattered. They are the Blue Man, an early, inadvertent victim of Eddie's; the Captain, who taught Eddie about war; Ruby, the patroness of the amusement park; Eddie's wife, Marguerite, who died young (the couple never had a child, which may help explain why Eddie takes care of kids at an amusement park); and Tala, the little girl who finally brings peace to Eddie.

The connections between these five form the core of a story meant to uplift and comfort. *The Five People You Meet in Heaven*, it seems, is designed to make you feel good. After all, at the end, Eddie transcends his ordinariness and, with the help of these talismanic figures, discovers he's not a bad guy, after all.

Doesn't everybody want that? Don't we all hope people see us as kind, connected and caring? The touchy-feely story Albom tells, in a narrative sticky with clichés, aims to be a tonic for these nasty, nasty times. All we have to do, Albom suggests, is find Ruby's Pier, where Eddie works. Once we find Eddie, he might let us in on the meaning of life.

About the Contributors

David Wallis is the founder and editorial director of Featurewell.com, a syndicate that markets articles by more than one thousand prominent writers. An outspoken advocate for independent journalists, Wallis has lectured at Columbia University's Graduate School of Journalism, New York University, and The New School, and appeared on CNN, Fox News, and Book TV. Wallis, himself a journalist, has written for *The New Yorker*, *Wired*, London's *Observer*, the *Washington Post*, and the *New York Times Magazine*, among other publications.

T. D. Allman is a renowned war correspondent and author of three books: *Miami: City of the Future* (Atlantic Monthly Press) *Mayhem and Illusion in American Foreign Policy* (Doubleday), and *Rogue State* (Nation Books). Mr. Allman was the foreign correspondent for *Vanity Fair* and a staff writer for *The New Yorker*.

Ann Louise Bardach is the author of *Cuba Confidential: Love and Vengeance in Miami and Havana* (Random/Vintage). She has covered Cuba for the *New York Times* and *Vanity Fair*, where she served as a contributing editor. Bardach currently writes for *Newsweek International* and is a commentator for National Public Radio's *Marketplace*. She is also a visiting professor of international journalism at University of California–Santa Barbara.

Rich Cohen is the author of three books: *Tough Jews: Fathers, Sons and Gangster Dreams* (Simon & Schuster), *The Avengers: A Jewish War Story* (Knopf), and *Lake Effect* (Knopf). He lives in New York City.

Larry Doyle, formerly an editor at *Spy* and *New York Magazine,* has contributed to *Esquire, GQ, Rolling Stone,* and *The New Yorker,* among others.

Jon Entine is a scholar-in-residence teaching journalism at Miami University (Ohio) and an Emmy-winning network television news producer formerly at NBC and ABC News. His books include the forthcoming *Genetics and Biblical Ancestry* (Gotham Books/Penguin) and *Taboo: Why Black Athletes Dominate Sports and Why We Are Afraid to Talk about It* (PublicAffairs). Entine writes a column for *Ethical Corporation* magazine.

Robert Fisk is Middle East Correspondent of *The Independent,* based in Beirut. Educated in Britain and Ireland, Fisk holds more journalism awards—twenty-four—than any other foreign correspondent for his reporting of the Iranian revolution and wars in Lebanon, the Gulf, Kosovo, and Algeria. He won the 2000 Amnesty International award for his reports from Serbia on NATO's bombardment of Yugoslavia and received the 2001 David Watt Memorial Award for his reporting from the Middle East.

Betty Friedan was born in Peoria, Illinois, in 1921. In 1963, Friedan wrote *The Feminine Mystique,* a groundbreaking book that challenged assumptions about the role of women in American society. Friedan helped establish the National Organization for Women in 1966, serving as its president for four years. In 2000, Friedan published her autobiography, *Life So Far* (Simon & Schuster).

Tad Friend has been a staff writer at *The New Yorker* since 1998, and writes the "Letter from California" column for the magazine. He is the author of *Lost in Mongolia: Travels in Hollywood and Other Foreign Lands* (Random House), a collection of his articles, which was published in 2001.

Todd Gitlin is the author of ten books, most recently *Letters to a Young Activist* (Basic Books). Gitlin is a professor of journalism and sociology at Columbia University.

Gerald Hannon learned journalism, and much else, through his involvement with *The Body Politic*, a Canadian gay liberation magazine that lasted from 1971 to 1987. During that period he was charged and tried several times for indecency, immorality, and obscenity, but was acquitted at trial each time. Since then, he has freelanced, winning four Canadian National Magazine Awards (though he remains prizeless as a "ho").

Erik Hedegaard is a contributing editor at *Rolling Stone* and in 2000 was nominated for a National Magazine Award in the profile-writing category. He currently lives, and smokes, in Narragansett, Rhode Island.

Christopher Hitchens is a visiting professor of Liberal Studies at New School University in New York, and a columnist for *Vanity Fair*. His most recent book, *Why Orwell Matters* (Basic Books), was published in 2002.

Jamie Malanowski has been an editor at *Spy* and *Time*. He has contributed to more than forty publications in the United States and Britain, including the *New York Times*, where he writes frequently about film and pop culture.

P. J. O'Rourke has written for such publications as *American Spectator, Playboy, Vanity Fair,* and *Rolling Stone,* where he was the magazine's Foreign Affairs Desk Chief. Three of O'Rourke's books—*Parliament of Whores* (Atlantic Monthly Press), *Give War a Chance* (Atlantic Monthly Press), and *Trouble in the World* (Atlantic Monthly Press)—have been *New York Times* hardcover bestsellers. Both *Time* and the *Wall Street Journal* have called him "the funniest writer in America."

George Orwell (1903–50) wrote nine books, including the classics *Animal Farm* and *Nineteen Eighty-Four*.

Jan Pottker is the author of eight books, most recently *Sara and*

Eleanor: The Story of Eleanor Roosevelt and Her Mother-in-law, Sara Delano Roosevelt (St. Martin's Press).

Ted Rall, one of three finalists for the 1996 Pulitzer Prize for his cartoons, has written four prose and graphic books. Rall last published *To Afghanistan and Back* (Comics Lit) an instant graphic travelogue chronicling his harrowing experiences covering the Afghanistan war for the *Village Voice*. His most recent book is *Wake Up America! You're Liberal: How We Can Take America Back from the Right* (Soft Skull Press).

Daniel Asa Rose recently wrote the critically acclaimed book, *Hiding Places: A Father and his Sons Retrace Their Family's Escape From the Holocaust* (Simon & Schuster). Formerly the Arts & Culture editor of the *Forward*, Rose has contributed to *Esquire*, the *New York Times Magazine*, and the *New York Observer*, among other publications.

Julian Rubinstein has contributed to the *New York Times Magazine Rolling Stone*, *Sports Illustrated*, and *Details*, among other publications. His work has been selected by *The Best American Crime Writing* (Houghton Mifflin) and twice sited *The Best American Sports Writing* (Houghton Mifflin). His first book, *Ballad of the Whiskey Robber*, will be published by Little, Brown in September, 2004.

Mike Sager is a writer-at-large for *Esquire*. A collection of his magazine work, *Scary Monsters and Super Freaks: Stories of Sex, Drugs, Rock 'n' Roll and Murder* (Thunder's Mouth Press) was published in January 2004.

Douglas Rushkoff is the author of eight best-selling books on new media and popular culture. His latest work is *Nothing Sacred: The Truth about Judaism* (Crown).

Mark Schone is a senior contributing writer at *SPIN* magazine. In 2002, he and coauthor Kent Walker won an Edgar Allan Poe Award for the bestselling true-crime book, *Son of a Grifter* (William Morrow). He has written for the *New York Times*, *Wired*, and *Outside*, among other publications. At present he and University of Oregon psychology professor Dr. Thomas Dishion are writing a book about the root causes of juvenile delinquency.

Nile Southern is a writer and filmmaker. His recently published book *The Candy Men* (Arcade) tells the saga of the novel *Candy*, from its French banning to its censorship, piracy, and best-sellerdom in the U.S. Southern is also the co-editor of *Now Dig This: The Unspeakable Writings of Terry Southern: 1950-1995,* and author of the forthcoming cyber-tale, "The Anarchists of Eco-Dub." He lives with his wife and two daughters in Boulder, Colorado.

Terry Southern (1925–95) was described by the *New York Times* as "the hippest guy on the planet." Aside from practically inventing the New Journalism in his magazine articles for *Esquire,* Southern co-wrote the screenplays for *Doctor Strangelove* and *Easy Rider.* Southern was no stranger to issues of censorship. In addition to his battle to get *Candy* published, after he protested the Vietnam war and testified for the Chicago Eight, his voice was deemed too "political" and he was no longer sought after by the literary editors of America's magazines.

Neil Steinberg is a columnist and member of the editorial board at the *Chicago Sun-Times*. His work has appeared in publications such as *Rolling Stone, Sports Illustrated,* and the *New York Times Magazine.* He is the author of four books, including *Complete and Utter Failure* (Doubleday). His fifth book, on John F. Kennedy and the decline of men's hats, will be published by Penguin.

Carlo Wolff, an independent journalist in Cleveland, reviews books for newspapers, including the *San Francisco Chronicle,* the *Boston Globe,* and the *Christian Science Monitor.*

Acknowledgments

Killed would have likely languished on my computer if not for the guidance of three skillful magazine editors—Gerald Jonas, Jonathan Black, and Daniel Asa Rose—and the tireless work of Jess Wisloski, who fact-checked the unpublished articles.

Many colleagues generously offered advice, contacts and reassurance. I owe favors to Amy Alkon, Brian Cullman, RaNae Merrill, Daniel Horowitz, Andrew Mayer, Melvin Jules Bukiet, Mark Frankel, Melvin Jules Bukiet, Stan Mieses, David Margolick, Will Blythe, Michael Shelden, Bill Steigerwald, Evan Elkin, Peter Alson, Robert Sawyer, Jessica Seigel, and Alec Wilkinson.

The legendary literary agent, Sterling Lord, graciously gave me access to his papers at NYU's Fales Library so I could search for correspondence between *Esquire* and Terry Southern.

Many thanks to my courageous editors Carl Bromley and Ruth Baldwin and to my determined agent Lisa Hyman, who championed *Killed,* not because she envisioned a big payday, but because she understood the project's significance.

Betty Friedan, her biographer Daniel Horowitz, her assistant, Hildie Carney, and Giordana Mecagni of The Arthur and Elizabeth Schlesinger Library at Harvard University have my gratitude for helping me track down "Are Women Wasting Their Time in College?"

A sweet kiss to Penny Blatt, who gave me unwavering support before, during, and after the editing process.

I am forever indebted to my cherished parents, who taught me early "elbows out, chin up," my brother Stephen Wallis, and my late granny Ida Drancz, who sat me on her wooden sewing table most weekday evenings so we could both watch, and discuss, NBC's *Nightly News*.

Finally, let me acknowledge Jim Mauro, ever so briefly the editor of *Spy*. I never forgot the inspiring words he wrote to me after we clashed over a contract: "Consider all future possibilities canceled."